More p
THE STOR

"Silber, a many-sided professor at New York University's Stern School of Business, is a gifted story-teller."
—DAVID WARSH, *Seeking Alpha*

"A page-turner of a financial-political multi-generational thriller worthy of, say, John Grisham, filled with larger-than-life speculators, businessmen, manipulators, crooks and politicians."
—PETER GORDON, *Asian Review of Books*

"Silber's book is insightful and enjoyable. It deserves to be read widely."
—GARY RICHARDSON, *Regulation*

"*The Story of Silver* is a wonderful, broad book, full of verve and insight into why various generations—from Queen Elizabeth I to Warren Buffett, Alexander Hamilton to, especially, the infamous Hunt brothers— have been so focused on this slippery stuff."
—PETER CONTI-BROWN, *Business History Review*

"Enlightening as well as fun to read, William Silber's *The Story of Silver* reminds us that the economic history of the world is inseparable from the history of this precious metal. As Silber recounts, politicians and business leaders, idealists and scoundrels have long found it irresistible."
—ROBERT J. SHILLER, Nobel Laureate in Economics

"Successfully combining key episodes throughout American financial history with some investment advice, this sound and impressive book examines the political economy and monetary role of silver."
—RICHARD SYLLA, author of *Alexander Hamilton: The Illustrated Biography*

"A fine economist with a keen eye for historical facts and episodes, Silber analyzes the economics and politics that determined the value of silver and its role in monetary systems and asset markets."
—THOMAS J. SARGENT, Nobel Laureate in Economics

"Full of riveting information and colorful details, *The Story of Silver* is an apt companion to Peter Bernstein's classic *The Power of Gold*."
—BENJAMIN M. FRIEDMAN, author of *The Moral Consequences of Economic Growth*

Silver Prices for 200 Years

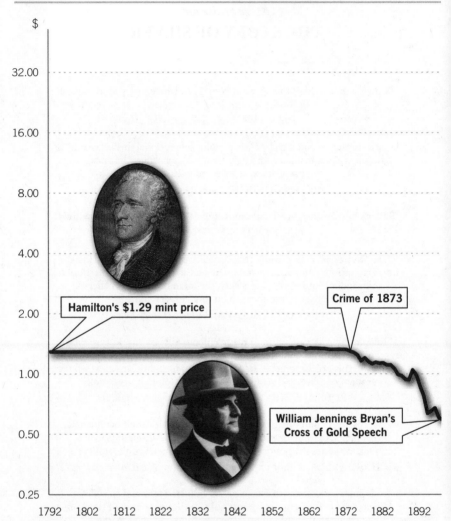

This semi-log chart shows the annual average price per troy ounce of pure silver in U.S. dollars from 1792 through 2015 and some of the major events influencing the white metal during that period. The data are spliced from the following sources: 1) The U.S. Mint price from 1792–1833; 2) The average market price reported by the Department of the Mint, 1834–1909; 3) The average of monthly prices reported by the CRB database, 1910–1946; 4) The average of daily prices reported by the

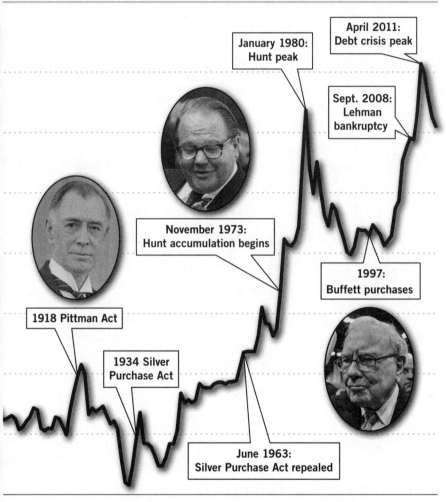

April 2011:
Debt crisis peak

January 1980:
Hunt peak

Sept. 2008:
Lehman
bankruptcy

November 1973:
Hunt accumulation begins

1997:
Buffett purchases

1918 Pittman Act

1934 Silver
Purchase Act

June 1963:
Silver Purchase Act repealed

1902   1912   1922   1932   1942   1952   1962   1972   1982   1992   2002   2012

CRB database, 1947–2015. The annual average price in 1980 is lower than in 2011, even though the daily peak price ($50) was higher in 1980, because daily prices fell more precipitously during 1980 compared with 2011. Note: Because of inflation, the value of $1.29 in 1792 is equivalent to $31.30 in current dollars of 2011, when silver hit a peak of $48 (based on the consumer price index calculator from the EH.net website of the Economic History Association).

By the Same Author

Volcker: The Triumph of Persistence

When Washington Shut Down Wall Street:
The Great Financial Crisis of 1914 and the Origins of
America's Monetary Supremacy

Financial Options: From Theory to Practice (coauthor)

Principles of Money, Banking, and Financial Markets (coauthor)

Financial Innovation (editor)

Money (coauthor)

Portfolio Behavior of Financial Institutions

THE STORY OF
SILVER

HOW THE WHITE METAL SHAPED
AMERICA AND THE MODERN WORLD

WILLIAM L. SILBER

PRINCETON UNIVERSITY PRESS

Princeton & Oxford

LCCN 2018941299

First paperback printing, 2021
Paperback ISBN 9780691208695
Cloth ISBN 9780691175386

British Library Cataloging-in-Publication Data is available

Editorial: Peter Dougherty and Jessica Yao

Production Editorial: Natalie Baan

Text and Cover Design: Leslie Flis

Production: Jacqueline Poirier

Publicity: James Schneider

Cover Credit: 1879 US silver dollar

This book has been composed in Sabon LT Std Roman

Printed in the United States of America

To
Danny
You left us too soon

CONTENTS

From the Author   xiii

Main Characters   xvii

INTRODUCTION
Obsession   1

CHAPTER 1
Hamilton's Design   10

CHAPTER 2
Solving the Crime of 1873   17

CHAPTER 3
Free Silver   27

CHAPTER 4
Seeds of Roosevelt's Manipulation   38

CHAPTER 5
FDR Promotes Silver   45

CHAPTER 6
Silver Subsidy   52

CHAPTER 7
China and America Collide   60

CHAPTER 8
Bombshell in Shanghai   71

CHAPTER 9
Silver Lining   90

CHAPTER 10
Costly Victory   99

CHAPTER 11
JFK's Double Cross   104

CHAPTER 12
LBJ Nails the Coffin Shut   119

CHAPTER 13
Psychiatrist's Meltdown   131

CHAPTER 14
Battle Lines   146

CHAPTER 15
Nelson Bunker Hunt   150

CHAPTER 16
Heavyweight Fight   165

CHAPTER 17
Saudi Connection   175

CHAPTER 18
Silver Soars   183

CHAPTER 19
Collapse   202

CHAPTER 20
The Trial   224

CHAPTER 21
Buffett's Manipulation?   236

CHAPTER 22
Message from Omaha   242

CHAPTER 23
The Past Informs the Future   249

Notes   253

Selected Bibliography   317

About the Author   327

Illustration Credits   329

Index   331

A lover of silver will never be satisfied with silver.
—Ecclesiastes 5

FROM THE AUTHOR

ACKNOWLEDGEMENTS

I DID NOT KNOW NELSON BUNKER HUNT, WHOSE DEATH IN 2014 spawned this book project, but many who knew him well shared their insights and recollections. I could not have written the story of silver without them. Phil Geraci of the Kay Scholer law firm that represented the Hunt brothers during their silver manipulation trial was a young lawyer back then and provided key personal observations from his six-month interaction with the Hunts. His assistant Patricia Apuzzo made it easy to use the related material. Henry Jarecki, whose business dealings with the Hunts while chairman of Mocatta Metals Corporation lasted more than a decade, gave me access to his unpublished manuscript that offered details unavailable elsewhere. His assistant Emily Goodnight made the process enjoyable and productive. Professor Jeffrey Williams served as an expert witness for the Hunts at their 1988 trial and provided copies of plaintiff and defendant expert reports that had been stored in his garage since then. I also relied on his excellent book on the economic testimony at the trial.

But this book is more than just about the Hunts. It is the story of silver, so at the beginning I spent a day with silversmith Geoffrey Blake at Old Newbury Crafters in Amesbury, Massachusetts, watching him mold the white metal into sterling silver flatware with the same tools and techniques that Paul Revere might have used. The ancient craft practiced in Blake's dusty basement workshop contrasted with the modern spectrograph used by Don and Angelo Palmieri in their Gem Certification & Assurance Lab to determine whether sterling silver jewelry contains the required 92.5% pure silver. But some things do not change. I watched Albert Robert (Irina and Gabriel's cousin) of the New York Gold Refining Company turn a silver coin into molten metal by heating it in a blackened crucible over an open flame as in ancient times.

My research work benefited from the cheerful effort of many individuals. I owe Carol Arnold-Hamilton, Alicia Estes, and Robert Platt, librarians at NYU's Bobst, for recovering source material that challenged Google's algorithms. Jack Shim, an outstanding PhD student at NYU Stern, and Omer Morashti, a great Stern MBA, analyzed the data with surgical skill. Bob Oppenheimer shared firsthand observations of the silver ring at the Commodity Exchange (Comex). Bernard Septimus, my friend for as long as I can remember, applied his biblical expertise to keep my references consistent with modern scholarship. Seth Ditchik and Bruce Tuchman read an early draft and molded the framework of the story for the better. Dick Sylla, Ken Garbade, and Paul Wachtel read the entire manuscript as if it were their own and scrubbed the fuzzy logic from the final product. Peter Dougherty, my editor at Princeton University Press, offered sage advice and gentle encouragement throughout the process. His e-mails at 5 a.m. were just the tip of the iceberg. My wife, Lillian, let me work on the book whenever I wasn't playing golf, read every word, and excised most (but certainly not all) of the annoying metaphors. And I apologize to my children and grandchildren for not calling the book "Silber on Silver," a unanimous recommendation at our family gatherings that fell to the cutting room floor like so many other gems.

SOURCE MATERIALS

No one needs to read the notes appearing at the end of the book, but they are there to expand on historical details and to provide technical information. The notes contain citations to newspapers, periodicals, academic articles, and books to support specific opinions and quotations appearing in the text. Statistical tests and a precise explanation of silver price data also appear in the notes. Silver prices usually refer to the price of physical silver in the form of bullion bars. These are sometimes called cash prices to distinguish them from prices in the futures market that become important in the second half of the book. The silver price data come from a variety of sources: 1) annual data during the nineteenth century come from the *Annual Report of the Director of the Mint*, Washington, DC: Government Printing Office, 1936; 2) daily data on silver prices during the 1930s were hand-collected from the *Wall Street Journal*, which published cash market quotations by bullion dealer Handy & Harman; 3) daily data on cash prices since 1947 and futures prices since 1963 were purchased from the Commodity Research Bureau (CRB), an independent data distributor that was a division of Knight-Ridder Financial Publishing and is now a division of Barchart.com, Inc., a Chicago-based vendor of financial data; and finally, (4) daily data on the London silver fix since 1968 come from the London Bullion Market Association as published by Quandl, an internet provider of economic and financial data.

A CONFESSION

The outline of this book when I started five years ago differs considerably from the final product. History surprised me with events and personalities that changed my thoughts and perceptions. I have shared those stories with you throughout this book and hope they are as pleasurable, instructive, and exciting for you as they were for me.

w.l.s.

MAIN CHARACTERS

Alexander Hamilton

America's first secretary of the Treasury recommended both gold and silver definitions for the U.S. dollar in 1791 and chose the $1.29 price that the mint would pay per ounce of silver bullion. He recommended bimetallism, the coinage of both gold and silver, to promote economic growth and "to avoid the evils of a scanty circulation."

John Sherman

U.S. senator from Ohio, chairman of the Senate Finance Committee, used deception and misrepresentation to pass the Coinage Act of 1873, demonetizing silver and establishing gold as the sole backing for the U.S. currency. Sherman later served as secretary of the Treasury, secretary of state, and is most famous for the Sherman Antitrust Act but was vilified for the so-called Crime of 1873, downgrading silver, which shadowed American politics for a century.

William Jennings Bryan

The thirty-six-year-old U.S. congressman from Nebraska captured the 1896 Democratic nomination for the presidency with the electrifying "Cross of Gold" speech at the convention. Despite its name, the speech was all about silver, a response to twenty-five years of deflation in America since the Crime of 1873, pitting rural westerners favoring easy credit against the hard-money urban East. *The Wonderful Wizard of Oz*, published in 1900, memorialized the class battle and portrayed Bryan as the cowardly lion whose roar was greater than his bite. Bryan ran three times for the presidency and lost.

Key Pittman

Elected U.S. senator from Nevada, the Silver State, in 1913 and made a career with legislation to promote the white metal. He became the influential chairman of the Foreign Relations Committee in 1933 and led the Senate's "silver bloc" of western mining states to convince the newly elected president, Franklin D. Roosevelt, to subsidize the price and production of the white metal. His support of silver debuted in 1918 with what was called the Pittman Act, authorizing the sale of silver to Great Britain to support the Indian rupee and then subsidizing the repurchase of the metal at above-market prices.

Franklin Delano Roosevelt

Elected U.S. president in 1932 in a landslide, pushed legislation with the help of Key Pittman and his allies to cure the Great Depression, including taking the United States off the gold standard. FDR repaid Pittman with a December 1933 proclamation to subsidize domestic silver production and by signing the Silver Purchase Act of 1934. FDR's programs doubled the price of the white metal, a boon to American mines but a catastrophe for Nationalist China. Smugglers drained the white metal from Shanghai banks for sale at inflated prices on world markets and forced the Asian giant off the silver standard.

Henry Morgenthau

Roosevelt's neighbor in Dutchess County, New York, and a personal confidante, became FDR's Treasury secretary and implemented the Silver Purchase Act for the president. Morgenthau nationalized the white metal and led a buying program to make silver 25% of America's monetary reserves but warned Roosevelt that this made Nationalist China, led by American ally Chiang Kai-shek, vulnerable to an internal threat from Mao Tse-tung's communist insurgents and an external threat from Imperial Japan. Morgenthau abandoned the aggressive buying program in December 1935, with the approval of Key Pittman, but failed to save China. The Silver Purchase Act tipped the balance of power in Japan away from the diplomats and towards the military, contributing to the outbreak of the Sino-Japanese War in 1937.

John Fitzgerald Kennedy

Elected U.S. president in 1960 and assassinated on November 22, 1963, by Lee Harvey Oswald before his main legislative initiative on civil rights could be enacted by Congress. He succeeded in repealing FDR's Silver Purchase Act in June 1963, a small step in making the white metal more readily available to industry. As a former senator from Massachusetts, home to silversmiths since the time of Paul Revere, Kennedy had long favored eliminating any monetary use of the white metal. The Warren Commission investigation into the assassination concluded that Oswald acted alone but failed to consider whether Kennedy was murdered for dropping the silver subsidy, a conspiracy theory no worse than the rest given the metal's power to provoke passion and fury in the American heartland for more than a century.

Lyndon Baines Johnson

Succeeded Kennedy as U.S. president and completed much of JFK's unfinished legislation, including freeing the white metal from government influence and eliminating in 1968 the connection between both gold and silver and domestic money and credit. Severing the link between precious metals and money allowed America's central bank, the Federal Reserve System, to deliver easy credit in response to political pressure, spawning the Great Inflation of the 1970s. The absence of government influence turned silver into a hard asset, unleashed a wave of speculation that drove the price above Alexander Hamilton's $1.29, and roiled financial markets.

Henry Jarecki

A German-born psychiatrist in his midthirties on the faculty of Yale University Medical School, pioneer in the drug treatment of depression, abandoned his medical career in the late 1960s to capitalize on the silver frenzy. Jarecki made millions by arbitraging between the U.S. Treasury's obligation to redeem silver certificates at the fixed price of $1.29 and the free market price of bullion on the Commodity Exchange. He spent the 1970s building Mocatta Metals Corporation into one of the biggest bullion trading companies in America and battling the Hunt brothers' alleged attempt to manipulate the silver market.

Nelson Bunker Hunt

A member of the right-wing John Birch Society, Bunker became the richest man in the world at age forty in 1966 when oil was discovered in Libya, where he owned the drilling rights. His ultra-conservative politics made him distrust government and its paper currency and favor real investments, such as oil, land, racehorses, and precious metals. His preference for silver became an obsession in 1973 after Libya, under Muammar Qaddafi, nationalized his oil fields. He and his brothers, Herbert and Lamar, accumulated 200 million ounces of the white metal between 1973 and 1979, more than the combined annual output of the four largest producing countries in the world. Skyrocketing silver prices during 1979 raised the value of their holdings from $2 billion to $10 billion, bringing charges of price manipulation and leading to retaliation by the Exchanges that eventually forced Bunker into bankruptcy.

Warren Buffett

The most successful investor in the second half of the twentieth century, famous for buying and holding companies that are understandable and run by outstanding people and avoiding assets like gold, which he said will "remain lifeless forever." Buffett, CEO of Berkshire Hathaway, had been monitoring silver, which he considered more industrial than precious, for longer than Bunker Hunt. He finally plunged into the white metal in 1997, buying more than 100 million ounces, driving up the price, and triggering headlines that the Hunts were back in town. Buffett's integrity quieted the uproar, but his investment strategy failed to match his reputation. He sold too early, leaving more than $4 billion on the table, and returned to investments like Coca Cola, which he has held forever.

INTRODUCTION

OBSESSION

LAMAR HUNT, THE THIRTY-FOUR-YEAR-OLD OWNER OF THE KANSAS City Chiefs football team, negotiated the merger of the upstart American Football League with the older and well-established National Football League in 1966, creating the most successful sports enterprise in America. Hunt also invented the name Super Bowl, originally the championship game between the two leagues, and now the most popular single sporting event in the country. He explained the origin of his inspiration: "My daughter, Sharron, and my son, Lamar Jr., had a children's toy called a Super Ball, and I probably interchanged the phonetics of 'bowl' and 'ball.' "[1]

The first Super Bowl was played in January 1967 and pitted Hunt's Kansas City Chiefs against Vince Lombardi's Green Bay Packers. The Packers walloped the Chiefs 35–10 and were awarded the Super Bowl trophy, a seven-pound sterling silver football made by Tiffany & Company. Winners of the annual Super Bowl since then have received an identical creation, now called the Vince Lombardi Trophy, with the winning team's name engraved on the pedestal by Tiffany craftsmen.

Lamar was proud of his franchise, especially after his Chiefs won the Super Bowl in January 1970, but he had no way of knowing that ten years later the trophy itself would be worth twenty-five times its original value, and not just for sentimental reasons. In January 1980 the price of silver had jumped to $50 an ounce, a modern record that still stands, and Lamar, together with his older brothers Nelson Bunker Hunt and Herbert Hunt, would be accused of rigging the price of the white metal in the boldest commodities market manipulation of the twentieth century.[2]

Lamar, Nelson Bunker, and Herbert were sons of H.L. Hunt, a poker-playing oil tycoon whose right-wing political outlook equated New York's liberal Republican governor, Nelson Rocke-feller, with Cuba's Fidel Castro. The family patriarch taught his children to distrust government, especially its paper currency, and to invest in real things, such as oil, land, and precious metals. He established trusts for his children, including shares in the family's billion-dollar crown jewel, the Placid Oil Company, which served as a funding source for their business ventures. The tall and trim Lamar, as mild mannered as an accountant, concentrated on foot-ball during the 1960s, while his outspoken older brother Bunker, as Nelson was called, concentrated on racehorses and oil fields. Bunker was a pear-shaped 250-pounder who enjoyed the limelight that came with being the family spokesman. A speculator like his father, Bunker may have been the richest man in the world after oil was discovered in Libya, where he owned the drilling rights. Bunker had made his deal with Libya's King Idris, but before he could en-joy all the fruits of his speculations, insurgents led by Muammar Qaddafi overthrew the monarchy in 1969 and soon after nation-alized the oil fields. Bunker was still a billionaire, when a billion dollars was real money, but the incident increased his distrust of government.

Bunker affirmed his conservative credentials by joining the John Birch Society, the Tea Party of its day, and began investing in silver because he feared government spending would produce inflation and erode the value of the U.S. dollar.[3] He also thought he could store his cache of the precious metal on his two-thousand-acre Cir-cle T ranch near Dallas without worrying about Qaddafi. But his speculation quickly turned into an obsession, and even Texas was not big enough for his holdings. Between 1973 and 1979 he led his brothers in accumulating almost 200 million ounces of the white metal, stored in New York, London, Switzerland, and other loca-tions that may not have been publicly disclosed. The Hunt silver was worth about $2 billion in September 1979. Four months later, when silver hit $50 an ounce, it came to nearly $10 billion.

Then it all disappeared. Within a year Bunker Hunt was forced to pledge his shares in Placid Oil as collateral for a billion-dollar loan to avoid bankruptcy. He had personally borrowed heavily to buy silver and the value of his leveraged holdings collapsed when prices fell back to $10 an ounce, a drop that rivaled the decline in the Dow Jones stock index during the Great Depression. He and his brothers were then found liable for conspiring with Saudi Arabian sheikhs to corner the silver market during their speculative binge. Bunker Hunt declared personal bankruptcy after the trial and lost prized possessions to his creditors, including fifteen ancient Greek vases and a collection of silver coins dating from the Roman Empire.[4] When an older sister asked what had happened, he answered, "I was just trying to make some money."[5]

The Hunts were not the first nor the last to be seduced by the white metal. In 1997 Warren Buffett, perhaps the most successful investor of the past fifty years, bought more than 100 million ounces, almost as much as the Hunts, and drove the price of silver to a ten-year peak. In 1933 Franklin Delano Roosevelt raised the price for silver at the U.S. Treasury to mollify senators from western mining states while ignoring the help it gave Japan in subjugating China. And in 1918 Senator Key Pittman of Nevada subsidized his home state constituents by sponsoring legislation to sell silver to India during the Great War. But the white metal has been more than just a vehicle for personal advancement to Americans; it has been part of the country's monetary system since the founding of the Republic and is woven into the fabric of history like the stars and stripes.

Perhaps the most famous speech in American electoral politics, Nebraska Congressman William Jennings Bryan's "Cross of Gold" sermon at the 1896 Democratic convention, was all about silver. Bryan became the party's nominee for president after delivering an address that would make a modern televangelist blush: "I come to speak to you in defense of a cause as holy as the cause of liberty— the cause of humanity . . . that all believers in free coinage of silver in the Democratic Party should organize and take charge of and control the policy of the Democratic Party . . . We do not come as aggressors. Our war is not a war of conquest. We are fighting in the defense of our homes, our families, and posterity."[6] Bryan's cause, the resurrection of silver as a monetary metal, aimed to rectify the injustice perpetrated by the Crime of 1873, which discontinued the coinage of silver dollars that Congress authorized in 1792 and established gold as king of American finance. The demonetization of silver sparked a great deflation in the United States during the last quarter of the nineteenth century, with declining agricultural prices provoking resentment among midwestern farmers against East Coast bankers. *The Wonderful Wizard of Oz*, which has entertained millions since it was published in 1900, is an allegory of the contemporary class warfare.

The abundance of silver in America during the 1870s made it the metal of the people, synonymous with cheap money compared with the more restrictive supply of currency under the gold standard. Bryan viewed remonetizing the white metal as a way to promote inflation to reduce the burden of mortgages owed by farmers to the banks. A century later, during the 1970s, the Hunts invested in silver as a bulwark against inflation, a rock-hard asset to protect their fortune against the spendthrift ways of the government. This is the story of silver's transformation from soft money during the nineteenth century to hard asset today, and how manipulations of the white metal have altered the modern world; but to understand the attraction of silver to politicians and its vulnerability to speculators and schemers requires historical perspective.

Silver is the preferred protection against government defaults, political instability, and inflation for people in most countries, a place to hide when conventional investments sour. In the three years following the financial crisis of 2008, when banks teetered on the brink of insolvency and the government debts of Italy, Ireland, and Greece resembled junk bonds, anxious investors drove up the price of silver by almost 400%, an increase greater than ten years of Warren Buffet's Berkshire Hathaway stock.[7] But the precious metal is more than just another safe-haven investment. For centuries it has been hammered by silversmiths into serving platters, candlesticks, and wine goblets for the upper classes. Families display these heirlooms with pride in their dining room cupboards to highlight an affluent past, but during bad times they are quietly sold for cash.

Silver has also been the monetary standard of almost every country in the world, including China and Saudi Arabia in the twentieth century, Great Britain in the seventeenth, and Biblical Egypt. Britain dominated world commerce with the gold standard during the nineteenth century, but its currency is still called "the pound sterling," a paradoxical reference to sterling silver as the standard. The word "sterling" means that a coin, candelabra, or Super Bowl trophy contains 92.5% pure silver, with the remaining 7.5% usually consisting of copper for strength. A mixture of nitric acid and potassium dichromate produces a different color on a sample scraping of "fine" silver, which is 99.9% pure, compared with sterling, and there is little to dispute once the sample has been assayed (tested) professionally.[8] Governments guarantee the purity and weight of coins minted from precious metals to make the currency generally accepted without further testing, and silversmiths engrave 925 or the word sterling on their work to certify its quality. Queen Elizabeth I, daughter of Henry VIII and Anne Boleyn, ascended the throne in 1558 and two years later made the metal backing the British currency one pound of sterling silver.[9] This so-called "ancient right standard of England" originated in the eleventh century under William the Conqueror, but had been debased by the gluttonous Henry before Elizabeth's rescue.[10] The sterling reference stuck despite Britain's switch to gold and survives today even though the silver content of the pound is long gone.

The clash between ornamental demands by silversmiths and government coinage often had surprising consequences. Louis XIV, the absolute monarch of France for seventy years until his death in 1715, turned the magnificent silver furniture and tableware in the Palace of Versailles into bullion bars for minting by his Treasury.[11] Silver dishes with matching place settings became common currency. The remaining French nobility had little choice but to follow the king's example—Louis is famous for the proclamation, "L'État, c'est moi" (I am the state). The results were fiscal credibility in France and a scarcity value in the surviving silver antiques.

Governments no longer coin silver as currency but rising industrial demands compete with silversmiths for the available supply of the white metal. Photographic film produced by the camera company Eastman Kodak usually consumed more silver in a year than the jewelry industry.[12] Now that digital cameras have made photographic film obsolete (driving Kodak into bankruptcy in 2012), the electronics industry dominates commercial uses. Silver, called a noble metal, along with gold and platinum, because it resists corrosion, is the best conductor of electricity and is used in circuit breakers, switches, fuses, and other electrical components. Modern technology has also exploited silver's antibacterial properties. In 2006 the giant Korean manufacturer Samsung introduced a washing machine that releases silver ions in the wash cycle to help sanitize the laundry.[13] Specialty retailer Sharper Image advertised a plastic food container infused with silver nanoparticles to keep food fresher, which received positive feedback on Amazon from users.[14] And in 2017 Colgate University in central New York state sprayed its locker rooms with a decontaminating fog of hydrogen peroxide and silver to combat the deadly MRSA staph infection.[15] The white metal's industrial demand now exceeds its combined use in jewelry, bullion bars, and commemorative coins.[16]

Silver attracts manipulators because occasional bursts of speculative fever clash with rising commercial use, especially when citizens fear political unrest. The resulting price gyrations allow conspirators to promote higher prices with relatively little effort while also camouflaging their manipulation. On November 4, 1979, during the height of the alleged Hunt conspiracy to corner the silver market, Iranian students invaded the U.S. embassy and took American citizens hostage.[17] The ensuing political crisis contributed to the tripling of silver prices during the next three months, masking the footprints of the manipulators.[18]

Gold is the primary store of value for those who mistrust the government, but silver remains the refuge of choice for most people because it is cheaper and more accessible. A standard 100-ounce bar of silver, about the size of three Hershey bars stacked on top of each other, costs about $1,700 today compared with a price of $130,000 for a 100-ounce gold bar. The relatively small dollar size of the silver market makes the white metal more volatile than the yellow, where a million-dollar order from anxious buyers and sellers makes a bigger impact.[19] Silver led the jump in precious metals after the 2008 financial crisis with nearly a 400% increase compared with almost 250% for gold.[20]

For most of recorded history paper currency was acceptable in everyday transactions because governments promised to exchange those pieces of paper for gold or silver, which gave money intrinsic value. U.S. citizens could exchange dollars for gold at the rate of $20.67 per ounce at the U.S. Treasury until 1933, and foreign governments could do the same at $35.00 per ounce between 1934 and 1971. President Nixon suspended the Treasury's gold obligations on August 15, 1971, ending the last connection between the dollar and precious metals.

All countries now issue fiat currency, paper money backed only by the creditworthiness of the government. The verdict remains uncertain on this relatively new worldwide experiment in pure paper currency because governments have often abused their right to print money, destroying its value, as in the 1920s hyperinflation in Germany.[21] Those concerned that the experiment will fail, such as the Hunts in the 1970s and the Tea Party today, seek refuge in the ageless storehouses of gold or silver. The great English economist David Ricardo, who learned a lot about money as a successful speculator, wrote almost two hundred years ago, "Experience, however, shows that neither a State nor a Bank ever have had the unrestricted power of issuing paper money, without abusing that power."[22] Ricardo recommended that "the issue of paper money ought to be under some check and control; and none seems so proper for that purpose as that of subjecting the issuers of paper money to the obligation of paying their notes, either in gold [or silver] coin or bullion."[23] Anchoring currencies to precious metals promoted price stability but caused controversy as well.

The United States, at the urging of Secretary of the Treasury Alexander Hamilton, established the silver dollar alongside gold in 1792 as America's currency. The two metals vied for public attention under this bimetallic standard until Congress passed the Coinage Act of 1873, eliminating the official status of silver and making gold the sole backing of America's money.[24] The scarcity of the yellow metal caused widespread price deflation over the next twenty-five years, and the reduced government demand for silver contributed to its decline in value of more than 50%.[25] The subsequent outcry in western mining states for Congress "to do something for silver" made headlines throughout the country.[26] William Jennings Bryan rode a silver train of resentment to the 1896 Democratic nomination for the presidency that ended in his defeat by William McKinley. Bryan ran twice more for the White House and lost, but none of those setbacks muffled the agitation for silver, which continued well into the twentieth century.

During the Great Depression, after the price of silver hit a record low of 24¢ an ounce, Democratic Senator Key Pittman of Nevada, the powerful chairman of the Senate Foreign Relations Committee, urged President Roosevelt to restore the white metal's full monetary status.[27] In exchange, Pittman promised the support of fourteen senators from western mining states for Roosevelt's controversial New Deal legislation. FDR responded with a series of purchase programs for silver, beginning with an executive order on December 21, 1933, directing the U.S. Treasury to buy the domestically produced metal at 64.5¢ an ounce, a premium of 50% above the free market price of 43¢.[28] The subsidy and the doubling of silver prices during Roosevelt's first administration gave "the silver miners and speculators much for which to be thankful," according to contemporary financial observers.[29] Senator Pittman agreed and described FDR's benevolence as a "Christmas present."[30]

Pittman made good on his promise. He delivered the "silver bloc" senators in support of FDR's 1933 pump-priming legislation, helping to jump-start the domestic economy, but U.S. diplomacy suffered a major blow. The higher price paid by the Treasury attracted silver from the rest of the world, especially from China, whose currency was backed by the precious metal. Despite local laws restricting exports, speculators smuggled silver out of Shanghai to profit on world markets and ultimately forced China to abandon the silver standard when that country was most vulnerable.[31] It was 1935 and China, led by American ally Chiang Kai-shek, faced an internal threat from Mao Tse-tung's communist insurgents and an external threat from Imperial Japan. Roosevelt's Treasury secretary, Henry Morgenthau, worried that China's insecure government, weak economy, and susceptibility to Japanese aggression made her especially vulnerable to the dislocations arising from American silver policy.[32]

Morgenthau was right to worry. Roosevelt's pro-silver program to please western senators helped the Japanese military subjugate a weakened China and boosted Japan's march towards World War II, demonstrating the danger of formulating domestic policy without considering international consequences. Was FDR's price manipulation less criminal than Nelson Bunker Hunt's? Reading this book will let you make an informed judgment.

CHAPTER 1

HAMILTON'S DESIGN

ALEXANDER HAMILTON KNEW MORE ABOUT MONEY AND FINANCE than just about anyone at the Constitutional Convention. He was born out of wedlock in the West Indies around 1755, came to New York City in 1773, where he studied at King's College, now Columbia University, and became an American patriot. He joined the New York militia to fight the British during the Revolution and served on George Washington's Continental Army staff for most of the War. Following the victory, he helped found the Bank of New York, which survives today as Bank of New York Mellon, but soon turned his attention to remedying the loose connection among the states under the Articles of Confederation. He championed the establishment of a strong central government in the Federalist Papers, authored with James Madison and John Jay, and during the Constitutional Convention proposed a lifetime term for the American president like Britain's King George III. Washington disagreed with Hamilton's royalist instincts, of course, but put his young protégé's financial skills to work by appointing him Treasury secretary in his first cabinet.[1]

Hamilton had more success implementing British traditions in his new job. He prepared a 1791 report "On the Establishment of a Mint" that recommended defining the U.S. dollar in terms of gold and silver, like the legal bimetallic standard prevailing in England.[2] The resulting legislation of April 2, 1792, created a number of American coins, including a silver dollar weighing about three-quarters of an ounce and a ten-dollar gold eagle weighing about half an ounce.[3] The precious metal content was specified precisely as 371.25 grains of pure silver for the dollar and 247.5 grains of pure gold for the ten-dollar eagle, and Hamilton recommended a version of Britain's Trial of the Pyx to ensure accuracy.[4]

FIGURE 1. Hamilton graces the Treasury.

The British trial dates back to the thirteenth century and was designed to protect the King's currency from being debased by the Master of the Mint producing coins with less precious metal content than the sterling standard. Coins were randomly selected from the mint's production, locked in a chest (called the pyx) from one trial to the next, and were assayed by independent experts. A favorable verdict assured the public of its currency's intrinsic value, while a negative outcome led to an indictment of the Master of the Royal Mint. Giles de Hertesbergh, who became Master of the Mint in 1316, was convicted of shortchanging the currency and spent six weeks in London's Marshalsea Prison along with smugglers, debtors, and pirates.[5]

The 1792 act followed Hamilton's proposals and required that an annual sample of coins be "assayed under the inspection of the Chief Justice of the United States, the Secretary and Comptroller of the Treasury, and the Attorney General of the United States," a jury that rivals the best of Britain, but the punitive stage of the legislation took on a distinctly American flavor.[6] Section 19 provided that if any of the coins were "debased or made worse . . . every such officer or person who shall commit any or either of the said offenses shall be deemed guilty of felony, and shall suffer death."[7]

Capital punishment has always been serious business in the United States, with somber witnesses to executions on death row heading the list. Although no one was put to death in almost two hundred pyx trials (at least not publicly), the potential remained until President Jimmy Carter effectively ended the drama in 1977 by abolishing the U.S. Assay Commission, the agency charged with testing the coins.[8] The Carter Administration called it a much-needed cost-cutting move, but voters failed to appreciate the president's penny-pinching and, for other reasons too numerous to mention, rejected his reelection bid in 1980.

Most of Hamilton's 1791 Mint Report focused on tying the U.S. dollar to gold and silver so that anyone with either metal could bring in bullion and receive coins in exchange, which is how currency was created back then. Hamilton considered gold by itself because of its stability and "greater rarity" but concluded that eliminating either metal from coinage would "abridge the quantity of circulating medium" and expose the country to the "evils of a scanty circulation."[9] A successful medium of exchange treads gently between scarcity and excess, like the ebb and flow of a mighty river, and nurtures commerce when the forces balance. Silver dominated as money in ancient times because it was valuable and remained the key circulating currency throughout Europe for hundreds of years because it never became too valuable.[10] Hamilton promoted silver to avoid deflation and to sustain economic growth, and Congress made both precious metals legal tender in America, acceptable in the payment of debts and taxes. Gold's greater value made it especially useful for large business transactions, like importing a case of French champagne, while silver was better for smaller social events, like buying a round at the local tavern.

Hamilton agonized over the relative gold and silver content of the dollar, knowing that incorrect ratios resulted in circulation of the overvalued coin while the undervalued would remain bullion. This well-known pitfall, called Gresham's law after Sir Thomas Gresham, who helped Queen Elizabeth I reestablish the purity of the British pound, goes by the popular phrase "bad money drives good money out of circulation."[11] Sir Isaac Newton, the great scientist who had a second career as Britain's Master of the Mint in the early eighteenth century, fell victim to Gresham's law by inadvertently overvaluing gold and driving silver out of circulation.[12] Many doubt that Gresham ever said the phrase, but history has been kind to Sir Thomas and his law just as it has been to Mr. Murphy and his law—If anything can go wrong, it will—whether or not he said it.

A simple example illustrates Gresham's law. Suppose jewelers and silversmiths are willing to pay one dollar per ounce of gold or silver bullion and the mint follows suit and establishes a dollar coin containing an ounce of either metal. Owners of bullion would come to the mint to have the metal assayed for free and receive a dollar coin, so both metals would circulate as currency. Now suppose gold bullion rises in value to $2 per ounce because doctors say that eating gold flakes for breakfast makes you skinny.[13] The mint continues to pay one dollar for either metal because that is the legal definition of each coin but now everyone hoards gold and brings only silver to be coined. Gold would no longer serve as currency because it is more valuable as a diet supplement.

Both coins circulate under a bimetallic standard, avoiding the "evils of a scanty circulation," only when mint prices reflect market values. After much discussion Hamilton proposed a price ratio of fifteen-to-one at the mint because gold bullion was worth about fifteen times an equal weight of silver in 1791.[14] The precious metal content of each coin in the 1792 Coinage Act resulted in a mint price of $1.29 per ounce of silver and a gold price fifteen times larger, $19.39 per ounce.[15] These relative prices worked perfectly

FIGURE 2. A familiar Alexander Hamilton.

for about ten years, until the market value of gold relative to silver rose to almost 16 to 1, and citizens hoarded the yellow metal and brought only silver to the mint, just as Gresham predicted.[16]

The emergence of a silver standard from the framework of bi-metallism probably displeased Hamilton, but not for long. He was killed in America's most famous duel on July 11, 1804, by Aaron Burr, the sitting vice president of the United States. Bad blood had soured their relationship over many years. Hamilton supported Thomas Jefferson over Burr in the contested presidential election of 1800 and the former Treasury secretary supposedly denigrated the vice president, who ran for governor of New York in 1804. But the underlying tension probably began much earlier: Burr had studied at the College of New Jersey, now Princeton University, making the King's College (now Columbia)-educated Hamilton a natural Ivy League rival.

Hamilton could not amend his handiwork but Congress did it for him in 1834 (with further adjustment in 1837) by redefining the gold content of the dollar and increasing the mint price per ounce to $20.67.[17] The new mint price ratio of gold to silver of 16 to 1 ($20.67 divided by $1.29) overvalued gold compared with the bullion market and encouraged Americans to turn the yellow metal into coins, which they did.[18] Going forward gold served as the primary medium of exchange in America even though both silver and gold were legal tender, acceptable in payment of debts and taxes. Silver was relatively more valuable as bullion than as coins at 16 to 1, with an average price in the metals market greater than the mint price of $1.29 per ounce in every year from 1834 through 1873.[19] The highest annual average price per ounce of silver was $1.36 in 1859, when the discovery of the giant Comstock Lode was publicized, marking a peak in value for the white metal. The average yearly price of silver would fall well below that level for the next hundred years and make the 16 to 1 price ratio a distant memory.[20]

The Comstock Lode, centered in Virginia City, Nevada, a rocky outcropping in the middle of nowhere, produced more silver in its first ten years of operation than America had ever seen. Thousands of settlers from across the country, plus immigrants from countries such as Ireland, France, Germany, and China, swarmed into the barren wasteland to seek their fortune, transforming the slopes of Mount Davidson into the bustling metropolis of 30,000 called Virginia City.[21] The steep grade of the mountainside made daily life an adventure, frequently forcing citizens to take cover when they heard the rumble of runaway wagons rolling down C Street in city center. But vigilance and perseverance paid dividends to those who survived the dust and dirt of frontier living. Mining companies such as Keystone, Ophir, Yellow Jacket, and Uncle Sam (of course) extracted about $30 million in silver from the Comstock Lode from 1861 through 1870 compared with less than $2 million produced in the entire United States from the founding of the Republic until then.[22]

This mining bonanza had a much broader impact on American life than simply turning a few pick axes into silver spoons. It launched the career of America's most famous nineteenth-century humorist, Samuel Clemens, who took the name Mark Twain as a reporter for Virginia City's *Territorial Enterprise*; it brought Nevada into the Civil War on the Union side as America's thirty-sixth state on October 31, 1864; and a century later it spawned the NBC TV hit western *Bonanza*, which aired from 1959 through 1973 and whose title references the giant discovery in the region called the Big Bonanza.[23] Some blame the Comstock Lode with triggering a collapse in silver prices that ultimately led to the 1896 presidential candidacy of William Jennings Bryan and the confrontation between East Coast bankers and midwestern farmers. The evidence shows that the Virginia City mines were a sideshow.

Despite the jump in silver production from the Comstock Lode during the 1860s the price of bullion remained remarkably constant, averaging between $1.35 per ounce in 1860 and $1.33 in 1869.[24] The 50% price decline during the remainder of the nineteenth century began in 1873, when silver fell below $1.30 per ounce for the first time in almost thirty years, and continued to slide like those runaway wagons in Virginia City.[25] The year 1873 was the date of an alleged crime, when Senator John Sherman, chairman of the Senate Finance Committee, guided the Coinage Act through Congress, eliminating the silver dollar as legal tender in the United States. Silver's vulnerability began with the California gold rush a generation earlier, and Sherman fed the avalanche with deliberate deception.

SOLVING THE CRIME
OF 1873

REPUBLICAN JOHN SHERMAN OF OHIO SPENT ALMOST HALF A century in Washington, D.C., as an influential legislator and cabinet member. He was elected to Congress in 1854 and then to the U.S. Senate in 1861, becoming a staunch supporter of Abraham Lincoln during the Civil War. He would later serve as secretary of the Treasury under Rutherford B. Hayes and as secretary of state under William McKinley but is most famous for sponsoring what became known as the Sherman Antitrust Act passed in 1890, the favorite legislation of trust-busting President Teddy Roosevelt. Few remember Sherman's role as chairman of the Senate Finance Committee in the alleged Crime of 1873, which is exactly what he wanted.

Sherman was born in Lancaster, Ohio, in 1823, one of eleven children, to Charles and Mary Sherman.[1] His father was a successful lawyer who died when John was six years old but still served as an example. John became a lawyer like his father and then used his legal training, like many before and since, to launch a political career. He accumulated considerable legislative power during his tenure in Washington and twice pursued, but failed to become, the Republican presidential candidate. Throughout his career, he suffered in the shadow of an older brother, Civil War General William Tecumseh Sherman, who replaced Ulysses S. Grant as Commanding General of the Army after Grant became president. General Sherman had gained fame for his brutal "march to the sea" through Georgia during the war but soon became an engaging and entertaining public speaker. He turned down subsequent requests to become a presidential candidate by famously saying, "I will not accept if nominated and will not serve if elected."[2] Sibling rivalry

FIGURE 3. A relaxed Senator John Sherman.

aside, Senator Sherman, known as the "Ohio icicle" for his austere personality, would have denied allegations of deception in the Coinage Act of 1873, but public admiration for his gregarious brother, called "Cump" by family and friends, must have encouraged the cover-up.[3]

The Crime of 1873 refers to legislation passed by Congress on February 12, 1873, negating Alexander Hamilton's favorite law, that both gold and silver be monetary standards in the United States, and establishing gold as sole legal tender for all obligations.[4]

The new law omitted the free and unlimited coinage of silver dollars at the mint, an option since 1792, and restricted the legal tender status of subsidiary silver coins, like dimes, quarters, and half-dollars, to five dollars or less.[5] The U.S. Constitution allows Congress to "coin money" and "regulate the value thereof," so no legislator voting for the act committed a crime in the technical sense. Senators and congressmen could even make their favorite coins of Great Britain, France, Spain, and Portugal legal tender in the U.S., which they did in 1793, without violating the law.[6] The allegations of impropriety arose because few people realized the full consequences of the shift to gold when the law was passed. Moreover, Senate Finance Committee Chairman John Sherman, who introduced the legislation, not only failed to sound the warning bell but also soft-pedaled the bill despite knowing its importance.

Sherman said on the Senate floor during an early discussion of the Coinage Act,[7] "This is a bill to codify the mintage laws of the United States. It does not adopt any new principles; it makes but very few changes in the general laws, except to transferring the head of the Minting Bureau to Washington."[8] Sherman should have stopped after the first sentence, which accurately described the legislation. More than fifty of the sixty-seven sections of the Coinage Act of 1873 deal with the minting process, including the salaries and responsibilities of the assayer, melter, refiner, and coiner, as well as administrative matters, such as making the mint a bureau within the Treasury Department rather than a free standing agency.[9] Much of the associated debate in Congress focused on whether the mint should charge a fee for coining bullion.[10] These housekeeping details on minting pushed the legislation's substantive change in the monetary standard beneath the radar of even sophisticated observers, like Francis A. Walker, a professor of political economy who had been lecturing on the topic of money at Yale in 1873. An avid newspaper reader with close friends in New York business circles, Walker confesses not to have "learned of the demonetization of the silver dollar" until long after it had happened.[11]

The word "crime" to describe the 1873 Act was first used by George M. Weston, secretary of the U.S. Monetary Commission of 1876, who wrote, "It is impossible to doubt that the laws of the country have been tampered with. Who the perpetrators of this crime were is not likely ever to be satisfactorily known."[12] Senator John P. Jones of Nevada called it a "grave wrong" to remove silver as a monetary standard "under the guise of regulating the mints of the United States."[13] Others called it a "fraud" and "conspiracy," but Professor Walker, who would become president of MIT as well as the founding president of the American Economic Association, set the proper tone of condemnation: "No man in a position of trust has a right to allow a measure of such importance to pass without calling attention sharply to it, and making sure that its bearings were fully comprehended. And no man who did not know that the demonetization of silver by the United States was a measure of transcendent importance, had any right to be on such a committee or to put his hand to a bill which touched the coinage of a great country." [14]

◆ ◆ ◆

John Sherman had become chairman of the Senate Finance Committee in March 1867 and knew almost immediately that silver's role as a monetary standard would disappear like the recently extinct dodo bird.[15] He toured Europe during the spring of 1867 and spent considerable time in Paris attending both the Universal Exposition, a world's fair organized at the suggestion of French Emperor Napoleon III, and the international monetary conference, where representatives of twenty countries gathered to promote uniformity across borders in weights, measures, and coins.[16] Sherman was treated like visiting royalty, referred to as "Monsieur le Senateur" while joining a reception given by the Emperor at the richly decorated Tuileries Palace adjacent to the Louvre.[17] He donned evening attire, including dress coat, formal trousers, and black silk stockings, and was presented to the Empress of Russia, the Prince of Wales, the King of Prussia, and Bismarck, who Sherman proudly recalls, "recognized me with a bow and a few words."[18] But state formalities took a backseat to the international monetary conference for the future of silver in world commerce.

Amidst the distractions of Parisian nightlife, the conference focused on narrow questions like the universal adoption of the metric system and broader issues like the appropriate international monetary standard. Spurred by massive discoveries of gold in California and Australia in the 1850s, which cheapened the yellow metal and led to its dominance as the circulating medium (courtesy of Gresham), conference participants recognized that gold had become sufficiently plentiful to support growing world trade and no longer suffered from excessive scarcity compared with silver. Moreover, they cited the easy portability of gold relative to the white metal as an advantage for "international coins," providing an ideal medium of exchange to settle trade among countries.[19] The conference voted by "a great majority" that gold be "the sole monetary standard of value" and recommended abandoning "the system of double monetary standard [bimetallism] . . . wherever it exists."[20]

Within six years of the Paris Monetary Conference nearly every major European country had moved towards the gold standard, and John Sherman wasted little time implementing its recommendations in the United States. He submitted a bill to Congress in 1868, based on the report of Samuel Ruggles, America's representative to the international conference, called "In relation to the coinage of gold and silver."[21] The legislation headlined demonetizing silver and promoted a new five-dollar gold coin that would be interchangeable with a French coin of twenty-five francs. Section 3 of the bill emphasizes "that the gold coins to be issued under this act shall be a legal tender in all payments to any amount; and the silver coins shall be a legal tender to an amount not exceeding ten dollars in any one payment." Opponents of the bill, led by Senator Edwin Morgan of New York, a former chairman of the Republican National Committee, ambushed the initiative by observing, "A change in our national coinage so grave as that proposed by the bill should be made only after the most mature deliberation."[22]

Sherman learned from this battlefield setback and countered with a diversion strategy worthy of study at West Point. He introduced new legislation prepared by the Treasury in April 1870, called "Revising the laws relative to the mints, assay offices, and coinage of the United States."[23] The bill quietly buried the demonetization of silver under mind-numbing instructions to the mint, such as "the assayer shall assay all metals and bullion whenever such assays are required in the operations of the mint."[24] The proposed legislation also removed the link to the French franc. Most newspapers ignored the 1870 bill, as well as the resulting Coinage Act of 1873, and those publications that commented put the withdrawal of the silver dollar at the bottom of the pyramid.[25]

No one cared about the mint, other than residents of Philadelphia (where the main branch was located), and fewer worried about the silver dollar in 1873, which was an "unknown coin" in the country according to Sherman.[26] And the senator was right.[27] For more than a generation silversmiths had turned the white metal into forks and knives rather than letting it circulate as currency. The value of shiny cutlery at the dinner table was worth more per ounce than the mint price of $1.29. Sherman added a personal observation in his memoirs: "Although I was quite active in business which brought under my eye different forms of money, I do not remember at that time ever to have seen a silver dollar."[28]

From Sherman's perspective the legislation simply ratified the status quo, suggesting that no one would miss the silver dollar, and justifying his early observation that the bill "does not adopt any new principles." But that perspective ignores an important aspect of bimetallism even when one metal dominates, as gold did in the decades before the Coinage Act of 1873. Alexander Hamilton made both gold and silver legal tender primarily to avoid the scarcity of circulating currency, to serve as a buffer against deflation, but that also gave taxpayers and debtors the option to pay their obligations in the cheaper metal. Everyone likes options, which, by definition, confer the right but not the obligation to do something, and are valuable even if they remain unused.

For example, homeowners value the right to refinance their mortgages, such as replacing a 6% loan with one costing 4% as interest rates decline, and that right facilitates the initial decision to borrow and buy a home. Few homeowners refinanced their mortgages in the United States during the 1970s because interest rates rose throughout the decade, and some may have forgotten how profitable refinancing could be, but no mortgage borrower would willingly abandon that option without a fight. Congressmen who quietly passed legislation to remove the refinancing option because it had fallen into disuse would have to find alternative employment after the next election.

During the decades before the Coinage Act of 1873 few Americans exercised the option to pay obligations in silver because the white metal was more valuable as bullion. In the colorful horseracing language of finance professionals, it was an out-of-the-money option because it failed to pay off, like the losing thoroughbreds in the Kentucky Derby, and that explains the giant yawn greeting the Coinage Act of 1873. But the market price of silver declined sharply soon after, making those out-of-the-money options quite valuable. The price of $1.29 per ounce at the mint looked cheap in 1872, when silver bullion averaged $1.32, but when silver hit $1.16 in 1876 that same mint price would have been a bonanza.

The Coinage Act was passed with the help of Sherman's subterfuge, but that legislation did not precipitate the price slide that led to the outcry of criminal behavior. The price of silver had already reached the lowest point in more than twenty years in the London bullion market in December 1872, two months before the act became law.[29] European countries dominated the demonetization of silver and the switch to gold, beginning with the Imperial Coinage Law in Germany, passed on December 4, 1871, at the urging of Chancellor Bismarck, and followed by Sweden and Denmark adopting gold in 1873.[30] Belgium, Italy, France, and Switzerland moved towards the gold standard by restricting the free coinage of silver.[31] France cut the maximum silver coinage to 250,000 francs per day in September 1873 and reduced it further to 150,000 francs in November.[32] Holland ended the practice of buying silver at a fixed price in 1872 and stopped all silver coinage in 1873.[33] In what appears like a coordinated ambush, massive sales of silver by Germany, which had been on a silver standard until then, combined with the absence of buyers from the rest of Europe, pushed down the price of the white metal to then unprecedented levels.[34]

The unlikely provocation for this European offensive against silver began in the gold mines of California, Russia, and Australia in the 1850s. Silver dominated gold as the preferred currency for most of recorded history primarily because it was scarce but not too scarce, so that it held its value but was sufficiently abundant to support expanding trade. But the explosion in gold production beginning in 1848 at Sutter's Mill, California, coupled with discoveries in Russia and Australia, appeared to solve the gold shortage.[35] Total world production in the twenty-five years between 1850 and 1875 matched the entire gold output of the previous 350 years.[36] The growing circulation of gold coins and the natural advantage of gold as international money, settling large transactions in world trade because it is compact and inexpensive to ship, convinced representatives in 1867 at the international monetary conference to recommend the gold standard.[37] And four years later, after Germany defeated France in the Franco-Prussian War, Bismarck rushed to adopt the conference recommendations. The Iron Chancellor wanted to create a German Goliath and what better initiative than to emulate Britain, the dominant economic superpower, which had been on the gold standard since 1816.[38] The other European countries followed like anxious freshmen pledging for a fraternity.

✦ ✦ ✦

Sherman's removal of the silver dollar from the Coinage Act of 1873 did not trigger the metal's price decline, but the snub eroded its value and altered the course of American history. The worldwide switch to gold supported the price of the yellow metal despite the increased supply and created waves of silver selling that, combined with renewed output from the Comstock Lode, cut silver's value in half by the mid-1890s.[39] The pro-silver forces fought to prop up the white metal throughout this period but failed.

Representative Richard Bland of Missouri and Senator William Allison of Iowa sponsored legislation to restore the legal tender status of silver. The Bland-Allison Act of 1878 made the silver dollar acceptable once again in all payments, both for private debts, unless otherwise specified, and for public obligations, like taxes.[40] But the act stopped short of free and unlimited coinage at the U.S. Mint and instead made the Treasury buy between two and four million ounces of silver per month to support the price. Twelve years later, in an ironic twist, silver's archenemy, Senator John Sherman, sponsored what was called the Sherman Silver Purchase

Act of 1890, repealing the purchase clause of Bland-Allison and ordering the U.S. Treasury to buy even more silver, 4.5 million ounces per month, to help boost demand.[41] Sherman explained his apparent about-face: "A large majority of the Senate favored free silver . . . [and] some action had to be taken to prevent a return to free [and unlimited] silver coinage, and the measure [that] evolved was the best attainable. I voted for it, but the day it became law I was ready to repeal it, if repeal could be had without substituting in its place absolute free coinage."[42] The Sherman Silver Purchase Act was repealed in 1893.

Neither Bland-Allison nor the Sherman Act restored Alexander Hamilton's free coinage of silver under which the U.S. Treasury was obligated to purchase the white metal in unlimited amounts at the mint price of $1.29 per ounce. The United States would have pegged the price at $1.29 with unlimited purchases, the country would have been on a silver standard courtesy of Sir Thomas Gresham and avoided some of the turmoil plaguing America during the last quarter of the nineteenth century.[43]

No one knows the pitfalls of the path not taken, but the gold discoveries of the 1850s failed to deliver as expected, creating the feared consequences of insufficient circulating currency in America. The outcome was twenty years of price deflation beginning in 1876, including the declining price of silver, but more importantly increasing the burden of debts like mortgages, which remained fixed in dollar terms even though home prices declined.[44] The drop in wages and agricultural prices launched a generation of social combat, pitting "silverites" against "goldbugs," debtors versus creditors, and midwestern farmers against East Coast bankers, all combining to darken the political landscape like a dust storm.

Many consider L. Frank Baum's children's story, *The Wonderful Wizard of Oz*, an allegory of the contemporary class warfare.[45] The cyclone that carried Dorothy to the Land of Oz represents the economic and political upheaval, the yellow brick road stands for the gold standard, and the silver shoes Dorothy inherits from the Wicked Witch of the East represents the pro-silver movement. When Dorothy is taken to the Emerald Palace before her audience with the Wizard, she is led through seven passages and up three flights of stairs, a subtle reference to the Crime of '73 which started the class conflict in America.[46] The story scares some children, and with good reason. It was a turbulent time.

Veiled threats of violence emerged from unlikely places during that period. At the National Convention of the American Bimetallic League, held in Chicago's First Methodist Church on August 1, 1893, the group's president, General A.J. Warner of Ohio, delivered the opening address. Referring to the Act of 1873, he said: "The members of Congress, the Speaker of the House who signed that bill, the President who approved it, never knew that it demonetized silver. There was but one man in the United States Senate who knew that the Act of 1873 demonetized silver, and yet he has never been hanged or shot for treason. . . . The Act will be known in history as the Crime of 1873."[47] The great applause following Warner's reference to John Sherman's fate anticipated the acclamation of William Jennings Bryan as the Democratic Party's presidential candidate in 1896.

CHAPTER 3

FREE SILVER

WILLIAM JENNINGS BRYAN, A NEBRASKA CONGRESSMAN WHO RAN unsuccessfully three times for the American presidency, made headlines soon after arriving in the capital. The *Washington Post* reported Bryan's speech on tariffs in the House of Representatives in March 1892 under the banner "Fame Won in an Hour."[1] The newspaper ignored the congressman's detailed attack on protectionism, which would have put its readers to sleep, and focused instead on Bryan's delivery, his "eloquent words in picturing his thoughts."[2] Bryan's theme was, "We are demanding for the people equal and exact justice to every man, woman, and child. We desire that the laws of the country shall not be made, as they have been, to enable some men to get rich while many get poor."[3]

Bryan's biographer Paxton Hibben expanded on his subject's way with words: "If anyone knew how to give emotional expression to a practical matter it was William Jennings Bryan."[4] But even Bryan's eloquence failed to sway the electorate in favor of "free silver," which meant the free and unlimited coinage of silver, the dominant issue in the 1896 presidential campaign between Democrat Bryan and Republican William McKinley. The defeat of William Jennings Bryan buried silver as a monetary standard in the United States, forcing the white metal to battle for price respectability at the dinner table.

Billy Bryan was born in Salem, Illinois, on March 19, 1860, to a frugal mother, Mariah Elizabeth, and a disciplinarian father, Silas, whose religious outlook shadowed the household. Young Bryan recalled, "My parents were quite strict with me and I sometimes considered the boys more fortunate who were given more liberty."[5] His father's favorite quote was from the Book of Proverbs: "Foolishness is bound in the heart of a child; but the rod of correction

FIGURE 4. A William Jennings Bryan performance.

will drive it from him." Despite the severity, young Billy idolized his father, a district judge in Marion County, who disciplined himself as well. The Honorable Silas Bryan would interrupt judicial proceedings three time a day, fall to his knees and pray in full view of his courtroom, and then resume deliberations.[6]

Billy Bryan attended court as a young boy, sitting like an obedient puppy on the steps leading up to the bench, watching his father rule. Silas resembled an Old Testament prophet dispensing justice and Billy knew then that he wanted to be a lawyer, although some of his teachers would say otherwise. When he first arrived in school the teacher asked, "'Well, little man, . . . What do you mean to be when you grow up?' 'President of the United States,' gravely replied Billy Bryan."[7] No one could accuse him of not trying.

Bryan grew up on a farm just outside of Salem, a small community in southern Illinois that had more in common with citizens of adjacent Missouri and Kentucky than with Abraham Lincoln's Illinois. The locals may not have been outright segregationists as in the rural regions of those neighboring states, but they surely believed in the evils of the East Coast banking elite, a prejudice that permeated Bryan's brain by osmosis. It would bubble forth later in life with complaints like "We simply say to the East take your hands out of our pockets and keep them out."[8]

Young Billy built a muscular back baling hay on the family farm and then sharpened his tongue in the debating society at Illinois College in Jacksonville. He benefited from a clear baritone voice that commanded attention but usually came in second during debating competitions, a yellow caution sign ignored by the Democratic Party.[9] When he returned to Salem on vacation and addressed the crowd during a Saturday night rally at the courthouse, the men dressed in their best denim overalls were overheard saying as they left the gathering, "Well, Billy Bryan's got a nice voice, but he ain't the man his father was—and never will be."[10]

Bryan learned to support both sides of an issue during his debating days, often taking the unpopular position simply for the sake of argument.[11] His life as a politician, which began when he moved to Lincoln, Nebraska, in 1887 after failing to prosper as an Illinois lawyer, benefited from this rhetorical flexibility. Bryan separated his personal preferences from what mattered to his constituents. The Prohibition Party, which had been active in the United States since 1869 and would sponsor a candidate for the presidency in the 1890s, threatened Nebraska's thriving brewing industry. Bryan personalized his teetotalism during the 1890 congressional elections: "Although I do not touch liquor myself, I do not endorse the prohibition amendment."[12] He won with support from the brewers, despite a finding by the Nebraska legislature of fraud by the liquor interests.[13]

Soon after arriving in Washington Bryan witnessed the dislocations of the Panic of 1893, including the suspension of almost five hundred banks in the United States, more than ten times the previous decade's annual average, and causing the bankruptcy of popular rail companies, such as the Union Pacific Railroad and the Atchison, Topeka, & Santa Fe.[14] The unemployment rate of 18% in 1894, combined with falling industrial output and sinking agricultural prices, resembled the conditions of the Great Depression that would prevail some forty years later.[15] In a preview of the 1930s, voters turned their backs on prohibition and towards the money question, whether America should remain on the rigid gold standard, which gave the dollar international credibility, or remonetize silver under Hamilton's bimetallic system, which would expand U.S. currency and promote easier credit to support the domestic economy.

Bryan knew what to do. He had told a crowded gathering of his constituents in September 1892, "I don't know anything about free silver. . . . The people of Nebraska are for free silver and I am for free silver. I will look up the arguments later."[16] It sounded good and got a laugh, but Bryan had already studied the silver coinage question when he was first elected to Congress in 1890, reading popular pamphlets issued by the Bimetallic League and wading through a dense academic critique by Professor J. Laurence Laughlin of the University of Chicago.[17] Bryan knew all the arguments and had adopted the free silver motto long before his public quip, but he was a ham and could not resist.

William Jennings Bryan not only favored the restoration of bimetallism in the United States, but he also wanted free and unlimited coinage of silver at the pre-1873 ratio of 16 to 1, which meant sixteen ounces of silver would be equivalent in value to an ounce of gold.[18] In 1894 the price of silver averaged 64¢ an ounce, so with gold fixed at $20.67 per ounce by the U.S. Treasury, the prevailing gold to silver price ratio was 32:1, making an ounce of gold worth thirty-two ounces of silver.[19] Restoring the 16 to 1 ratio meant raising the price of silver through unlimited purchases by the Treasury until it reached $1.29, the mint price established in the Act of 1792, which would have enriched mine owners and diluted the currency according to Bryan's critics. The *Chicago Tribune* raised the obvious question: "Silver mining has never been one of the interests of Nebraska. It has raised wheat, corn, hogs, sheep, and some statesmen like Bryan, who are sillier and 'absurder' than sheep, but it has produced no silver. Why then should Nebraskans run their legs off to give the miners to the west of them more for their metal than it is worth in the world's markets?"[20]

The congressman's constituents favored the free coinage of silver because they believed more circulating currency would bring higher prices for wheat, corn, hogs, and sheep, not to mention higher prices for their heavily mortgaged farmlands, which were threatened with foreclosure. The *New York Times* reported that "the most powerful argument [for silver] . . . is wheat at 35¢ per bushel on Kansas farms. At this price no Kansas farmer can get either a gold or a silver dollar or a day's labor to say nothing of [paying] interest on either farm mortgage[s] or cost of machinery."[21] The superintendent of the New York State Banking Department had criticized investments by "some of the savings banks of the eastern states" in "western farm mortgages" because "the market value of real estate . . . has at times depreciated to such an extent as to induce borrowers to surrender their holdings in preference to paying the mortgage loans."[22]

Bryan supported silver for the same reason that it dominated gold as the medium of exchange in ancient times, because the white metal was valuable but sufficiently abundant to support growing economic activity. Silver was a softer and more elastic currency than gold. Throughout history the supply of silver fed the sea of commerce like an underground spring, keeping prices and production afloat. Gold had been too scarce to serve the masses until the discoveries of the 1850s, which led to the worldwide switch to the yellow metal in 1873. But gold failed to flow as expected, and the resulting currency shortage in America sank prices. The burden of deflation fell primarily on debtors, farmers, and small businessmen who had to repay fixed dollar obligations like mortgages and bank loans with lower revenues. A typical Bryan supporter, Louis Kohnstamm, who ran a small meat market in New York City, commented, "There is not money enough in circulation, and unlimited issue of silver dollars will throw more money into business, and that's what I want."[23]

Bryan's pro-silver sentiments were most popular west of the Mississippi but reflected more than just a hometown bias. He thought that the power to create money belonged to the government and "can no more with safety be delegated to private individuals than we could afford to delegate to private individuals the power to make penal statutes or levy taxes."[24] This may sound obvious today but back then America had no central bank to manage its currency and much of what passed as money were national bank notes, direct obligations of privately owned commercial banks, such as the Bank of California, the Bank of New York, and the First National Bank of Birmingham, Alabama. Bryan acknowledged the creditworthiness of bank currency, which was backed by U.S. government bonds, but he wanted the government to control the quantity in circulation to promote economic growth. He believed "the great thing desirable in a dollar is stability" and the free coinage of silver would promote that goal.[25] Carter Glass, a delegate to the Democratic convention in 1896, and a future congressman from Virginia who would sponsor the legislation in 1913 to create the Federal Reserve System, America's central bank, supported the presidential candidacy of William Jennings Bryan.[26] Bryan would return the favor by publicly supporting Glass's currency bill creating the Fed.

Resurrecting silver to full monetary status was not the only radical proposal Bryan supported at the Democratic Convention in Chicago in July 1896. He also favored an income tax, direct election by voters of U.S. senators, and women's suffrage; radical ideas that branded him a socialist at best and an anarchist at worst but would soon become conventional wisdom. He was ahead of his time, like Barry Goldwater, the Republican Party's presidential candidate in 1964 whose conservative stance on welfare and defense led to Democrat Lyndon Johnson's landslide victory, but whose ideas triumphed a generation later with Ronald Reagan. Bryan and Goldwater would surely recoil at their shared fate.

Bryan arrived at the Democratic convention without a national campaign organization but his famous "Cross of Gold" speech on July 9, 1896, turned the delegates into a volunteer army of true believers. Bryan presented himself as a humble citizen "clad in the armor of a righteous cause," and said that "the money question was the paramount issue of the hour."[27] He claimed that free coinage of silver would promote prosperity for the common man, mark U.S. independence from the gold standard countries of Europe, and "is the issue of 1776 over again."[28] His closing plea to "not crucify mankind upon a Cross of Gold" added religious thunder to the revolutionary spirit. An eerie silence greeted Bryan's final words in the convention hall, as though a lightning bolt had stunned the audience, and then a boisterous celebration exploded. Cheering delegates rose to their feet, threw hats, umbrellas, and newspapers into the air, while two sturdy members of the Georgia delegation raced across the floor, lifted the bulky six-foot Bryan on their shoulders, and paraded him through the hall.[29] It was as though he had just hit a walk-off home run to win the World Series.

The emotional outburst to bimetallism, with both gold and silver serving as monetary metals, a topic usually as exciting as a debate over the Malthusian Theory of Population, lay in Bryan's oratorical skills and in the growing resentment to deflation following the Crime of 1873. Bryan had refined his message through repetition, like the preparation of a professional athlete, and had used the Cross of Gold metaphor during an earlier speech in the House of Representatives.[30] No one took notice back then, but his message resonated more forcefully with the ravages of the depression that began in 1893. Unemployment was still 14% in the election year of 1896, down from 18% two years earlier but higher than anything America would experience until 1931 during the Great Depression.[31]

And yet he lost the election.

William McKinley defeated William Jennings Bryan for many reasons. Republican expenditures were fourteen times bigger than the Democrats even though McKinley never left his front porch during the campaign, while Bryan crisscrossed the country like a travelling salesman.[32] McKinley, aged fifty-three, was an experienced executive as governor of Ohio and had served in the Union

Army during the Civil War, while Bryan, aged thirty-six, had served two terms as a congressman and was holding a rattle rather than a rifle during the War Between the States. *Harper's Weekly* magazine lampooned the contrast in a cartoon entitled "The Deadly Parallel," showing a soldier in full dress facing a nearly naked toddler.[33] McKinley's carefully scripted speeches never missed their mark while Bryan's impromptu remarks often gave the opposition explosive ammunition. The Nebraska congressman explained that he launched his campaign in New York's Madison Square Garden so that "our cause might be presented first in the heart of what now seems to be the enemy's country."[34] Newspapers skewered Bryan on that final divisive phrase, helping the Republicans win every state in the Northeast as well as four southern border states— Maryland, Kentucky, West Virginia, and Delaware—that had been Democratic strongholds since the Civil War.[35]

But the man who orchestrated McKinley's victory, campaign manager Mark Hanna, an Ohio millionaire businessman with interests in coal, steel, and railroads, said it best early in the campaign: "[Bryan's] talking silver all the time and that's where we've got him."[36] Newspapers throughout the country denigrated Bryan's obsession with the free coinage of silver, running stories promoting a sound currency backed by gold rather than silver dollars filled with bullion worth half its face value. The *New York Times* quoted an immigrant cabinet maker, M.E. Thoesen from New York City, "I am for gold through and through and all the time and do not want any fifty-three-cent dollars. What good would such money [do] to the workman?"[37] The *Washington Post* followed up: "These jokes about the 53-cent dollar won't go any more. It's only a 50-cent dollar now. The price of silver has dropped."[38] Senator James K. Jones of Arkansas, chairman of the Democratic National Committee, was not amused: "The thing which hurts us most is the constant statement that free silver means a fifty-cent dollar."[39]

The Republican arithmetic was right. Silver sold for an average of 63.5¢ an ounce in 1896 and the silver dollar contained three-quarters of an ounce of the white metal, so the silver dollar was worth about 49¢ of bullion.[40] But Bryan should have said that the value of a dollar depends on how much it can buy and not on its intrinsic value, an obvious fact today in a world of fiat currency, where dollars are worth more than the paper they are printed on because the government promises to keep them scarce. But back then almost everyone believed, and many still do, that making the currency convertible into a precious metal keeps the government honest, ensuring that it will not debase the currency by printing too much money and causing inflation. Concern over the intrinsic value of money may seem like a medieval superstition similar to ghosts and goblins, but John Maynard Keynes, who considered the gold standard a barbarous relic, worried at the start of the Great War that a break with gold would undermine the credibility of the British pound.[41]

Bryan answered his fifty-cent critics by saying "free and unlimited coinage by the United States alone will raise the bullion value of silver to its coinage value and thus make silver bullion worth $1.29 per ounce."[42] And he invoked the law of supply and demand for support: "Any purchaser who stands ready to take the entire supply of any given article at a certain price can prevent that article from falling below that price. So the Government can fix a price for gold and silver by creating a demand greater than the supply."[43] Bryan was right about purchases and sales by the mint setting the price of precious metals and he added an analogy about eggs for the common folk: "If any man in this community would offer to buy all the eggs produced at 25 cents a dozen . . . nobody would sell eggs for less, no matter what the cost of production, whether one cent or five cents a dozen. So with silver."[44]

Students at the Metropolitan Business College in downtown Chicago tossed eggs at a Bryan campaign parade as it passed the corner of Michigan Avenue and Monroe Street but that was a minor indignity compared with the splatter greeting Bryan's metaphor in the press.[45] The *Chicago Daily Tribune* offered the following narrative:[46] "Let us see what would happen with the eggs. First, everybody would want to sell eggs. . . . Second, eggs would be sent in from Mexico, from Canada, and from every country which had eggs. . . . Third, people could not afford to eat eggs kept so dear. . . . Fourth, . . . the man [buying the eggs] would have his hands full and his barns full of rotten eggs. . . . The man would be bankrupt long before he bought all the eggs. [And] any government would be bankrupt long before it bought all the silver. The eggs would rot. The 'dollar' would be rotten too."

The eggs analogy laid bare the consequences of Bryan's proposal to raise the price of silver to $1.29 per ounce from the 63.5¢ prevailing in the bullion market in 1896. Mexico and Canada would have shipped silver at its inflated value to the United States in exchange for gold. And so would every European country on the gold standard, which included Britain, France, and Germany. Bryan had touted the support of the Iron Chancellor, Prince Otto von Bismarck, to bolster his campaign for free silver until the press headlined Bismarck's ulterior motive: to dump Germany's store of pre-1870 silver at the U.S. Mint.[47] Recall that Bismarck had triggered the run on silver by adopting the gold standard after the Franco-Prussian War ended in 1871.

Bryan's campaign to coin silver at the pre-1873 ratio of 16 to 1 would have increased the domestic stock of money in the United States and promoted easier credit, a desirable outcome in the 1870s, when America faced decades of deflation, but was counterproductive in 1896, when gold became more plentiful and fueled an emerging inflationary spiral.[48] His timing was bad, like selling umbrellas during a drought, and the economic resurgence kept the Democrats out of the White House until Woodrow Wilson was elected in 1912. Bryan served as Wilson's secretary of state between 1913 and 1915, which was the closest he ever got to being president. At that time the secretary of state was second in line, after the vice president, to succeed an incapacitated or impeached president.[49]

During the final years of his life, Bryan applied the righteous fervor he felt for silver to fighting the teaching of Charles Darwin's theory of evolution. His most famous confrontation was the 1925 battle with prominent lawyer Clarence Darrow, who defended John Thomas Scopes, a substitute science teacher accused of violating a Tennessee law forbidding the teaching of evolution in public schools.[50] Bryan's prosecution brought a guilty verdict in the Scopes Trial, fictionalized in the hit 1960 movie *Inherit the Wind*. William Jennings Bryan died less than a week after the trial ended

FIGURE 5. Bryan as statesman.

and did not live to see the verdict overturned by the State Supreme Court. His death may have been merciful from that perspective, but he also never lived to see the resurrection of his 16 to 1 war cry for silver during the Great Depression and its influence on master politician Franklin Delano Roosevelt.

CHAPTER 4

SEEDS OF ROOSEVELT'S MANIPULATION

PRESIDENT FRANKLIN ROOSEVELT AND NEVADA SENATOR KEY Pittman seem like an odd couple of financial coconspirators. "Young Roosevelt knows nothing about finance," California politician Franklin K. Lane said, which sounds terrible, but most people know even less.[1] The problem went deeper according to Lane, who served as Woodrow Wilson's interior secretary: "But he doesn't know he doesn't know." FDR's aristocratic upbringing on a country estate in New York's Hudson Valley infused a self-confidence in the future president that served him well in politics but undermined his business decisions. His optimism seduced the public during his campaign tours but left him vulnerable to Wall Street scams.

Franklin Roosevelt, the pampered only child of James Roosevelt and Sara Delano, both coming from inherited wealth, was born on January 30, 1882. He went to Groton, an elite boarding school, and to Harvard, where he was an average student, and then followed his fifth cousin, President Theodore Roosevelt, into public service. The Roosevelt name was already political royalty at the dawn of the twentieth century, and although Teddy was a Republican and Franklin a Democrat, the family moniker worked its magic. In 1910 FDR won election to the New York State Senate from his Dutchess County district that had last chosen a Democrat in the 1850s. His support of Woodrow Wilson in the 1912 presidential election brought him to Washington. He served as assistant secretary of the Navy in the Wilson administration, where he impressed Interior Secretary Lane with his financial acumen and supported America's entry into the Great War in 1917. His strong chin, sunny disposition, and East Coast pedigree helped him secure the Democratic vice-presidential nomination in 1920 alongside presidential hopeful James Cox of Ohio. They lost to the Republican ticket of Warren Harding and Calvin Coolidge.

Roosevelt was stricken with polio in 1921 and withdrew from public life to battle the disease. He launched a number of business ventures during the 1920s, but the outcomes were as predictable as if a crown prince were running a flea market. FDR's misadventures included investing in a fleet of blimps to fly passengers from New York to Chicago, introducing vending machines that dispensed premoistened postage stamps, trading in the German mark, and trying to corner the live lobster market.[2] His losses in lobsters should have restrained his foray into manipulating the silver market after he was elected president in 1932, but he never made the connection.

Key Pittman, on the other hand, learned finance because he needed money. He was born on September 12, 1872, on a farm in Vicksburg, Mississippi, and lost both of his parents before becoming a teenager.[3] He lived with relatives and then studied law at Southwestern University in Clarksville, Tennessee, where he took required Bible classes from Dr. Joseph Wilson, father of Woodrow Wilson, but was only an average student. His impulsive instincts and good looks could lead to drink and trouble, so it is no surprise that Dr. Wilson took little interest in him. The future president, however, would promote Pittman's Senate career as a reward for his outspoken support.

Pittman dropped out of the University in 1890 before graduating and on a whim moved west to seek his fortune, using his legal training to support land and mining speculations. He settled in a small town near Seattle but after a string of bad investments filed for bankruptcy in 1897, leaving an overdrawn checking account and unpaid bills from a physician and a clothing store. He moved to Alaska in 1897, joining the Klondike gold rush, but earned more from his legal fees than his mining skills. In 1902 he followed a former law partner to Tonopah, Nevada, a frontier town located midway between Reno and Las Vegas, after rich gold and silver mines were opened. He told his wife, Mimosa, a California beauty he had met and married while in Alaska, "I am going to make money here."[4] He did.

Pittman learned from his earlier mistakes and profited by following his well-connected clients, including Charles M. Schwab, president of the Bethlehem Steel Company and part-owner of the Tonopah Extension Mining Company. He bought shares in Schwab's companies and by 1907 became a major investor in the Pacific State Telephone Company and in the Nevada Hills Extension Mining Company.[5] But he wanted more and told Mimosa, "[William Jennings] Bryan at my age had been two terms in Congress and two years later was the nominee for president of the United States."[6] Local Democratic politicians recognized Pittman's potential and in 1908 offered to back his candidacy for Nevada's seat in the House of Representatives. Key rejected their initiative: "I do not believe that there is any chance of the next Congress being Democratic and for that reason any Congressman we may elect will be a nonentity in that body."[7]

Key Pittman was ambitious.

His patience paid off in 1912 when he was elected U.S. senator from Nevada. Pittman's timing was perfect. He took office when the Democratic Party gained control of both houses of Congress and Democratic Governor Woodrow Wilson of New Jersey became president. He would capitalize on the opportunity.

The freshman senator from Nevada began his congressional career by preparing for reelection. He became chairman of the Senate Committee on Territories because no one with seniority wanted it and then explained to friends, "I am in a position to do more for this State than anyone else. I am preparing stuff for my constituents all the time. . . . I want my constituents to know that I am busy."[8] But he also knew that party loyalty mattered: "I am thoroughly in accord with the Administration and am pleased that I am in a position where I can assist in carrying out its policies." As a result, his recommendations for federal appointments in Nevada were quickly accepted, leading a local newspaper to write that Pittman, "could smell a job across a township and was singularly adroit in getting it for one of his constituents."[9]

Pittman's support for the administration benefited his own career as well as favoring voters back home. In 1916, while still lacking seniority, he was chosen by the Democratic leadership to fill an opening on the prestigious Senate Foreign Relations Committee. Pittman's guile had helped his cause. He had confided to Mimosa soon after arriving in the Senate: "I am trying to establish a reputation for modesty that I can overdraw on my next term—I am still playing the game, and deceiving my associates. They commenced to believe that I am satisfied with silence and peace."[10]

The Washington press reported that President Wilson viewed the appointment "with the broadest of favor."[11] And so did Pittman. He told Mimosa, "There were seven applicants for the vacancy so I consider it a great honor for us."[12] It was more than just an honor. Pittman would become chairman of the Senate Foreign Relations Committee in 1933 and find a new friend, Franklin D. Roosevelt, the newly elected president.

✦ ✦ ✦

Pittman's path to power began during the Great War when his outspoken support for Woodrow Wilson paid dividends to Nevada mining interests. Isolationists had objected to Wilson's aggressive stance after the sinking of the *Lusitania*, the British ocean liner torpedoed by a German submarine with the loss of 128 American lives. But Pittman rallied behind the president: "I would rather that we lost a few hundred men, if necessary, in cooperation with the allies at the present time, than lose millions of men in a war that we alone might have to fight. We have got to fight Germany. We will either fight Germany now or we will fight Germany later on."[13] Pittman underestimated the sacrifice, but his support facilitated America's entry into the war in April 1917.

Silver prices had been on a roller coaster since the outbreak of hostilities in Europe, fluctuating with supply and demand just like any other commodity. Prices sagged at the outset because it was not needed by the military, but as the expanding economy created shortages of silver-based small change like dimes and quarters, the white metal increased from 55¢ an ounce in mid-1914 to a dollar at the end of 1918, almost doubling like most raw material prices.[14] Pittman contributed to the price rise by introducing legislation in

FIGURE 6. Key Pittman dressed for work.

the Senate to accommodate Britain's need to borrow hundreds of millions of ounces of silver from the U.S. Treasury. After all, it was his patriotic duty to help an American ally.

Britain's unusual request was on behalf of India, a British colony at the time and still on a silver standard like its Asian neighbor, China. India was having difficulty redeeming its currency, the rupee, with the white metal, and the U.K. worried that a suspension of convertibility would lead to unrest or rebellion, impairing the war effort. The British ambassador asked the Treasury Department to melt 350 million silver dollars held in its vaults and lend the bullion to India. The legislation, known as the Pittman Act, authorized the sale at the prevailing price of a dollar per ounce of pure silver, and the Treasury's Bureau of the Mint delivered as promised.[15] The Philadelphia and San Francisco branch mints handled most of the order, shoveling silver dollars into furnaces by the thousands and molding the liquid metal into bullion bars, which were shipped to the Calcutta mint.[16]

The Pittman Act pleased almost everyone—Britain, India, and especially America's miners—because the legislation also required the U.S. Treasury to replenish its inventory of coins by purchasing domestically produced silver at that same one dollar per ounce, irrespective of the free market price. Congressman Edward Platt of New York warned that this repurchase clause was "a plain case of holdup by the silverites."[17] He was right. When the war ended and demand for silver declined, the world market price dropped below a dollar and American silver mines sold to the U.S. Treasury rather than on the open market. U.S. producers, including small mining companies in the West and industrial giants like the American Smelting and Refining Company, reaped a handsome subsidy between mid-1920, when the free market price fell below a dollar, and mid-1923, when the Treasury completed its purchases under the Act.[18] The legislation could have been labelled Made in Nevada.

Two prices for silver prevailed in the United States during this period, a free market price averaging 68.8¢ and the fixed $1 price in the Pittman Act for domestic production.[19] Metal dealers like Handy & Harman advertised the subsidy by posting two quotes for silver, one for U.S. production and the other for imports.[20] Representative L.T. McFadden of Pennsylvania introduced congressional legislation to repeal the repurchase clause of the Pittman Act to eliminate the boondoggle.[21] The *New-York Tribune* headlined an editorial called "Doing Something for Silver" and recommended that "the 'joker' in the Pittman measure should be eliminated at the next session of Congress."[22]

Key Pittman never doubted the wisdom of the act that bore his name: "I am confident the future of silver is safe. The Pittman Act will never be repealed. What little opposition there was . . . to the purchase of domestic silver at $1 an ounce . . . was dying out as a result of intelligent opposition on the part of engineers and mining men all over the country."[23] Pittman had the votes of other senators from western mining states to prevent a repeal so the subsidy to American producers remained. He also thought it marked the beginning of a new era for the white metal: "Foreign demand with domestic consumption would be ample . . . for many years as soon as conditions in Europe return to normal."[24] His forecast of a bright future for silver makes British Prime Minister Lloyd George's prediction, "Germany is unable to wage war," look good.[25]

The fingerprints of the Pittman Act faded with the expiration of Treasury purchases. The act's support of India's silver standard may have helped the British war effort, but it failed to retain India as a permanent customer of American mines. In mid-1926 a royal commission appointed by King George V recommended that India switch the backing of its currency to gold.[26] The announcement caused a 10% decline in silver.[27] The white metal then averaged 56¢ an ounce until the Great Crash in October 1929, when a new round of selling ultimately cut the price in half.[28]

The Pittman Act failed to boost the price of silver permanently but became a model for future manipulations of the white metal. The two-tier pricing strategy subsidized American mines with relatively little spillover elsewhere, making it an attractive political tool. President Roosevelt would adopt that approach during his first year in office, but his efforts forced China, the last major country on the silver standard, to reject the white metal, and Japan would capitalize on China's misfortune.

CHAPTER 5

FDR PROMOTES SILVER

In a campaign speech on October 20, 1932, in Pittsburgh's triple-tiered Forbes Field, with thousands cheering as though the Pirates had won the National League pennant, Franklin D. Roosevelt said, "If the nation is living within its income, its credit is good. . . . But if, like a spendthrift, it throws discretion to the winds . . . and continues to pile up deficits, it is on the road to bankruptcy."[1] Marriner Eccles, a Utah banker who would soon become chairman of the Federal Reserve System, America's central bank, suggested that the conservative rhetoric in Roosevelt's speeches read like "a giant misprint" in which FDR delivered Hoover's lines.[2] Eccles had nothing to worry about, of course. What Roosevelt said and what he did often had little in common, especially when it came to America's money.

The Democratic Party nominated New York Governor Franklin Roosevelt as their presidential candidate at the convention in Chicago at the end of June 1932, but it was hardly a landslide despite his having the most committed delegates at the outset. It took four ballots to overcome determined opposition, including from the party's 1928 presidential nominee, former New York Governor Al Smith, who refused to join the bandwagon even after the final vote. When a member of the Democratic National Committee asked Smith to make the nomination unanimous, he folded his arms in front of him like a petulant teenager and said, "I won't do it. I won't do it. I won't do it."[3] Roosevelt was considered weak, a "feather duster," according to syndicated columnist Heywood Broun.[4] Another reporter wrote, "The Democrats have nominated nobody quite like him since Franklin Pierce."[5]

A young Chicago lawyer at the convention, Leon Despres, recalled decades later, "Nobody could work up much enthusiasm for

Roosevelt," he was a "flip-flopper" on the League of Nations, Prohibition, and "sound money."[6] Sound money was a code word for the prevailing gold standard in the United States, permitting Americans to exchange dollar bills for gold at a fixed price of $20.67 per ounce at the U.S. Treasury. The gold standard insured that America's paper money retained its value, keeping consumer prices in check by restraining the supply of money and credit. But the Great Depression was more than a speck on the horizon in mid-1932, and America's problem was too little money and credit, not too much; deflation rather than inflation. Since the Great Crash in 1929, consumer prices had declined by more than 20%, the money supply had declined by almost 30%, and one in four workers was unemployed.[7] A shortage of money, the ancient scourge that had made silver the preferred circulating medium for thousands of years, had cursed business activity in the 1930s. No wonder restoring the monetary status of silver dominated remedies to cure the economy.

Delegates to the Democratic convention had placed the resurrection of silver in the party platform, third in the list of seventeen solemn promises to implement after the election: "We advocate . . . A sound currency to be preserved at all hazards and an international monetary conference called on the invitation of our government to consider the rehabilitation of silver and related questions."[8] Roosevelt later elaborated on this point in a nationally broadcast radio address, the first of many talks delivered as though he were a guest in American living rooms. "The United States could well afford to take the lead . . . to determine what can be done to restore the purchasing power of that half of the world's inhabitants who are on a silver basis. . . . Nothing could do more to create stable relations in which trade could once more be resumed."[9]

Roosevelt's reference to "half of the world's inhabitants" using silver probably was an exaggeration, but it echoed the words of Winston Churchill, who was a member of the British Parliament at the time and had practiced finance as chancellor of the Exchequer, the rough equivalent of America's secretary of the Treasury. Churchill blamed the worldwide depression on money, anticipating the thesis of American economist Milton Friedman: "I believe something has gone wrong with the monetary system. It no longer affords men and nations an adequate means of exchanging what they are capable of producing." [10] He continued by focusing on the white metal: "Silver is the money of all Asia. Silver is the money of a billion human beings, and it ought not to be treated with as little regard as if it were a sack of potatoes. . . . Surely we would do well to consider more carefully the part it has to play in our world housekeeping." Roosevelt and Churchill would become close allies in battling Hitler, but even in 1932 they shared much, including an aristocratic upbringing, an attachment to the sea (Churchill was first lord of the Admiralty during the Great War and Roosevelt was assistant secretary of the Navy), and an affinity for the white metal.

Silver had plunged in price to an all-time low of 24.25¢ an ounce in 1932, not quite as cheap as Churchill's sack of potatoes but an embarrassing value for what had once been a proud monetary metal.[11] Rehabilitating silver in the United States would reverse the price decline by adding to the demand for bullion in at least two ways.[12] Purchases of the white metal by the Treasury to create silver dollars would increase demand directly and would also add to the circulating currency in America, expanding the economy and increasing demand indirectly. In January 1932 liberal Democratic senator Burton Wheeler of Montana combined those two ideas with a page from American history that made Roosevelt blush at its audacity.

Wheeler sponsored a bill in the Senate to raise the price of silver to $1.29 per ounce that the press headlined as "Wheeler to Offer a 16–1 Silver Bill," a reference to the legal price ratio of gold to silver before the Crime of 1873, when sixteen ounces of silver were worth an ounce of gold.[13] Wheeler wanted to restore 16 to 1, just like William Jennings Bryan, and recalled having taken Bryan's side during a high school debate in 1896, saying, "I had been for the remonetization of silver ever since."[14]

Senator Wheeler wanted to create more circulating currency in the United States to counter the deflation and, according to the *New York Times*, claimed, "Such a law would double the volume of world primary money and within a year the world price of wheat, cotton, and all agricultural products would be more than trebled."[15] Wheeler never substantiated those estimates nor did he highlight the upheaval of moving from the existing price ratio of 85 to 1 to Bryan's 16 to 1. The prospect of an uncertain increase in currency and uncontrolled inflation scared most members of Congress. The chairman of the House Committee on Coinage, Weights and Measures, Brooklyn congressman Andrew Somers said, "Any man who stood up and said remonetize silver at 16 to 1 was looked upon as being something of an idiot."[16]

FDR did not want to be called an idiot and had no intention of remonetizing silver at 16 to 1 or any other fixed ratio. He had pledged during the campaign to maintain a "sound currency," a euphemism for the gold standard, and committed only to calling an international conference "to consider the rehabilitation of silver and related questions." But none of that bothered his fellow Democrat Burton Wheeler. He was already called a crackpot for running in 1924 as the vice-presidential candidate on the Progressive Party ticket headed by Wisconsin Senator Robert La Follette. They were endorsed by the Socialist Party of America. Wheeler's 16 to 1 bill came to a vote in the Senate in January 1933, after FDR was elected but before he took office. The bill was defeated by a vote of 56 to 18, but Wheeler did not give up.[17] He would reintroduce his 16 to 1 proposal in the new Senate, a month after Roosevelt took office, and the more favorable reception would force a reluctant FDR to compromise.

+ + +

A day after he was inaugurated on Saturday, March 4, 1933, Roosevelt announced a bank holiday throughout the country, which, despite its festive name, imposed drastic restrictions on Americans. The holiday suspended all banking operations in the U.S. for ten days, and banks were ordered specifically not to permit withdrawals or transfers of "any gold or silver coin, or bullion or currency."[18] This was Roosevelt's opening remedy to cure the bank insolvencies that had swallowed the life savings of millions of Americans since the beginning of the Great Depression. FDR gave his first "fireside chat" on Sunday, March 5, 1933, to explain the extraordinary measures so that everyone understood them, "even the bankers," quipped humorist Will Rogers.[19] The stock markets were closed during the bank holiday, preventing investors from registering their response, but silver bullion continued to trade. The white metal jumped by more than 8% on Monday, March 6, a significant reaction to the president's initiatives.[20] It was just the beginning.

April is the cruelest month according to the poet T.S. Eliot, but not for the silver bloc in Congress in 1933.[21] The economic depression had given FDR a landslide victory in November 1932 and had also swept Republicans from office, creating large Democratic majorities in the House and Senate willing to try the untried to fix the economy. With the prices of wheat, corn, and cotton at depressed levels, inflation was now the solution, not the problem, and Wheeler was no longer on the lunatic fringe. He knew that coining silver at Bryan's favorite price ratio would be "somewhat inflationary" but said it would be "far better than cutting the gold content of the dollar, or going to paper money, as some were advocating."[22] Wheeler added, "[T]here wasn't enough gold to form an adequate base for our money."[23]

Wheeler dismissed Roosevelt's continued opposition to "16 to 1." He would often battle FDR going forward, derailing the president's attempt at packing the Supreme Court in 1937 and siding with the isolationist "America First" movement to maintain U.S. neutrality in mid-1941.[24] Wheeler's fight to remonetize silver in 1933 was just the first skirmish in a long war. He attached his proposal as an amendment to Roosevelt's Agricultural Adjustment Act hoping the president would swallow "16 to 1" along with the administration's most important farm support legislation.[25] But when the amendment came to a vote on Monday, April 17, Arkansas Democrat Joseph Robinson, the Senate majority leader, announced that "President Roosevelt does not approve of any of the amendments pending."[26] The president's opposition persuaded at least ten pro-silver senators, including Nevada's Key Pittman, to abandon Wheeler, sending the amendment to defeat by a vote of 43 against and 33 in favor.[27]

It was just a temporary setback for the white metal. Inflationary sentiment dominated in the House of Representatives and now, with 33 favorable Senate votes compared with only 18 supporters four months earlier, in January 1933, the contagion had spread to the upper chamber despite Roosevelt's arm twisting. On Tuesday, April 18, a day after Wheeler went to defeat, Democratic Senator Elmer Thomas of Oklahoma, who had campaigned for William Jennings Bryan in 1896, proposed an alternative inflation plan for the same farm bill. He had been worried all along about the collapse in agricultural prices, saying, "We've got a surplus of everything but money."[28] The Thomas Amendment gave the president various options, including the right to reduce the gold content of the dollar and to establish "machinery for the remonetization of silver at any ratio he may determine."[29]

Roosevelt remained opposed despite the flexibility, but Senate leaders warned that the new amendment would pass over his objections. FDR met with Thomas at the White House on the afternoon of April 18 and flattered the Oklahoma senator into withdrawing his amendment temporarily to give the administration a "breathing spell."[30]

The breath of fresh air swept away Roosevelt's anti-inflationary restraint, mostly because he had no choice.[31] Political commentator Walter Lippmann remarked that the only questions left were "how inflation was to be produced and whether or not it would be managed and controlled."[32] At 10:30 the following morning, Wednesday, April 19, 1933, the president took the United States off the gold standard. He announced to more than one hundred reporters crowded into his oval study in the White House that going forward "no more licenses would be issued for export of gold."[33] Roosevelt relished the surprise during his press conference, bantering with reporters like a mischievous schoolboy, but refusing to divulge his next steps. FDR compared himself to a quarterback with a flexible game plan: "If the next play gains ten yards obviously the succeeding thrust will be a different one than . . . if the team is thrown for a loss."[34]

Despite uncertainty about the ultimate fate of the gold standard, financial markets responded immediately to the inflationary news. Agricultural commodities, such as wheat and cotton, had the biggest trading sessions of the year on April 19, and prices rose between 4 and 6%, but those gains paled compared with the precious metals.[35] Preventing the export of gold from the United States meant that the international value of the dollar would fall, as did the British pound when it was decoupled from gold in September 1931. By the end of the day the U.S. dollar declined by 9% against the French franc, the only major currency still tied to gold, making Americans pay that much more for an ounce of the yellow metal.[36] Silver jumped by more than 11% even though Roosevelt had said nothing about it; speculators expected a revised version of the pro-silver Thomas Amendment.[37]

They did not have to wait long. On Thursday, April 20, 1933, Elmer Thomas introduced an amendment to the farm bill cater-ing to FDR's more conservative taste.[38] The amendment had been rewritten by Roosevelt's so-called "brains trust," led by speech writer Raymond Moley, with the assistance of Nevada Senator Key Pittman, now the president pro tempore of the Senate as well as chairman of the Foreign Relations Committee.[39] Pittman moder-ated Thomas's demands, focusing the amendment on expanding the supply of money by the Federal Reserve, giving the president discretion to devalue America's currency by lowering the gold con-tent of the dollar, and by allowing foreign governments to repay World War I debts with silver valued at the premium price of 50¢ an ounce, which would then be used for silver dollars and silver certificates.[40] Senate Majority Leader Robinson suggested that this would "stabilize the price of silver around 50¢ an ounce."[41]

The *Washington Post* described the watered down version of the Thomas Amendment as a "sop to the silverites," but the white metal rose by a significant 9% on April 20 to over 35¢ an ounce.[42] The combined 20% price increase on April 19 and 20 was more than double the percentage price increase in gold over the same period, consistent with silver's reputation as the more volatile metal, and lessening the sting of Roosevelt's tepid support.[43] Raymond Moley credits Key Pittman with implementing the president's program: "It was Pittman who 'sold' the revised amendment to Thomas. No one but a known friend of silver could have accomplished that."[44] FDR owed Pittman and would repay the debt.

CHAPTER 6

SILVER SUBSIDY

KEY PITTMAN PRACTICED THE LOW ART OF CHAMELEON POLITICS. Early in his career he campaigned for women's voting rights in Nevada and supported a resolution in the state legislature in favor, but as a U.S. senator he voted against the national amendment. Pittman explained on the Senate floor, "I believe that [women's suffrage] is essential for good government in our State. . . . I do not know whether it is essential for good government in the States of the South . . . [to] add to the negro vote that of the negro women."[1] Suffragettes disapproved but a hometown newspaper considered it a political master stroke: "When Nevada's junior senator needs the votes of southern representatives for issues of vital importance to Nevada he is pretty apt to know where to find them."[2]

Pittman favored higher silver prices for his Nevada constituents, such as the Tonopah Mining Company in Esmeralda County and the Bristol Silver Mines in Lincoln County, but cared little about silver's role in the nation's money supply. He voted against Montana Senator Wheeler's "16 to 1" bill in January 1933, saying it "would turn the whole East against us."[3] But he marshalled international support for silver after becoming a member of the U.S. delegation to the World Monetary and Economic Conference in London, where representatives of sixty-six countries gathered for six weeks beginning June 12, 1933, to discuss financial solutions to the depression. FDR appointed Pittman to the committee representing the U.S. without consulting Secretary of State Cordell Hull, who chaired the American delegation.[4]

The Nevada senator led a one-man cavalry charge for the white metal during the London meetings that summer. James Warburg, a Wall Street adviser to FDR and financial consultant to the American delegation, noted that Pittman "was really a wild man when drunk, but he was drunk so often that he was often wild. . . . If he ever got the idea that you weren't on his side God help you because that was the end."[5] At one point during the meetings Pittman brandished a bowie knife while chasing a technical adviser down the corridor of the Claridge Hotel, the preferred lodging for visiting dignitaries, because the man showed inadequate enthusiasm for silver.[6] In one of the sessions Pittman's insistence on an agreement caused the German representative Hjalmer Schacht to wave his hands in surrender and say, "All right, we agree about silver."[7]

The press was less graphic, perhaps because they feared the senator from the Wild West, and simply credited Pittman's "unsleeping efforts for silver."[8] The silver treaty signed on Saturday night, July 22, 1933, promoted higher prices by restricting sales of silver by countries that were disposing of the demonetized white metal, such as India, and capped the output of producing countries, such as Australia, Mexico, and the United States, by requiring those governments to buy excess production from domestic mining companies.[9] The agreement, which the respective governments had to ratify before April 1, 1934, was considered by many "the only tangible result of the World Monetary and Economic Conference."[10] Pittman said, "This is the biggest thing that has ever happened in my life."[11] The market for silver bullion responded favorably within a day of the signing, rising a significant 5% from 35.5¢ an ounce to over 37¢.[12]

Pittman's victory fell short of Burton Wheeler's goals, and the Montana senator denigrated the London proposals as "the most backward step that has been taken by the United States since the demonetization of silver in 1873."[13] Wheeler then repaid Pittman for abandoning "16 to 1" by adding, it is "a sad commentary" on the United States delegates' "grasp on the fundamentals underlying the money questions."[14] The ever practical Pittman avoided a confrontation and asked Farm Credit Administrator Henry Morgenthau Jr., a Roosevelt confidante who would soon become Treasury secretary, to convince FDR to avoid a formal Senate vote on the London treaty. Pittman suggested a presidential proclamation: "The instrument is not a treaty, or even an agreement that requires ratification by the United States Senate. It is simply a written memorandum of agreement."[15]

FIGURE 7. FDR gives his neighbor Henry Morgenthau a lift.

The president enjoyed driving a loophole in the law and was often helped by Morgenthau, his former neighbor in Dutchess County, New York. Henry Morgenthau was born in 1891 on Central Park West in New York City to a wealthy family but loved the land more than his father's real estate empire and could afford to follow his heart. He bought several hundred acres in Fishkill, New York, near Roosevelt's Hyde Park estate, and became a farmer, although his bald pate and pince-nez made him look anything but.[16] Like Roosevelt, Morgenthau was active in Democratic politics. They both supported Woodrow Wilson in 1912, although the two men did not meet until 1915, when Roosevelt tried unsuccessfully to convince Morgenthau to run for county sheriff.[17] Henry was flattered and contributed time and money to Roosevelt's successful campaign for governor of New York in 1928. FDR said that Henry was the only man he knew who had made a profit farming and appointed him conservation commissioner for New York state.[18] The relationship between the two men was far more intimate than the title implied. When Morgenthau asked Roosevelt for the most opportune time to discuss a new funding request, he answered, "While I am shaving."[19] Henry arrived days later to discuss his project just as FDR lathered up.

After arriving in Washington in March 1933, Roosevelt appointed Morgenthau the first director of the newly established Farm Credit Administration (FCA), but as in New York his duties extended well beyond his title. In October 1933, six months after FDR had taken America off the gold standard, the president decided to push the country towards devaluation by buying gold in the bullion market. Congress had not yet changed the official $20.67 price of the yellow metal and Undersecretary of the Treasury Dean Acheson questioned the legality of Roosevelt's plan.[20] Morgenthau consulted his legal counsel at the FCA and proudly disclosed a favorable ruling to FDR. He summarized the discussion in his diary: "Called on the President at Hyde Park and showed him a longhand memo by Herman Oliphant suggesting various ways the President might, through an Executive Order, have a free gold market in this country."[21] After reading the memo Roosevelt raised the stakes a notch: "I have a method of my own to break the law which I think is much simpler."[22]

Morgenthau's eyes widened at Roosevelt's words, but he listened to the subterfuge of using the Reconstruction Finance Company (RFC), a government corporation established in 1932 to support banks, to buy gold. It may have been simpler, but it was no less controversial to Acheson, who wanted the president to write a letter absolving him of the personal risk.[23] According to Morgenthau, "The President and Acheson almost came to blows," but FDR withheld firing him on the spot, waiting a month before forcing his resignation.[24]

Morgenthau then enlisted the attorney general in getting a favorable ruling for the president's plan, and FDR announced the gold-buying program in a fireside chat on Sunday, October 22, 1933: "I am going to establish a government market for gold in the United States. Therefore, under the clearly defined authority of existing law, I am authorizing the Reconstruction Finance Company to buy gold newly mined in the United States at prices to be determined from time to time after consultation with the Secretary of the Treasury and the President. . . . We shall also buy or sell gold in the world market."[25] The Reconstruction Finance Company began buying gold at ever-increasing prices beginning Wednesday, October 25, 1933.[26]

Roosevelt's emphasis on the legality of his gold plan, as subtle as a sledgehammer, became the template for ratifying without Senate approval Pittman's London silver program. On Thursday evening, December 21, 1933, the president announced: "Under the clear authority granted to me by the last session of Congress, I have today, by proclamation, proceeded to ratify the London agreement with regard to silver."[27] Roosevelt's proclamation authorized the Treasury to pay 64.5¢ per ounce for all newly mined domestic silver and to coin the bullion into standard silver dollars.[28] The new program gave miners a subsidy of 50% above the prevailing market price of 43¢ an ounce, leading Key Pittman to say he "never took part in any legislation that gave me more satisfaction and happiness."[29]

Bullion dealer Handy & Harman immediately began posting two prices for silver: the Treasury's price for new U.S. production and a free market price for everything else, such as foreign silver destined for manufacturing or the arts.[30] The free market price rose to 44.25¢ immediately after FDR's announcement because the proclamation not only subsidized miners but also diverted the supply of American silver away from industry. The overnight price increase of almost 3% is significant compared with normal daily price changes, but it is much smaller than the price jumps earlier in the year following favorable government initiatives.[31] The withdrawal from commercial use of U.S. silver production, totaling about 20% of world output, should have had a bigger price impact.[32] And it did, except a leak in the chain of command produced a response *before* the December 21 announcement.

The *Washington Post* headline, "Gold Plan Aids Speculations in U.S. Silver," appeared on Tuesday, November 7, 1933, six weeks before the silver proclamation and two weeks after FDR's fireside chat announcing the gold-buying program.[33] The newspaper reported that "silver prices have pushed up to the best level in three years . . . [and] the new upturn has been accompanied by rumors that Washington might do something for silver."[34] It was more than rumor. At noon on Thursday, October 26, during his daily meeting with Morgenthau, Roosevelt confided, "I am worrying about silver . . . we have entered into a gentlemen's agreement to buy a certain portion of world's supply of silver each year and I have not the faintest idea what we have done about it."[35] FDR suggested that they discuss it with Senator Pittman, but Morgenthau, like the perfect handyman, replied, "Leave it to me and I will take care of it for you."

Early Wednesday afternoon, November 1, Morgenthau reported back to FDR, "We were about ready to go ahead on silver but instead of taking it up with [Undersecretary of the Treasury] Acheson, I suggested that we get the Attorney General to rule on it first and then tell Acheson about it afterwards."[36] Roosevelt broke into a grin, "You Devil—you are just as bad as I am." And Henry said, "Well, who taught me?" Roosevelt roared, "That will be simply grand. Go ahead and get the information and let me know." Morgenthau then spoke to Ugo Carusi, special assistant to the attorney general, who agreed to assign the task "in strict confidence."

Later that evening Morgenthau met with Key Pittman for an all-night discussion of silver. He told the Nevada senator about his marching orders from FDR and the forthcoming ruling by the attorney general. Morgenthau made the following entry in his diary: "I impressed on [Pittman] the importance of secrecy. However, there must have been a leak earlier in the day as metal stocks went up 4 to 6 points."[37]

Between FDR's fireside chat on Sunday, October 22, 1933, and the *Washington Post* rumor article on Tuesday, November 7, 1933, the price of silver rose from just under 37¢ an ounce to 41.5, a significant increase of more than 12%.[38] The gold-buying program accounts for part of the jump, and part belongs to anticipation of a policy to "do something for silver," which was announced on December 21, 1933, with a further increase in price.

Key Pittman called Roosevelt's December 21 proclamation "a Christmas present."[39] He should have added: Christmas came early this year.

The new silver program triggered all-night celebrations in the once-proud mining camps of the Rocky Mountain states. Jesse McDonald, president of the Colorado Mining Association, called the program "the best news the silver camps have had in years."[40] In Leadville, Colorado, unemployed miners from surrounding silver-rich settlements like Aspen joined the locals to toast "Roosevelt, silver, and Santa Claus." Wild talk of "going back to the hills" to earn millions coaxed revelers into the streets, firing six-shooters into the air to sound the revival. In Tonopah, Nevada, Key Pittman's territory, the hoopla was more restrained:[41] free drinks kept everyone inside the saloons, where the local women climbed atop the bars to dance with their men. The town would have paraded had there been a town band.

But not everyone celebrated. Senator Elmer Thomas of Oklahoma, author of FDR's favorite amendment, said the new program "is good as far as it goes . . . it will satisfy the silver miners and help foreign trade a little but it is not enough. . . . Congress undoubtedly will demand further action if the government's moves do not restore commodity prices."[42] Roosevelt's least favorite Democrat, Senator Burton Wheeler, said he would offer another bill for the free coinage of silver at 16 to 1: "This proclamation is in no wise a substitute for those who believe that commodity prices must be raised by means of reflation. . . . The remonetization of silver . . . would immediately raise the price . . . throughout the world to $1.29 . . . [and] American manufacturers would no longer have to fear the competition of depreciated currency of the Orient."[43]

Burton Wheeler's reference to the Orient meant China, a relatively new interest for the Montana senator, but Nevada's Pittman had been a China watcher ever since joining the Senate Foreign Relations Committee and had used that country to advance his recent pro-silver arguments. Pittman had pointed to America's declining trade with China during the first two years of the depression and wrote: "The chief cause for the abnormal and sudden decrease in our commerce with China during the latter part of 1929 and 1930 was the . . . unprecedented fall in the price of silver . . . [which is] the only money in China."[44] But his claim that China would benefit from higher silver prices ignored the relative prosperity that country enjoyed during the early years of the depression. China experts like Sir Arthur Salter, former head of the League of Nations economic section, had explained that the Asian country had escaped the worst of the depression precisely because the decline in silver helped it avoid domestic deflation.[45]

The test would come soon enough.

CHAPTER 7

CHINA AND AMERICA COLLIDE

PITTMAN FANCIED HIMSELF AN EXPERT ON CHINA'S MONEY AND shared his perspective with his Senate colleagues: "The people of oriental and tropical countries are suspicious of paper money. They have always used silver as money because it is practically indestructible. They preserve it by burying it in the ground, by manufacturing it into jewelry, and wearing it as ornaments, and by carrying it in their loin cloths. They contend that paper money is subject to destruction, and when placed in their loin cloths, in a very few hours it is in a condition beyond circulation."[1]

Key Pittman was right about silver serving as China's money, but loin cloths went beyond his expertise. Silver had been the main Chinese currency for at least a thousand years though almost none of the white metal was produced domestically.[2] China was a major buyer of America's silver exports after the Great War, taking between 10 and 75% of U.S. bullion shipments abroad.[3] And China had imported silver during the sixteenth and seventeenth centuries, for example, by exchanging silk and tea with English and Portuguese merchants for silver coins, including the famous Spanish pieces-of-eight, which circulated throughout the world and had been legal tender even in the United States.[4] Until 1933, however, the main Chinese medium of exchange was the "tael," a measure of weight roughly the equivalent of an ounce, rather than a standardized coin.[5] Bullion shaped like a shoe, sometimes called shoes of sycee, containing about fifty tael, were used for large transactions, although the precise size and worth of the silver sycee varied across the country.[6] The disparity in value, a boon to Chinese bankers, hindered internal commerce and provoked domestic discord.

The yuan, a standardized silver coin, was first introduced into China in May 1910 and became the official monetary unit by proclamation of the Chinese Ministry of Finance in Nanking, the nation's capital, on April 6, 1933.[7] The government's effort to unify the currency and to stabilize the economy came too late. China's currency is still called the yuan, but the silver content disappeared in 1935 when China was forced off the silver standard, a victim of efforts by Pittman and FDR to "do something *more* for silver."

The president inadvertently began the second leg of his silver program with gold. On Monday, January 15, 1934, Roosevelt asked Congress for legislation to transfer gold held by the Federal Reserve to the U.S. Treasury, the last step in nationalizing the yellow metal.[8] No private citizen in America would be permitted to own gold except for artistic or industrial purposes, such as jewelers for making bangles or earrings and dentists for implanting fancy false teeth (gold inlays have been a status symbol to eastern Europeans for centuries and to jet-setting celebrities, like Madonna and Justin Bieber, in the twenty-first century).[9] The law would forbid Americans from investing in gold, not to mention speculation, and would remain in force for forty years.[10] FDR also asked Congress to restrain within narrower limits his authority to devalue the dollar granted by the Thomas Amendment of May 1933, a clever tactic to broaden support. And Roosevelt hailed silver as an important monetary metal, saying, "I look for a greatly increased use," but recommended no action until we "gain more knowledge of the results of the London agreement and of our other monetary measures."[11]

Congress gave the president everything he asked for by passing the Gold Reserve Act on Tuesday, January 30, 1934.[12] FDR raised the price of the yellow metal to $35 an ounce the following day but ignored the Thomas Amendment's authorization to "fix the weight of the silver dollar . . . at a definite fixed ratio in relation to the gold dollar . . . and to provide for the unlimited coinage of such gold and silver."[13] For the twelve months ending January 31, 1934, the prices of gold and silver had increased by 70%, the yellow metal from $20.67 to $35 an ounce and the white from 25.875¢ to 44¢ an ounce, leaving the price ratio between the two unchanged at about 80 to 1. To Burton Wheeler that meant no progress at all and he was joined in that sentiment by almost half the Senate.

Wheeler had challenged Roosevelt's request to put silver on the back burner in a proposed amendment to the president's gold bill that would have required the Treasury to buy silver until it purchased one billion ounces or until the price rose to restore the 16 to 1 ratio.[14] World annual silver production averaged about 250 million ounces, so the price impact of buying a billion ounces at the proposed rate of ten million per month would have been substantial.[15] Wheeler added that raising the price of silver would be "like putting a tariff wall against China" because the price of its currency would rise with silver and make Chinese imports more expensive.[16] A Senate supporter chimed in, "It will mean something in terms of trade, business and improvement, and it will mean something to the American people."

Forty-five senators voted against the amendment and forty-three voted in favor, including Key Pittman, who ignored Roosevelt's opposition to the program's mandatory provision and sided with his fellow silverites.[17] The press reported that Wheeler's supporting remarks before the final roll call contained "no flaming oratory [like Bryan's] . . . Cross of Gold" and added that a senator complimented him on "making such a conservative speech that those who vote against the measure are made to look like radicals."[18] The president's slim two-vote victory emboldened the silver bloc in the Senate and raised the white metal to the top of FDR's shopping list.

Roosevelt followed up by supporting the Silver Purchase Act introduced in the Senate on May 22, 1934, saying "it would be helpful to have legislation broadening the authority for the further acquisition and monetary use of silver."[19] Key Pittman negotiated the compromise bill permitting, but not requiring, the president to purchase silver bullion until it comprised one-fourth of the combined value of gold and silver reserves for America's money and to issue paper dollars called silver certificates redeemable in the white metal.[20] In addition, the bill authorized the president to nationalize at his discretion all the silver bullion in the United States as had been done with gold. Henry Morgenthau, who had become Treasury secretary in January 1934 and would implement the purchase program, said that he would buy surplus stocks of silver and treat the "permissive provisions" as though they were mandatory. According to Colorado Senator Alva Adams, a moderate in the silver bloc, "This is the longest step taken for the rehabilitation of silver since its demonetization in 1873."[21]

Alva Adams correctly identified the importance of the Silver Purchase Act, especially its proposal to make the white metal 25% of America's monetary reserves. Even Alexander Hamilton, who had established American bimetallism by defining the dollar in terms of both gold and silver, had never set precise targets for the two metals. He just wanted both gold and silver to back the dollar to avoid the "evils of a scanty circulation." The Silver Purchase Act marked a rebirth of bimetallism that exceeded the reach of the original.

The price of silver jumped from 43.75¢ an ounce to 45.125¢, a significant increase of more than 3%, when a detailed description of the Silver Purchase Act surfaced two weeks before the bill was introduced.[22] The U.S. Treasury would need to purchase more than a billion ounces of the white metal to make silver a quarter of total monetary reserves, but a flexible timetable restrained the price increase.[23] Treasury Secretary Morgenthau said, "What we want is a rise in the price of silver, but we don't want a sensational price rise, because the worst thing that could happen would be to have silver go up and then have a collapse."[24] The secretary was just a farmer from Fishkill, but he could have taught the professionals how to manipulate prices.

Roosevelt helped Morgenthau smooth the uptrend. The president had insisted on a 50% excess profits tax on transactions in silver bullion as part of the Silver Purchase Act, forcing speculators to mask their speculations.[25] In addition, section 3 of the act prevented the Treasury from paying more than 50¢ an ounce when acquiring silver bullion held in the United States, blunting the upside pressure. Key Pittman did not care because *newly mined* domestic silver still received the 64.5¢ an ounce promised in the December 21 proclamation. And before Roosevelt left Washington for a summer vacation beginning Monday, June 30, 1934, he left further instructions to prevent speculators from capitalizing on the government's purchase plans.

FDR would be gone for six weeks, travelling aboard the 10,000-ton navy cruiser, USS *Houston*, to visit Puerto Rico, the Virgin Islands, the Canal Zone, and Hawaii. The warship was outfitted especially for the president, including accommodating his tall frame with a seven-foot-four-inch-long bed which had been tested for durability by a number of adventurous midshipman until a sign was prominently posted, "Lay off this bed, please."[26] The press reported that the ship contained the latest wireless communications facilities for the chief executive so that "within a few minutes he can dispatch any orders he may choose to give after receiving information."[27] Roosevelt could govern from the high seas, but he prepared in advance for silver in a memo dated June 28, 1934, two days before his departure. The president instructed Morgenthau to implement section 7 of the Silver Purchase Act and to nationalize the white metal when the free market price reached 49.5¢ an ounce.[28]

Morgenthau viewed the president's memo like a blueprint for acquiring an estimated 100 million ounces of silver bullion sitting in speculator vaults, the first step in making silver a quarter of total U.S. monetary reserves. On Wednesday, August 1, 1934, he wrote in his diary that when silver exceeded 46¢ an ounce, he would "personally take charge of the buying and expected to run it up to 49½ cents and then nationalize."[29] When prices advanced to 48¢ the following week the *Wall Street Journal* correctly identified Morgenthau's fingerprints: "Renewed government activity is believed to be responsible. . . . There has been no public demand for silver . . . [because] under the terms of the Silver Purchase Act an upper limit of 50 cents per ounce has been placed upon official purchases."[30] And at 11 a.m. on Thursday morning, August 9, Morgenthau made a bid of 49.5¢ for silver in the New York market, which triggered the order to nationalize the white metal.[31]

The government takeover of silver bullion in the United States rippled the market like a giant rock thrown into a small pond. The U.S. Treasury had pushed silver to the highest level since 1929 and bullish speculators had made a bundle. The nationalization order ended trading in silver futures contracts on New York's Commodity Exchange and would not be resurrected for thirty years, but anyone betting on further price increases could turn to the London bullion market, which is where Morgenthau would direct his purchases of silver to expand its backing of U.S. currency (the act's 50¢ price limitation applied only to domestically held bullion). Key Pittman hailed the nationalization order as "a process that will hasten the complete absorption of the silver surplus in the world [and] . . . as this surplus is absorbed . . . the price of silver will steadily rise until it reaches $1.29."[32]

Handy & Harman continued to quote prices in the United States for industrial uses, which mirrored the free market price in London and also reflected the demand for silverware and decorative items by American households. The press assured the public that the government would not confiscate "silver coins, silverware, bric-a-brac, antiques, [or] golf cups."[33] As a result, the nationalization order stimulated record retail sales of sterling silver tea services, ash trays, vases, and flatware, as consumers scrambled to beat expected price increases and tried to stash some bullion for a rainy day in the dining room cupboard, just like in the Middle Ages.[34] Wall Street hailed the Silver Purchase Act as a boon to silverware companies such as Gorham Manufacturing and International Silver, but the reception was less welcome in Shanghai, where the fallout from rising silver prices worried Chinese government officials.[35]

✦ ✦ ✦

The formal protest from China's Finance Minister H.H. Kung, delivered less than two months after Roosevelt's nationalization order, arrived through normal diplomatic channels on Secretary of State Cordell Hull's desk. The message was described in the press as written in "frank terms," which in diplomatic language means a tirade.[36] Kung, known as "Chauncey" during his student days at Oberlin and Yale, was a brother-in-law to Chinese leader General Chiang Kai-shek, so his missive carried even more weight than his title implied.[37] He wrote that the U.S. program presents "a potentially serious monetary situation resulting from the present rise in the price and the drain of silver" and urged "American cooperation to prevent a further rise in the price."[38] This objection may have been a surprise to those who had heard Key Pittman claim that higher silver prices benefited China because of its huge reserves of the white metal, but that argument had been dismissed earlier in the year as "not economically sound" by Li Ming, chairman of the Bank of China.[39] And Ming was right.

Higher silver prices threatened to deflate the Chinese economy with two puncture holes. Higher world prices for the white metal encouraged speculators to withdraw silver from Chinese banks for profitable sale in London. Silver reserves in Shanghai, in fact, declined to new 1934 lows a month after the U.S. nationalization order, and with fewer reserves the banks would curtail lending and discourage business activity.[40] The rise in silver prices also lowered Chinese exports. The yuan, which was linked to silver just like the dollar was to gold, became more expensive in the foreign exchange market as the white metal increased in value. The appreciating yuan meant that Chinese goods cost more to Americans and Europeans, which curtailed sales abroad and increased unemployment in China's export industries. Princeton economist Richard A. Lester analyzed the record and concluded, "An increase in the value of silver . . . would blight their commerce."[41] Countries battled for a share of world trade with competitive devaluations during the Great Depression and viewed an appreciating currency like a deadly plague. The contemporary press confirmed that everyone understood this: "The Chinese may be peculiar, but economic laws are no respecters of nationality. Like other people, they find their ability to export reduced by the higher exchange value of their currency."[42]

The *Washington Post* chided the silver bloc in the Senate: "Those philanthropic members of Congress who strove so valiantly to aid the Chinese by increasing the price of silver and presumably increasing Chinese purchasing power have been cruelly rebuffed by the very people whom they sought to benefit."[43] But not everyone was convinced. Raymond Moley, a charter member of FDR's brains trust who had been an undersecretary of state until mid-1933, wrote that the protest "reflects the point of view of a very small minority of the Chinese people. . . . It is still believed that the increase in the value of silver . . . affords a genuinely improved position to the masses of the Chinese."[44] Perhaps Moley believed what he said but more likely it was another installment payment to Key Pittman for implementing FDR's version of the Thomas Amendment.

Secretary of State Cordell Hull responded to Finance Minister Kung's protest note with a diplomatic dance worthy of Fred Astaire: "In conducting operations under the Silver Purchase Act this government, while necessarily keeping within the general purposes of enactment, will give the closest possible attention to the possibilities of so arranging the time, the place, and the quantity of its purchases as will keep in view the considerations put forward by the Chinese Government."[45] Hull juggled his words to satisfy both the Chinese and the silverites in Congress, but the secretary of state had little influence implementing the Silver Purchase Act. Treasury Secretary Morgenthau controlled the program and the two cabinet members disliked each other.

Hull, a tall Tennessee lawyer known for his patient political skill, was said to carry "a long knife" by those who knew him well.[46] Hull resented Morgenthau's encroachment into State Department turf and his influence with Roosevelt: "The Secretary of the Treasury . . . often acted as if he were clothed with authority to project himself into the field of foreign affairs and inaugurate efforts to shape the course of foreign policy. . . . I mentioned this habit to the President from time to time; but Mr. Roosevelt had a way of quietly easing by such complaints relating to his intimates."[47] Morgenthau thought that Hull favored Japan over China in the Far East by deferring to the Japanese Amau Doctrine, articulated in April 1934, asserting Japan's interest in any developments in China.[48] A month after the Japanese declaration Hull wrote, "It is and has been the policy of the United States . . . to cooperate with the efforts and professed desire of the Japanese Government to strengthen the traditional relations of friendship between the two countries."[49] He then rebuffed a suggestion by Morgenthau's economic emissary to China, Yale Professor James H. Rogers, with the following note to the State Department's consul general in Shanghai: "Please inform Rogers urgently that discussion with Chinese officials of [a] possible loan involves traversing delicate political ground . . . he should under no circumstances receive or discuss any proposal for [a] loan."[50]

Morgenthau wanted to balance the scales. He telephoned Roosevelt on Monday, November 26, 1934, when the free market price of silver approached 55¢ an ounce, and reminded FDR that the president had wanted silver "to be 64½ cents by the time Congress met."[51] Morgenthau then told him that the silver purchase program was doing "everything possible to help Japan" by "deflating China." He said that silver was "being smuggled out of Shanghai" and asked for permission to abstain from bidding "above 55 cents for silver for the rest of the week" until they had a chance to talk. FDR agreed to the temporary halt and Morgenthau wrote in his diary that he wanted to ask the president to "think over the idea that we should tell China that when silver reached 64½ cents that we would try to stabilize it" and that he would "try and sell this idea to the silver block senators showing them that contrary to their prognostications our export business with China has been falling off."

In the beginning of December the *New York Times* headlined "Deflation in China Gains Momentum" and explained that the country is "slowly being drained of its circulating medium."[52] The Chinese Ministry of Finance had levied a silver export tax to curtail outflows but an estimated $50 million of the white metal had been smuggled out of China in less than two months, and many observers blamed Japan, but high world prices also attracted legitimate American business to the silver-backed "yuan dollar."[53] Goldsmith Brothers Smelting and Refining Company in Chicago paid the 10% tax and imported twelve tons of Chinese coins engraved with the revered likeness of Sun Yat-sen, founder of the Chinese republic, which were then unceremoniously melted into silver nitrate used to manufacture movie film and electrical circuitry.[54] Dealers commented: "The total cost of refining and shipping charges for Chinese and other foreign metals is not sufficiently large [to discourage] silver purchases abroad."[55]

After two Shanghai banks closed their doors Morgenthau went into emergency mode.[56] On Thursday, December 13, 1934, he telephoned Professor John Henry Williams, an international economics expert at Harvard, and said:[57] "I'm calling you up confidentially . . . the Chinese situation seems to come to a head . . . and over the weekend I'm going to take a hand at writing a financial program for China. . . . I wondered if you could come down and spend a couple of days with us and help us." Williams agreed to join the task force, which included the distinguished University of Chicago economist Jacob Viner, but Morgenthau wanted a practitioner as well and, following his call to Williams, he telephoned Siegfried Stern, a vice president at the Chase National Bank, for an in-house recommendation:[58]

MORGENTHAU (M): I'm calling you to talk to you very confidentially.

STERN (S): Yes.

M: We're going to try to see if we can do something to help China with her troubles.

S: Yes.

M: Who in your opinion, knows the most about . . .

S: We had one specialist in the bank here who handles the actual trading and exchange . . .

M: It isn't a question of buying and selling.

S: I see.

M: I mean a man that just deals with it wouldn't help much, would it?

S: Not much. . . . Well we have one man who has been out there for six months or so.

M: Who?

S: Mr. Frank, our Treasurer. I think he knows quite a little about the currency. He isn't a trained economist.

M: Well, we have plenty of those.

S: Yes, plenty of those.

M: But he knows the currency?

S: He knows the currency. . . . I imagine he would be the best we have. He has had actual experience in China.

M: What's his name?

S: N.R. Funck—F-U-N-C-K.

M: Funk?

S: Yes, Funck. Assistant Cashier

M: Can he be here tomorrow morning?

S: He'll be there tomorrow morning.

M: Fine.

S: Alright if there is anything else we can do here, we'll be glad to do it, Mr. Secretary.

Pause . . .

M: Funck?

S: Yes, Funck . . . F-U-N-C-K.

M: Right. . . . Thank you.

S: Thank you. . . . goodbye.

M: Goodbye.

Morgenthau knew what he needed to help formulate a cure for China's money troubles, and it was not a currency trader and certainly not another economist; he needed someone with practical experience, but he had trouble believing a man named Funck could be the answer.

Henry!

CHAPTER 8

BOMBSHELL IN SHANGHAI

THE WORDS "VERY CONFIDENTIAL" TOPPED THE SEVEN-PAGE "Silver Problem" report Morgenthau's committee of China experts completed over the mid-December weekend.[1] He submitted the detailed document to the president at 2 p.m. on Sunday, December 16, 1934, but the only concrete outcome was an invitation to the Chinese to send a representative to Washington for discussions.[2] Morgenthau rejected the report's suggestion to keep the price of silver at 55¢ an ounce until reaching an agreement with China, explaining in his diary: "I had given my word to the silver senators . . . that I would carry out the purchase of the silver enthusiastically."[3] Morgenthau invoked a higher authority by adding, "The President also made a similar statement although I do not remember the exact words he used."

At a follow-up lunch at the White House, Morgenthau asked FDR whether he would like to suggest names to the Chinese for their representative, and the president said, "Yes, tell them either Kung, Minister of Finance, or T.V. Soong."[4] Roosevelt knew both were prominent in China. Soong, a forty-year-old graduate of Harvard, whose round black-rimmed glasses made him look professorial, had served as Minister of Finance immediately before H.H. Kung. He had worked in New York City at what is now Citibank and was as fluent in English as in Chinese.[5] Soong had three sisters: one had married Kung (and probably helped him get the job); another was married to Dr. Sun Yat-sen, founding father of modern China, who died in 1925; and the third married General Chiang Kai-shek, successor to Sun as leader of the Republic of China, who would rule the country until the communist takeover in 1949.[6] The Soongs rivaled the Roosevelts as political royalty.

When Morgenthau conveyed the president's preference for Kung or Soong to the Chinese ambassador to the United States, Alfred

Sao-ke Sze, he responded with: "What would the Japanese [think] if one or two such prominent men would come over here?"[7] Ambassador Sze's question stunned Morgenthau into saying, "I know nothing about world politics," which may have been true but was certainly nothing for a Treasury secretary to confess unless it was to a priest administering last rites. Morgenthau claims that when he repeated the Sze conversation to Roosevelt, the president was equally surprised that the Chinese were worried about what Japan would think. The truth is they both knew.

Morgenthau and Roosevelt were warned about Japan by William C. Bullitt, a charming and debonair upper-class Philadelphian, Yale educated, who had been a special assistant to Secretary of State Cordell Hull, and now served as America's ambassador to the Soviet Union.[8] Bullitt had worked on Russian matters with Morgenthau and had cultivated a special relationship with Roosevelt through extensive personal correspondence from Moscow, encouraged by the president's words: "I am anxious to hear all that has happened. Do write."[9] The ambassador visited China and Japan on his return trip to Washington in late 1934 after FDR confirmed, "I think it is a fine idea for you to come back via the Far East where you will be able to get at least a cursory view of things in Siberia, Manchuria, China, and Japan.[10] A confident Bullitt arrived in Washington in December and shared his insights about the Far East in a long and delicate telephone conversation with Morgenthau:[11]

MORGENTHAU (M): How are you?

BULLITT (B): How are you, old scoundrel—I called you three times.

M: Are you talking from the State department?

B: No, I'm not. . . . Why, do you want to say anything?

M: Well, I'll just ask you this. . . . How critical do you think the Chinese situation is?

B: Extremely.

M: Extremely.

B: I can tell you very, very briefly. . . . I have this from ten or fifteen people. . . . They expect or fear . . . a collapse before the Chinese

settlement day, which is the 1st of February. . . . My secretary
has just handed me something . . . an opinion of . . . a competent
banker in that entire country—would you like me to read it to
you for a second?

M: I've got plenty of time.

B: Well, just let me read you this. . . . Very much disturbed about
the present financial situation in China . . . the foreign banks
in Shanghai and throughout China were withdrawing from all
commitments which were throwing an unprecedented strain on
the Chinese banks . . . the flow of silver out of the country was
beginning to make everyone extremely nervous . . . there was
already a flight of capital from the country and it was impossible
to say when a panic might start . . . we can't stop the export of
silver . . . because the Japanese are smuggling it out by way of
the [Tientsin] Railway.

M: Let me ask you this. How much of what you're telling me have
you had a chance to tell the president?

B: I've talked at great length about that—much more than on anything else, but I don't remember how specifically I went into this
particular thing. I may have explained it fairly well. We were
talking about different aspects of the Far East thing.

M: I've been terribly embarrassed about the thing—I've been just
directed as an agent . . . [but] to sum up my feelings . . . I was
on the pay of the Japanese [and] I've been earning my pay.

✦ ✦ ✦

The "thing" that embarrassed Henry was his role as purchasing
agent for silver to bring it to one-quarter of U.S. monetary reserves
as proposed by the Silver Purchase Act of 1934. He felt as though
he was working for Japan by buying the white metal, driving up its
price, and encouraging renewed Japanese aggression by weakening
the Chinese economy. In 1931 Japan had invaded China's province of Manchuria, established a puppet state called Manchukuo,
and then withdrew from the League of Nations after the League
condemned its conquest. Perhaps Morgenthau was guilty of excessive enthusiasm in implementing America's silver policy, but FDR

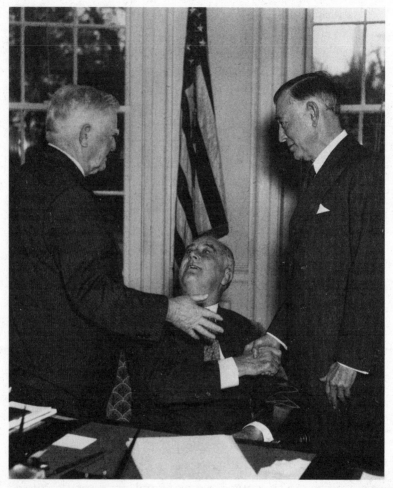

FIGURE 8. FDR holds Pittman close while talking to Vice President Garner.

deserved greater blame. The president had given a juicy subsidy to the silver senators in his 1933 proclamation, called a Christmas present by Key Pittman, but he now gave the Nevada senator the final say over how to deal with China's troubles. When Pittman heard that T.V. Soong might visit the United States he told Morgenthau: "It should be understood that he is not coming here to discuss our silver policy."[12] Henry delivered Pittman's message to FDR and the president then said it was "much better that Soong did not come."[13]

Senator Pittman may have had more on his mind than T.V. Soong. On January 2, 1935, the *Chicago Daily Tribune* headlined: "Mining Deals by Pittman and Baruch Bared."[14] The article reported that the Nevada senator together with Bernard M. Baruch, "the Wall Street speculator and economic adviser to President Roosevelt," have joined with others to purchase "rich gold and silver mining properties in a new California bonanza. . . . This action by two New Deal leaders places them in a position to profit handsomely from the New Deal's own monetary manipulation." Pittman and Baruch had "quietly purchased mining properties" two weeks earlier, and the newspaper quoted estimates by engineers that the mine would earn a profit of $13 per ton of ore compared with $7 without the New Deal gold and silver programs. Pittman confirmed the reports to the *Tribune* and said that he, Baruch, and their associates "have not given any interviews on the new gold and silver discovery lest the announcement attract a flood of poor persons seeking to get rich quick."

Key Pittman succeeded in disinviting T.V. Soong but could not silence the former Chinese finance minister, who was still very much in the public eye. He was now running the China Development Finance Corporation, an entity designed to attract foreign capital to promote China's industrialization, and had met William Bullitt during his trip to the Far East.[15] Soong knew of Bullitt's relationship with FDR and sent him a note on January 31, 1935, knowing it would be shared with Roosevelt (which it was). Soong wrote that he was "taking a hand in [the] currency and financial problems because of the extreme gravity [of the] situation."[16] He explained that a "currency collapse while unfortunate need not be so disastrous, but . . . with Japan now pressing for [a] showdown . . . in order to dominate China, [our] Government would then have to choose between accepting a Japanese loan under onerous political and economic conditions or [face] the emergence of provincial governments . . . under Japanese protection." Soong concluded with a request for American aid to mitigate the silver problem "in view of the impending danger to China and the world."

Soong may have been overly dramatic, perhaps because he had studied in the United States and watched too many westerns, but his warning reflected Japanese gunfire. A week before his message to Bullitt a four-thousand-strong Japanese-Manchukuoan force, supported by Japanese aircraft, attacked three towns in the Chahar region of Inner Mongolia, a Chinese province adjacent to Manchukuo, killing forty-four Chinese citizens.[17] Although the attack was labelled a border dispute and came after Japanese foreign minister Hirota called upon China to join Japan in "safeguarding the peace of East Asia," the *New York Times* suggested that it gave the Chinese reason to "reflect on past Japanese advances" and to fear "that Japan's next objective is the absorption of all Inner Mongolia into the Manchukuoan Empire."[18]

The Japanese wanted more than Inner Mongolia, which was just a small piece of territory in a giant jigsaw puzzle of intrigue. Following the attack, they sent Minister Akira Ariyoshi and two military attachés to Nanking to confer with General Chiang Kai-shek, the first meeting for the Generalissimo with the Japanese minister since the Manchurian conflict of 1931. The press reported that the Japanese wanted the two countries to form an "economic bloc" which, "if consummated, would be highly prejudicial to commercial relations with American and European nations."[19] As an incentive the Japanese offered to "extend financial assistance to China with the purpose of offsetting the adverse effects of American silver policy." High Chinese officials refused to speak publicly but journalists leaked private comments that this arrangement "would amount to China's submission to Japan's claim of military and economic hegemony in Asia."

The Japanese understood that the worsening silver crisis would bring the Chinese government into conflict with its citizens. Silver ornaments dominated the accumulated wealth in China and the central bank needed to replenish the depleted stock of the white metal that had been smuggled out of the country. The Finance Ministry issued regulations to get families to exchange their silver plaques, vases, trays, dishes, and jewelry for standard Chinese silver dollars at the below-market official rate.[20] The Chinese elite might prefer capitulation to Japan to losing their favorite silver heirlooms.

Newspapers sometimes exaggerate the facts to promote sales but on Sunday evening, February 17, 1935, two weeks after the meetings between General Chiang and Minister Akira, William Bullitt brought a message to Roosevelt from Ambassador Sze confirming the substance of the negotiations between China and Japan. Bullitt arrived at the White House unannounced, which was unusual even by Bullitt's self-assured standard, but not as unusual as what he told FDR, who was meeting with Morgenthau. He said that the Chinese ambassador had shown him "a very confidential cable which he did not feel he could show the State Department" but asked Bullitt to get the information to the president. Morgenthau just listened but said to himself, "This procedure seemed most irregular and I should think would be frowned upon by Hull" (probably the understatement of the year).[21]

Bullitt relayed details of the telegram to the president like a secret agent, saying it was meant for FDR even though it was sent to Ambassador Sze from Finance Minister Kung. It confirmed the earlier note from Soong and said that Japan was offering a "large loan" as part of an extensive "so-called economic cooperation which amounts to economic domination particularly [in] North China."[22] The message added that Japan would help make "joint representations against American silver policy." The president thanked Bullitt for the information but waited until the following day, at a lunch with Hull and Morgenthau at the White House, to discuss the contents. He told Cordell Hull all about Bullitt's conversation of the previous night, perhaps to take the secretary of state down a peg, which delighted Morgenthau who considered Hull soft on Japan, and then said, "In view of the information that Bullitt has brought us, I am now convinced that I am right that somehow or other our silver policy is hurting Japan."[23] FDR then nodded towards Morgenthau, "I have told this to Henry and other people but nobody seems to know why it should hurt Japan, but I maintain that it does."

No one understood the president's argument because it made no sense. Japan had crafted a plan to exploit China's weakness inflicted by the Silver Purchase Act and agreed to fight the American program to wrangle further concessions from China. The Japanese preferred victory by appeasement to bloodshed just like most neighborhood bullies. FDR had deluded himself in the service of Key Pittman and the silver senators but would recognize his error too late.

◆ ◆ ◆

Skyrocketing silver prices in mid-April 1935 inflamed China's troubles after the State Department rebuffed its appeal for American aid.[24] The free market price had already advanced from 55¢ an ounce on January 2, 1935, to 61¢ on April 1, 1935, thanks to Henry Morgenthau. He had been an aggressive buyer of the white metal since the 1934 Silver Purchase Act proposed that America's monetary reserves consist of three-quarters gold and one-quarter silver. However, after accumulating all U.S. mine production at a monthly rate of 3.5 million ounces and buying an average of 25 million ounces per month on the London bullion market, Morgenthau's objective remained unfulfilled.[25] He still had over a billion ounces to buy and on Tuesday, April 9, 1935, speculators pushed Handy & Harman's free market price to 63¢ an ounce, almost equaling the subsidized 64.5¢ offered to newly mined domestic silver under FDR's 1933 proclamation.[26] The press reported that Treasury Secretary Morgenthau gave "official assurance that whenever the world price exceeded the Treasury price to domestic producers, the latter would receive the world price"[27] Traders bid up the free market price to over 64¢ on Wednesday, April 10, in a significant response to Morgenthau's pledge.[28] It was just the beginning.

A speculative frenzy greeted the president's announcement late that Wednesday evening that going forward the subsidized price for newly mined domestic silver would be 71¢ an ounce.[29] Buyers loved FDR's revised proclamation and pushed up the free market price over the following two days to 68.5¢, a significant jump that brought silver to its highest level in almost ten years.[30] FDR's subsidy adjustment confirmed the power of the silver bloc in the Senate and suggested a game of leapfrog between the two silver prices. Morgenthau inadvertently fed the speculation when he justified the president's action by saying to reporters that American silver mining interests "were entitled to that price." When asked, "Why?" in a follow-up question, Morgenthau answered, "Because."[31]

The press recognized the fallout for China. An April 12 headline in the *Manchester Guardian* sounded the alarm: "Higher U.S. Price for Silver 'Bombshell' to Shanghai."[32] The *Wall Street Journal* explained "that drastic action by China will be necessary to stem the deflationary effect . . . discussions are being heard on the possibility of China cutting loose altogether from the silver standard."[33] And the *Boston Globe* added a new wrinkle of concern: "The heavy buying of silver for American account last year and early this year has swept the market almost bare of supplies and made speculative manipulations that much easier."[34]

The clash between speculators wanting to make a killing and Morgenthau wanting to satisfy Congress exploded in the last week of April. Traders pushed up the free market price to over 71¢ on Wednesday, April 24, and the government responded the following day with a new proclamation making the subsidized price 77¢, which encouraged another round of speculation and a jump in the free market price to 81¢ an ounce on Friday, April 26.[35] The *New York Times* headlined: "Speculators Rule in Silver Market," confirming what most traders already knew and forcing Morgenthau and FDR into emergency consultations.[36]

Henry had told FDR the week before that he wanted to "spank some of the speculators" and began the process by refusing to announce a new subsidized price following the free market price increase of April 26.[37] Morgenthau and Roosevelt met that Friday morning and agreed to wait until Saturday afternoon before taking any action. The president suggested making the following statement to explain the pause: "We do not like the speculative interests in silver, that the American mining interests are not speculating and that we realize that the Silver Purchase Program of the United States Government had lent itself to the support of speculation."[38] FDR then told Morgenthau, "Personally, I would be glad to see the price of silver stay around 75 cents for a few months as I think the advance has been entirely too rapid. . . . I think it would stay there the balance of this year and in to 1936." The president grinned and fluttered his eyebrows like Groucho Marx when mentioning 1936, and Morgenthau understood "that he had the election in mind."

Silver and politics nurtured each other in America since the Crime of 1873 fed William Jennings Bryan's 1896 presidential campaign, so Morgenthau followed up FDR's signal with a courtesy meeting at the Treasury that very same day with Key Pittman and other silver senators. Morgenthau summarized the problem: "The speculators have taken this thing away from us and the market is going up too fast. There will be a sudden drop and this will hurt the whole recovery program."[39] He then added a new twist, "We [also] have the Mexican situation on our hands. Their problem is that silver in pesos is worth 72 cents." Mexico was not on a silver standard but its citizens had been hoarding coins and melting them for sale as bullion at higher prices, so the country now had a shortage of currency that was hurting business. Pittman pursued the Mexico problem.

PITTMAN: Has Mexico got silver bullion?
MORGENTHAU: Yes, about 25 million ounces of newly mined silver.
PITTMAN: Why doesn't she sell some silver?
MORGENTHAU: I suggested that to them but they are withholding it. . . . They have been speculating themselves.
PITTMAN: The only thing that will stop speculation is to give the speculators a loss. . . . I think you ought to sit tight and do nothing and wait four or five days.

✦ ✦ ✦

Both Morgenthau and Pittman wanted to spank the speculators, and Mexico obliged by changing sides and abandoning her speculative ways. President Lazaro Cardenas declared a bank holiday for Saturday, April 27, just as Roosevelt had done upon taking office, ordered all silver pesos surrendered to the Treasury in exchange for paper currency, and banned exports of the white metal.[40] Mexico, the largest producer and exporter of silver in the world, had suddenly become a potential seller of even more silver.[41] In a very private meeting arranged at Henry Morgenthau's Washington home with Roberto Lopez of the Mexican Finance Ministry, Lopez told Morgenthau, "We wish to assure you that we will positively not speculate any more in silver in New York or London and that we would like to sell you our silver in London."[42] The promise pleased Morgenthau, especially since he had asked Mrs. Morgenthau to witness the discussion that had taken place in their living room.

The price of silver reacted immediately to the events of April 27, which included an announcement by Morgenthau of no change in the government's subsidized price.[43] The white metal declined from 81¢ an ounce on Friday, April 26, to 77¢ on Saturday, a significant drop even by the more recent volatile standard.[44] Mexican banks reopened the following Monday with little disruption from the bank holiday, and the country benefited as the free market price of silver stabilized between 71¢ and 77¢ an ounce over the next month.[45] Unlike most silver-producing countries, where the white metal is a byproduct of other mining operations, such as lead, copper, and zinc, most Mexican mines specialized in silver, so that production responded to higher prices and employment in the industry soared.

A stable and high price for silver was very good news for Mexico but was very bad news for China, which continued to suffer from a drain of the white metal. The *Boston Globe* noted that the world market is "rigged by the buying operations of the Treasury . . . but Mexico—as compared with China—has very little to complain about in the outworking of our enigmatic policy."[46] The high price of silver bullion accelerated smuggling out of China during 1935, siphoning about 140 million ounces from the country, worsening the financial crisis, and encouraging further Japanese aggression.[47]

✦ ✦ ✦

Japanese troops advanced about ten miles beyond the Great Wall into the demilitarized zone of Northern China on May 22, 1935, as though summoned by a beacon of shining silver, and killed more than three hundred Chinese soldiers.[48] The Japanese force greatly outnumbered the Chinese and sent the surviving defenders fleeing into the surrounding hillside. Japanese losses were six killed and three wounded. A War Office spokesman in Tokyo said after the incursion, "The sole object of the present drive is to clear away the bandits . . . Japanese troops will be recalled within the Great Wall once the bandits are defeated. The Japanese army has not the slightest intention of starting another military operation."[49] Observers were not so sure, and according to the *Washington Post*, "watched developments closely through the bars of censorship."

The Japanese War Office's denial of further military action masked threatening messages to China and to diplomats in Japan's Foreign Office. The army insisted that China remove the anti-Japanese governor of Hopei province and put an end to anti-Japanese propaganda, longstanding demands that were quickly granted by the Chinese authorities.[50] The generals also launched an internecine battle to show diplomats in their Foreign Office "that peaceful persuasion alone will never induce China to give Japan the opportunities she desires."[51] A telegram to Secretary of State Cordell Hull from U.S. Ambassador to China Nelson Johnson confirmed that the Japanese military "have been skeptical of the efficiency of the Japanese Foreign Office policy . . . [and] that the military would be content to watch only for a limited time the direction of Japanese policy in China by Japanese civilians."[52] Local Japanese commanders dispatched troops to Peiping (Beijing) to emphasize the point.[53]

A fragile tension rose in Northern China like a gathering storm cloud until it burst on Sunday, November 3, 1935, making front page headlines throughout the world. China surrendered to the silver smugglers and severed the connection between its currency and the white metal. Finance Minister H.H. Kung announced that all silver yuan must be delivered to the central bank in exchange for new banknotes, an edict that mimicked FDR's order in April 1933, forcing Americans to turn in their gold coins for Federal Reserve notes. Kung justified the surprising turnaround because "the rapid rise in the price of world silver" caused China's currency to become seriously overvalued, leading to "severe internal deflation, growing unemployment, [and] widespread bankruptcies."[54]

China's move to fiat currency required the skills of a gymnast. The government could now expand money and credit to jumpstart the economy, but it had to avoid overexpansion to assure citizens that the new banknotes would remain valuable even without silver backing. Kung's currency reform took a double-barreled approach to promote compliance with the decree. It warned that illegal possession of silver "shall be punishable in accordance with the law governing acts of treason," but it also promised to keep "the exchange value of the Chinese dollar stable" at present levels against the major currencies of the world.[55] Shanghai businessmen and peasants alike would willingly hold the new legal tender if they knew it could be reliably exchanged for American dollars at a bank or currency kiosk. But that was easy to say and hard to do, like diet and exercise, because China's central bank needed American dollars to offer for yuan or the new banknotes would decline in value on the foreign exchange market. And the need for American dollars had brought the Chinese ambassador to Morgenthau's doorstep a week before the November 3 announcement.

At ten o'clock Monday evening, October 28, 1935, Alfred Sze arrived at Morgenthau's home to outline the new currency program. He asked on behalf of Finance Minister Kung that America purchase 100 to 200 million ounces of silver, which China would no longer need, so the central bank would have dollar reserves to support the value of their new currency. Morgenthau viewed this as an opportunity to link the yuan to the U.S. dollar and made that a key condition for the silver transaction. He told the president afterwards, "This is our chance ... to hook them up to the dollar instead of the pound sterling," which would enhance U.S. export business to China. Britain also valued China trade, preferred a link between the yuan and the pound, and had the advantage that Sir Frederick Leith-Ross, an economic adviser to the British government, was already in China for consultations.[56]

Long distance negotiations between Morgenthau and Finance Minister Kung during the following week failed to produce an agreement, and Morgenthau began to worry about his silver program. He told Herman Oliphant, his chief legal counsel, and other advisers at Treasury, "We do not want to find ourselves with several billion ounces of silver and no one interested in buying silver except ourselves. . . . Inasmuch as Sze has informed me . . . that at this time they considered it impolitic to tie the yuan to the dollar . . . there is no real pressure on us to do anything."[57] Henry then added an eye opener: "If we can get away with it politically . . . I think the nicest 'out' would be to drop the [free market] price to around 40 cents, [at] which I understand . . . there would be no profit to export silver from China." The U.S. Treasury would still pay the subsidized price for domestically mined silver but this radical departure from current policy required approval from FDR.

Henry arrived at the White House the next day and found the president in a jovial mood, which quickly turned in a direction Henry had not anticipated.[58]

> FDR: Well, what have you brought me today?
>
> MORGENTHAU: Since I talked to you yesterday morning I have altered my ideas somewhat regarding the plans for the purchase of silver. . . . China has asked us to purchase 100 or 200 million ounces of silver. . . . This means that they are willing to give up silver as a monetary base and that is not in accordance with [our] idea of a wider use of silver.
>
> FDR: Have you heard anything further from Dr. Sze?
>
> M: Yes. He called yesterday afternoon and said that Dr. Kung could not give any promises as to linking the Chinese yuan to the United States dollar.
>
> FDR: Did he give any reasons?
>
> M: Yes. He said that owing to political pressure they could not announce the linking of the yuan to any other currency and simply repeated that they were stabilizing it at the present level.
>
> FDR: Internal or external pressure?
>
> M: External pressure. The Japanese.

✦ ✦ ✦

The president knew that Japan had objected to China's failure to consult on the silver decree, but neither he nor Morgenthau anticipated the extent of Japanese fury. A front page news story on November 5, 1935, led with "China's Money Plan Angers Japanese," and explained that according to Japanese bankers, who were taken completely by surprise, it "reveals a British intention to seize control of Chinese trade" because of the alleged role played by U.K. adviser Sir Frederick Leith-Ross in the decision.[59] An editorial in Tokyo's *Nichi Nichi Shimbun* claims it shows China's "complete insincerity."[60]

The rhetoric escalated the next day in a *New York Times* headline, "China Threatened by Japanese Anew: Wrathful Over Nanking's New Monetary Plan, War Minister Says Army Is Ready to Act."[61] The news article reported that Japan's War Minister Yoshiyuki Kawashima turned high finance into politics by saying that China's monetary reform has proved her "insincerity," and the Japanese army may act alone in China to protect Manchuria from "the Communist menace," a reference to neighboring Russia and to China's internal communists led by Mao Tse-tung. The paper suggested that "Japan may be ready to replace Foreign Minister Koki Hirota's 'negative' policy of a conciliatory attitude toward Nanking by the army's positive policy of forming a North China bloc to allow Tokyo to achieve its aims."

Joseph Grew, America's ambassador to Japan, had anticipated an emerging conflict between civilian and military authorities in Japan that could threaten regional peace. He wrote in his diary a year earlier, "The pendulum of chauvinism throughout Japanese history has swung to and fro in periodic cycles of intensity and temporary relaxation, [and] the armed forces of the country are perfectly capable of overriding the restraining control of the Government and of committing what might well amount to national hari kiri in a mistaken conception of patriotism. . . . There is a swashbuckling temper in the country, largely developed by military propaganda, which can lead Japan during the next few years . . . to any extremes unless saner minds in the Government [prevail]."[62] Events would soon confirm Grew's prediction.

China's monetary decree of November 3, 1935, robbed Japanese politicians of their sugarcoated strategy for dominating China. The Japanese government had promised a "large loan" to aid China's finances and promised to help make "joint representations against American silver policies," according to the telegram leaked by William Bullitt to FDR. But now that China was free of its silver obligations, Japanese politicians needed to find a new candied carrot, and during their search the army could march ahead unchallenged. The Japanese military should have been shopping for a Christmas gift to send to FDR, but they were too busy preparing to advance into Chinese territory.

On Friday, November 22, 1935, War Minister Kawashima debated Foreign Minister Hirota before the Tokyo cabinet over the proper way to subjugate the five northern provinces of China, including the key cities of Tientsin and Peiping.[63] Five days later everyone knew who had prevailed. A front page story headlined: "Japanese March Into North China; Seize Rail Centre," adding that "3,000 move southward," and "after taking the railway station . . . took over the Chinese military telephone lines."[64] On Thursday, December 5, Secretary of State Cordell Hull issued a formal statement objecting to the effort being made "to bring about a substantial change in the political status and condition of several of China's northern provinces."[65] Hull's lukewarm rebuke never mentioned Japan, but the British Foreign Office requested a "frank statement" from Japan on its intentions in Northern China.[66] The *Manchester Guardian* reported Japanese government officials saying "the 'autonomy' movement is a purely Chinese movement and that any idea that Japan is planning a military intervention is entirely unfounded." No one told the Japanese Air Force to stand down, so they sent planes over Peiping to drop leaflets, "calling upon the people of North China to rise and establish an autonomous Government." Major General Kenji Doihara of the Japanese Army, known as "Lawrence of Manchukuo," supported the autonomy movement with troops stationed at the Japanese garrison at Tientsin.[67]

Two days after Hull's warning, described by historians as having "tiptoed around the issues . . . almost to assure Japan of noninterference," a new autonomous state was born in Northern China that marched in step with Tokyo rather than Nanking.[68] The new entity planned to have its own currency, would reestablish passenger and mail airplane links with the Japanese puppet state of Manchukuo, and would conclude an agreement for cooperation with Japan against communist military action.[69] The *Washington Post* reported that Major General Kenji Doihara, who would be executed in 1948 for crimes committed in World War II, was expected to become a principal adviser to the new regime.[70]

✦ ✦ ✦

Japanese aggression began before the Silver Purchase Act, but the American program helped shift the balance of power in Japan towards the military by driving China off the silver standard. U.S.

Ambassador to China Nelson Johnson wrote, "My opinion [is] that the Japanese military faction is forcing Japan along a road of compulsory piecemeal domination of China."[71] Japan would invade China proper in mid-1937 and the long Sino-Japanese conflict escalated globally during World War II, but a robust China with its ancient silver heritage intact would have been less vulnerable at the outset.

Many countries survive a currency crisis. Britain recovered after cutting ties with the gold standard in 1931, but a country like China, divided internally by Mao Tse-tung's communist insurgency and threatened externally by militarist Japanese expansionism, needed currency stability. George Roberts, a contemporary economist at National City Bank of New York (now called Citibank), anticipated the problem in early 1936: "China in her present state of economic development, with a large part of the population accustomed to the use of hard money, is poorly adapted to a managed currency."[72] The transition to fiat currency boosted the Chinese economy for a while but the fragile foundation succumbed to skyrocketing inflation under wartime pressure, leading ultimately to the communist takeover with Mao's victory over Chiang Kai-shek in 1949.[73]

The irony is that a month after the silver smugglers defeated China, the United States abandoned the strategy that had drained the white metal from that country's coffers. At five o'clock, Saturday afternoon, December 7, 1935, Henry Morgenthau called the president to discuss his recurring silver program nightmare.[74] America resembled a rogue elephant trampling the countryside, bulldozing China off silver and feeding a scavenging Japanese lion by paying them a 50% profit on smuggled silver.[75] Henry worried that unless America lowered the price it was willing to pay, he would "buy up all the floating silver in the world [and] drive all the silver-using countries off silver."[76] He said to himself, "The best joke is that today . . . with one possible exception, Ethiopia is the only country on the silver standard. It is a joke that we should continue our silver purchasing program to maintain the silver standard of Ethiopia." On a more serious note he worried that "we are giving Japan the necessary money with which to stabilize her currency and build up her fleet."

When Morgenthau told the president that he wanted to "drop the price of silver," Roosevelt stunned him with a detailed suggestion of how to do it.[77] Henry thought that FDR must have been "getting a little tired" of paying up for silver without getting any concrete benefits now that China refused to tie the yuan to the dollar. The president suggested that, instead of the usual daily procedure, which was for the United States to specify a price at which it would buy silver in the London bullion market and accept all offers at that price, America turn the tables on the sellers. He told Henry that going forward tell London "that you are ready to buy [say] two million ounces and that *they* [italics added] should quote you a price and . . . you will let them know whether or not you accept the offer." Perhaps the president had learned a thing or two about trading from his losses in the live lobster market because the new tactic worked to perfection.

The free market price of silver had remained virtually unchanged at a little over 65¢ an ounce for almost four months, from Tuesday, August 13, 1935, through Saturday, December 7, 1935.[78] The U.S. Treasury had pegged the price by absorbing record volumes thrown onto the market by Mexico and India liquidating excess inventories of the white metal and by Japan selling the silver smuggled out of China. Beginning Monday, December 9, 1935, FDR's new defensive strategy allowed the price to find its natural level and silver collapsed to a shade under 50¢ an ounce by Tuesday, December 24, 1935. Speculators and smugglers were grateful for the Christmas holiday, which put an end to the nearly 25% rout in prices over the two-week period.

Newspapers identified the U.S. Treasury as the culprit in the silver crash. A *Wall Street Journal* headline read, "Silver Collapses as U.S. Treasury Removes Support."[79] Morgenthau remained silent, so rumors spread that the Treasury was refusing to buy the "large quantities of silver which had been smuggled from China to Japan," and that it refused to buy from China itself "which was selling to acquire dollar or sterling balances with which to stabilize its currency."[80] The press urged Morgenthau to hold a news conference to discuss the situation, but he released the following statement instead: "The Treasury is still fulfilling the provisions of the Silver Purchase Act and will not discuss day-to-day developments in the world's silver markets, nor the tactics we will employ in meeting the situation."[81]

Henry Morgenthau had spent eighteen months servicing FDR's silver interests in the Senate and knew not to implement the new plan without first covering that most important base. Before the collapse in silver had gathered steam, he met with Key Pittman to describe what was coming. After hearing the plan Pittman asked one question: "You are not thinking of changing the domestic price?"[82] Morgenthau smiled, knowing that the 77¢ subsidized price paid under the December 1933 proclamation would look even better to domestic miners if the free market price declined. He said, "I had no such intention." Pittman replied, "I do not care what you do with the world price as long as you leave the domestic price alone."

His change of heart was too late to save China. Roosevelt's program to please the silver bloc seems to have been misdirected but the damage was done. Worldwide buying of the white metal under the Silver Purchase Act had helped Japan subjugate a weakened China. The Asian giant might have succumbed to Japanese aggression or to communist forces even with its silver-backed currency, but FDR deserves blame for his willingness to sacrifice China by focusing on domestic considerations without weighing international consequences.

CHAPTER 9

SILVER LINING

WEST POINT BECAME THE FORT KNOX OF SILVER ON WEDNESDAY, July 6, 1938, when a fleet of ten trucks arrived at 3:30 in the afternoon carrying 114 tons of the white metal belonging to the U.S. Treasury.[1] The trucks had left the New York Assay Office in lower Manhattan early that morning, travelling fifty miles north along the scenic Hudson River to the U.S. Military Academy, each truck loaded with about 320 standard, one-thousand-ounce silver bars. Members of the Coast Guard, a unit of the Treasury Department back then, armed with submachine guns and side arms, rode shotgun on each vehicle. There was, however, little threat of anyone hijacking a truck's $137,000 payload; a bar of pure silver, unpolished and gray, about a foot long and slightly thicker than an ordinary brick, weighs almost seventy pounds. The only tempting cargos were Spanish and Chinese silver coins, also belonging to the Treasury. A daily caravan over the next few months would transfer 45,000 tons of the white metal accumulated by Henry Morgenthau under the Silver Purchase Act to the new depository at West Point, a secure one-story facility about the size of a football field, with a two-foot-thick steel door, built for safekeeping America's silver reserves.[2] The new vault, which would eventually hold 70,000 tons of silver worth about $1 billion at prevailing prices, was protected by armed Treasury guards twenty-four hours a day, who could summon assistance from the nearby military barracks.

Unearthing silver from the mines of Mexico and Nevada and reburying the hoard in a reinforced-concrete building promoted full employment in the mining industry, a worthwhile objective for the likes of Key Pittman, but a travesty according to George Roberts, editor of the *Monthly Economic Letter* published by the National City Bank of New York. Roberts wrote that purchases of silver by the U.S. Treasury initially succeeded in raising the price of the white metal, just like the silver senators intended, but the price increase "attracted huge quantities of secondary silver from all over the world" that ultimately neutralized the price jump.[3] Secondary silver refers to any source of the white metal other than the newly mined variety, such as scrap reclaimed from the jewelry industry and bullion from melted coins. According to Roberts, price increases brought secondary supplies to the bullion market from silversmiths and coin hoarders, which eventually overwhelmed the manipulations. Silver sold for about 45¢ an ounce before the Silver Purchase Act of June 1934 and returned to that level at the end of January 1936, a testimony to the power of the ancient forces of supply and demand.

Roberts also negated the claim by silverites like Senator Burton Wheeler that Treasury purchases of the white metal expanded money and credit, an important objective during the Great Depression. The Treasury paid for bullion under the Silver Purchase Act either by creating silver dollar coins containing about three-quarters of an ounce of silver or by issuing silver certificates in one-dollar, five-dollar, and ten-dollar denominations. The Treasury's certificates closely resembled Federal Reserve notes issued by America's central bank, the dominant form of money in the United States, except the label "Silver Certificate" instead of "Federal Reserve Note" appeared at the top. The different types of money were equally accepted everywhere, such as paying for groceries at the local supermarket or settling obligations with the IRS, and were used interchangeably except for silver dollar coins, which were too bulky to carry. Roberts claimed that "the new silver certificates in circulation simply have taken the place of some other kind of money."[4] Congressional testimony by Treasury Secretary Morgenthau confirmed that silver dollar coins were in circulation only in "the Rocky Mountain States [where] the miners still carry 'cart wheels' as they call them," but everywhere else "we have replaced Federal Reserve notes with silver certificates."[5]

Silver certificates issued under the Silver Purchase Act felt just like crisp Federal Reserve notes, smelled the same, and had pictures of Lincoln and Hamilton gracing the five-dollar and ten-dollar bills, respectively. But there was a difference: Treasury currency carried a claim to silver held at West Point while Federal Reserve notes did not. A person with a one-dollar silver certificate could demand from the U.S. Treasury a silver dollar coin containing .77 ounces of silver, which translates into getting an ounce of silver at the official mint price of $1.29.[6] A ten-dollar Treasury certificate would exchange for ten silver dollar coins, of course. No one chose to exercise the exchange option back then because buying silver at about 45¢ an ounce in the bullion market was cheaper. But this option to get the underlying metal gave silver certificates a whiff of pre-1933 American currency, when all dollar bills could be exchanged for gold at the rate of $20.67 per ounce.[7] If silver prices rose above $1.29 in the bullion market, however, that faint silver lining would suddenly become valuable because holders of Treasury certificates could earn a profit by exchanging the paper for coins at the Trea-

FIGURE 9. A $10 bill distinguished by "silver certificate" across the top.

sury and then selling them as bullion. It was as though an invisible silver thread were woven into Treasury currency, which might someday spring to life; until then the white metal remained sealed in the West Point crypt.

The *Washington Post* lampooned the silver vault at West Point as "an enduring memorial to the world's most efficient racket," explaining that it is a "monument to the Senate rule which enabled the representatives of seven states to hold up the country for a selfish subsidy" and that "few of their [Senate] colleagues were aware that jelly-making was listed by the Commerce Department as more important than silver mining."[8] Some evidence suggests that the Silver Purchase Act stimulated faster economic recovery from the Depression in the silver states—Arizona, Colorado, Idaho, Montana, Nevada, New Mexico, and Utah—but the white metal mattered little to the overall American economy.[9] During the robust five years before 1929, total mining production contributed less than 3% of economic activity in the United States and silver amounted to less than 1% of that.[10] For example, iron mining contributed an average of $700 million to U.S. income per year; copper, $263 million; lead, $93 million; zinc, $80 million; and silver averaged $37 million dollars per year.

World War II changed everything.

✦ ✦ ✦

On Monday, January 5, 1942, a month after Japan attacked the United States at Pearl Harbor, President Roosevelt outlined a plan in his Annual Budget Message to Congress to defeat the Axis powers: "Powerful enemies must be out-fought and out-produced. . . . We must out-produce them overwhelmingly, so that there can be no question of our ability to provide a crushing superiority of equipment in any theatre of the world war. And we shall succeed."[11] Ten days later FDR issued an executive order establishing the War Production Board (WPB) to mobilize America's resources to win the war.[12] At that time more than 1.5 billion ounces of silver bullion were stacked like bricks of gray clay in the West Point depository waiting to serve the country, but the humble copper penny stood first in line.[13]

The president's executive order conferred broad authority on the WPB to "exercise general direction over the war procurement and production program," and the Board quickly responded with instructions as nit-picking as the tax code to economize on war material.[14] On Tuesday, January 27, 1942, the WPB set the standard by warning that "fewer newspapers are in prospect for America" because "copper and bronze parts in [paper] mills' equipment are wearing out faster than shortages in these materials will permit their replacement."[15] The Board's obsession with the base metals, such as copper, nickel, lead, and zinc, continued the following day when it lowered by 50% the production of "lamps designed primarily for Christmas trees or for advertising" in order to save an estimated 221,000 pounds of nickel, 295,000 pounds of copper, and 2,874,000 pounds of brass.[16] The WPB valued the giant savings in brass because the shiny alloy combines some zinc with mostly copper. The press also reported that the Board secured the agreement of shoe manufacturers to use "substitute metals instead of brass eyelets," which made Christmas lights seem important by contrast, until the news article confirmed that the eyelet substitution "will save enough brass to make one million artillery shell cases a year."[17]

The copper component of munitions, from full-metal-jacket bullets to cannon shells, made the red metal a priority in the early stages of the war and brought the WPB into conflict with civilians of both sexes by banning "copper and copper base alloy in the manufacture of slide fasteners (zippers), hooks and eyes, brassiere hooks, snap fasteners, and grippers."[18] In case a fashion designer tried to beat the ban, the Board also forbade any "other garment closures . . . including buckles, corset clasps, [and] garter trimmings."[19] The public's willingness to sacrifice and undress encouraged the U.S. Mint to start replacing the familiar copper penny with a steel coin but that became a disaster.[20] The zinc-plated 1943 steel penny created a backlash from the start: its white coating made it resemble a dime, allowing the unscrupulous and unpatriotic to pay a penny for 10¢ worth of fruit at the corner stand; and the steel coins confused bubble gum vending machines because the new pennies were often rejected as worthless slugs.[21] The complaints brought an unceremonious halt to the experiment after 700 million of these steel imposters were coined and, in an incestuous twist, were replaced by new copper pennies made from discarded cartridge shells unsuitable for recycling as munitions.[22]

The use of copper electrical wiring in almost every civilian and military appliance, from refrigerators to radios, heightened the critical shortage of the red metal and opened the way for silver, a better but more expensive conductor of electricity, to join the war effort. The U.S. Treasury owned more than 1.3 billion ounces of "free silver" that had accumulated over the years in the General Fund and was not needed to back Treasury certificates.[23] Officials at the War Production Board asked Henry Morgenthau to consider lending this silver to "industrial defense plants, both government and privately owned, in substitution for copper."[24] The *Washington Post* syndicated columnist Ernest K. Lindley urged that "silver can be put into a uniform" and added "the law requires the Government to amass the silver . . . but does not specify where it shall be kept."[25] Instead of West Point the government could "store it in electric equipment, like that at . . . Niagara Falls."

Morgenthau would soon tell Congress, "We would be in favor of striking all silver legislation off the books and make it possible for us to make use of the silver . . . for war purposes."[26] He responded quickly to the more limited request from the War Production Board.[27] On Wednesday, April 1, 1942, he wrote to Attorney General Francis Biddle for a formal legal opinion and attached a lengthy memorandum from Treasury's General Counsel Edward Foley that concluded "It is within the President's powers . . . to direct that 'free silver' contained in the available stocks of the Government be transmitted to industrial plants engaged in defense production for use . . . in a manner which will permit substantially all of it to be returned at the termination of the war."[28] Biddle concurred on Tuesday, April 7, and Donald Nelson, chairman of the War Production Board, announced that same day to the press that 40,000 tons of Treasury silver would be loaned for use in defense plants.[29] Nelson assured the public that the silver would be used "as 'busbars,' the main conductors of electric generating plants," and "the silver would be 100 per cent recoverable and could be replaced by copper when the emergency is over."[30]

Transfers of silver from the West Point depository began with 4.8 million ounces shipped to the Defense Plant Corporation on Monday, June 29, 1942, but the program mushroomed to highest priority on Saturday, August 29, 1942, with a letter from Secretary of War Henry Stimson to Treasury Secretary Morgenthau.[31] Stimson, a blue-blood Republican who had been Secretary of War under William Howard Taft, was seventy-three years old when Roosevelt appointed him to the job, but he still had the energy of a marine recruit. He was especially proud of his service as an artillery commander in World War I and still enjoyed being called Colonel Stimson by those who knew him best. Stimson wrote a three-page letter to Morgenthau that included the following:

"In an effort to conserve critical materials and at the same time expedite construction of a war project, the Manhattan District of the Corps of Engineers requires 6,000 tons of silver to be used as a substitute for copper in the construction of that project. . . . The War Department has obtained clearance for the tonnage required from the War Production Board. . . . The transfer proposed herein is in general accord with the procedure recently followed by the Defense Plant Corporation. . . . Any silver received by the War Department will be returned in the quantity, form and fineness in which . . . it was received. . . . The War Department will take reasonable precautions [to] . . . maintain such mechanical or custodial safeguards . . . to protect such silver."[32]

Stimson added one clarification in his letter, translating the War Department's request of 6,000 tons of silver into the Treasury's preferred measure, 175,000,000 troy ounces, but left the time and place of delivery to be determined by "written notice signed by the District Engineer, Manhattan District, Corps of Engineers."[33] The Treasury would carry the silver on its books after it was withdrawn from the West Point depository and, unlike the publicity accorded earlier deliveries to the Defense Plant Corporation, agreed with Stimson's request for silence on its cooperation with the District Engineer.[34] Henry Morgenthau had no training as a nuclear physi-

FIGURE 10. Treasury Secretary Morgenthau joins the war effort.

cist but he just became a silent partner in the top secret atomic bomb program, although he did not know it because Stimson insisted that he had no need to know.[35] It was still early in the war, before Winston Churchill's famous "end of the beginning speech" in November 1942, and an allied victory was still very much in doubt. The birth of the Manhattan Project brought a glimmer of hope, a silver lining, in the race for atomic weapons between scientists in America and Germany that the United States could not afford to lose.

On Friday, October 30, 1942, Colonel John C. Marshall, the Manhattan district engineer, withdrew an initial installment of white metal from the West Point depository.[36] He had the shipment of one-thousand-ounce silver bars trucked under heavy guard seventy-five miles south to a U.S. Metals Refining Company facility in Carteret, New Jersey, the first step in their transformation into powerful electromagnetic coils needed to separate fissionable uranium-235 from uranium-238.[37] The program would eventually use about one thousand of these giant magnets, each about one hundred times more powerful than anything ever built.[38] Plant workers in production facilities at Oak Ridge, Tennessee, who worked near the coils were supplied with special nonferrous tools to avoid hammers and screwdrivers flying out of their hands. Sneakers became the favored footwear for workers after the magnets pulled out the steel nails attaching the sole to the upper part of their shoes.

The Manhattan Project would eventually use 400,000 silver bars containing 400 million troy ounces, which comes to 14,000 tons, or more than double the original 6,000-ton estimate, and all of it had to be returned to the depository at West Point.[39] Armed guards monitored every phase of production to insure that nothing disappeared, and they often helped preserve the precious metal. When workers bored holes in strips of silver to prepare for fastening them together, the guards stood by with pieces of paper positioned to catch the drill dust; and then the workers' coveralls were vacuumed clean to recapture the residue.[40]

But useless restrictions were avoided, according to General Leslie Groves, who was in charge of implementing the project. Stimson had told him to produce the bomb "at the earliest possible date so as to bring the war to a conclusion."[41] Any time "that a single day could be saved . . . save that day." Groves sought to strike a balance between security and economy: "The precautions that we took were aimed primarily at concealing our interest in silver, and included the use of coded commercial bills of lading, the direction of all shipments to nonmilitary personnel, and the requirement that our officers wear civilian clothing in many of the plants they inspected."[42] Groves reported after the war that "throughout the entire operation we lost only .035 of one percent of the more than $300 million worth of silver we had withdrawn from the Treasury."[43] The missing $100,000 in silver was a small price for the Treasury to pay compared with civilian sacrifices of zippers and brassiere hooks.

CHAPTER 10

COSTLY VICTORY

SILVER HAD LOST ITS GUARDIAN ANGEL WHEN KEY PITTMAN DIED on November 10, 1940, but Pat McCarran, the junior senator from Nevada, continued the battle with no less fanaticism, like Stalin picking up where Lenin left off. McCarran was born in Reno in 1876 and spent his entire life in Nevada practicing law and running for political office.[1] He made William Jennings Bryan his personal hero and put the white metal on a pedestal: "The greatest value in the world is human energy—and brains, brawn, and muscle are represented in every ounce of silver we produce."[2] The beefy and broad-shouldered McCarran was first elected to the U.S. Senate in 1932, when there were about 90,000 people in Nevada and he may have known everyone by name. McCarran told his daughter after the election: "I visited every water hole, town, hamlet, valley and place within the State. There was scarcely a man, woman, or child . . . that I did not see personally."[3]

McCarran was an admirer of Spain's fascist dictator Francisco Franco and joined Wisconsin's disgraced Senator Joseph McCarthy on a communist witch hunt after World War II, but like Pittman he knew how to please his constituents.[4] He spent much of the war battling Senator Ted Green of Rhode Island over America's silver policy. The seven big western states in the silver bloc made the odds 14 to 1 against Green in the upper chamber of Congress, but the senator from the tiniest state made some headway. McCarran would have the last word, of course.

Theodore Green was born in 1867 in Rhode Island and could trace his lineage back to its founder, Roger Williams.[5] Educated at Brown University and Harvard Law School, Green was governor of Rhode Island before being elected to the U.S. Senate in 1936 as an FDR liberal. Like Roger Williams, tolerance ran deep in Green's blood, and he was a strong supporter of civil rights and religious freedom, but he also favored cheap silver to please his constituents. A thriving silverware and jewelry industry populated Rhode Island and surrounding states. The New England Manufacturing Jewelers and Silversmiths Association was founded in Providence and included about 30,000 workers before the war.[6] The restrictions on scarce raw materials imposed by the War Production Board beginning in 1942 threatened those firms in the jewelry industry that could not convert to war production. The abundance of silver at West Point was a tempting target to sustain employment.

On Wednesday, October 14, 1942, a subcommittee of the Senate Banking and Currency Committee approved a bill introduced by Green to "permit the Treasury to sell non-monetary silver to private industry for consumptive use and to lend monetary silver for non-consumptive purposes."[7] This meant that the Treasury could, for example, sell free silver to the Progressive Ring Company on Sabin Street in Providence, which employed about ninety workers, to make wedding bands and engagement rings, and could lend the silver that backed silver certificates to the Niagara Hudson Power Company to substitute for copper busbars in their generating plants servicing upstate New York. Henry Morgenthau had already begun lending free silver for the Manhattan Project, but the expansive Green bill permitted outright sales as well as lending monetary silver to anyone if it remained under Treasury control. Morgenthau supported the new legislation but specified that the average sale price of silver under the act "shall not be less than 50¢ per fine troy ounce."[8]

Morgenthau's 50¢ sale price covered the 48.5¢ average cost of free silver to the Treasury, but that did not satisfy Pat McCarran, who said that senators from the silver states would oppose the Green bill "most heartily."[9] Failure to pass it would mean the Treasury could sell only at $1.29 per ounce or higher as specified in the Silver Purchase Act.[10] McCarran met with Morgenthau at his home with a counterproposal that would have permitted sales of free silver for war purposes at 71¢ an ounce if going forward the Treasury paid $1.29 for domestically mined silver. Morgenthau said, "I don't think you can get away with it."[11]

He almost did. McCarran led a one-man filibuster against the Green bill on Tuesday, December 8, 1942, by reading in a hoarse voice a report on the activities of the Reconstruction Finance Company for 1932 to an empty Senate chamber.[12] McCarran's stocky frame became a human roadblock on the Senate floor and succeeded in preventing the bill, which had the support of the Treasury, the Navy, and the War Production Board, from being considered before the Christmas recess.[13] The *New York Times* editorialized: "This is strictly a war measure which goes no further than a minimum of common sense requires. It would break the ridiculous impasse now existing in which industry is being denied badly needed silver while the Government sits on a huge hoard buried in the ground. It would be better to repeal the whole discredited mess of selfish silver legislation which now requires the Government to continue endlessly to purchase silver at inflated prices and forbids it to sell the metal outright even for urgent war needs, except at prohibitive prices."[14] The editorial probably brought a smile to McCarran's lips.

Six months later the Senate voted for the Green bill after it was amended to make the selling price of silver 71¢ an ounce, the same price the Treasury paid for newly mined domestic silver, perhaps because the symmetry appealed to four silver bloc senators on the Banking Committee who switched sides to break the deadlock.[15] Senators Abe Murdock of Utah, Worth Clark and John Thomas of Idaho, and James Scrugham of Nevada joined forces with Senator Green, who said this would "prevent the closing of silversmiths throughout New England."[16] McCarran did not like the bill (or the four turncoats) but failed to rally enough support to withhold scarce resources during the war. He viewed it as a temporary setback, like a strategic military retreat that would turn into victory after hostilities ended and the permissive regulations expired.

McCarran prepared for a counterattack.

✦ ✦ ✦

When the Green bill expired on December 31, 1945, four months after Japan surrendered to end World War II, the white metal had become a scarce commodity. Much of the Treasury's stock was still leased to industry, and silver bullion stored in the West Point depository had dwindled to about 200 million ounces compared with 1.5 billion ounces four years earlier.[17] Use of the white metal in electrical equipment, photographic film, silverware, and jewelry exceeded domestic mine output by almost 100 million ounces in each of the previous four years, and the U.S. Treasury had supplied much of the difference with outright sales.[18] And as America shifted production from war to peace the shortfall promised to get worse, further shrinking the coverage of the Treasury's readily available supply of bullion.[19]

Soldiers returning from war wanted to get married and raise families, which meant greater demand for sterling place settings as wedding presents and more silver baby spoons nine months later (the natural order of things back then). The demand for apartment furnishings like stoves, refrigerators, chandeliers, and wall mirrors exploded, but R.H. Turner, president of the Mirror Manufacturers Association, warned that without any silver "some in that industry also are facing [a] shutdown."[20] The *Wall Street Journal* focused on the shortage of the white metal in business: "Film for medical and industrial photography is being shut off."[21] In April 1946 William Thurber, spokesman for the Silver Users Association, said, "Unless Congress grants new authority to dispose of some of the Government's excess of 225 million ounces underground at West Point, a lot of silversmiths are going out of business."[22]

Senator McCarran rode to the rescue with silver bullets in his gun belt. He proposed an amendment that would fix the value of the white metal at 90¢ an ounce, allowing the Treasury to sell silver to industry at that price and also pay the same for newly mined domestic silver.[23] This jump from the prevailing 71¢ subsidized price would last for two years, according to McCarran's bill, when it would increase to the distinguished $1.29 of Alexander Hamilton and William Jennings Bryan. McCarran urged the return of silver to its full monetary value with an appeal to history: "This does not end the long fight which began with the 'Crime of 1873,' when silver was demonetized, but it brings the end of that fight in sight."[24]

McCarran got much but not all of what he wanted. The battle between western miners and eastern silversmiths, a legacy of the class warfare between Bryan's Democrats and McKinley's Republicans, had brought congressional appropriations to a standstill, preventing postal workers from receiving their paychecks, but on July 19, 1946, each side compromised to allow the mail to be delivered.[25] The legislation raised the price for domestically mined silver to 90.5¢ an ounce, extending the tradition of subsidy established by FDR in December 1933, but avoiding any mention of further increases.[26] Congressman Herman Kopplemann, representing silverware companies in central Connecticut, and a member of the House-Senate conference committee negotiating different versions of the bill, considered the omission a victory: "At least we stopped them from putting over the $1.29 an ounce price."[27] Moreover, unlike FDR's original Christmas present to the silver bloc, which simply paid 64.5¢ per ounce to American mines, the new bill made 90.5¢ a two-way street as long as the Treasury held enough bullion to cover its silver certificate obligations. The Treasury would buy domestically produced silver at 90.5¢ an ounce and could also sell the white metal to industry at that price.[28] Few realized at the time that this provision would destroy silver's monetary crown.

McCarran died in 1954 and did not live to see President Kennedy lead the coup.

CHAPTER 11

JFK'S DOUBLE CROSS

CONSPIRACY THEORISTS HAVE TURNED THE ASSASSINATION OF President John F. Kennedy in Dallas on Friday, November 22, 1963, into big business. Hundreds of books have been written attributing JFK's murder by Lee Harvey Oswald to complicated plots by the CIA, the KGB, the mafia, the John Birch Society, and anyone from Texas, including the sitting vice president, Lyndon Baines Johnson.[1] None of these stories impressed the Warren Commission appointed by President Johnson to investigate the assassination, although it did examine the connection between nightclub owner Jack Ruby, who murdered Oswald, and the right-wing John Birch Society.[2] The commission concluded that Oswald acted alone but failed to consider whether Kennedy was murdered for downgrading the silver subsidy, a theory worth investigating given the metal's power to provoke passion and fury in the American heartland.[3] It is at least as plausible as the rest.

John Fitzgerald Kennedy defeated Richard M. Nixon in the 1960 presidential race with little room to spare. Rumors circulated that the Democrats stole the election in Illinois courtesy of Mayor Richard Daley, who performed a miracle of Biblical proportions on the banks of the Chicago River, getting dead people to rise from their graves to vote for JFK, some more than once. But young Americans ignored Kennedy's shortcomings and embraced the forty-three-year-old president, the youngest ever elected to the office. JFK came from a rich Boston family, went to Harvard, and had a Hollywood leading-man's full head of hair. His major legislative agenda, which included tax cuts and civil rights, was bottled up in an unfriendly Congress, but like FDR he used presidential executive orders to circumvent the roadblocks.

In November 1961, less than a year after taking office, JFK announced a major change in America's silver policy in response to an alarming report from Treasury Secretary Douglas Dillon. A wealthy former investment banker, who went to kindergarten with the *Wall Street Journal* under his arm, Dillon wrote to the president on Monday, November 27, 1961, that the Treasury's supply of free silver had dwindled to 22 million ounces. He explained that continued sales to industry under McCarran's July 1946 compromise caused an unprecedented decline in free silver of more than 80% in less than a year and warned the president of further shortages: "It is clear that under present procedures this stock would soon be entirely exhausted and that the Treasury would thereafter have no further silver available for public sale."[4] Dillon attributed the long-run problem to expanding "industrial consumption of silver" while production "falls far short." Between 1959 and 1961 industry and foreign coinage used an average of 285 million ounces per year while mine production delivered 198 million ounces.[5] Kennedy responded to Dillon on November 28, 1961, writing, "You are directed to suspend further sales of free silver."

A *New York Times* headline greeted Kennedy's directive with the Lone Ranger's "Hi-Yo, Silver" and added gravitas with some history: "Silver is back in the news again—shades of William Jennings Bryan and '16-to-1'!"[6] The president's message, released in the evening of November 28, made its mark like those western heroes, driving up the price of silver bullion the following day from 91¢ to over $1.00 per ounce. The one-day increase of over 10% matched the price jump when FDR announced the suspension of the gold standard on April 19, 1933.[7] The Treasury's withdrawal from the market meant that major users like the Eastman Kodak Company of Rochester, New York, makers of camera film, and the International Silver Company of Meriden, Connecticut, manufacturers of sterling silverware, would have to bid for the limited supply of the white metal from American and foreign mining companies rather than taking delivery at the nearest office of the U.S. Mint. Western mining men cheered the president's action, including Robert Hardy, president of the Sunshine Mining Company in Coeur d'Alene, Idaho, who said it was "a good thing for the silver market" and Charles Steen, a minerals speculator from Reno, who said "the law of supply and demand finally caught up with the Treasury."[8] Silver bloc Senator Frank Church of Idaho called Kennedy's action "the most important step the administration has taken to help the mining industry."[9]

Westerners praised Kennedy's action for raising the price of silver towards the historic $1.29 until they read JFK's entire message. Kennedy framed his directive to Treasury Secretary Dillon by writing, "I have reached the decision that silver metal should gradually be withdrawn from our monetary reserves," and predicted that "our new policy will in effect provide for the eventual demonetization of silver," statements that should have rousted William Jennings Bryan from his grave to challenge JFK's leadership of the Democratic Party.[10] Democrats have elected dead people to office, but Bryan probably stayed put because JFK was so popular and because it was Treasury Secretary Dillon, an East Coast banker and gold standard advocate, who developed the plan to purge silver from America's monetary reserves.[11]

Douglas Dillon, a strapping and strong-jawed financial aristocrat, whose father founded the Dillon Read & Company international banking firm, made a name for himself with keen intellect and a facility with numbers.[12] He could read and fully comprehend what he read by the time he was four years old, was educated at the Pine Lodge School in Lakehurst, New Jersey, where his schoolmates included Nelson and Laurence Rockefeller, and received an A.B. degree magna cum laude from Harvard College in 1931. After graduating he became a member of the New York Stock Exchange and at the end of World War II was appointed chairman of Dillon Read, where he doubled the firm's profits after just a few years.[13] Dillon became active in Republican politics and was appointed ambassador to France in 1953 by President Eisenhower and then became undersecretary of state, but his financial prowess convinced JFK to make him secretary of the Treasury.

Kennedy had been taught by his father that "a nation was only as strong as the value of its currency," which at the time meant redeemable in gold.[14] Foreign central banks could exchange dollars for gold at $35 per ounce in 1961, even though American citizens could not, and this vestige of the gold standard had come under attack by international speculators betting that expansionary economic policies under the new president would provoke inflation and undermine the dollar. According to future Federal Reserve Chairman Paul Volcker, Kennedy chose Dillon to head the Treasury Department as a "reassuring symbol of financial rectitude."[15] Dillon did not waste any time. On October 9, 1961, after less than a year at Treasury and six weeks before his memo on silver to JFK, Dillon quietly reorganized the department's domestic gold and silver authority, transferring these longstanding policy functions of the director of the mint to Undersecretary of the Treasury Robert Roosa.[16] There was no formal announcement of this reorganization, except a routine publication in the *Federal Register*, but it was a masterful stroke with a double-edged sword to cut silver from the monetary base.

Roosa was an East Coast banker like Dillon whose support for the yellow metal would have made William McKinley blush. He had been a senior executive at the Federal Reserve Bank of New York, where he taught everyone passing through, including a young Paul Volcker, that gold was just one letter away from god.[17] Dillon knew that Roosa would downgrade silver as a monetary metal, but that was not the main reason he neutered the mint director in policymaking. On Saturday, September 23, 1961, the Senate had confirmed President Kennedy's appointment of Eva Adams as the new director of the mint.[18] The redheaded Adams was born in Wonder, Nevada, and moved to Washington, D.C., in 1940 when she joined the staff of the late Senator Pat McCarran. At the time of her appointment as mint director she was the administrative assistant to McCarran's successor, Senator Alan Bible, and her new position promised jubilant silver bloc senators an inside advocate for the white metal. The press questioned why Kennedy made the appointment, considering his statement years earlier as a Massachusetts senator that "there is no longer any sound economic and social justification" for silver subsidies.[19] Kennedy's sympathies lay with Massachusetts silversmiths who had favored cheap raw material for their wares since the Revolutionary War, when Paul Revere practiced the trade. But the journalists had forgotten that Nevada was one of the few western states to vote for JFK in the 1960 presidential election and Kennedy owed Bible. The president paid his obligation when Adams was confirmed as director of the mint on September 23, 1961, but two weeks later, on October 9, his Treasury secretary delivered the double cross by removing silver policy from her portfolio.

Douglas Dillon softened the blow by telling Adams at her installation on Monday, October 30, 1961, "I can confidently predict that your business will continue on the upgrade," which was true because she would oversee the growing production of nickels, dimes, and quarters for use in the expanding population of vending machines and parking meters fed by maturing baby boomers.[20] But manufacturing small change was not what the silver senators had in mind when they celebrated Eva Adams's appointment to the mint, even though an emerging coin crisis would soon threaten their interests. They expected her to carry on the Nevada tradition of boosting miner subsidies that began with Key Pittman and continued with Pat McCarran, but Dillon's knockout punch before the installation neutralized his warm words, quieting the celebration.

✦ ✦ ✦

JFK declared war on silver subsidies in his November 28, 1961, directive, promising "to recommend to Congress, when it reconvenes, that it repeal the acts relating to silver," including the most important of all, the Silver Purchase Act of June 19, 1934.[21] Kennedy followed up in his Economic Report to Congress in January 1962 by saying, "Silver—a sick metal in the 1930s—is today an important raw material for which industrial demand is expanding steadily. It is uneconomic for the U.S. Government to lock up large quantities of useful silver in the sterile form of currency reserves. Neither is any constructive purpose served by requiring that the Treasury maintain a floor under the price of silver. Silver should eventually be demonetized, except for its use in coins."[22]

The 1934 Silver Purchase Act targeted the white metal to become 25% of America's monetary reserves, and although that goal remained unfulfilled, it resulted in $2.1 billion silver certificates outstanding at the beginning of 1962, a quintupling since the act was passed.[23] The Treasury held almost 1.7 billion ounces of silver bullion to redeem these certificates, which were a small but integral part of America's money.[24] Federal Reserve notes issued by America's central bank dominated U.S. currency, just as they do today (check your wallet), but by law all one-dollar bills were silver certificates back then, rather than Federal Reserve notes, and were secured by about three-quarters of the Treasury's silver.[25] The remaining bullion at the Treasury backed five-dollar and ten-dollar silver certificates that mixed seamlessly with Federal Reserve notes of the same denomination. Kennedy would have to fight a nuclear war with the silver senators to repeal the Silver Purchase Act, but he could start to remove the white metal as monetary reserves without congressional approval by finding and withdrawing the five- and ten-dollar silver certificates and replacing them with Federal Reserve notes. Kennedy told Dillon to begin this search and destroy mission, and Dillon turned to Elizabeth R. Smith, the treasurer of the United States, to implement the plan.

The treasurer of the United States, an officer within the Treasury Department, is most famous for signing every piece of American paper currency (check your wallet again to see the signature on the front-left side of any bill) and is also responsible for maintaining the physical integrity of America's cash. The treasurer oversees the removal of frayed or worn dollars and the substitution of crisp new bills, with technical assistance from banks and the Federal Reserve System. In the first six months of 1962 Elizabeth Smith withdrew enough five- and ten-dollar silver certificates to free 45 million ounces of bullion.[26] The unencumbered silver was used to manufacture subsidiary coins, such as dimes, quarters, and half-dollars, precisely as Kennedy had directed.[27]

Freeing silver bullion by making five- and ten-dollar Treasury certificates disappear was just a minor skirmish in a full-scale battle that erupted on Tuesday, February 20, 1962. The Treasury submitted a bill to Congress to repeal the 1934 Silver Purchase Act as well as the July 1946 bill establishing 90.5¢ as the subsidized price for the white metal.[28] The proposed legislation also authorized the Federal Reserve to issue one-dollar notes so that the Treasury could withdraw the same denomination silver certificates and free the bulk of its bullion for coinage purposes. In case Americans thought this was a technical adjustment that would put anyone but a dismal scientist to sleep, the *New York Times* focused on the politics:[29] "The Administration has made its formal bid to break the Democratic Party's historic ties to silver." The *Times* then added a dark cloud, "But some important Democrats are not disposed to make the change."

Senator Alan Bible wasted no time settling the score with JFK, urging his fellow senators investigating "Gold and Silver Production Incentives" to reject the president's proposal: "I would think that this subcommittee . . . should speak out very strongly on the present legislation which is pending before the Banking and Currency Committee. . . . It seems to me that now is not the time to repeal the Silver Purchase Act."[30] Bible then reminded his colleagues of Kennedy's trickery at their expense: "As you well recognize . . . the President of the United States without congressional enactment called in silver certificates . . . and replaced them with Federal Reserve notes. . . . I hope this Hearing will throw some light on this." Senator John Carroll of Colorado, an important mining state, echoed Bible's concern, saying it is "a good time to put to rest the ghost of a possible repeal in this session of Congress of the Silver Purchase Act."[31] The Senate bowed to the still powerful silver bloc in March 1962 by tabling the president's proposed legislation.[32]

❖ ❖ ❖

An acute shortage of small change in supermarkets and department stores throughout the country during the 1962 Christmas shopping season helped JFK battle the silver senators. The *Boston Globe* began a news story with "Santa Claus is being short-changed," and quoted John Lowe, cashier at the Federal Reserve Bank of Boston, a branch of America's central bank: "The coin shortage is not only a local or area problem. The whole country is crying for more nickels, dimes, quarters and halves."[33] Lowe complained that "the mints, with the machinery and personnel they have, just aren't able to meet the demand for coins." But Mint Director Eva Adams, now wearing a hard hat as production manager, claimed that her employees "are working weekends" and the Denver Mint "has been working around the clock" to ease the shortage.[34] Lowe, ever the cashier, suggested, "If people would just break open their piggy banks . . . it sure would help."[35]

Douglas Dillon had a better idea. JFK's Treasury secretary acknowledged on Wednesday, January 30, 1963, the need for "extra mint facilities sometime this year," but warned of a worse coin shortage "unless outmoded silver legislation is changed."[36] In a get-acquainted meeting with Texas Democrat Wright Patman, the new chairman of the House Banking and Currency Committee, Dillon urged passage of the administration's bill to repeal the silver subsidies and to authorize the Federal Reserve to issue notes in one-dollar denominations because it would give the government more flexibility "and make more silver available for coinage."[37] He added, "The government may soon be forced to buy silver from foreign producers to make its coins. Vending machines just gobble coins and the mints have difficulty keeping up with the demand."[38]

Dillon blamed voracious vending machines for the coin shortage, but Mint Director Eva Adams cited increased accumulation by numismatists: "They seem to be collecting in large quantities on the hunch that some of the coins will be worth more ten years from now."[39] A.W. Wadsworth, manager of the cash department at the Federal Reserve Bank of Cleveland, made younger Americans the culprits just like his Boston colleague: "More people are stuffing coins in their dresser drawers and more kids are putting them in piggy banks." These educated guesses were not mutually exclusive, and they explained the Treasury's growing appetite for silver. During the previous three years U.S. coin production increased by more than the combined rise in all other uses of the white metal. America's coin output rose by 31 million ounces, a jump of more than 60% between 1960 and 1962; world demand for silver by industries like photography and electronics increased by 23 million ounces, a rise of 10%; and coinage by all other countries rose by 2 million ounces, an increase of 4%.[40] Treasury Secretary Dillon was right to worry.

Congressman Wright Patman expedited hearings in the Banking and Currency Committee as a courtesy to Dillon, and the Treasury's bill passed the House of Representatives on Wednesday, April 10, 1963. The legislation repealed the silver subsidies, eliminated the 50% tax on trading silver bullion, and authorized the Federal Reserve to issue one-dollar notes, but the heavyweight match lay in the Senate where the silver bloc had pinned legislation in the past.[41] The *Wall Street Journal* reported that Democratic Senate Majority Leader Mike Mansfield of Montana agreed to support the administration and "not to block the measure if it can be eased through the legislative machinery without stirring up a big controversy."[42] Mansfield sounded as though he were navigating a minefield even though the white metal had increased to $1.25 in the bullion market, which should have eased western senator objections to losing the 90.5¢ floor price. The *Journal* confirmed the danger after the vote in the House: "The Kennedy Administration's bill to sever the link between silver and paper currency met unexpected hostility in passing the House, 251 to 122. Supporters, who had anticipated a much bigger margin, now are worried opponents will redouble efforts to sidetrack the measure in the Senate."[43]

Formal hearings began in the Senate Banking and Currency Committee on Monday, April 29, 1963, and Committee Chairman A. Willis Robertson of Virginia opened by referencing past misdeeds in the upper chamber of Congress. He distanced himself from Senator John Sherman's quiet demonetization of silver: "We are not doing anything about silver like they did—I think it was in 1873 when they amended a silver act and whoever was in charge of the bill conveniently omitted the power to coin silver dollars. . . . That change in the law slipped through the Senate with the silent tread of a cat. . . . We have no silent tread of the cat in this bill."[44]

The Virginia senator's evenhandedness encouraged a member of the House of Representatives, Compton White of Idaho, to make a strange request of the Senate committee on the first day of hearings: "I would not be here this morning to urge your attention to the drastic consequences of reporting this bill in the form it passed the House if I believed the proposed legislation had received adequate consideration. . . . As you know, there were but four days of hearings on this very difficult issue. Of those four days only two hours were given to witnesses for the opposition."[45] White had no way of knowing whether the Kennedy administration had suppressed the naysayers, but he certainly suspected it. "I do not know if it was by design or accident that so little time was given to

FIGURE 11. This $1 silver certificate gets competition in 1963.

the study of H.R. 5389. I fear that it was the former, because the more understanding gained by Members concerning the effects of enacting the Treasury Department's proposed solution to the silver shortage problem, the more the opposition grew. . . . I ask the committee's permission to have inserted in the record a letter that I sent to House Members concerning H.R. 5389."

Compton White represented Idaho, which produced twice as much silver as any other state, but he avoided parochial arguments in his missive and sounded the alarm for the world reputation of the American dollar:[46] "I oppose this demonetization because . . . [it] would be a triumph for those who advocate a monetary system based solely on fiscal credit. Ancient and modern history have repeatedly proved that money systems based solely on the promissory notes of governments, which continued to spiral themselves deeper into debt, have ruined not only the economy of those countries, but their political systems as well."[47]

Senator Alan Bible appeared before the Senate Banking Committee to support Congressman White and began with a disclaimer: "I am deeply concerned with certain provisions of this bill, H.R. 5389, now before your committee. Representing a famous state, known as the Silver State, one perhaps could draw an erroneous conclusion that my concern lies only with silver producers . . . [but] there is not one single operating silver mine in the great Silver State of Nevada."[48] Bible failed to mention his displeasure with JFK for the Eva Adams deception and focused his comments on section 3 of H.R. 5389, authorizing the Federal Reserve to print one-dollar bills: "The framers of our Constitution recognized that gold and silver were metals of intrinsic value and should be used in our monetary system, and the history of all nations will show that, wherever these basic metals have been done away with, the historical experience is inflation and the value of the currency goes down. I know of no exception to this historical fact. . . . I believe removal of silver from our silver certificates will be an inflationary move on the part of our Government. . . . History will again show that paper money is not valued by other nations of the world. . . . For the above reasons I must strenuously object to section 3 of the proposed legislation."

Both Bible and White sounded as patriotic as Francis Scott Key, but preventing inflation by retaining silver backing for dollar bills made sense only if the Federal Reserve was similarly constrained in issuing $100 bills. The Federal Reserve Act as amended required the central bank to hold gold equal to 25% of its liabilities to prevent it from running a printing press, but that constraint was under attack. White had warned his colleagues that the proposal to substitute one-dollar Federal Reserve notes for silver certificates was just "a step toward the complete demonetization of not only silver but of gold as well."[49] He then explained: "The [House] Banking and Currency Committee now has pending before it a bill to eliminate the requirement for the 25 percent gold backing for Federal Reserve notes." Congressional opponents of JFK's demonetization of silver feared an avalanche of paper money and inflation. Unfolding events would prove them right.

◆ ◆ ◆

Treasury Secretary Dillon testified before the Senate committee and sidestepped the inflation scare by touting the benefits of the bill: "We presently hold 1,300 million ounces of silver as backing for one-dollar [Treasury] certificates" and allowing the Federal Reserve to issue one-dollar bills to replace these certificates would assure the "adequate supply of silver to meet our coinage needs for the next ten to twenty years."[50] He told the committee that "the ultimate replacement of silver certificates with Federal Reserve notes does not in any way debase our currency," and his assurance carried the day. On Thursday, May 25, 1963, the Senate passed the bill "To repeal certain legislation relating to the purchase of silver, and for other purposes," erasing from the books the Silver Purchase Act of 1934 and allowing the Federal Reserve to issue one-dollar bills.[51]

Support by senators from eastern silver-using states, including Thomas Dodd of Connecticut, Claiborne Pell and John Pastore of Rhode Island, and Kenneth Keating of New York, combined with lobbying by the administration, defeated the western silver bloc by a margin of more than six-to-one.[52] The *Washington Post* put the fall of the white metal from its monetary pedestal into context: "The historic link between silver and the country's paper currency was unceremoniously severed when the Senate by a lopsided vote passed an act which provides for the gradual replacement of the Treasury's silver certificates by Federal Reserve notes."[53] The *Post* then added a requiem usually reserved for third-world dictators: "Save for the fulminations of a few anachronistic demagogues, the silver issue has been dead since Bryan went down to defeat at the hand of McKinley, and it will be formally interred when President Kennedy signs what is probably the last major piece of silver legislation."

New Yorkers celebrated. A week after President Kennedy signed the bill repealing the Silver Purchase Act, trading of futures contracts on the white metal resumed on the Commodity Exchange, called Comex, located back then at 81 Broad Street in the heart of Manhattan's financial district. On Wednesday, June 12, 1963, just before the bell rang to begin the trading day, Simon Strauss, vice president of the American Smelting and Refining Company, explained the significance of the historic moment, saying it was "28 years, 10 months, and three days" since trading was suspended by FDR's nationalization order, and pointing out that "this was a short period in the life of silver," one of the oldest metals known to man.[54]

Commodities trading was a physical activity back then and more than one hundred traders, all dressed in jacket and tie for the festive occasion, stood shoulder-to-shoulder around a circular railing waiting anxiously to shout their buying and selling interests to each other. A piercing ring triggered an explosion of bids and offers from suddenly animated traders, making the cavernous room sound as though a championship boxing match were underway. More than 2 million ounces of the white metal for future delivery changed hands that day, with buyers rooting for prices to increase and sellers hoping they would decline. For the first time since the Great Depression Americans could buy silver bullion like citizens of other countries to protect themselves against political uncertainty or inflation rather than hiding their intentions behind candlesticks or tea sets in the dining room cupboard. The legislation signed by JFK on June 4, 1963, repealing the Silver Purchase Act, and the launch of trading on Comex on June 12, 1963, signaled the end of silver as a dull monetary metal and its birth as a shiny hard asset.

The free market soon accomplished what a century of political intrigue and manipulation had failed to do. On Monday, September 9, 1963, rising demand for silver spurred traders to push the price of the white metal to $1.29, the legendary monetary value established by Alexander Hamilton.[55] Metal fabricators like Engelhard Minerals & Chemicals Corporation of Newark, New Jersey, a New York Stock Exchange listed company, suddenly found silver certificates the easiest way to accumulate the white metal; according to law the certificates could be exchanged for Treasury bullion at the rate of $1.2929 per troy ounce. On Thursday, September 12,

Engelhard delivered a check for $65,000 and received 50,000 troy ounces of Treasury silver, the first purchase from the government since JFK suspended sales in November 1961.[56] Engelhard did not, in fact, own the certificates needed to make the purchase. The formal instructions from Secretary of the Treasury Douglas Dillon permitted requests for the government's silver bullion to be made by check to the Federal Reserve Bank of New York, a branch of America's central bank, which would then accumulate the silver certificates to present to the Treasury.[57] Access by industrial users to more than 1.5 billion ounces of Treasury silver would prevent the free market price of the white metal from rising above $1.293 per ounce . . . at least for a while.[58]

The silver senators were unhappy. Senator Frank Church of Idaho tried to restrain the government's sales by introducing an amendment to prohibit the secretary of the Treasury from selling silver above its monetary value, and Senator Peter Dominick of Colorado wanted to prevent the Treasury from providing silver to other government agencies.[59] Both initiatives were defeated by margins of more than two-to-one. Republican Senator Gordon Allott of Colorado lamented to his colleagues, "This may be a step along the way towards devaluation of our currency," a sentiment shared by right-wing organizations throughout the country.[60]

JFK did not live to see the consequences of demonetizing silver. He was assassinated in Dallas, Texas, less than six months after he signed the bill authorizing the Federal Reserve System to substitute its paper currency for silver certificates. Concern for Kennedy's safety in his Texas visit had increased after U.S. Ambassador to the United Nations Adlai Stevenson was "jeered, jostled, and spat upon" after a speech in Dallas in late October 1963.[61] The day before Kennedy arrived an "anonymous handbill" appeared on Dallas streets fashioned like a sheriff's circular with the words "Wanted for Treason" printed below frontal and profile pictures of the president. And on the day of the assassination, November 22, 1963, the *Dallas Morning News* published a black-bordered "Welcome Mr. Kennedy to Dallas" advertisement, addressing a series of unfriendly questions to the president. Supporters of the right-wing John Birch Society, including Texas billionaire oilman and future silver speculator Nelson Bunker Hunt, paid for the advertisement.[62] The John Birch Society was dedicated, first and foremost, to destroying a perceived communist menace in the United States and to eliminating anything not sanctioned by the Founding Fathers, including the Federal Reserve System.

The Warren Commission concluded that Lee Harvey Oswald acted alone and dismissed any connection with the John Birch Society, pushing to the bottom of the conspiracy scrap heap the theory that Kennedy was murdered because he demonetized silver, a suggestion as fanciful to contemporaries as putting a man on the moon. Nevertheless, the phrase "Wanted for Treason" recalls the words of General A.J. Warner of Ohio, who delivered the opening address at the National Convention of the American Bimetallic League on August 1, 1893. Warner said in reference to Senator John Sherman, architect of the Crime of 1873: "There was but one man in the United States Senate who knew that the Act of 1873 demonetized silver, and yet he has never been hanged or shot for treason."[63]

Virginia Senator Robertson had distanced himself from Sherman's treachery at the opening of hearings on JFK's demonetization bill but the century-old misstep still shadowed the upper chamber of Congress and continued to pit East against West in a battle for economic dominance. However, murder for the sake of silver dollars seems excessive, a primitive response to a commercial conflict, perhaps understandable in the more violent nineteenth century but inconsistent with the more civilized twentieth. Or not?

CHAPTER 12

LBJ NAILS THE COFFIN SHUT

At 2:38 p.m., Friday, November 22, 1963, a somber Lyndon Baines Johnson raised his right hand like a reluctant volunteer and was sworn in as president of the United States aboard Air Force One, the plane taking him and JFK's body from Dallas to Washington, D.C.[1] Jacqueline Kennedy, wife of the slain president, stood by Johnson's side watching Judge Sarah Hughes administer the oath of office and the orderly transfer of power in midst of an unfolding trauma.[2] It also meant that LBJ inherited the unfinished work of John Fitzgerald Kennedy, a bequest that resembled a vial of nitroglycerine.

Five days later, Wednesday, November 27, 1963, Lyndon Johnson gave his first formal address as president of the United States to a Joint Session of Congress. His full six-foot-four-inch frame standing erect behind the lectern on the dais of the House Chamber, he began with the now-famous words, "All I have I would have given gladly not to be standing here today."[3] It may have been an exaggeration, but he followed with a promise to continue JFK's legislative agenda, including an item that would test the sincerity of his commitment: "No memorial oration or eulogy could more eloquently honor President Kennedy's memory than the earliest possible passage of the civil rights bill for which he fought so long."[4]

Fervent opposition by Southern Democrats in the Senate had throttled JFK's civil rights initiative, suppressing the legislation with the genteel protocol of the upper chamber of Congress. LBJ, who had served as Senate majority leader and wrote the book on political persuasion, succeeded where JFK failed, using his Texas drawl to convince wavering former colleagues from border states to vote for the Civil Rights Act of 1964. The legislation was Johnson's crowning achievement as president. LBJ also inherited Kennedy's

Vietnam brush fire but stoked that misadventure into an unpopular war. Vietnam was a failure that would tarnish his legacy. Historians have scrutinized Kennedy's and Johnson's records on civil
rights and Vietnam but have ignored another joint venture of these
two men who remain tethered by fate: the war against silver. LBJ
finished what Kennedy started by burying the remaining link between money and precious metals in the United States, a discon-
nect that fueled the Great Inflation of the 1970s and almost ruined
the American economy.

❖ ❖ ❖

Treasury Secretary Douglas Dillon had testified in the Senate on
April 29, 1963, that passing JFK's legislation authorizing the Federal Reserve to print one-dollar bills would assure the "adequate
supply of silver to meet our coinage needs for the next ten to twenty
years."[5] Less than a year later, on Monday, March 23, 1964, a
crowd of more than a thousand people ignored Dillon's prediction
and surrounded the historic U.S. Treasury building in Washington,
D.C., like it was Macy's on Black Friday, waiting to buy silver dollars.[6] Few Americans used the bulky coins in daily life, but they had
been last minted in 1935, and the growing population of numismatists found them irresistible. According to Franklyn R. Bruns,
sales manager for coin and stamp collecting at the Woodward and
Lothrop department store in Chevy Chase, Maryland, "People are
just hoping they will come across some of the silver dollars with
rare dates or rare mint marks. . . . For instance, . . . one of the
756,000 silver dollars minted in 1879 in Carson City, Nevada,
would bring a good price. One dealer said . . . he would pay from
$40 to $70 for an '1879CC' which was uncirculated."[7] America's
obsession with coin collecting rivaled the craze for a new music
group, the Beatles, who had arrived in America a month earlier.

Failure by the House of Representatives to allocate funds for
new coinage of silver dollars had triggered the rush to get the remaining stock in Treasury vaults, but that was not the last word.
Support for the production of more silver dollars came from high
places beyond the Continental Divide, according to the *Boston*

Globe: "A posse of lawmakers, headed by Democratic leader Mike Mansfield (Montana), cantered onto the Senate floor Saturday to defend the cartwheel—the 'hard money' silver dollar which is the favored coin of the realm in the Great West."[8] Mansfield, the majority leader of the Senate, sounded as though he regretted supporting JFK's demonetization program, saying that cartwheels "should not follow the buffalo, the whooping crane, the eagle, and the gold piece into oblivion." He said that even thieves preferred "hard money," explaining that bank robbers recently took $20,000 in silver dollars from the bank in White Sulphur Springs, Montana.

But the public demanded more than just silver dollars. The U.S. Mint had inadvertently stoked the coin collecting frenzy by unveiling the Kennedy half-dollar on Tuesday, March 24, 1964, a day after the crowd stormed the Treasury building for the dwindling supply of cartwheels. The new fifty-cent piece with the profile likeness of the late president on the front gave the still-grieving public a sentimental reason to hoard the new coin, forcing banks to ration the supply among their depositors. The Charter Oak Bank and Trust Company in Hartford, Connecticut, limited one to a customer and distributed a thousand coins in one day. A man standing in line at the door said, "They're going like wildfire."[9] The Treasury, which had suspended distribution of silver dollars on March 24 to allow customers to get the Kennedy halves, put a limit of forty per person even though $26 million coins had already been produced and more were on the way.[10] Scarcity in the nation's capital led to rumors of bank tellers selling Kennedy halves above their face value, forcing Richard Norris, president of the Riggs National Bank to say, "It is possible," but none of their employees "would be allowed to engage in this sort of activity."[11] Few would have asked his permission, of course.

More than 160 million Kennedy half-dollars minted in 1964 would prevent the coin from becoming a valuable collector's item like the 1879 Carson City cartwheel, but people could not get enough of them, perhaps because word had spread that silver was a bargain at the Treasury's price of $1.293 per ounce.[12] According to the *Chicago Tribune*, "Many experts believe the silver hoarder is

FIGURE 12. Speculators collect silver coins.

the biggest single cause of the coin shortage plaguing the country."[13] The price of silver would have to go above $1.38 ¼ per ounce to make circulating dimes, quarters, and halves worth melting for their bullion value, but that was only 7% away and until then budding numismatists could enjoy their new hobby.[14] Coin collectors also searched for nickels minted between 1942 and 1945, when silver replaced the coin's nickel content, which was used in armor plating for combat vehicles.[15] Those wartime nickels had a little more than .05 ounces of silver, making them worth more than 7¢ at the current price of $1.293 per ounce.[16] Coin collectors had become closet silver speculators and the current profits were just an appetizer before the anticipated feast if silver exceeded $1.38. It was as though Americans had heard the opening bell at Comex signaling a new beginning for the white metal as a hard asset.

✦ ✦ ✦

Vanishing nickels, dimes, and quarters tested the ingenuity of American business. The renewed coin shortage hit supermarkets the hardest during the first half of 1964, according to Clarence Adamy, executive vice president of the National Association of Food Chains: "Our stores have been spending countless hours working deals and running around to locate the coins they need but the situation is now desperate."[17] The Jewel Tea Company, with 350 supermarkets in the Midwest and New England, proposed issuing its own scrip, private paper currency in various denominations. The notes were about the size of a personal check and were color-coded to avoid confusion: blue for nickels, green for dimes, and orange for quarters. Stores did not require customers to accept scrip, but the company promised to redeem the colored notes for real money (in dollar increments) or in exchange for other purchases. The treasurer of the Kroger Company of Cincinnati, a 1,400-store Midwest chain, confirmed a similar plan for their customers. This clever response to the coin crisis displeased the U.S. Treasury.

Treasury rules prohibit private groups or individuals from issuing any "note, check, memorandum, token or other obligation for a sum less than $1 intended to circulate as money."[18] A week before the Jewel Tea proposal the Treasury had impounded wooden "nickels" about the size of a poker chip issued by the First National Bank of Monroe, Wisconsin, which were circulating among local merchants. The bank president, Edward R. Adams, said, "The Mint was unhappy," but he ignored the reprimand because he was about to retire for the same reason he authorized the ersatz nickels—the coin shortage.[19] The Treasury confiscated most of the 20,000 wooden coins that had been issued except for those hoarded by collectors who were paying $11 per chip now that the supply had been cut off.[20] The U.S. Treasury then rejected the Jewel Tea Company proposal even though their notes were not designed to circulate.[21] Uncle Sam does not like competition.

President Johnson had been preoccupied with the civil rights bill, but in May 1964 he responded to the accelerating coin shortage by allocating funds to permit the Denver and Philadelphia mints to work around-the-clock, seven days a week, as though they were fighting a war.[22] He resorted to some budget trickery to pay the mint workers because Congress, deadlocked over civil rights, had failed to appropriate the necessary funds.[23] The president also favored Majority Leader Mike Mansfield and other western senators by signing legislation on Monday, August 3, 1964, to produce forty-five million silver dollars at the Denver mint.[24] LBJ often displayed his western roots, wearing a fawn-colored Stetson hat like the Texas rancher he was, and promoted the Denver mint because the nearby Nevada casinos feasted on the cartwheels fed into their slot machines. To force the silver dollars into circulation and keep them away from collectors, who valued uncirculated coins, the mint proposed to distribute a few thousand new cartwheels each month to banks in the Rocky Mountain states. LBJ also signed a bill authorizing the Treasury to freeze the 1964 date on all new coin production, minimizing future scarcities that enhance a coin's value to numismatists.[25]

It was a losing battle.

Silver speculators masquerading as coin collectors knew that the Treasury had been disposing of its vast supply of bullion, holding the price of the white metal at $1.293, but when that ended the excess demand would blow the roof off the government-imposed ceiling. The Treasury's stock of silver declined by 366 million ounces during 1964, a drop of almost 25% compared with annual average declines one-third the size since 1960.[26] The bulk of the 1964 decline—203 million ounces—went into increased production and distribution of dimes, quarters, and half-dollars, almost triple the annual average increase in coinage since 1960.[27] The *Wall Street Journal* reported on December 28, 1964, that the Treasury would delay minting the silver dollars LBJ had authorized five months earlier "so that all the department's equipment can be used to make quarters, dimes, and other lesser coins . . . for which there is no substitute."[28] But that was like battling a forest fire with a water pistol.

The Treasury's 1.2 billion ounces of silver bullion looked respectable in December 1964, but about 950 million ounces of that hoard backed the more than $1.2 billion silver certificates still outstanding.[29] The Treasury retired $645 million certificates during the year, exchanging most of them for Federal Reserve notes as planned, but speculators and industrial companies like Engelhard Minerals & Chemicals Corporation had used certificates to acquire more than 140 million ounces of the Treasury's white metal.[30] Worldwide consumption of silver exceeded new mine production by 200 million ounces a year since 1960, compared with an annual average of less than 75 million ounces during the 1950s, and the excess demand rose despite the increase in prices.[31] Prospects for further price appreciation encouraged long dormant producers like the old Smuggler Mine near the ski slopes of Aspen, Colorado, to reopen, described in the press as "It's Silver Time in the Rockies as Mines Come Alive," but that activity would not restore balance.[32]

The *New York Times* showed a picture of jagged mountain peaks framing Ouray, Colorado, where five hundred men rode clattering rail cars around a snow-covered pine forest and into the Camp Bird Mine of the Federal Resources Company.[33] Benton Bailey, a long-time engineer at the Camp Bird Mine, recalled when caravans of two hundred pack horses carried ore from the mines and said that "the industry is in for good times again" because many mines "were shut down before the coming of modern technology."[34] But mechanization could not overcome the cold calculations of hardened speculators, who knew that price increases in the white metal failed to expand production significantly because most silver was a by-product of mining base metals. When lead and zinc rose from 8¢ a pound to 15¢, silver production expanded alongside those metals, and miners simply scooped up the extra profits from high silver prices.[35] A Treasury staff study confirmed, "Variations in pure silver production . . . do not seem to bear any simple relationship with silver prices."[36]

The headline "Silver Shortage Nearing Crisis" greeted readers in the nation's capital on January 1, 1965.[37] The *Washington Post* story described the problem: "The demand for silver by industry has put the U.S. Treasury on the spot. It mints silver coins by the billions and is using more and more of its own stockpile to try to get ahead of the coin shortage." The article warned "consumers simply began tapping" the Treasury when the price reached $1.293 but "if the stockpile were depleted the lid would be off." The *Post* then hinted at a New Year's resolution: "Congress . . . is expected to act well before the Treasury's stockpile vanishes," but the president would have to deliver the marching orders.

◆ ◆ ◆

On Thursday, June 3, 1965, Lyndon Johnson began his coinage message to Congress by reminding legislators of America's great monetary history: "Our coins, in fact, are little changed from those first established by the Mint Act of 1792," and "the long tradition of our silver coinage is one of the many marks of the extraordinary stability of our political and economic system."[38] He then switched to the sad facts: "Silver is becoming too scarce for continued large-scale use in coins. . . . We expect to use more than 300 million troy ounces—over 10,000 tons—of silver for our coinage this year. That is far more than total new production of silver expected in the entire free world this year." He said reform was needed "to maintain an adequate supply of coins or face chaos . . . from using pay telephones, to parking in a metered zone, to providing children with money for lunch at school."

Legislation for parking spaces and lunch money had broad support in Congress and presidential politics made the Coinage Act of 1965 resemble a well-stocked smorgasbord. It recommended new dimes and quarters that looked like the old but were made of a copper and nickel alloy and no silver, pleasing the Northeast industrial users who wanted to eliminate government demand for the white metal. The new Kennedy half-dollar remained a combination of copper and silver in deference to public sentiment but reduced the white metal content from 90% to 40%. The president satisfied western preferences by keeping the cartwheel at 90% silver but left in place the Treasury's indefinite delay in minting the silver dollars that Congress had authorized a year earlier.[39] And he asked for authority to buy domestically mined silver bullion at $1.25 an ounce, spreading a safety net beneath the prevailing $1.293 price to comfort Rocky Mountain producers and to prevent a revolt by the silver bloc senators. To implement the new coinage system LBJ asked for "standby authority to institute controls over the melting and export of coins" but left the embarrassing details about manipulating the silver market to his new Treasury secretary, Henry Fowler.[40]

Two months earlier, when Douglas Dillon resigned after four years in the job, the president appointed the bespectacled, white-haired Fowler as his successor. Henry Fowler, a fifty-six-year-old courtly Virginian, called "Joe" ever since classmates at Yale Law School dubbed him Gentleman Joe for his snappy dress, had served as Treasury undersecretary to Dillon, and was described as a "middle-roader both politically and economically."[41] His soft southern manners smoothed his testimony in Congress.

Fowler appeared before Texas Congressman Wright Patman's House Committee on Banking and Currency to promote LBJ's Coinage Act and anticipated the contradiction of banning silver from dimes and quarters but keeping it in the half-dollar: "One reason for retaining some silver in our coinage is a desire to continue the 173-year-old tradition of American silver coinage . . . [but] we could, if unforeseen difficulties developed, do without the half dollar temporarily. It can be replaced in use by two quarters."[42] Fowler ignored why the same logic did not apply to the dime, which could be replaced by two nickels, and focused instead on the delicate task of keeping the old 90% silver coins in circulation alongside the new debased currency. Speculators may not have heard of Sir Thomas Gresham, but they knew the potential value of those precious dimes and quarters if the price of silver rose above $1.38¼ per ounce. The New York Times quoted Dr. Franz Pick, a foreign exchange market observer, saying that "dimes and quarters now in circulation will completely disappear, and maybe even half-dollars too."[43]

Joe Fowler revived the Democratic Party's penchant for manipulating the price of silver but this time to keep it down rather

than to perk it up: "The continued use of coins that are 90 percent silver also requires protection of this high silver content coinage from hoarding or destruction. . . . It will be necessary for the
Treasury to protect the monetary value of our silver coinage by
supplying silver to the market upon demand at the present monetary price."[44] He added clarity for Committee Chairman Patman:
"Treasury had been doing this since 1963 by exchanges of silver
bullion against silver certificates," but section 6 of the new law
went further, providing for "sales by the Treasury of silver in excess
of what is needed to back silver certificates" with the objective of
keeping the price at or below $1.293.

Peter Dominick, the tall and athletic Republican senator from
Nevada, warned that the Johnson administration's efforts to sup-
press the price of silver were doomed: "The law of supply and
demand wants to raise silver prices substantially" and the current
situation resembles "an overheated pressure cooker with a blocked
release valve."[45] But Democratic Committee Chairman Patman,
perhaps unfamiliar with the warning whistle of the stainless steel
cooking pot, ignored the potential explosion. He had known LBJ
ever since the president's father, Sam Johnson, had shared a desk
with Patman when they both served in the Texas legislature. The
chairman considered LBJ "one of the most loyal friends I ever
had."[46] He accepted the administration's plan and led Treasury
Secretary Fowler on a duet defending the new law.[47]

PATMAN: Mr. Secretary . . . we would not debase our coinage at all
    by this bill because the monetary value attributed to silver is
    merely that accorded by the people's elected representatives.
FOWLER: That is correct sir.
PATMAN: So, these coins, regardless of the commodity value of the
    metal that is in them, will have the stamp of the United States
    recognizing that each coin is legal tender for the payment of all
    debts, public and private.
FOWLER: Yes, sir.
PATMAN: I know one fellow who owed a considerable amount as
    alimony, about $1,500, and he took it all in pennies and deliv-
    ered it to his former wife.

Fowler ignored Patman's Texas humor and simply assured the chairman that the Coinage Act of 1965 made subsidiary coins legal tender, ending an ambiguity that had plagued small change for almost a century.[48] He also understood the reason for Patman's responsive reading of the virtues of fiat currency. Three months earlier Patman's House Committee on Banking and Currency, and its Senate counterpart, had urged passage of an administration bill to remove the required 25% gold backing for Federal Reserve deposits, freeing the central bank's credit creation ability from external restraint.[49] A vigilant Senator Dominick had warned back then:[50] "It is an obvious first step toward a completely managed monetary system . . . making the value of the dollar thereafter subject to the arbitrary decisions of the fiscal managers." Dominick acknowledged "there may be valid objections to a complete return to a gold standard" but urged "a gold reserve high enough to give stability and firmness to an expanding currency and to provide a series of warning lights against inflation." Dominick supplemented his argument with an analogy to congressional control of the national debt ceiling: "While the Congress has traditionally given in to the administration by repeatedly increasing the debt limit, it has in recent years become more and more obstinate about doing so. The very nature of this situation has forced upon the administration certain fiscal restraints and requirements for justification of its economic policies."

Dominick, a Yale Law School graduate like Fowler, made considerable sense. The Johnson administration had convinced Congress to remove monetary speed bumps by passing the Coinage Act of 1965 and by eliminating gold backing against Federal Reserve deposits.[51] The central bank could now pursue an easy monetary policy to accommodate fiscal deficits without braking to explain. In a retrospective on the Great Inflation of the 1970s, Harvard's Robert Barro, an influential monetary economist, referred to "the removal of silver from most United States coins minted after 1964 . . . as one of President Johnson's most significant policy moves."[52] Barro dignified this obvious exaggeration by adding that he said it "only partly in jest" and explained that the demonetization of silver was a "continuation of the well-established tendency of all unrestrained monarchs to secure revenue by debasing the currency."

Debasing the monetary standard leads to inflation, but economic circumstance and a history of price stability can often delay the consequences. A mid-1965 *Wall Street Journal* article warned, "Inflation's bag of tricks includes the fact that it doesn't necessarily explode into a wage-price spiral the moment or the year the government lights the fuse."[53] President Johnson had loosened the restraints on monetary expansion and speculators would roil the silver market in response, but few politicians listened to the subsequent warning whistle.

CHAPTER 13

PSYCHIATRIST'S MELTDOWN

THE MARCH 1965 ISSUE OF *FORTUNE* MAGAZINE, THE MONTHLY business publication most famous for ranking America's largest companies, called the Fortune 500, did not belong on Henry Jarecki's desk. He was a thirty-two-year-old psychiatrist at Yale Medical School, who had published research studies in the *Journal of Nervous and Mental Disorders* and had pioneered the use of drugs such as Tofranil for depression and Thorazine to help patients overcome delusions. Nevertheless, Henry, a six-footer with well-endowed eyebrows, remained fixated on the *Fortune* article with the playful title "Our Silver Dolors," a lamentation on the sorrows of the white metal.[1] It began, "The U.S. economy is literally running out of silver, and the U.S. Treasury doesn't have much time left in which to do something about it." The article reminded readers that former Secretary of the Treasury Douglas Dillon "had miscalculated the extent of the coin shortage" and pointed out the stupidity of Congress authorizing the mint to issue 45 million new silver dollars: "From the Treasury's point of view this had to be madness."[2]

Henry knew that his older brother Richard, a physician who made a living as a professional gambler, had been collecting silver certificates, exchanging them for cartwheels at the Treasury, and selling them at a profit to Las Vegas casinos for use in slot machines. Henry mailed the article to Richard after the Treasury renewed its ban on cartwheel production, but what he got in return, a shoebox filled with cash, changed his life forever.[3] A confident Henry would abandon his medical career like his brother, become a multimillionaire when silver exploded above the historic $1.293 to a new all-time high in 1967, and then continue the confrontation between East and West by battling the oil-rich Hunt family of Texas for control of the white metal. Henry Jarecki's transformation from pioneering psychiatrist to precious metals arbitrageur was no surprise to those who had watched him grow up.

◆ ◆ ◆

Henry was born in 1933 in Stettin, Germany, a thriving seaport about one hundred miles northeast of Berlin that became part of Poland after World War II.[4] His father, Max Jarecki, was a forty-year-old dermatologist with a medical degree from Heidelberg University when he married Gerda Kunstmann, the twenty-one-year-old daughter of shipping magnate Arthur Kunstmann. The marriage did not last. Gerda disappeared for three weeks on an African safari with a young shipping executive when Henry was a year old. After the divorce, Gerda took Henry and his brother Richard, who was eighteen months older, to live with her parents in their mansion on Falconwood Street in Stettin. The Nazi regime had just come to power in Germany, but the family fortune and Arthur Kunstmann's status as a former president of the German Shipowners Association shielded them from the early brutality. Those happy days dominated Henry's memory except for the incident with the family chauffeur, a man by the name of Streussel, who had entertained Henry and his brother during his downtime until he quit to join the Nazi Party. When Henry and Richard saw Streussel on the street a few days later, they ran up and hugged him but were rebuffed with, "Get away from me, little Jew boys."[5]

Henry left Germany with his family in 1937, moved to London, where he became fluent in English, and then came to the United States after his mother remarried. Henry's father, Max, was already in America, and Henry spent his formative years shuttling between his father, who lived in Asbury Park, a small seaside town in New Jersey, and his mother, who settled in the Forest Hills section of Queens in New York City. Both parents doted on him. Max introduced Henry and Richard to skat, a German card game they often played through the night. Henry struggled to stay awake and track his wins and losses, learning a lesson he never forgot: "He who keeps score will win."[6] His mother wanted him to be a movie star and sent him to audition for the show *Quiz Kids*.

Henry never made it to the movies but managed to graduate from high school at age sixteen. His first major disappointment came when the University of Michigan rejected him because of poor grades, but he fought back. He reapplied after doing well on the College Board exams and was accepted. Henry enjoyed campus life, especially the women, the beer, and the leftist youth organization Young Progressives of America (in that order), but the outbreak of the Korean War in 1950 interrupted his carefree ways. The draft of eighteen-year-olds into the army forced Henry to accelerate his medical school plans to avoid military service.

American medical schools had quotas for Jewish students back then, so Henry turned to his father's alma mater, Heidelberg University, to pursue a six-year MD program. The holocaust was a fresh wound in 1950, a barbarity that would dissuade many American Jews from buying anything made in Germany, but Henry embraced the thought of studying there. His fond childhood memories made him feel as though he were "going home" and guilt-ridden Germans made it easy, but above all "it was a practical decision."[7] It allowed him to study medicine, which pleased his father, and kept him out of the army, which made Henry happy.

Henry studied physiology, chemistry, and anatomy at Heidelberg, just like every other future doctor, but a foray into arbitrage, buying a commodity where it is cheap and simultaneously selling where it is expensive, supplemented his medical education, earned spending money, and made him happier than most other medical students. During vacations he would buy British gold sovereign coins in Switzerland at their intrinsic metallic value and sell them at a 10% premium in Germany, where the coins were in short supply because such cross-border transactions were forbidden to German citizens. Henry referred to this straightforward arbitrage as "fixing up asymmetries," but it really verged on smuggling except for the power of his American passport.[8] A more elaborate scheme that really was smuggling involved Nescafé coffee, which sold for the equivalent of five marks per can in Basel but would fetch eight marks in Heidelberg. Henry identified a loophole in the customs inspections process that allowed him to ship suitcases filled with cans of coffee between the two cities duty free, earning three marks per can.

Henry observed that when customs inspectors boarded a train at the crossing between Switzerland and Germany they would go from one compartment to another demanding that each traveler remove their bags from the overhead rack and open them. But the customs agents never looked at the overhead rack and asked, "Who owns the yellow valise?" And that procedural error sparked a plan. Henry would buy cans of Nescafé in Basel, stuff as many as would fit in a tattered old suitcase, and put the bag on the train to Heidelberg. He would then call his partner in Germany and say, "Grandma is arriving on the 4:40 in the second compartment of the third car. Please help her off."[9]

After six profitable years in Heidelberg, Henry received his MD degree, and married Gloria Friedland, a former classmate at Michigan, who had been working for the U.S. military newspaper *Stars and Stripes* in Germany. Henry says, "She was a civilizing influence on me."[10] The couple returned to America, where Henry was offered a residency in psychiatry at Yale Medical School. He jumped at the opportunity, even though his father would have preferred that he become a real doctor rather than a psychiatrist. He recalls, "Psychiatry wasn't very scientific back then," a lesson he learned personally from one of his first patients at the West Haven Veteran's Administration Hospital.[11] A young man came in for a scheduled consultation, sat down in a chair in front of Henry, bent his head between his knees, and rocked back and forth like a mystic at prayer. Henry asked, "What's the matter?" The patient lifted his head, looked at him and said, "How should I know, Doc? Am I a mind reader?" The response stunned Henry and set the tone for his views of psychiatry. "We don't know why people get depressed . . . and the patient knew I didn't know."

Soon after that encounter the lure of an arbitrage like Nescafé coffee diverted Henry's attention. He discovered that used Mercedes cars in Germany cost $12,000 and could be sold in the United States for $22,000, so he went into the import-export business again, but this time it was perfectly legitimate (which he didn't mind).[12] The proceeds from the Mercedes arbitrage dwarfed his resident's salary and pleased Henry: "Much of my relationship with money is about the satisfaction and excitement I get from earning it, especially when . . . it helps fix asymmetries in the world."[13] But his supplementary activities came to a premature end after his Yale department chairman Fritz Redlich asked him somewhat dismissively, "Are you really dealing cars on the side?"[14]

His days as a psychiatrist were numbered.

◆ ◆ ◆

Henry was only mildly surprised that he had not heard from Richard for two years since sending him the March 1965 *Fortune* article on the silver shortage. He knew Richard had been pursuing his passion for roulette before most casinos in Las Vegas and Monaco banned him for making too much money. Back then roulette wheels were made of wood and were slightly unbalanced so there were small but significant regularities in the supposedly random outcomes. Richard's careful observation and money management made him millions, just like the early "card counters" at blackjack, but also left him on the street after casino owners tossed him from the fanciest establishments. One casino operator said, "Dr. Jarecki is a very nice man with a very clear mind and strong nerves, but he wins too much."[15] He said, "If the casino directors don't like to lose, they should sell vegetables."

In early spring 1967 Richard arrived at Henry's home in Woodbridge, Connecticut, where many Yale faculty members lived, carrying a shoebox filled with silver certificates. It was the residue of his collection after the Treasury decided to redeem certificates in bullion rather than silver dollars.[16] The Las Vegas casinos paid up for cartwheels, not bullion. Richard was on his way abroad, wanted to exchange the certificates for a less bulky stash, and thought Henry might be interested, considering the article he had sent. Henry recalls, "I didn't know he had paid any attention to it," but since he had, "I took the shoebox."[17]

Henry was still teaching psychiatry at Yale and running a community clinic, but he always scrutinized the financial pages of the newspaper. He knew that silver had been stuck at $1.293 per ounce since mid-1965 because the U.S. Treasury had been selling the white metal to all comers at that price to discourage hoarding the old-style silver coins. A chart of silver prices was as flat as the desert horizon and about as exciting, but Henry suspected that might not continue, and if prices rose, the shoebox would produce a windfall. Richard had told him there were $1,293 Treasury certificates inside, just enough to get a one-thousand-ounce bar of bullion from the government. The detail-obsessed Henry wanted to see exactly how that worked, so he conducted a trial run as though he were preparing a million-dollar heist. He brought the cash to the Federal Reserve Bank of New York on Liberty Street in Lower Manhattan, got a receipt for the certificates which he took to the New York Assay Office a few blocks away, and then lugged a seventy-pound bar of 99.9% pure silver back to his house on Rimmon Street in Woodbridge.[18] Satisfied that it could be done, Henry left the dull-gray elongated brick on his front porch, using it as an occasional doorstop, until a neighborhood jogger questioned his common sense. The jogger smiled after Henry said he was a psychiatrist.

Henry's preparation paid a giant dividend on Thursday, May 18, 1967, when the U.S. Treasury changed its silver policy. Demand for the government's bullion had soared since the beginning of May, perhaps because President Johnson had just appointed the Joint Commission on the Coinage, which would recommend when the Treasury should stop defending the $1.293 price.[19] The Treasury had received orders for more than 30 million ounces of silver during the first two weeks of May, compared with a monthly average of 13 million ounces since the beginning of the year.[20] To stem the outflow of the white metal the Treasury announced that going forward it would sell free silver only to those "legitimate domestic concerns which use silver in their business," and it also prohibited the export or melting of silver coins.[21]

The new policy created two prices for silver bullion, $1.293 at the Treasury for companies like the American Smelting and Refining Company and a free market price determined by competition among speculators, hoarders, and exporters. Within a day of the news, traders drove up the free market price of silver bullion to $1.49 an ounce, easily surpassing the old record of $1.38¼ made on November 25, 1919, in the aftermath of the Pittman Act.[22] It was the beginning of a shining era for the tortured white metal, a turnaround in the fortunes of silver buffs that would have pleased William Jennings Bryan, and there was more to come.

The new regime brought an immediate smile to Henry Jarecki, who knew that two prices for the same commodity invited arbitrage, whether it was for Nescafé coffee or silver bullion. Domestic industrial companies could get silver from the Treasury at the preferred $1.293 price but so could holders of Treasury certificates. Henry also knew that the Commodity Exchange (Comex), which had reopened courtesy of JFK in 1963 after a thirty-year hiatus, sponsored trading in silver for future delivery. For example, the buyer of a July 1967 futures contract agrees to take delivery of silver in July and the seller agrees to make delivery in July and both parties agree on the price today. Speculators on Comex bid up the price of those futures contracts after the May 18 Treasury announcement and by the following week, on Wednesday, May 24, silver for July delivery settled at $1.544 an ounce.[23] Henry's eyes widened at the thought of selling a July contract for $1.544, paying $1.293 for bullion at the Treasury using silver certificates, and delivering the white metal about a month later to a Comex warehouse. He sat down after dinner that evening at the kitchen table with his hand-cranked adding machine and was still there in the morning when his wife Gloria interrupted him, saying, "What have you been doing?" Henry grinned, trying to impress her: "I just made a million dollars." She shrugged her shoulders—show me.[24]

A million dollars was a lot of money in 1967. Baseball Hall of Famer Willie Mays earned $125,000 that year, the highest in the major leagues, and the average baseball player's annual salary was $19,000.[25] Henry knew that to make a million dollars he would need $6,465,000 silver certificates to get 5,000,000 ounces of silver at the Treasury. He would then deliver the 5,000,000 ounces on Comex at $1.544, which was 25¢ more per ounce than the $1.293 price at the Treasury. Subtracting about 5¢ an ounce for delivery costs would mean a net profit of 20¢ an ounce, or a million dollars on 5,000,000 ounces.[26] More than $500 million Treasury certificates remained outstanding at the end of May 1967, and all he needed was to get hold of some.[27] And that proved much harder and more costly than his sample calculations suggested, which, strangely enough, made his million dollar boast to Gloria an underestimate. It discouraged competitors.

♦ ♦ ♦

Henry found almost no silver certificates at the local New Haven banks, so he placed a tiny advertisement in the *New York Times*: "We Will Buy Silver Certificates. . . . Call Mr. Benson," and to further camouflage his arbitrage activities from his Yale colleagues, he put the New York telephone number of a friend in the ad.[28] The response to the advertisement produced more silver certificates in a day than Henry had acquired during a month in New Haven, perhaps because he offered to pay a premium above face value for each certificate. More importantly the ad put Henry into contact with Nat Shane and Sol Amelkin, owners of the Terminal Trading Company, who responded that first day with 156 Treasury certificates, the largest single transaction.[29] Henry went to their headquarters on 14th Street in Manhattan, a storefront check-cashing business housed in a rectangular room with a bulletproof glass separating the workers from the friendly clientele. When Henry learned they had ten such locations throughout New York City, ideal collection points for silver certificates, he asked whether they wanted to go into the arbitrage business with him. They thought it was a scam and responded politely with "it's much too complicated," confirming Henry's instincts that arbitrage profits lay in executing the details.

He established a company called Federal Coin & Currency, Inc., rented a one-room office in Manhattan, hired an assistant named Susan Silverman, and bought silver certificates from Terminal Trading and from coin dealers throughout the country. Whenever he accumulated 12,930 silver certificates, enough to get 10,000 ounces of 99.9% pure silver from the Treasury, he would sell one Comex futures contract, allowing him to deliver those 10,000 ounces and locking in the price difference. The arbitrage activity soon brought press coverage and forced Henry to pay an increasing premium over face value per certificate, narrowing his profit margin. The

Washington Post headlined: "N.Y. Speculators Pay $1.12 for $1 Silver Bill" and explained that a "$1 silver certificate . . . is redeemable for 77/100ths of an ounce of granulated silver."[30] Henry did not like being called a speculator, thinking he was more businessman than gunslinger, but the publicity attracted individual entrepreneurs to his collection network, softening the indignity. A Pan American Airlines pilot named Paul Gibson, who flew regularly to Liberia, where the U.S. dollar was the national currency, became an especially valuable resource, bringing sacks of silver certificates to Henry's office that had been "buried beneath the mud huts of tribal chieftains."[31] Henry recalls that you could smell Paul coming "the moment he got off the elevator three hundred feet away."

The government acted to cool the overheated silver market as spring turned into summer, pressuring Henry to accelerate his arbitrage. On June 24, 1967, President Johnson signed a bill limiting the right to exchange Treasury certificates for silver bullion to one year.[32] The arbitrage game would end after June 24, 1968, when holders of silver certificates would receive Federal Reserve notes rather than bullion. The arbitrage became potentially more profitable, however, after the Treasury announced on Friday evening, July 14, 1967, that it would no longer sell silver to domestic firms at $1.293 because there was a sufficient supply of the new copper-nickel coins to eliminate a threatened shortage "even if some of the silver coins should be illegally melted down."[33] The *New York Times* quoted a high Treasury official explaining helpfully that sales of silver had to end at some time and "now that time has arrived."[34]

The price of silver jumped by almost 6% to $1.80 per ounce when the Treasury announced the sales suspension, putting an end to the two-tier market that began on May 18, 1967, and making Treasury certificates more valuable as well.[35] Each certificate was worth about .77 times the price of silver, or $1.39 when the price was $1.80. The *Wall Street Journal* trumpeted the bonanza: "The 'gold rush' is on again only this year it's for silver. Newcomers needn't pack picks, shovels, and Klondike maps; just have wads of paper money (silver certificates to be specific)."[36] The publicity forced the price of each certificate to reflect the value of the underlying bullion, so Henry began paying .72 times the price of the Comex spot silver contract for each certificate, equal to $1.30 when the price of spot silver was $1.80. His gross profit margin was $1.39 minus $1.30 or 9¢ an ounce. Subtracting delivery costs of 5¢ per ounce left him with a net profit of about 4¢ on the outlay of $1.30, or about 3%, which sounds small. Henry had to sharpen his arbitrage pencil to make a million dollars and impress Gloria, which he did through the magic of leverage.

Borrowing money to buy an asset, which is the definition of leverage in finance, can turn pennies into millions. Three cents per dollar invested does not sound like much, but borrowing $10,000,000 and completing the arbitrage in a month produces $300,000, which is a nice start. Subtracting borrowing cost of about 5% per annum on $10,000,000 removes $41,666 for a month's interest, giving a net monthly profit of $258,334. Repeating the process every month generates more than $3 million for the year, confirming the power of the arbitrageur's mantra: "Do it as often as you can, as quickly as you can." It is not appropriate for every activity but that is how arbitrageurs become multimillionaires.

Henry had the right idea but the wrong degree: a banker could get fired for lending $10 million to an overconfident Yale psychiatrist with delusions of alchemy. His scheme to turn silver certificates into a gold mine managed to raise only $200,000 from the Bankers Trust Company in New York City, and only because John Weisman, a successful businessman who had come to Henry for marital advice, vouched for the plan.[37] The small-scale arbitrage left Henry well short of his million-dollar goal, but that was just the beginning of trouble. On Thursday, October 12, 1967, the government almost put Henry out of business. The U.S. Treasury announced that it would no longer redeem certificates with bars of 99.9% pure bullion, the grade of silver required for Comex deliveries.[38] The Treasury said it would meet its obligations in full but with silver from its West Point Depository, which is between 99.6 and 99.8% pure, rather than from the San Francisco Assay Office, which is 99.9% pure silver.[39] At first Henry thought he could simply refine the metal, separate the copper impurities from the silver, and make good delivery on Comex, but he learned that U.S. refineries were on strike with no resolution in sight. Henry's arbitrage boat had sprung a leak.

But he persisted, just like after being rejected by the University of Michigan, and solved both his refinery and money problems in a single master stroke. Henry recalled reading *Silver: How and Where to Buy and Hold It* by currency consultant Franz Pick, who had predicted years earlier the disappearance of the old silver coins and now advocated investing in precious metals to hedge against inflation and dollar debasement. Pick reminded U.S. silver speculators of their thirty years in the wilderness after President Roosevelt nationalized the white metal in 1934 and warned of America's "tendency to punish the precious metals operator for his foresight."[40] To avoid the political risk he suggested using the London forward market in silver rather than Comex futures. Forward markets and futures markets provide similar delivery mechanisms for silver, but the key for Henry was the absence of a refinery strike in London.

Henry reopened Pick's book and saw a sample forward contract from Mocatta & Goldsmid, a three-hundred-year-old London bullion dealer that had been broker to the Bank of England and was now a division of Hambros Bank, a major player in London's Eurobond market.[41] He stared at the telephone number at the top of the page and knew that financing would not be a problem if they accepted the arbitrage argument. Never shy, Henry called Mocatta and asked to speak with someone about the silver market and was put through to Managing Director Keith Smith:[42]

JARECKI: My name is Henry Jarecki. I am a psychiatrist in New Haven, Connecticut, and I would like to talk to somebody about the silver market.

SMITH: Go ahead.

JARECKI: Well, I have this idea to buy silver certificates, hedge them in the forward market in London, and ship the silver to London. . . .

SMITH: (after listening for about forty-five seconds) That's very interesting Dr. Jarecki. We will support you completely.

Henry had practiced being charming and convincing all his life but even he was stunned at the speedy decision. He also knew that his plan involved a commitment of millions, which required a personal touch.

JARECKI: Would it be possible for us to meet?
SMITH: Sure, I'd be happy to see you. Come on over.

✦ ✦ ✦

The beauty of the arrangement between Mocatta and Henry Jarecki was that each side contributed expertise to enhance the outcome. Henry collected the certificates through his New York network, transferred them to a Manhattan vault owned by Mocatta, who then sold the underlying bullion in the London forward market. Mocatta financed the entire operation and could borrow money very cheaply, so Henry became an aggressive bidder for the dwindling supply of Treasury currency. He collected silver certificates not only from retailers like Terminal Trading Company but from other arbitrageurs who found Henry's price better than they could get. His potential competitors became suppliers and delivered so many certificates wrapped in hundred-dollar packs to Henry's office that he decided to weigh the bundles instead of counting the individual bills. Henry's workers used a finely tuned apothecary scale to balance a precounted hundred-dollar pack against an incoming lot but were careful to match old and dirty bills against a similar standard, following the same procedure with crisp new bills. Older bills weighed more because of accumulated dirt and sweat.

The booming partnership between Mocatta and Jarecki, an unintended consequence of the Treasury's decision on October 12, 1967, to redeem certificates with bars less than 99.9% fine, matched an explosion in silver prices. Bullion rose from $1.74 before the Treasury's announcement on Thursday, October 12, to $2.10 an ounce on Friday, December 29, 1967, the last trading day of the year, a 20% increase that the press hailed as restoring the credibility lost by the white metal almost a century earlier in the Crime of 1873.[43] The *New York Times* celebrated the revival with

FIGURE 13. Henry Jarecki talking arbitrage.

the headline: "Silver Now at Bryan's 16 to 1 Ratio," adding for the arithmetically challenged "that the free market price of silver . . . was almost exactly 1/16th of the $35 an ounce price of gold for the first time in almost a century."[44] It showed a picture of William Jennings Bryan being "carried in triumph after his 'Cross of Gold' speech" at the 1896 Democratic convention, where he championed the restoration of silver as a monetary metal. The *Times* noted: "The Great Commoner must be smiling in his grave."

Bryan's victory was, in fact, bittersweet. He had promoted monetizing silver at $1.29 per ounce, but the white metal rose to over $2 for the first time in history precisely because it had been *demonetized*. American citizens could use silver to protect against inflation and a debasement of the currency because the Treasury stopped fixing the price at $1.293, its monetary value established by Alexander Hamilton. The *Washington Post* headline, "Price Rise Beginning to Worry Experts," confirmed that inflation had become a serious concern.[45] The *Post* pointed out that "consumer prices, under the stimulus of the Vietnam War, jumped 3 per cent from 1965 to 1966 . . . [and] threaten to rise nearly as much this year."

That may not sound big by later standards, but the *Post* compared it with the "period 1958 through mid-1965 [that] saw an average yearly increase of only 1.3 percent." A review of 1967 by President Johnson's Council of Economic Advisers admitted that "the most disturbing economic news was the continuation of the creeping inflation that began in 1965."[46] FDR's ban on owning gold remained in force in 1967, making silver America's preferred hard asset to hedge against the eroding value of the dollar. The *New York Times* attributed silver's "string of record prices" to speculators coming "under the spell of inflation fears."[47]

In their annual review of the silver market, Handy & Harman added that the price of silver "has climbed to record high levels in the face of very large physical supplies. There is no shortage of silver for industrial uses."[48] The review estimated that speculators had accumulated "200 million ounces . . . as a hedge against devaluation of the dollar."[49] U.S. inflation dimmed the outlook for the U.S. currency in the foreign exchange market, suggesting the dollar might go the way of the British pound, which was devalued on November 18, 1967.[50] In an article entitled "How Sound Is Your Dollar?" the *Chicago Tribune* quoted European bankers saying they "no longer believe budget estimates announced by the United States government," and big budget deficits forced the Federal Reserve to expand credit and inflate, undermining the currency both domestically and internationally.[51]

The overheated price of the white metal sounded a warning like Senator Peter Dominick's whistling pressure cooker: monetary accommodation of U.S. budget deficits threatened American finance. The crescendo intensified in March 1968, when declining gold reserves forced the United States to abandon support of the $35 price, allowing the yellow metal to trade freely among speculators and limiting the official price to government transactions with foreign central banks.[52] The new policy created two markets for gold, just like for silver in May 1967, but Americans citizens were still unable to buy the yellow metal and stayed with silver for protection. The spillover from the disruption in gold pushed silver prices even higher so that when the redemption period for Treasury certificates ended on June 24, 1968, the white metal reached $2.47. The price of gold in the London bullion market had also increased to $41.05, leaving the ratio at Bryan's 16 to 1 when Henry Jarecki and Mocatta ended their arbitrage.[53]

Mocatta & Goldsmid had committed more than $100 million to the joint venture, and Henry's share of the profit was well above the million dollars he had promised Gloria, but he had neglected his medical practice. In addition to teaching at Yale, he was the director of Psychiatric Associates, a walk-in clinic serving the New Haven community that he founded with his friend and partner Gene Eliasoph, a gifted psychotherapist. In one memorable incident, Henry was supposed to lead a discussion among represen-tatives of five welfare agencies concerning a fifteen-year-old girl whose family members were all in trouble.[54] Henry arrived late and apologized to the group: "I'm awfully sorry but as some of you know I have some outside interests." Gene was not happy and reprimanded his partner as everyone stared: "Yes, Henry, we know you have outside interests. This practice for one."

It was time for Henry to repair the damage. He flew to London, thanked Keith Smith for having faith in a psychiatrist with a split personality, and they parted ways.

But not for long.

CHAPTER 14

BATTLE LINES

THE U.S. SECRET SERVICE ARRESTED TWO MEN ON TUESDAY NIGHT, December 3, 1968, for running a makeshift coin smelting plant in the basement of 63 Dekalb Avenue in the heart of downtown Brooklyn, where they illegally turned pre-1965 dimes and quarters into bullion bars.[1] Nathaniel Robinson and Arthur O'Leary melted the coins in crucibles over gas flames and then poured the mercury-like molten silver into ingots. Investigators found partially melted dimes at the bottom of a steel sink that held the molds. The two men were caught after trying to sell 50 one-thousand-ounce bars to Engelhard Minerals & Chemicals Corporation, the big refinery located in Newark, New Jersey. They had explained to the company that the ingots, which had no engraved certifying marks, came from melting sterling silver scraps. Engelhard workers tested the bars, which failed to pass the 92.5% sterling standard, and reported their suspicions to the Secret Service. The Secret Service has been enforcing the currency laws since it was established in 1865 as a unit of the Treasury Department, and investigators thought this was "the biggest case of illegal coin melting ever uncovered in the U.S."[2] The Service did not start to protect the president and other government officials, its most famous job, until after William McKinley's assassination in 1901.

The U.S. Treasury banned melting the high-silver-content coins on May 18, 1967, and violations carried a penalty of up to five years in prison and a $10,000 fine. Perhaps that is why Robinson and O'Leary could buy the coins for only a 10% premium above face value even though silver sold for $2 an ounce in December 1968, a premium of almost 50% above the silver content of the coins.[3] The threat of incarceration restrained the competition, giving Robinson and O'Leary a hefty profit if they had remained out of jail, which would have been easier had they remembered that U.S. coins were only 90% silver and not up to the sterling standard.

Everything changed less than six months later, on Monday, May 12, 1969, when the Treasury lifted the ban on melting the pre-1965 coins. Richard Nixon had become president on January 20, 1969, and a Republican philosophy had taken hold. The new Treasury secretary, David Kennedy, a white-haired former commercial banker, recommended at the first meeting of the Joint Coinage Commission after he had taken office "that the current administrative ban on the melting and export of silver coins be discontinued."[4] He explained, "In contrast to the situation in the past, the melting ban no longer either keeps silver coins in circulation or contributes to the Treasury's supply of silver coins." At the previous meeting of the commission, on December 5, 1968, when the Democrats still ran the country, outgoing Treasury Secretary Fowler recommended that "the Congress enact legislation to make the current administrative ban on the melting of silver coins permanent."[5] He explained that "any profits resulting from the sale of silver in U.S. coins should be realized by the public as a whole through their Government rather than to individual hoarders of these coins." Laissez-faire had prevailed instead.

Henry Jarecki approved of deregulation, despite his youthful flirtation with the leftist Young Progressives of America, and was tempted by the more than $2.6 billion pre-1965 silver coins waiting to be plucked.[6] The coins contained almost two billion ounces of silver, more than four times the amount in silver certificates when Henry went into the arbitrage business with Mocatta's Keith Smith.[7] He hesitated because another prolonged distraction from his medical practice could be fatal. Susan Silverman, his former office manager at Federal Coin & Currency, who was now working at an advertising agency, had no doubt. She left him a note saying: "I read about the lifting of the melt ban this morning. I have given notice at my job and I'll be in on Monday."[8]

Henry watched the price of old coins rise immediately after the ban was lifted. On Tuesday May 13, 1969, the day after the announcement, New York coin wholesaler Joel Coen offered to pay a 12.5% premium for large quantities to coin dealers throughout the country. William Crowl, proprietor of a coin shop in Arlington, Virginia, commented, "I may melt them in the back of the shop."[9] It was an idle threat for much of his inventory, however, because coins with numismatic value would remain with collectors. No one knew how many of the $2.6 billion coins outstanding had been thrown into piggy banks ready to be raided versus those with aristocratic lineage, like the uncirculated 1879CC cartwheel, guarded like the family jewels in velvet-lined boxes.

Susan was right, of course. Henry knew that the logistics for the coin arbitrage "were sure to be harder than they were with silver certificates," and the harder it was for everyone else the better it was for him.[10] He recalls: "I was sure there would be a great need for the gathering, payment, and hedging system I had developed for silver certificates." He called Keith Smith, who agreed to support establishing a joint venture in the United States between Hambros Bank, owner of Mocatta & Goldsmid, and Jarecki. The first task would be to execute the arbitrage between coins and bullion and then to expand the business and become a dealer in precious metals in America. Jocelyn Hambros, chairman of the Bank, laid down one condition: Henry would have to leave medicine and run the company full time.

It was not an easy decision. He was in the middle of a ten-year book project on psychopharmacology, *Modern Psychiatric Treatment,* with his Yale friend and colleague, Tom Detre, and he wanted to finish.[11] When he mentioned his dilemma to his father, Max, the old man looked as though he had just swallowed arsenic and said, "You are thinking of giving up a profession to go into business?"[12] But the attraction of a joint venture with Mocatta & Goldsmid, a company with a storied history, proved irresistible. The firm was organized in 1684 by Moses Mocatta, ten years before the Bank of England was chartered, and became bullion broker to the bank in 1720.[13] In 1937 the *Wall Street Journal* referred to Mocatta as a "leading London firm of bullion dealers."[14] In 1954, when the London gold market reopened after being closed for fifteen years, Mocatta & Goldsmid was one of five bullion-dealing firms invited to participate in establishing the daily reference price for gold, known as the "gold fixing."[15] And in January 1961 the *New York Times* reported the company's prediction that "the continued demand for silver would lead to a shortage" and "that the United States Treasury . . . might stop selling silver to American industry."[16] Two centuries of experience had polished Mocatta & Goldsmid's crystal ball to perfection.

Henry could not resist becoming chairman of Mocatta Metals Corporation, a partnership with Hambros Bank that conferred a sense of history and provided access to the deep pockets of the London money center bank. He was also fortunate to meet the bank's controller, Pat Brennan, a tall and austere man, who asked a somewhat embarrassing question early on: "Tell me do you have any practical business experience?"[17] The answer, of course, was no. A successful arbitrageur does not necessarily know how to meet a payroll. Brennan gave Henry a crash course in management to complement the Hambros money and the Mocatta & Goldsmid heritage. He would need it all to confront Nelson Bunker Hunt, the Texan who had given a celebrity-filled party at London's famed Claridge Hotel the week before America lifted the melting ban in May 1969.[18] The five hundred guests were witness to Bunker's arrival on the international scene—and that was just his opening act.

NELSON BUNKER HUNT

THE *WALL STREET JOURNAL* HEADLINE ON APRIL 25, 1966, "BIG Oil Well Discovery Is Completed in Libya by British Petroleum . . . Dallas Man Has 49% Interest," was not Nelson Bunker Hunt's first taste of publicity.[1] Two years earlier he had been implicated by the *Washington Post* as one of "three wealthy Dallas businessmen" responsible for financing the hostile "Welcome Mr. Kennedy" advertisement in the local press on the day of the president's assassination.[2] Both stories brought an unwelcome glare to the ultraconservative Texan, a member of the right-wing John Birch Society, who was the wealthiest man on the planet at age forty after the Sarir oil field discovery. No one knew exactly how much oil lay beneath the sand, but Britain's *Daily Telegraph* trumpeted "The Biggest Pipeline" in describing the 320-mile, 34-inch-diameter pipe "laid jointly by British Petroleum and by Nelson Bunker Hunt" to transport oil from the desert to Tobruk, site of a decisive World War II battle and now a Libyan seaport on the Mediterranean.[3]

None of the uncertainty muffled fascination with the size of Bunker's wealth. His older sister Margaret said, "He owned billions of barrels of reserves, making him richer than Daddy," which meant a lot since family patriarch H.L. Hunt was the richest man in the world according to J. Paul Getty, who had been given that title by *Life* magazine.[4] Surpassing Haroldson Lafayette Hunt, called H.L. by everyone, meant that Bunker now had the evidence to disprove his father's taunt, "Stupid boy . . . I can't believe you've got my genes in you," one of many put-downs H.L hurled at his least-favorite son.[5] Subsequent estimates put a contemporary value of between $6 and $8 billion on Bunker's share of the Libyan discovery at a time when the number of billionaires in the world could be counted on one hand.[6] Bunker enjoyed the uncertainty over his fortune and would respond years later to a related question during one of many congressional investigations into his alleged manipulation of the silver market: "People who know how much they are worth, generally aren't worth much."[7]

The party in May 1969 at the Claridge Hotel, site of Senator Key Pittman's bowie-knife rampage for silver thirty-five years earlier, resembled an international debutante ball. The gossip columnists chirped, "American and oil-rich, Mr. Hunt and his wife Caroline, just gave a ball for 500 . . . with three bands, including Woody Herman's crew, which they flew over from the United States."[8] The extravaganza turned a giant spotlight on the 250-pound Bunker, whose large oval glasses matched his pie-shaped face, illuminating every stain and blemish. He continued to wear rumpled brown suits, fly coach on commercial airlines, and drive an old Cadillac DeVille that had left its hubcaps on the highway, but his passions became obsessions, especially his purchases of Australian farmland, silver, and racehorses.

Bunker already owned over two hundred thoroughbreds in 1969, and most were housed in Europe, which explains the London venue of his coming-out party, but he was far from finished. At eight o'clock on Thursday night, December 4, 1969, Bunker bought Decies, a two-year-old Irish colt, for what the London *Times* described as "the second highest price ever to have been paid at Tattersalls' sales ring at Newmarket."[9] *The Times* reported additional Hunt purchases, which it called "a spending spree." The newspaper then cautioned, "Whether or not Mr. Bunker Hunt has secured a bargain is another question," an observation that would also apply to his silver buying frenzy that began in 1973. Bunker was a risk-taker, like his father, always trying to prove he was a Hunt.

✦ ✦ ✦

Nelson Bunker Hunt was born on February 22, 1926, to H.L. and Lyda Bunker Hunt in El Dorado, Arkansas, an appropriate hometown for a future tycoon. He broke the scales at birth and arrived four weeks late, leading his sister Margaret to say when he was older: "Poor Bunker, he really can't help being overweight because he came into this world a month old and weighing twelve pounds."[10]

Bunker's father, H.L., was a successful gambler who used his winnings at the poker table to finance oil exploration. He had an uncanny ability to drill gushers and in 1938, after accumulating a small fortune and six children, moved his family to a fourteen-room mansion in Northeast Dallas called Mount Vernon because it resembled George Washington's Virginia home. H.L. and Lyda took adjoining bedrooms on the second floor so Bunker and his younger brothers, Herbert and Lamar, shared the large master bedroom and often played games using the laundry chute as a slide (it was a tight squeeze for Bunker).[11] There were six safes in the house that remained empty except one Lyda used for canned goods and another where Lamar stored his footballs and baseballs. Bunker had a soft spot for Lamar's sports obsession and helped him learn to shoot a basketball both left-handed and right-handed. Later on, after Lamar barely made the football team at Southern Methodist University, Bunker drove his mother to the stadium an hour early on game days to watch Lamar warm up on the field with the rest of the team before he took a permanent seat on the bench during the game.[12]

H.L.'s oldest son, Haroldson Lafayette III, called Hassie by everyone, was five years older than Bunker and had already joined his father's oil exploration business when they moved to Dallas. He and H.L. shared a rugged look, broad shouldered with bright blue eyes, and had won the father-son look-alike contest at Hassie's high school.[13] The youngster could also smell the best oil drilling sites like his father, and when Bunker joined the business he suffered in comparison. Not only did Bunker resemble his mother more than his father, he sounded slow and plodding when he spoke, enjoyed taking midafternoon naps, but, most disagreeably from H.L.'s standpoint, he drilled one dry hole after another and could barely find an oil slick at the local gas station. H.L. let everyone at the office know his feelings, screaming, "The boy's an idiot. I can find more oil with a road map than he can with a whole platoon of geologists. His brother Hassie's a towering genius compared to him."[14]

But Hassie had a problem. He was mentally unstable, perhaps schizophrenic, and would behave erratically, sometimes leaving the car during a stop in an oil field to roll around in the mud pits.[15] He received a medical discharge from the army during World War II,

FIGURE 14. Herbert, Lamar, and Bunker Hunt.

and H.L. tried every therapy known at the time to cure him, including a prefrontal lobotomy, but nothing helped.[16] The failure nearly destroyed H.L. but did nothing to help Bunker, who heard a new refrain from his father: "Get out of my sight, you dimwit. Your younger brothers have more sense in their feet than you have in your whole body. Herbert and Lamar are my true sons. You're not fit to be my heir."[17] H.L. was right about one thing: Herbert and Lamar bore no outward resemblance to Bunker; they both were as rectangular and neat as Bunker was round and relaxed.

H.L. had already established irrevocable trusts for his six children, so Bunker remained a beneficiary despite his father's rejection. And none of the insults dimmed Bunker's reverence for the old man, who he considered "much smarter than my brothers and me because he'd been out in the school of hard knocks. He was street smart."[18] Bunker felt that his father "had courage" and was "an unusually honest man," who would never, for example, contribute to both sides in an election.[19] H.L. considered communism public enemy number one, dating the danger, according to his daughter Margaret, from Roosevelt's and Churchill's concessions to Stalin at the Yalta Conference during World War II.[20] A Hunt employee thought that the boss believed America's flirtation with the evil empire started much earlier: "H.L. thinks that communism began in this country when the government took over the distribution of the mails."[21]

Bunker adopted his father's outlook, sharing a xenophobia that targeted communists and Jews. He was not shy about the family's view of the communist menace: "I consider communism to be socialism with a gun. [My father] saw it as sophisticated slavery."[22] Bunker was less willing to concede he was anti-Jewish, saying only: "They are a little different, like a Chinaman or whatever is different; you do have to say that."[23] His employees may have sidestepped his half-joking instruction to "Never hire a Phi Beta Kappa. They all turn into communists."[24] But that warning did not apply to Jews, who he thought were all smart and could help him. He said, "Never look a gift-Jew in the mouth."[25]

Bunker wanted to prove to H.L. that he was worthy of the Hunt name. The Libyan oil concession, negotiated with King Idris in 1957, was his last chance, but when it needed a cash infusion to continue exploration, Bunker had no money left.[26] He had already spent everything he had—perhaps $250 million—on failures.[27] Although Bunker was close with his two older sisters, Margaret and Caroline, they were not risk-takers in the Hunt tradition, so he turned to Herbert and Lamar for help. He sold them a 15% interest in the Sarir oil field in exchange for their contribution, which eventually made them even richer than they already were.[28] The deal also solidified their familial bond, which they needed after learning about their father's two other families.

H.L. Hunt had difficulty keeping his pants zipped, but that was not the biggest factor in his extracurricular activities. According to his biographer Harry Hurt, he had more than enough casual opportunities to satisfy his outsize libido, but he had another agenda. He confided to a business associate that he carried a genius gene and "believed that by fathering children he was doing the world a favor, providing the human race with its future leaders."[29] In addition to his six children with Lyda, H.L. sired another eight by two women, four with Frania Tye, who he met in 1925, and four with Ruth Ray, who he met around 1941, all conceived while he was married to Lyda Bunker.[30]

Perhaps H.L. should have received lofty recognition for his accomplishments, a Nobel Peace Prize for creating potential world leaders or an Olympic Gold Medal for avoiding prison for bigamy, but the "second" and "third" families had one very practical impact: they brought Bunker and his siblings, now known as the "first family," closer together to promote their joint interests, especially in the most valuable trust, the Placid Oil Company. The three families would fight in court for a share of the Hunt fortune, even though Herbert would say, "We do not want one penny more than we really are supposed to have."[31] A member of the second family joked after several years of litigation: "We only see each other at weddings and at trials."[32] Bunker would need Placid Oil to keep afloat after the silver market debacle so he did not think it was so funny.

+ + +

A cloud of doubt darkened Bunker's world on Monday, September 1, 1969, just four months after his celebration at the Claridge. A group of Libyan army officers overthrew King Idris and the press warned, "U.S., British Rights Threatened by Coup."[33] A twenty-seven-year-old Colonel Muammar Qaddafi emerged as leader of the bloodless takeover, promising a new republic with "unity, liberty, and socialism" as its watchwords.[34] He expelled the Americans from Wheelus Air Base near Tripoli and forced the British to remove their troops from Tobruk, but he allowed the major oil companies favored by the King to remain.[35] Qaddafi realized the Libyans needed the technical expertise of Big Oil, including Mobil, Esso, British Petroleum (BP), Shell, Marathon, Gulf, and Phillips, to continue the revenues from the black gold.

But the restraint did not last. On Thursday evening, December 7, 1971, the Libyan government announced it was nationalizing British Petroleum's oil operations in retaliation for Britain's alleged pro-Iran, anti-Arab activity in a territorial dispute over islands in the Persian Gulf.[36] The petroleum minister appointed a compensation committee, composed of Libyans, to determine reimbursement to BP, but it was not expected to recommend payment for oil reserves in the ground. The Libyan government denied "other oil companies were threatened," explaining that "our action was political and in response to the occupation of the islands."[37]

Bunker began to worry as soon as they said not to worry. On Friday, June 9, 1972, he travelled to Tripoli for consultations with his representatives after the government summoned local officials of the Bunker Hunt Oil Company for a high-level meeting.[38] The negotiations dragged on for months and led to Petroleum Minister Ezzeldin Mobruk demanding half of Bunker's production from the Sarir oil field, which had been operating jointly with Libya's state-owned Gulf Exploration Company since the expulsion of British Petroleum.[39] Oil analysts suggested that instead of going after one of the major U.S. firms in Libya, like Mobil, Esso, or Marathon, the government was "picking out one of the smaller American companies to bargain with and then demanding that the others fall in line."[40] Bunker felt like a guinea pig, richer than any other, but still a guinea pig that biologists use for scientific research. He refused to participate in the experiment.

It did not end well.

On Monday evening, June 11, 1973, Qaddafi announced in a speech marking the third anniversary of the American evacuation from Wheelus Air Base that Libya was nationalizing Bunker Hunt's half of the Sarir oil field.[41] He began with a jab at the U.S.: "The time has come for us to deal America a strong slap on its cool, arrogant, face."[42] Qaddafi then justified expropriating Hunt's operation, saying, "The right to nationalize comes under our sovereignty over our land. We can do whatever we want with our oil."[43] In Dallas Bunker released a prepared statement saying that he had "tried to work with the Libyan national oil company and its subsidiaries" but it was "impossible due the unjustified demands." He added that he "will pursue all available legal remedies" and complained that the Libyan government had "chosen Hunt as an example" because he was in a "vulnerable position following the nationalization of the British Petroleum half of the field." Bunker had been much more succinct when receiving the phone call in his office, breaking the news. He smashed down the receiver and said, "Fuck."[44]

Bunker's expletive understated the personal calamity. Qaddafi's speech on June 11, 1973, demoted him from wealthiest man in the world to an ordinary multimillionaire, restoring his status as a rich man's son rather than wealthy in his own right. It cut Bunker down from adult to child's size. Moreover, the fall had come at a particularly bad time for a man worried that the American government was spending its way into bankruptcy and eroding the value of the dollar. The first six months of 1973 witnessed the highest rate of inflation since the Korean War, an increase in consumer prices of 8% per annum, eclipsed later in the decade but a peacetime record back then.[45] President Nixon's Council of Economic Advisers described the inflation problem as "a Hydra-headed monster, growing two new heads each time one was cut off" and warned "if we do not fight inflation effectively it will accelerate."[46] When Nixon responded to the problem with another freeze on prices, a *New York Times* headline described the new reality, "Controls as a Way of Life," confirming Bunker's suspicions that all American presidents were communists, not just Roosevelt, and Soviet-like repression was here to stay.[47]

Qaddafi had denied Bunker his oil reserves, which would have more than compensated for overall inflation going forward. Bunker sued for restitution but needed to hedge against the threat of runaway prices. He had no faith in fiat currency and disparaged the Federal Reserve, America's central bank, saying, "Just about anything you buy, rather than paper, is better. . . . Any damn fool can run a printing press."[48] Bunker had begun dabbling in silver soon after the 1969 Claridge party so it became his first choice.

✦ ✦ ✦

The beginning of 1970 was a bad time to start accumulating silver. The price of the white metal had declined from its peak of $2.50 per ounce in June 1968, when the U.S. Treasury ended the redemption rights of silver certificates, to $1.80 per ounce as the new decade began, and would continue to erode for two years to a low of

$1.28, a decline of almost 50% from its previous high.[49] Bullion dealer Handy & Harman described "a growing disillusionment on the part of speculators," but that sentiment did not stop Bunker, who had practiced patience and persistence in investing, from listening to a sales pitch by Alvin Brodsky, a commodities broker for Bache & Company, the second largest U.S. brokerage firm after Merrill Lynch.[50] In January 1970 the short and voluble Brodsky flew from New York to Dallas to meet with the celebrity Texan to drum up business.[51] It was worth the time and expense. He sat across the table from Bunker in the kitchen of his home, pointed to the dishes, napkins, forks, and knives set for dinner, and asked: "Do you believe you're going to have to pay more for these things next year?" When Bunker agreed, Brodsky stifled a smile and said, "Well, then, you should consider silver."[52]

The simple argument appealed to Bunker, and Alvin Brodsky reaped the benefits. He would become a major player in the silver ring on the Commodity Exchange, a force to be reckoned with on Comex thanks to the Hunt connection, but at the outset Bunker bought only a few hundred thousand ounces of the white metal, the equivalent of pocket money, perhaps just to see what a stack of bullion bars looked like. Nelson Bunker Hunt had too much oil and too many other diversions to make silver a high priority in the early 1970s. He owned large tracts of land, including 10,000 acres in Mississippi for a new town projected to house 125,000 people, and 2,000 square miles of virgin property in Australia's Northern Territory just for show.[53] The *Wall Street Journal* reported Bunker's boast that he "will become the largest American landholder in Australia."[54] Bunker enhanced his horseracing colors by buying the French stables at Chantilly owned by the late Jean Stern, which led the press to comment: "Nelson Bunker Hunt will take over . . . as Europe's 'Mr. Racing.' He has built up an enormous horse empire."[55] And in early 1973 he joined a consortium of fifteen men led by George Steinbrenner in buying the most famous American baseball franchise, the New York Yankees.[56]

None of these investments made much money for Bunker, but they put him on world display, especially his ownership of a horse named Dahlia. The three-year-old filly had a royal pedigree and

FIGURE 15. Queen Elizabeth presents Bunker Hunt with the winner's trophy.

won the King George VI and Queen Elizabeth Stakes at the Ascot racecourse on Saturday, July 28, 1973, the richest race in English history at the time.[57] Dahlia received $208,000 for winning the prestigious competition, a nice prize, but not even worth a footnote to the loss Bunker incurred when Qaddafi nationalized his share in the Sarir oil field a month earlier. Bunker needed to replace his Libyan oil investment and to protect his remaining Texas-size fortune from government misbehavior, both foreign and domestic, and that is why he began buying silver in bulk on the Commodity Exchange in late 1973.

Comex had come a long way since President Johnson suspended U.S. Treasury sales of silver at $1.293 per ounce in July 1967. In the first full year after the price ceiling was removed trading on the Commodity Exchange set a record of 4.8 billion ounces.[58] By 1973 trading volume more than doubled to 12 billion ounces, making it a full-service cafeteria worthy of Bunker Hunt's appetite.[59]

The Commodity Exchange now dominated the silver market the way the New York Stock Exchange ruled stocks.[60] Handy & Harman had been quoting silver prices in the United States since the 1890s, publishing daily quotations, described as "the lowest price at which offers can be obtained by Handy & Harman for silver in commercial bar form."[61] By the end of 1973 Handy & Harman had switched the basis of its quotes to "prices obtainable for futures contracts on the New York Commodity Exchange," explaining that nowadays "commercial users base their daily offers of silver for prompt delivery on prevailing quotations for futures on Comex."[62]

The Commodity Exchange became the main source of price discovery for the white metal even though the big commercial users like the camera giant Eastman Kodak rarely took delivery of silver on the Exchange.[63] Comex, like every other futures exchange, sponsored trading in a standardized product to promote wide participation among investors, speculators, and industry so that the resulting price reflected a broad consensus among many buyers and sellers. The silver contract called for delivery of 99.9% pure silver at a Comex approved warehouse, but the Rochester-based photo company wanted the white metal delivered to its doorstep and perhaps with even fewer impurities than the "three-nines fine" standard. Kodak, like other commercial users, bought a futures contract on Comex as a first step in the production process, to hedge against a future price increase in the raw material. Kodak used the standardized contract because open competition among many potential buyers and sellers on the Comex floor determined the price. But as soon as Kodak took delivery of silver in Rochester from its favorite supplier, perhaps Henry Jarecki's Mocatta Metals Corporation, which had become one of the largest bullion dealers in the United States, Kodak sold its futures contract.[64] If the white metal had become more expensive and they had to pay more to Mocatta, Kodak would also have an offsetting gain in value on the purchase and sale of its futures contract.

Bunker Hunt used Comex to buy silver for the same reason as Kodak—it was the premier market for trading the white metal—but his objective was simply to make money. He chose silver because it would protect against inflation and could not be confiscated like his Libyan oil, at least if he stored it where no one could find it. After the Qaddafi disaster he trusted only himself and his brothers, but with Lamar chasing Super Bowls with his Kansas City Chiefs football team Bunker joined with Herbert to pursue silver. The Hunt brothers often invested together, sometimes through their jointly owned Placid Oil Company and sometimes because circumstances forced it, such as when Herbert and Lamar came to Bunker's rescue in the Sarir oil field exploration. But just as often they remained separate, such as Bunker's race horses and investment in the New York Yankees, and Lamar's lone pursuit of a football franchise.

In March 1959 the twenty-seven-year-old Lamar had asked Bunker to call Bud Adams, son of a Texas oilman, about meeting with Lamar for dinner to discuss the formation of a new football league after the established National Football League rebuffed Lamar's effort to buy a franchise.[65] Adams agreed to the dinner and then asked Bunker what it was about. Bunker said, "I don't tell Lamar my business. And he doesn't tell me his business."[66] A week after Lamar and Bud Adams announced the formation of the new American Football League, Bunker walked a few steps from his office to his brother's and said, "Hey Lamar, I'd like to invest in your team." Lamar said, "Oh, thank you. But I prefer to go this one alone." Bunker shrugged his shoulders and said, "Okay."[67]

Lamar wore his usual friendly smile while losing more than a million dollars a year at the beginning, leading a Dallas sportswriter to quip, "At that rate he can only afford to lose for the next 100 years," but by 1973 he had become a successful celebrity in the sports world.[68] Bunker's youngest brother had engineered the merger between the National and American Football Leagues, invented the name Super Bowl, and won the Tiffany-crafted silver trophy with his Kansas City Chiefs in January 1970. He had also orchestrated the formation of the World Championship Tennis tour in 1968, so Bunker and Herbert moved ahead on their own with silver.

Bunker and Herbert had offices next door to each other in their downtown Dallas headquarters in the First National Bank Building and lived a few blocks apart, although their work schedules differed considerably. Herbert, three years younger than Bunker, typically arrived in the office soon after dawn and left before dinner, while his brother tumbled in around lunchtime and stayed late. According to Herbert, who was as unassuming as Bunker was flamboyant, they complemented each other in other ways: "Bunker is very farsighted, very perceptive. . . . He prefers to conceive something and then step back. I get more involved in the details."[69] Herbert liked precision, including maintaining order in his full mop of wavy black hair and adhering to his early-morning jog to remain trim, while Bunker let nature take its course. Herbert elaborated, "He doesn't make hotel reservations and he just shows up at the airport and waits in line to fly standby." Herbert knew that Bunker rarely read anything beyond the racing forms, so he bought Jerome F. Smith's *Silver Profits in the Seventies*.[70] It became their blueprint.

Jerome Smith was one of many financial newsletter writers touring the country and giving seminars on how to avoid monetary ruin in an inflationary world, but his eighty-eight-page booklet gave a sophisticated analysis of the white metal as a compelling investment. He began with a tease: "If you have the patience to study this report and follow its logic, and if you have some money to invest—it could make you rich. If you are already rich, it can, at least, provide you a means to keep what you have."[71] Smith then drew a detailed demand and supply picture of silver similar to the 1965 report by the U.S. Treasury that had convinced LBJ to abandon silver as a monetary metal. The landscape remained the same, a growing commercial demand for the white metal, especially in making photographic film because silver is "one hundred times better than the second best light-sensitive substance," and in electronics, where "silver conducts electricity more efficiently than any other metal."[72] Despite the U.S. Treasury's withdrawal from the demand side of the silver market, completed on December 31, 1970, when the 40% silver half-dollar was replaced by a lowly copper-nickel alloy, total world demand for the white metal exceeded new mine production by more than 100 million ounces a year.[73]

The excess demand for silver drove up prices and attracted aboveground supplies to the market from speculator inventories, hoarders in China and India, and coin-melting arbitrageurs like Henry

Jarecki. These so-called secondary sources filled the gap between consumption and production, but Smith argued that prices had never fully escaped the drag from years of government intervention and manipulation.[74] He invoked the legendary 16 to 1 ratio of William Jennings Bryan to conclude that, with gold selling at $100 an ounce at the end of September 1973, silver should have been $6.25 and not $2.70.[75]

Jerome Smith's message made Herbert Hunt smile. He knew that Bunker had considered gold to hedge against inflation, even though Americans still could not legally invest in the yellow metal, but had rejected it as "too political" and "too easily manipulated" by outside forces.[76] Central banks throughout the world had substantial gold reserves they could dump on world markets to make a profit, dampening price increases. Smith confirmed the superiority of silver because the upward price pressure would be free of government influence. The white metal would outperform the yellow going forward, according to Jerome Smith, but he raised two red flags that caught Herbert's attention. He reminded readers that the government had confiscated silver bullion from American citizens in 1934 at the arbitrary price of 50¢ an ounce and suggested it could happen again: "In the U.S. there is a lack of freedom, a complete absence of privacy, and little safety for investors who hold their investments (especially silver) in the U.S."[77] He suggested storing silver in a Swiss bank because "there is a maximum of freedom, complete privacy, and a very high level of safety for investors." Herbert knew that Smith's suspicion of the U.S. government paled compared with Bunker's mistrust, so he would recommend they rent Switzerland as a big safe deposit box. But Herbert had trouble with Smith's second warning.

Jerome Smith did not like the Commodity Exchange. He began by saying, "Silver futures markets are a way of speculating in silver, not of investing in silver. Prices for future delivery are more volatile than bullion prices—the most distant months being most volatile."[78] Smith referred to Comex silver as a "paper market" because few buyers took delivery of the underlying metal, which meant that trading volume could far exceed the physical supply of bullion. He added that "this is a market for full time professional traders and floor brokers seeking short-term trading profits" and warned that a floor broker will "try to persuade you to buy and sell on short term price movements." He suggested ignoring Comex and using your favorite Swiss bank both as broker and for storage.

Smith was right about speculators trading on the Commodity Exchange and that trading volume surpassed physical supplies, but Bunker and Herbert had no alternative for the Hunt-size accumulation they had in mind. Comex was the most liquid market in the world in part because short-term traders attracted large orders from around the globe, producing a competitive price. Handy & Harman had switched to Comex for bullion quotes and Eastman Kodak used Comex to hedge their physical silver exposure. Speculators had replaced government bureaucrats in determining silver prices after the U.S. Treasury stopped wholesaling the white metal to industry. There was no escape, not even for the Swiss bankers who watched Comex for price discovery just like everyone else. Herbert designed a modified blueprint for accumulating silver on the Commodity Exchange, a buying program that nearly destroyed Henry Jarecki.

CHAPTER 16

HEAVYWEIGHT FIGHT

BUNKER AND HERBERT HUNT HAD 2,000 DECEMBER FUTURES contracts in their brokerage accounts on Monday, December 3, 1973, each contract conferring the right to take delivery of 10,000 ounces of silver, for a total of 20 million ounces of the white metal, the same amount that all of French industry consumed the year before.[1] During November Bunker's favorite floor broker on Comex, Alvin Brodsky, had purchased those contracts for the Hunts by lifting offers from willing sellers at prices ranging from $2.79 to 2.96 per ounce. On December 3 the price of silver stood at $3.04, so the Hunt brothers had a paper profit of more than three million dollars.[2] Any other speculator would have sold those contracts and taken the money to the bank rather than pay for the underlying bullion as required during the so-called delivery month, when December futures contracts expire. But not the Hunts, who wanted profits together with the underlying metal and considered their December holdings like an appetizer at a Texas barbecue. Bunker and Herbert remained in the background while brokerage firms like Bache & Company took delivery of the 20 million ounces on their behalf, paying the full $60 million as required.[3] The tactic made headlines.

On Wednesday, December 12 the business and financial correspondent of the *Christian Science Monitor* raised the question, "Who's trying to corner the market in silver?" and speculated that Bache had been instructed to pay for the metal by "Bunker Hunt, son of H.L. Hunt, Texas billionaire."[4] The word "corner" in the headline refers to when buyers of futures contracts accumulate the underlying commodity to prevent sellers of futures from delivering as required. It is sometimes called a squeeze, with the longs (buyers) squeezing the shorts (sellers) into a corner. If the shorts are forced to buy back their contracts at artificially high prices, it is called manipulation. Proving manipulation, however, requires demonstrating intent and suffers the same ambiguity as pornography, with an equally long history in commercial intercourse that gets resolved only in court. The press quoted Charles Stahl, publisher of *Green's Commodity Market Comments*, who claimed that Bache had acted for Bunker Hunt, saying that he noticed buying of the "nearby December" contract on Comex about a month ago, but he doubted a manipulative squeeze, adding, "Mr. Hunt is buying the silver as an investment, not as a speculation." Stahl was right but after a repeat performance by Bunker in February 1974, Congress took notice.

On Monday, February 11, 1974, *Barron's* newspaper, an influential financial weekly, reported that Bunker Hunt had recently bought 2,700 futures contracts giving him rights to 27 million ounces of silver over the next four months and suggested he was "willing to accept delivery of the bullion, an unusual stance."[5] The cash price of the white metal had jumped to a new world record, $5.37 per ounce on February 11, bringing the Hunt profit on the original 20 million ounces to $50 million, making even Bunker smile while reading the racing results.[6] Comex silver traders had learned to watch Alvin Brodsky, short in stature but with the clout of a giant, thanks to his Texas clients. The press described the action: "Each morning . . . just prior to the 10 o'clock bell that signals the opening of business in silver futures . . . traders' eyes flick almost involuntarily in the direction of Irv Brodsky [*sic*] . . . Is he buying or selling, the smart ones ask. When Brodsky buys, then they buy." *Barron's* offered this adult version of follow-the-leader as "one way to explain the incredible rise in the price of silver" and suggested that "Hunt would be the biggest single silver winner in recorded history" if he could realize a similar profit on his new contracts.

Silver prices rose following the *Barron's* article, reaching $6.70 an ounce on Tuesday, February 26, the highest level to date and marking a speculative frenzy that more than doubled prices since the beginning of December.[7] Some blamed the Hunts for the price bubble but even their massive purchases of almost 50 million ounces would have caused just a temporary boom, like a summer thunderstorm that quickly dissipates, without strong underlying fundamentals.[8] *Barron's* explained that the "Brodsky-Hunt Theory . . . is only one minor influence on silver's price" and listed fundamental forces driving up demand for the white metal, including runaway inflation, the Arab oil embargo following the October 1973 Yom Kippur War, silver's demand-supply imbalance, and the strength of gold.[9] The *New York Times* reported that "record prices for gold in Europe contributed to new highs in silver futures," which may have been true, although gold had risen from $100 to $175 since early December while silver eclipsed that rate of increase by jumping from $3.04 to $6.70.[10] Silver has always been more volatile than gold because it is a smaller market, so equal speculative dollars make a bigger impact, but many in Congress worried that the Hunt trading was designed to make a big splash, like a cannonball dive into a small pond.

Congress held hearings in 1974 to establish the Commodities Futures Trading Commission (CFTC) to regulate all futures trading to replace the Commodity Exchange Authority, established in 1936 with a mandate limited to futures markets in traditional agricultural products like wheat, soybeans, and corn. The growth of futures trading in nonagricultural goods like copper, silver, and lumber spurred the new legislation as did the potential for fraud and manipulation in these newer markets. Congressman Fernand St. Germain, representing Rhode Island, the center of silver manufacturing in the United States and home to the New England Manufacturing Jewelers and Silversmiths Association, clamored for relief. He cited the Hunt accumulation and revived the historic battle between America's East Coast manufacturing and western mining interests: "Silver is an unregulated commodity and apparently there is no way to prevent an individual from holding for personal gain an unlimited quantity. . . . I submit that these multimillionaires acting in unison should not be allowed to hold the silver-using industries at ransom."[11] He then added a broader concern: "It is difficult to be sympathetic to two oil barons whose thirst for personal gain and further enhancement are having the result of forcing silver prices upward, of adding another inflationary factor to the economy." Congressman St. Germain warned his House colleagues when debating the CFTC bill: "These practices raise the question as to whether an investigation should be made . . . to prevent the cornering of the market by a few individuals."

St. Germain made his constituents proud. Although the Hunts were never formally charged with manipulation, Congress gave silver special treatment in the Commodity Futures Trading Commission Act, requiring that "the Commission should take all steps necessary to ensure that on the effective date of the Act, silver futures trading will be effectively regulated."[12] The legislation specifically recommended "investigations" and regulations "on the proper speculative limits for silver futures trading." But many dismissed the danger, including Henry Jarecki, chairman of Mocatta Metals Corporation. When a reporter asked Henry whether the Hunts were behind the explosion in silver prices, he said, "I tend not to believe it."[13] He would suffer the consequences.

◆ ◆ ◆

Henry Jarecki had built Mocatta into a trading powerhouse after just four years in existence, growing the company into the largest bullion dealer in the United States according to his calculations.[14] Henry had expanded beyond the narrow arbitrage business that had lured him away from medicine and had become a dealer specializing in silver bullion. Jarecki courted all the major silver-producing countries in the world, including the big three, Mexico, Peru, and Canada, and visited the largest consuming companies, focusing on Kodak in Rochester, New York, and 3M, formerly Minnesota Mining and Manufacturing, in Maplewood, Minnesota. With contacts on both the production and consumption sides of the market, Mocatta became the premier middleman, buying at its bid price and selling at its offer to earn the spread, similar to the used-car business. A used-car dealer buys Chevrolets and Hondas from owners wanting a change and sells those cars to drivers who want to buy, making money on the price markup and rapid turnover. Dealers also try to avoid a big inventory of unsold cars.

Mocatta bought and sold physical bullion but it was usually for future delivery at a guaranteed price. For example, Henry's traders might arrange to buy silver from Mexico in three months at an agreed-upon bid price of $5.00 an ounce and to sell silver to Kodak in three months at an agreed-upon offer price of $5.10 an ounce. Mocatta earned the middleman's ten-cent spread with no risk if buying and selling interests balanced, but that was not always the case. Mocatta had to quote bids and offers continuously to attract business, to be a reliable marketmaker providing liquidity, but orders on either side could run fast or slow.[15] Excessive selling by Mexico and insufficient buying by Kodak increased Mocatta's silver inventory, bringing losses if prices declined, and less selling by Mexico and vigorous buying by Kodak left Mocatta short of silver inventory, producing losses if prices rose. Henry had been a pioneer in computerizing his business to stabilize inventory: when too much accumulated, his program recommended lower prices to buy less, and when inventory fell short, it recommended higher prices to buy more. But that delicate dance faltered just when he needed it most.

Henry romanced his potential business contacts to keep them close, especially Luis Chico, deputy manager of the International Division of Banco de Mexico, the Mexican central bank, which managed that country's considerable silver exports. Luis was thin, always well dressed, and the perfect gentleman. Henry recalls, "When we were out to dinner and a woman left the table for personal reasons, Luis would jump to his feet and escort her to the powder room."[16] Henry knew the women were pleased and envied Chico's skill at turning a cartoonish gesture into attractive manners. During one of those dinners in 1971, when Henry was just getting started, Luis said he wanted to sell a substantial accumulation of scrap silver in the bank's vault and wondered whether Mocatta would help. Henry recognized the opportunity to make a lasting friendship and bought the scrap silver at the closing price on Comex, a far too generous number considering the transportation and refining costs he would incur. Henry expected the gesture to pay dividends, which it did.

A Chicago banker introduced Henry to the Hunt brothers soon after his deal with Chico, and he flew from New York to Dallas to offer his brokerage services.[17] They picked him up at the airport in a beat-up old Cadillac, Herbert behind the wheel and Bunker riding shotgun in the front. Henry sat in the back, enjoying the wealthiest chauffeur service in the world, until they arrived at Bunker's two-thousand-acre Circle T ranch outside Dallas. Henry recalls the wide-open space, the endless herd of cattle, and the suddenly bumpy ride along a rutted dirt road. It was a bad omen, and he recognized a problem during his sales pitch when Bunker disappeared and was found later sound asleep on a couch.

The failure to corral the Hunts left Henry stranded when silver exploded in late 1973. With Comex prices reaching new highs just about every day, Mocatta's big silver-using clients, Kodak and 3M, began buying for future delivery at a much faster pace than producers like Mexico and Peru were selling. Mocatta's traders tried to restore balance by raising the bid price to buy more and raising the offer price to reduce sales. But their measured responses fell short as silver raced into uncharted territory just as it had after the Crime of 1873, a century earlier. This time prices went up rather than down but caused similar disruption. Towards the end of February 1974 Mocatta was short 5 million ounces of silver, meaning it had promised to deliver 5 million ounces more than it owned, and the run-up in prices had produced a loss of over $20 million.[18] Moreover, that loss would mushroom if Mocatta tried to buy the 5 million ounces on Comex to make up its shortfall. Floor traders monitoring the Hunt accumulation would force Mocatta to pay dearly for the silver needed to correct its error, squeezing the life out of Henry's young company. Mercy in the futures ring is as rare as at the poker table. The mistake hurt Henry's pride, and the loss would make his London partners think he had been speculating rather than running a reliable business, that he had misrepresented himself to Jocelyn Hambros. Henry recalls, "I was worried about damaging our still young relationship with Hambros Bank."[19] The crisis threatened Mocatta Metals Corporation with bankruptcy.

Henry needed 5 million ounces of silver without going public. He knew that Banco de Mexico had a vault full of the white metal so he called his friend Luis Chico, who agreed to sell him 5 million ounces directly but wanted a ten-cent premium over Comex.[20] Henry said yes before Chico could hang up the phone, knowing that trying to buy that amount quickly on the Exchange would cost much more.

He had escaped disaster because of who he knew, a lesson he would remember for the rest of his career. He also admitted feeling much better about "buying that lousy scrap silver from Chico."[21]

◆ ◆ ◆

Luis Chico bailed out Henry Jarecki and also slaked the speculative binge in silver. He had been sitting on 45 million ounces of the white metal and the lucrative sale to Henry was the first course in a sumptuous feast on fattened silver prices.[22] Henry handled the sale of Chico's remaining 40 million ounces on Comex, dumping the last 4 million at the peak cash price of $6.70 per ounce on Tuesday, February 26, 1974, into the anxious hands of Alvin Brodsky. But fewer speculators wanted the white metal now that it was in abundant supply and prices collapsed. On Tuesday, March 5, the cash price of silver hit $4.98, a 25% decline in a week, lopping $80 million off the value of Bunker and Herbert's 47-million-ounce position. The Hunts learned what Treasury Secretary Henry Morgenthau had discovered forty years earlier—the law of supply and demand applies to everyone. Bunker would need help to realize his dreams for the white metal.

Silver remained in the $5.00 range through April, leaving the Hunt brothers with a hefty paper profit on their overall position. They began to take delivery on their 2,700 expiring futures contracts when Bunker made a cameo appearance at the Commodity Exchange in Lower Manhattan just to view the combat zone. His presence momentarily silenced the haggling coming from the two big circular arenas where copper and silver traded, as everyone turned to see the round and rumpled Texan who had jolted the market. He remained unbowed in his conviction that anything is better than paper dollars, saying before he left the battleground: "If you don't like gold, use silver. Or diamonds. Or copper. But something."[23] Bunker made sense, even though commodities, especially silver, fluctuated in value like all risky investments. Consumer prices had risen by more than 3% during the first quarter of 1974, on pace for an annual rate of inflation exceeding 12%, which meant that during the year the dollar would shrink in value to about what 88¢ could buy.[24]

The white metal was $4 an ounce in late 1974, well below its recent record but, considering its long and wounded history, the equivalent of Pike's Peak. Silver had been a second-class monetary metal since 1873, begging for a political handout from the likes of Key Pittman and FDR, but had become a hard asset in a world of fiat currency, a hedge against inflation, and its elevated price compared with Alexander Hamilton's $1.29 reflected the new reality. Alan Greenspan, President Ford's chief economic adviser and a future Federal Reserve chairman, gave investors good reason to worry that inflation would continue. In the *Economic Report of the President* covering 1974, he documented an accelerating inflation since 1965 and attributed the new trend to "increasing government expenditures along with monetary policies that were appreciably more expansionary" than in the past.[25] Silver was an attractive hedge against inflation but would have to compete with gold in America after December 31, 1974, when the forty-year ban against U.S. citizens investing in the yellow metal ended. Silver remained the favorite of the Hunts, however, who worried that gold was vulnerable to political pressure, which is why they removed their hoard of the white metal from American soil.

After family patriarch H.L. Hunt died on November 29, 1974, and before the first and second families began to bicker, Bunker and Herbert put Randy Kreiling, a second family brother-in-law who had made money speculating in commodities, in charge of transferring their silver to Switzerland. Flying 47,000 bars of the white metal, each weighing close to seventy pounds, from New York to Zurich required attention to detail, especially with the Hunt version of military secrecy.[26] General George Patton, America's premier tank commander in World War II, gave logistics the highest priority by warning, "The officer who doesn't know his communications and supply . . . is totally useless."[27] Brother-in-law Randy, a square-jawed risk-taker in his midtwenties, took his job as seriously as if he were reinforcing front-line troops. He began by holding a sharpshooting contest among the cowboys he employed at the second family's Circle K Ranch to choose the guards who would accompany the white metal on its transatlantic journey. He

FIGURE 16. Silver bar pedigree: 999.9% pure.

then chartered a fleet of Boeing 707 jets, blocked out the vendor's name with tape so that only the registration numbers showed, and had the planes flown to New York in the middle of the night. A convoy of rented armored trucks brought the silver bars from Comex warehouses to the airport, and the guards then divided the bullion among the aircraft, making certain that the weight was evenly distributed within each plane to insure a safe flight. Another escort of armored trucks met the planes in Zurich and delivered the precious metal to six secret storage locations.

Bunker always flew commercial but did not blink at chartering aircraft to transport his silver out of the country. His mistrust of the U.S. government, a suspicion bordering on paranoia, justified the intricate operation. Some experts suggest that paranoia is a genetic marker for success but more likely it resembles a heightened sense of smell, detecting dangerous odors when everyone else perceives perfume in the air. Henry Jarecki suffered the same psychosis, suggesting that prolonged exposure to the white metal's tarnished history promotes the disease. But Jarecki's anxiety was more personal than Bunker's. He wanted to buy an island as insurance against chaos in the world and recalls, "I think I was motivated at least in part by my childhood experience fleeing Germany. I wanted a haven where I could be safe."[28] In early 1975 he bought Guana Island, 850 acres of tropical forest and white-sand beaches in the British Virgin Islands, which he proceeded to develop with a conservationist's eye. Bunker could have afforded a similar retreat but instead spent his time and money touring the globe to enlist allies in the silver struggle, a battle that would launch the white metal into the stratosphere. His courtship of the Arabs made him super rich and world famous but, like his Libyan oil venture, ended in disaster, with an assist from Henry Jarecki.

CHAPTER 17

SAUDI CONNECTION

KING ABDUL-AZIZ IBN SAUD SUBDUED THE BEDOUIN FACTIONS
OF the Arabian Peninsula and through a series of tribal marriages
to more than one hundred women, four at a time as permitted by
Islamic law, unified the desert country in 1932.[1] Well over six-feet
tall, with a warrior's mustache and pointed beard, framed by a kef-
fiyeh, Ibn Saud ruled like a medieval monarch over four million
subjects until his death in 1953, but his imprint endures in more
than just the name, Saudi Arabia. He left a legacy in power, religion,
and monetary affairs.

Ibn Saud spawned the oil wealth that sustains the country by
granting drilling rights to several major oil companies, including
Standard Oil of California and the Texas Oil Company. The black
gold began to flow in 1938 and has continued since. He belonged
to a strict religious Islamic sect, Wahhabism, which made him abstain from the pleasures of alcohol but encouraged conjugal pur-
suits that sired 140 known children. His insistence on adherence
to Sharia law remains a hallmark of the Saudi penal system, such
as punishing stealing by amputating a thief's right hand. And two
years before he died, Ibn Saud engaged Arthur Young, a former
financial adviser to the Chinese Nationalist government, to mod-
ernize the nation's monetary system. Until then the Saudi riyal,
containing .344 troy ounces of silver, was the only circulating currency in the country, two pounds of the white metal for each man,
woman, and child.[2] Young explained, "The people have relied upon
the 'intrinsic' metal content of money rather than upon government measures . . . and thus they tend to distrust paper money."[3]
Arthur Young modernized the financial system by establishing the
Saudi Arabian Monetary Agency, called SAMA, which still manages
the country's monetary reserves. But the full-bodied riyal had been
baked into the country's culture like the desert sand, so at the outset

SAMA linked the riyal to silver.[4] Young said, "Silver coinage was more basic than gold . . . the Riyal was the ordinary money of the people."[5] Nelson Bunker Hunt had good reason to visit the Saudi kingdom.

In mid-March 1975, after Bunker returned to the United States from Iran, where he failed to convince the Shah to invest in silver, he arranged through a trusted intermediary to meet with sixty-eight-year-old King Faisal of Saudi Arabia.[6] Faisal was the third son of Ibn Saud, had reigned over the desert kingdom since 1964, and could have been Bunker's fraternity brother. Although an absolute monarch like his father, Faisal was unpretentious, using a single car rather than the royal fleet, was married to one woman although permitted four, and was most famous as a staunch anti-communist and anti-Zionist. He dismissed the Soviet Union's pro-Arab policies with Machiavellian creativity: "Communism is a Zionist creation designed to fulfill the aims of Zionism. They are only pretending to work against each other in the Middle East."[7] Bunker needed barely a month of Faisal's oil revenues to make a major impact on silver, but on March 25, 1975, just days before Bunker's scheduled departure, King Faisal was shot to death in his palace in Riyadh.

The assassination smacked of a communist plot to destroy Faisal and Bunker in one shot, a reasonable suspicion from the Texan's perspective, but Faisal was gunned down by a thirty-year-old nephew who had undergone psychiatric treatment and had sought revenge for Saudi police killing his brother years earlier.[8] The royal family moved quickly to fill the void, naming Faisal's younger brother Khalid Ibn Abdul-Aziz as the new king. Khalid was not nearly as well known abroad as Faisal, so Bunker had to put the Saudi plan on the backburner, where it simmered while he cooked up a scheme to evade U.S. regulations.

✦ ✦ ✦

The United States ranks just below Mexico, Canada, and Peru in world silver production, but more than 65% of its annual output of about 35 million ounces is a by-product of base metal mining, especially lead, copper, and zinc.[9] The Sunshine Mining Company in the Coeur d'Alene region of northern Idaho is an exception, devoted almost exclusively to the white metal, which is why Bunker and Herbert, through their company Great Western United, tried to gain control of Sunshine Mining on March 21, 1977, by tendering for one-third of the outstanding stock.[10] Listed for trading on the New York Stock Exchange, Sunshine opened in the 1880s and became the largest silver producer in the United States, extracting as much as 6 million ounces a year in the mid-1960s.[11] Production had been interrupted by a fire in 1972 that killed ninety-one miners and by a strike in 1976 that lasted most of the year, but in 1977 the company regained its prominence as the nation's leading producer.[12] The *New York Times* explained, under the banner headline "Sunshine Mining: Why Hunts Want It," that some local shareholders believed "Sunshine Mining is the most poorly managed company in the state," and "stockholders have been looking for a way to rid the company of its inept leadership, and Great Western seems to be a sound solution."[13] All of which may be true, but Sunshine's main attraction to Bunker related to a bizarre connection between silver and soybeans.

Starting in mid-1976 and continuing into 1977, Nelson Bunker Hunt dreamt about soybeans, not because he considered switching to the protein-rich legume from his favorite diet of spareribs and vanilla ice cream, but because he thought the 1976 bean crop had been poor, which would boost prices. Soybeans traded alongside wheat and corn, the other two major U.S. agricultural crops, in the futures market on the Chicago Board of Trade (CBOT). Located at the intersection of LaSalle Street and West Jackson Boulevard in downtown Chicago, the CBOT is the oldest futures exchange in the United States, dating from 1848. It was also the largest futures exchange during the 1970s, with a trading room six-stories high and bigger than a football field. The Chicago Board of Trade had traditionally specialized in agricultural commodities, reflecting Chicago's stockyards and railroad connections, and viewed New York's Commodity Exchange as a newcomer to futures trading, a competitor to be discouraged like an unwelcome immigrant. Comex introduced the silver futures contract in 1963, and the CBOT countered with a competing contract in 1969.[14] New York retained its dominance in silver because an established liquid market usually prevails, but the competition between Comex and the CBOT pleased the Hunts, especially after the soybean caper.[15]

Bunker began buying soybean futures, anticipating prices would rise, but regulations at the CBOT restricting each speculator to 600 contracts, controlling 3 million bushels of beans, interfered with his banquet-size plans.[16] These so-called position limits prevent a speculator from becoming dominant, cornering the market, and manipulating prices. Bunker and Herbert viewed regulations as a minor nuisance, like a traffic detour, and circumvented them by making the soybean speculation a family affair. They opened brokerage accounts in their own names as well as for their adult children: Bunker's son Houston; Bunker's daughters, Elizabeth, Ellen, and Mary; and Herbert's son Douglas. Each chipped in as if buying a family birthday present, for a combined 22 million bushels, equaling about one-third of the entire U.S. crop. The Commodity Futures Trading Commission accused the Hunts of violating position limits, claiming that Bunker and Herbert manipulated prices by trading these accounts together, and demanded they sell contracts until they held only 3 million bushels, the maximum for a single speculator. The CFTC bolstered its argument by pointing out that Houston Hunt, at the time an undergraduate at the University of Tulsa, had allegedly "conducted his soybean trading from a public pay phone at the Phi Kappa Alpha Fraternity House."[17]

Bunker responded to the CFTC's friendly request by accusing the agency "of doing what they accuse the Hunts of," which is "manipulat[ing] the price of soybeans" by "trying to repeal the law of supply and demand. Soybeans are in short supply."[18] The dispute ended in court, with each side partially vindicated, but the episode convinced Bunker to pursue Sunshine Mining.[19]

Speculators in futures markets, like the Hunts, absorb risk from hedgers, helping companies like Kodak avoid volatile prices, but also resemble gamblers at the blackjack table, always looking for an edge. Futures exchanges impose position limits on speculators to keep them in line, so that prices reflect commercial value, but allow hedgers a free rein so they can conduct their business. Bunker wanted to control Sunshine Mining Company, a natural hedger in the silver market, either selling contracts to protect unmined reserves or buying contracts when production declines, to avoid position limits and to speculate surreptitiously. The CFTC had authorized position limits in silver but neither Comex nor the CBOT had imposed them in 1977 because the two exchanges were competing for business. Bunker's bid for Sunshine Mining prepared him for when the exchanges would be forced to act.[20]

Bunker added more insurance by shifting some of his silver buying from Comex to the CBOT, taking delivery of 50 million ounces in Chicago through Great Western United.[21] He discovered that Mocatta Metals owned a storage facility that was a Comex-approved warehouse for silver, and he wanted to avoid snooping by Henry Jarecki.[22] Bunker and Henry had already tangled in February 1974, the Texan pushing Mocatta to the brink of bankruptcy by driving up prices, and Henry counterpunching by selling Bunker 4 million ounces of the white metal at $6.70 an ounce, the highest level to date. But like most competitors, Bunker and Henry did business when it served their purpose. The Hunts borrowed money from Mocatta using silver as collateral because Henry made it attractive.

When the Hunts took delivery of silver, either on Comex or on the CBOT, they had to pay the full value of the underlying metal instead of just the good faith deposit, called margin, required on futures contacts. On March 1, 1977, for example, each Comex or CBOT contract covered 5,000 ounces of metal so at $5.00 per ounce the total bill came to $25,000 per contract.[23] Taking delivery on 2,000 contracts for a total of 10 million ounces cost $50 million, and not even the Hunts carried that in their wallet, so they usually borrowed part of what they needed. Borrowing $40 million and investing only $10 million of their own, for example, also magnified their potential returns. A 10% jump in the price of silver from $5.00 to $5.50 produced a profit of $5 million or a 50% return on their $10 million investment—the magic of leverage. When prices decline, however, leverage works in reverse and magnifies losses, but that did not worry the Hunts back then. They borrowed money from the usual sources to finance their silver—banks and brokerage houses—and from Mocatta Metals because it charged a low interest rate.

Mocatta had become a bullion department store by mid-1977, the Macy's of precious metals. The company still bought pre-1965 silver coins and melted them into bars, the arbitrage that had started Henry's new career, but it also bought and sold physical gold and silver throughout the world, stored bullion for investors, executed orders for customers on Comex and the CBOT, bought and sold customized gold and silver options, and leased the physical metal to those needing it temporarily. Mocatta had been unsuccessful in becoming the Hunt's floor broker on the exchanges, but the company's bullion-leasing operation helped Henry turn Bunker and Herbert into clients.

When Bunker borrowed money from a bank to take delivery of silver, he gave the white metal as collateral for the loan, which the bank held in its vault. When Bunker did the same transaction with Mocatta, Henry took the silver and leased it for a fee to his customers, perhaps to Kodak, 3M, or DuPont, who were temporarily short of the white metal needed for X-ray film production. If the bank charged Bunker 6%, Mocatta charged less, depending on how much it made on leasing Bunker's bullion, which is why the Hunts borrowed money from Mocatta even though they worried about Jarecki—it was cheaper. Henry never told the Hunts what he was doing, nor did he have to, since this was normal industry practice. After the price of silver rose, Henry used Bunker's silver as collateral to expand his own borrowing from the banks. When the Hunts discovered what Henry had done, Herbert, who was in charge of the fine print, complained that Jarecki "always had conflicts of interest" and "when he told you something you had to look at it with suspicion." [24] Herbert, the boss of details, should have read the loan agreement more carefully but he was right to worry.

◆ ◆ ◆

Silver perked up in October 1978, pushing above the $6 level for the first time since May 1974, just as Bunker renewed his pursuit of the Saudis.[25] The white metal's four-year slumber had bottomed in the first quarter of 1976, when it traded as low as $3.85 an ounce, and the climb since then mirrored the rise in gold, which increased from $130 an ounce to over $225.[26] The precious metals rode a wave of displeasure with the dollar throughout the world as American inflation hit record peacetime levels. International investors sold the greenback as though the U.S. currency were confetti so that a dollar cost only 1.8 German marks in October 1978, compared with 2.4 marks two years earlier, a decline of about 25%. Bunker's prediction that anything, but especially silver, was better than paper dollars found an eager audience in Paris following the prestigious Prix de l'Arc de Triomphe race on October 1, 1978. His horse Trillion, owned with his friend Edward Stephenson but bred in Bunker's Bluegrass Farm in central Kentucky and ridden by famed jockey Willie Shoemaker, came in second—a performance that gained attention from Saudi Arabian royalty.[27]

Horseracing had been a favorite pastime in the Arabian Peninsula for centuries, and the founding father of the country, King Abdul-Aziz Ibn Saud, had infused a passion for the sport in his bloodline. One of his sons, Crown Prince Abdullah, standing second in succession for the Saudi throne at age fifty-four in 1978, Commander of the National Guard, and an accomplished horseman, had founded the Equestrian Club of Riyadh in 1965. Abdullah had thirty wives (no more than four at a time, of course) and one of his former brothers-in-law, Mahmoud Fustok, had attended the October 1st Paris race on a mission for the Crown Prince that brought him into friendly competition with Bunker.[28]

Fustok was in his early forties, his face dominated by thick lips and slicked-back hair, someone who looked out of place at a friendly poker game, but a close business relationship with Abdullah made him quite popular. He came to Paris for the horse auction at the Polo de Bagatelle sporting club on the day following the big race, looking to buy a future winner for his sometime brother-in-law. He was joined by Naji Nahas, a debonair thirty-five-year-old, with a square face and thinning hair, who was born in Lebanon but had lived in Brazil for a number of years investing in real estate, including some deals through Fustok for the Saudis. Both Fustok and Nahas had taken advantage of the royal family's reticence to participate directly in commercial ventures, funneling sovereign wealth into preferred business activities in their own names, but returning the profits and principal, minus a finder's fee, to their imperial patrons. Wealthy merchants from Riyadh and bankers from the more cosmopolitan Jeddah, a port city on the Red Sea, would also front for princely undertakings.

The auction at the Polo de Bagatelle club was an annual affair that had brought Bunker to the French capital before, but this was one of the few times he lost the bidding war for a horse. Fustok had Abdullah's money to spend, and the Saudi royal family could easily match Bunker's wealth barrel for barrel. The loss may have paid for itself, however, when Fustok and Nahas agreed to join Bunker following the competition for drinks and a conversation about horses and oil, which somehow ended with silver. Judging by what happened next, Bunker had delivered an inspired message.

CHAPTER 18

SILVER SOARS

THE ARRIVAL OF ISLAMIC MILITANCY IN IRAN MADE LIFE EASIER for Bunker Hunt, driving the white metal above $7 an ounce for the first time in history on Monday, February 5, 1979.[1] According to James Sinclair, head of a brokerage firm bearing his name: "Anxiety has been heightened by the weekend events in Iran, which promises to raise the price of oil and reduce American and European influence in the Mideast."[2] The Ayatolah Khomeini, a white-bearded Muslim cleric wearing a black turban and flowing black robe, had arrived in Teheran from Paris on Thursday, February 1, two weeks after revolutionary demonstrators pushed the reigning Shah into exile. Khomeini greeted his supporters gathered at Teheran airport with, "Our final victory will come when all foreigners are out of the country. I beg God to cut off the hands of all evil foreigners and all their helpers."[3] Over the weekend the *New York Times* elaborated on the Ayatollah's return from his fourteen-year separation:[4] "Like Lenin returning to Russia after the overthrow of the Czar, Ayatollah Ruhollah Khomeini came home last week to complete his own very different form of revolution." The *Times* added a dark prophetic note: "The process in Iran could be as chaotic and bloody as the consolidation of Bolshevik power." When markets opened on Monday, February 5, investors grabbed for the white metal like it was a life preserver, starting a buying frenzy that would raise its value from $7 to $50 an ounce in less than twelve months, a sevenfold increase that has never been matched before or since. The difficulty of disentangling the role of worried speculators from scheming manipulators in the price explosion made Bunker smile.

◆ ◆ ◆

Silver's upturn in February 1979 raised concern over a potential squeeze, and Henry Jarecki responded to the anxiety as though he were still making rounds at the Yale-New Haven Hospital. He had dispatched Mocatta teams to cities throughout the country, such as Columbus, Ohio, Des Moines, Iowa, and Springfield, Illinois, to buy silver jewelry, tea sets, and flatware from people needing cash more than shiny antiques.[5] Three or four Mocatta employees would advertise their arrival in regional newspapers, rent a motel room for the weekend, and wait for locals carrying worn shopping bags filled with silver artifacts wanting premium prices for their metal. Henry described the heartbreaking scene of a teary-eyed elderly couple watching Mocatta employees stomp their family's soup tureen and tea set into flattened disks for efficient transport in a barrel. "We had no reason to do otherwise," he said. "Our job was not art preservation; it was to ship fully-filled barrels of silver to refineries."[6] He had heard rumblings of a corner in silver during his travels promoting Mocatta's expertise: "Silver traders have started to talk about a topic they find interesting and disconcerting: Can there be a squeeze in silver, and if so, what does this mean?"[7]

Jarecki answered the question by writing an article in the March 1979 issue of *Euromoney*, a popular monthly business and financial magazine with worldwide distribution, concluding that silver could be squeezed because "the low level of above-ground stocks . . . makes the market vulnerable to physical dislocation."[8] He suggested that there was "far less than a billion ounces" of the white metal in the world, and someone controlling "150 million ounces . . . might well succeed in achieving the price they ask."[9] He added that a squeeze required "a substantial enterprise willing to undertake a massive silver purchasing program."[10]

Henry may have sounded professorial, which he sometimes could not help, but to advertise Mocatta's skill he added a practical blueprint for how to do it. His article highlighted "Three Ways to Squeeze the Silver Market" in bold letters like on a highway billboard so that no one could miss the message.[11] The three methods were: first, outright purchases of futures contracts on a particular delivery month, say December 1979; second, balanced purchases and sales of different delivery months, called switches, spreads, or straddles, such as buying 150 million ounces of December 1979 futures and selling the same amount of March 1980 futures; and third, the most complicated scheme, unbalanced purchases and sales, such as buying 175 million ounces of December 1979 futures and selling 150 million ounces of March 1980 futures.

Henry admitted that the simplest method, outright purchases, was potentially the most profitable but was also the most expensive to implement because the good faith margin deposit required by the futures exchanges for outright purchases was much greater than for spreads. And while spreads did not add to the overall demand for the white metal, they did put pressure on the so-called long leg of the straddle, December in the example, forcing the shorts to deliver silver during that month. Jarecki promoted spreads as the best way to squeeze the market but warned of the danger when the speculator wanted to capitalize on the price increase. "The problem is that if he then wants to sell, his selling, and that of those who watch his activities, rapidly causes the price to fall; the price shoots downward even more rapidly than it rose."[12] He cited the price decline of 1974 after the Hunts stopped buying to illustrate the speculator's problem and suggested the more prudent unbalanced purchases and sales as the best strategy. Henry never disclosed how to avoid losses but advertised his expertise to do the job: "This route obviously takes the greatest amount of skill and (need one add?) the involvement of experienced market professionals."[13]

Henry had no interest in cornering the silver market but wanted the commissions the Hunts would generate in the process. In retrospect, he says the *Euromoney* article was "essentially an ad for Mocatta saying to the Hunts, 'You want to do this? Come and talk to us.' "[14] Henry was never accused of aiding and abetting a squeeze because, he says, "The Hunts followed my roadmap to the letter with one exception: they didn't ask us to help them." He then adds, "Not calling us might have been their biggest mistake."

✦ ✦ ✦

Bunker and Herbert Hunt did not follow Henry Jarecki's blueprint "to the letter," but they paid close attention. On Friday, May 18, 1979, Herbert wrote to Scott Dial, a commodities broker with Clayton Brokerage in Dallas, who he had done business with before: "Certainly appreciated receiving the copies of your talk and the article by Dr. Jerecki [*sic*]. Had the opportunity to read both of these last night and found them extremely interested [*sic*]."[15] During subsequent courtroom testimony Herbert did not recall reading the *Euromoney* article, despite his letter to Dial, which he pointed out had not been signed, but the Hunts changed their trading strategy going forward in a number of ways, including using straddles for the first time, option two in Jarecki's list.[16] They also abandoned their pursuit of the Sunshine Mining Company in June 1979, after the company's management rejected their takeover price as inadequate.[17] Bunker could have continued to battle by raising his bid but he no longer needed Sunshine's cover to avoid potential speculative limits on trading. He had new partners with money to spare to pursue the white metal.

On Tuesday, July 24, 1979, the Hunts quietly entered into an agreement with two Saudi businessmen, Sheikh Ali bin Mussalem and Sheikh Mohammed Aboud Al-Amoudi, establishing the International Metals Investment Company, known as IMIC, a Bermuda-based company with the objective of accumulating silver.[18] The two sheikhs were wealthy but their main attraction to Bunker and Herbert came from their friendship with fellow Jeddah resident Prince Faisal, son of Crown Prince Abdullah, commander of the Saudi National Guard.[19] Mohammed Affara, the man who brought the two sides together, told Herbert that "Sheikh Ali was involved in representing the Saudi Arabian government."[20] The Hunts paid Affara a finder's fee of $1 million for access to the royal court.[21] It gave the Hunts ammunition to stoke the already explosive surge in silver prices, which had increased above $9 for the first time earlier in July, reflecting the growing frustration with economic and political conditions in America.

The annual rate of inflation in the United States had accelerated to over 13% during the first six months of 1979, a new peacetime record, forcing President Jimmy Carter into a ten-day stay at Camp David, the presidential country retreat in Maryland's Catoctin Mountains, for consultations with a cross section of Americans, including industrialists, labor leaders, economists, and pastors (not necessarily in that order).[22] Anyone coming to Camp David by car endured the double indignity of higher gas prices and long lines of cars snaked around service stations waiting to get to the fuel pump. The president blamed the gas shortage on "less oil than expected coming from Iran" since the Khomeini revolution, but one angry Massachusetts motorist broadened the blame: "Jimmy Carter . . . ought to hit those Texans and sheikhs who started this mess."[23] The press commented, "Until President Carter comes up with new energy and inflation policies the uncertainty that has dominated the precious metals market . . . is likely to continue."[24] But instead of offering a credible plan to reassure the public, Carter descended from his mountaintop retreat and gave a thirty-three-minute talk to the nation that made Jeremiah, the Biblical prophet of doom, sound like an optimist. He said that the emerging "crisis of confidence" was "a fundamental threat to American democracy" and continued as though he were on Bunker's payroll: "The phrase 'sound as a dollar' was an expression of absolute dependability until ten years of inflation began to shrink our dollar and our savings."[25]

Investors worry when the president of the United States bad-mouths the U.S. currency so they paid special attention to the *Wall Street Journal* headline on September 6, 1979, a day after traders returned from the Labor Day weekend and silver breached $11 an ounce: "Gold, Silver Prices' Unfathomable Surge Stirring Rumors of 'Big Money' Invasion."[26] The article dismissed "rumors of manipulation" as premature and quoted Norton Waltuch, a member of Comex and director of ContiCommodity Investor Services, a major futures brokerage firm, pointing to economic fundamentals: "Just look at the vast pools of money floating around the world. Paper currencies are declining. People who have it have to put their money somewhere."[27] Waltuch knew what he was talking about, having led the bidding for silver on the Comex trading floor and, according to the *Journal*, was "instrumental in spurring prices skyward."[28] Norton refused to identify his clients, but the press cited "widespread belief among speculators that Arab interests" are behind the accumulation.[29]

Norton Waltuch, bald except for a fringe of black hair skirting the crown of an egg-shaped head, had been manager since 1970 of the New York branch office of ContiCommodity Services, the brokerage subsidiary of Continental Grain, a family-run commodities giant founded in Belgium in the nineteenth century. The growth in futures markets during the second half of the 1970s helped Waltuch become a major revenue producer for the company but the explosion of silver prices after the 1979 Labor Day holiday turned the stocky trader into a movie star. According to the *Wall Street Journal* his mere "presence on the Comex floor, whether he is buying contracts or just watching, has been enough to send prices soaring."[30] An eye witness recalls that traders posted clerks along the hallway leading to the trading room, a cavernous structure housing Comex and her sister exchanges on the eighth floor of Four World Trade Center, to gain an advantage before Waltuch arrived.[31] A glimpse of his yellow trading jacket emerging from the elevator would start a price rally in the silver ring. Some spotters went to the seventh floor, where ContiCommodity offices were located, for an additional edge, watching if he took the elevator up to trade or down for lunch.

Waltuch sounded as though he were visiting the dentist's office when Alabama Senator Donald Stewart extracted the identity of ContiCommodity's clients during testimony at one of many subsequent congressional hearings on silver.[32]

STEWART (S): Could you tell us where the Arab participants . . . came from?

WALTUCH (W): Are you asking me Senator?

S: Yes.

W: I met one Saudi Arabian, and two or three Lebanese.

S: What is the name of the Saudi Arabian?

W: Mr. Fustok.

S: Could you give me the name of the other individual?

W: Mr. Nahas is a Lebanese, although he is a Brazilian citizen.

S: Where did you meet these people?

W: Mr. Fustok in Paris. Mr. Nahas in Geneva.

Senator Stewart then searched for a connection between the two men.

S: Was anybody else present in the meeting besides you and these individuals?

W: Well, when I had the meeting with Mr. Fustok, Mr. Nahas was present. When I met with Mr. Nahas there were two people from a company called Advicorp, which is a Geneva based management company.

Advicorp represented Mahmoud Fustok, so the senator probed further.[33]

S: Have you ever met Nelson Bunker Hunt?[34]

W: Yes.

S: Where and when did you meet Mr. Hunt?

W: I met him once in Kentucky . . . in July [1979].

S: That is all that took place during that particular period of time?

W: No . . . I met him again in September in Paris and in October in Zurich.

S: What did you discuss at those meetings?

W: Well . . . he was picking my brain and asking me what I thought about silver.

S: Did you solicit his account at that time?

W: No, sir.

S: Did you indicate to him at all that you were . . . trading for other accounts at that time?

W: Well anyone who follows the financial pages would know that I was greatly involved in silver.

S: Who else was involved at that time in those meetings?

W: Mr. Nahas was present.

S: Who else?

W: That is all.

Senator Stewart had just identified Waltuch's most important client, Naji Nahas, closing the loop that began in Paris on October 1, 1978. The CFTC later charged that Nahas and Bunker Hunt were "the principal axis of communication and coordination" in the scheme to corner the market for the white metal.[35]

❖ ❖ ❖

Silver manipulators needed more than just communication and coordination to drive up prices without getting caught by the authorities.

Increased global tension in the second half of 1979 covered their tracks by boosting the safe haven demand for gold, which spilled over into silver. On Tuesday, September 18, 1979, a historic jump in prices began in Hong Kong, while New York still slept, and spread with the sunrise to Europe and America, registering new world records in every trading center.[36] No one could explain exactly what had triggered the explosion but Rainer Gut, chief general manager at Credit Suisse Bank, pointed to a simmering international pressure cooker: "With political changes in Iran, the whole Middle East had become more fluid and unstable. We don't know what might happen in Saudi Arabia and other areas around the Persian Gulf. So, we're observing Middle Eastern buyers moving out of dollars and other paper currencies into gold."[37] The chief economist of the Salomon Brothers investment bank, Henry Kaufman, known as Dr. Doom for his dire predictions for inflation and interest rates, said: "In effect it's a vote against the established economic and financial system."[38]

The increase in gold by almost $25 an ounce to $376 in New York on September 18 made front page headlines in the *Washington Post*: "Frenzied Trading Sends Gold Price to Record High."[39] The 6.7% overnight jump delivered a message to political leaders, according to the *Post*: "Investors big and small . . . doubt governments have the ability or willingness to control the inflationary spiral."[40] Gold sent the message, but the price movement on September 18, four times larger than its normal daily price volatility, resembled a plodding freight train compared with silver's Amtrak express.[41] The white metal rose almost $2 an ounce to close at $15.78 on September 18, a spectacular 12.7% overnight jump, almost double the percentage change in gold.[42] The press described the yellow metal as the price leader and suggested that silver "soared sympathetically," but the normally more volatile white metal became a lightning rod for trouble.[43] The *Wall Street Journal* wrote, "Chaos has struck the silver market," and quoted one trader saying, "The market is out of control. People are really going to get hurt."[44] Which is why Bunker and Herbert Hunt visited Henry Jarecki to check on their business arrangement.

The Hunts had borrowed $50 million from Mocatta, a loan they had taken out to buy more silver when it was selling for about $5.50

an ounce, and had left 10.7 million ounces of the white metal with Mocatta as collateral. The $10 price increase since then gave the Hunts a billion-dollar profit on their 100-million-ounce accumulation but spawned rumors that Jarecki had been caught short, as in 1974, and the Hunts worried about the safety of their collateral.[45] The gossip had reached Washington, D.C., where a member of the CFTC said, "How did Henry get caught short? Usually he's a little smarter than that."[46] If Mocatta went bankrupt, the Hunts would have to stand in line with other creditors to get their precious metal back, so they wanted to repay their loan and take their bullion, which turned out to be as complicated as putting a man on the moon.

Herbert surprised Henry by arriving unannounced with his attorney Bart Couzins at Mocatta's office on the fifth floor of Four World Trade Center. Henry was sitting at his desk in a glass-walled booth talking on the phone to a friend in London and blurted out, "My God, the Hunts have just walked in."[47] But no one agrees what happened after that. Herbert recalls, "Jarecki was in complete turmoil; he was getting eaten alive by margin calls. . . . Bunker and I had put up 10.7 million ounces of silver . . . for which we had obtained loans of $50 million. . . . But suddenly I discovered he had hocked our silver for as much as the banks would loan him—about $185 million, I believe."[48] Herbert called Bunker in Dallas and said, "You better come up here and look after your own interests."

Henry Jarecki denied that "Mocatta's solvency was ever in question," but Herbert's claim that rising silver prices forced Henry to borrow heavily at high interest rates to meet margin calls rings true.[49] Mocatta had amassed a huge stock of silver inventory by scouring the country for pre-1965 coins and sterling silver heirlooms, paying premium prices to pry the white metal from proud owners. Mocatta leased the coins and the sterling for a handsome fee and sold short silver futures on Comex and the Chicago Board of Trade (CBOT) to protect its inventory. Mocatta was short silver futures but it was a risk-reducing hedge rather than speculation. Price declines would lower the value of its inventory and the short futures positions would offset the loss; price increases would raise the value of its inventory which was balanced by a loss on futures. Henry slept well at night collecting fees, knowing that his silver inventory was protected, except for the occasional nightmare called variation margin payments.

Comex and CBOT futures do not require paying for the underlying silver until the delivery date, but price changes until then are settled every day in cash called variation margin payments. On September 18, 1979, for example, silver rose by $2 an ounce so a Mocatta short position of about 20 million ounces of futures required a payment of $40 million to the Comex and CBOT Clearinghouses for distribution to those who were long futures.[50] Mocatta's net worth remained the same because the value of its inventory increased by the same amount, but it still had to borrow the necessary cash and the bankers, who equated futures trading with casino gambling, were skeptical.[51]

The Hunts worried about Mocatta's finances and wanted to repay the loan to get back their silver collateral but ran into a roadblock erected by Jarecki's lawyers. Tom Russo, thin with an olive complexion, born and raised in New York, provided Henry with expert legal advice. He was a partner at Cadwalader, Wickersham & Taft, the oldest law firm in New York City, had been the first director of the CFTC's Division of Trading and Markets, and, more importantly, Tom thought like a businessman. Russo knew that Mocatta made money lending out silver inventory, including the bullion left as collateral by Bunker and Herbert, so he designed the loan contract to prevent the Hunts from repaying early and withdrawing their silver. It was a sensible business decision that turned the confrontation with the Hunts in Jarecki's favor, allowing Henry to play his cards like a finalist in the World Series of Poker.

Herbert says that he and Bunker spent a week in Jarecki's office working out a plan: "We did everything but sleep there. They brought in dinner about 10 or 11 each night. And each day we went out and bought another shirt."[52] The cash price of silver continued to rise during their negotiations, reaching $18 an ounce on Monday, October 1, 1979, a significant 9% jump following a speech on Sunday evening by former Federal Reserve Chairman Arthur

Burns blaming American inflation on "political currents that have been transforming economic life in the United States."[53] Herbert remembers Henry rushing into the conference room and saying, "When it hits $22.90 I'm broke—Mocatta is insolvent."[54] A few minutes later Herbert says Jarecki returned even more alarmed and said, "I've miscalculated. The figure's a little lower."[55]

Henry said later that the Standard Chartered Bank, which had taken over Hambros Bank's interest in Mocatta, had "infinite deep pockets" and would have extended credit to maintain his hedged portfolio, but he had every reason to feign panic to the Hunts.[56] The more nervous they were about Mocatta's solvency, the more anxious they became about getting back their precious metal. The negotiations settled on Mocatta transferring 23 million ounces of physical silver to the Hunts in exchange for an equivalent number of futures contracts, which Jarecki would then use to cancel his short position. The increase from the original 10.7 million ounces to 23 million gave the Hunts more physical silver, which they loved, and allowed Jarecki to cure his entire variation margin headache. It was a basic transaction called an EFP, exchange of futures for physicals, complicated by Mocatta's unique inventory of coins and silver-lease contracts with banks and industrial companies. The value of a standard sealed bag of coins, for example, with a face amount of $1,000, depends on the price of the white metal and also on the abrasion of the coins.[57] Hunt lawyer Bart Couzins complained, "We had to stay right on our toes" to keep from being outsmarted by Jarecki and admitted, "He got the best of us by three or four ounces per bag."[58] Tom Russo recalls Bunker accentuating his Texas drawl, "You're selling us the cow and keeping all the milk."[59]

A surprise in the EFP agreement signed on Friday, October 5, 1979, confirmed that the Hunts had recruited allies in the market. Bunker instructed Mocatta to deliver the 23 million ounces of silver to IMIC, the Bermuda-based company the Hunts owned with their Saudi Arabian partners. IMIC had purchased about 20,000 futures contracts between July and September, representing 100 million ounces of silver, helping to drive up prices and giving it a platform to squeeze the market higher by demanding delivery from

Comex warehouses.[60] But now that Henry was no longer short he seemed less concerned with allegations that the Hunts were cornering the market, except the lengthy negotiation had taken its toll.[61] He complained to a friend, "Bunker Hunt cost me a lot of sleep. But for every hour he's cost me I'm going to make him lose ten."[62] Bunker said, "I'm a very good sleeper. I may lose money, but I don't lose sleep."

Perhaps he should have bought an alarm clock. Henry Jarecki was a member of the Comex Board of Governors, and the exchange was not about to let the Hunts destroy their marketplace by artificially inflating prices.

✦ ✦ ✦

Comex, like most financial markets in the United States, including the New York Stock Exchange and the Chicago Board of Trade, is a self-regulatory organization that polices itself under the guidance of a federal authority, in this case the CFTC. The Board of Governors is elected by exchange members to maintain a fair and orderly market to attract hedgers and speculators, who generate orders and commissions for members.[63] The big brokerage firms, including Merrill Lynch, E.F. Hutton, and Bache Halsey Stuart Shields, were represented on the Comex board, as were industrial companies like Engelhard Minerals & Chemicals Corporation, and trading companies such as Mocatta Metals and J. Aron & Company. The Comex board also included a representative of the general public, Andrew Brimmer, former member of the Federal Reserve board, to ensure a fair deal for customers.

The Comex board established a Special Silver Committee under Brimmer's chairmanship to monitor the market and maintain order after the doubling of silver prices during August and September.[64] At one point the committee asked Walter Goldschmidt, chairman of ContiCommodity Services, to keep the firm's star broker, Norton Waltuch, away from the silver ring because of his disruptive impact.[65] Goldschmidt argued that Waltuch was a dues-paying exchange member in good standing and had every right to trade, but Norton agreed to make fewer appearances.

Comex increased the good faith margin deposit required for silver contracts to dampen the speculative frenzy and so did the Chicago Board of Trade. The CBOT also voted to impose position limits, a maximum of 600 futures contracts for each trader, which would force Bunker and Herbert to reduce their holdings. Position limits had worried the Hunts since the soybean saga, and Bunker complained to anyone who would listen, "This is like Libya. They're taking my property away."[66] But the exchange had every right to change the rules to protect the integrity of its market, and Bunker knew this from the beginning, which was one reason he took delivery of physical bullion and shipped it to Switzerland. Bunker added a broader complaint reminiscent of the battles between eastern bankers and rural westerners throughout American history, "The home-town boys who run the markets don't want anybody from out of town to make any money."[67] The outcry pushed the CBOT to delay position limits after Bunker and Herbert promised not to take delivery on their February 1980 futures contracts, but these were just the opening salvos in the white metal wars.[68]

The *New York Times* headline on October 29, 1979, "Squeezing the Market in Silver," exposed the alleged conspirators to public scrutiny.[69] Most traders refused to be quoted but currency consultant Franz Pick, whose book on silver had brought Mocatta & Goldsmid to Jarecki's attention years earlier, said, "I'm 82 years old and don't care how many more enemies I make." Pick listed his least-favorite manipulators, including Norton Waltuch who has "steadfastly refused to discuss his trading operations," the Hunt family "that has also refused all comment," and finally "the Kuwaiti element, which is actually a much broader group of Mideast oil money." Franz may have mislabeled some of the participants, but he warned, "By placing large orders . . . they could easily run up the price." Silver had already advanced relative to gold during the year, increasing by more than 150% in value compared with about 70% for the yellow metal, which the CFTC would later use as proof of manipulation.[70] The price ratio of gold to silver started the year at 36 to 1, meaning it took thirty-six ounces of silver to buy an ounce of gold, and now the ratio was 23 to 1.[71] Pick suggested that the manipulators had targeted the "historic ratio with gold of 16 to 1" that existed prior to the Crime of 1873. Bunker countered that the price ratio of gold to silver had nothing to do with manipulation but reflected normal supply and demand. Both precious metals rose in value because of economic and political uncertainty, but silver's industrial use compared with unproductive gold would ultimately drive the price ratio much lower, perhaps to 5 to 1, so that only five ounces of silver were needed to buy an ounce of gold.[72] Bunker picked 5 to 1 because it was lower than 16 to 1 but he could have gone further. In ancient Egypt silver's scarcity and medicinal properties had made it more valuable than gold.[73]

The Commodity Exchange Act prohibits manipulation but does not define it, so the courts must identify the ingredients.[74] One appeals court said it was "the creation of an artificial price by planned action," which is easy to say but hard to prove, especially with prices responding continuously to provocative news.[75] Disentangling the impact of alleged manipulators from legitimate speculators took extensive litigation in this case.[76] The CFTC argued that during the second half of 1979, Norton Waltuch and the Hunts, together with their Arab collaborators, coordinated a scheme to drive up silver prices by purchasing over 200 million ounces of the white metal, more than the combined annual output of Canada, Mexico, Peru, and the United States, the four largest noncommunist producing countries.[77] The manipulators pressured the market by controlling more than 40% of silver in exchange warehouses and by taking delivery of almost 50 million ounces of bullion. But the alleged manipulation was not the classic corner of futures markets, where the longs prevented the shorts from delivering. As silver prices accelerated in December 1979, for example, even the CFTC said that the shorts "anticipated no difficulties in making delivery on their positions."[78] Instead, some plaintiffs argued that the manipulation closely resembled the "pump and dump" scheme associated with "penny stocks."[79] Latecomer buyers claimed that the Hunts touted silver as a great investment, bought bullion to push up the price to convince others to join the bandwagon, which caused an artificial price spiral.

The Hunts denied manipulative intent, dismissed any coordination, even among themselves, and justified their demand for silver as a hard asset to protect against global risks, a view supported by David Rutledge, an executive vice president at Comex: "We don't have reason to believe that the resurgence in silver prices is due to anything other than the international political situation."[80] Bunker never sold to any "latecomers" and protested to anyone within earshot, "I am not a speculator. I am not a market squeezer. I am just an investor and a holder of silver."[81] The legal confrontation dragged on for years, but the unfolding battle snared some surprising victims.

James Sinclair, head of his own brokerage firm, complained that the "silver market has been all but destroyed by uncommonly greedy manipulators who have . . . driven the public out of this futures market."[82] A 50% decline in silver's average daily trading volume during October 1979, compared with the previous nine months, confirms Sinclair's complaint, but some of that decline resulted from increased margin requirements.[83] Not everyone stayed away, of course. Buying silver required money and conviction that it was the best hedge against economic turmoil, which explains why Bunker's youngest brother, Lamar, let the white metal distract him from his Kansas City Chiefs football team. Lamar says he first bought silver "because I thought it was a good investment based on things I had heard Bunker say [and] articles I had read."[84] But unlike his brothers, who began buying in 1973, Lamar entered the market in 1974 and admits, "I saw a price rise and [as] a typical naïve investor I was late getting in and I lost money."

But Lamar Hunt was not a typical investor and could hold a losing position until it became a winner, which it did by 1979. Lamar began to invest again, using a teaspoon compared with Bunker's steam shovel, but enough to make him pay attention in October 1979, except Sunday afternoons when he rooted for his Chiefs who had a promising 4–2 record.[85] It was almost ten years since their January 1970 Super Bowl victory, when Lamar proudly cradled the sterling silver trophy, whose value had increased almost tenfold with rising white metal prices, and he hoped the Chiefs might be ready to repeat.[86] A five-game losing stretch after the promising start destroyed their chances, but Lamar took comfort from silver's explosive 1979 finish.

✦ ✦ ✦

FIGURE 17. Lamar loved sports.

Escalating international tension beginning November 4, 1979, when Iranian students took U.S. embassy personnel hostage, combined with Russian troops in Afghanistan towards the end of December, helped turn the overheated market for the white metal into an inferno. On Monday, December 3, 1979, the *Wall Street Journal* headline, "Dollar Plummets as Mideast Crisis Triggers Jitters," marked the U.S. currency's decline to a record low against the German mark, and the accompanying article noted that silver made a new high at $20.05.[87] Later in the month a *New York Times* article titled "Price of Gold Tops $500 for First Time" explained that "Ayatollah Ruhollah Khomeini said that Iran's current conflict with the United States could worsen" and added concern over "reports that thousands of Soviet troops were in Afghanistan."[88] But none of those developments compare with silver's spectacular performance during the last few days of the year.

On Monday, December 31, 1979, silver closed at $34.45 an ounce, up almost 50% from Friday, December 21, 1979, the last trading day before the Christmas holidays.[89] Many traders take vacation during Christmas week so the market is thin, meaning prices often bounce around like a pinball, especially when surprised by the Soviet push into Afghanistan.[90] One trader said the obvious: prices spiraled higher "because there were just no sellers around." A financial analyst made a more fundamental observation: "The role of silver in investment activities is undergoing a dramatic revaluation."[91]

Anticipating the new sentiment, the Hunts had made more money than anyone but a Hunt could have imagined. At the end of 1979 they owned approximately 200 million ounces of silver at an average price of about $8.[92] Their profit at the year-end closing price of $34.45 was more than $5 billion, a number Bunker could use to erase his father's putdown, "You're not fit to be my heir." But with H.L. gone Bunker simply said he "could not understand why anyone would be short silver."[93] Unfortunately for a Peruvian civil servant named Ismael Fonseco, those words never reached his ears.

Ismael, a short and heavyset man in his early thirties, worked for Minpeco, a marketing corporation owned by the government of Peru and chartered to accumulate the country's silver and other minerals to be sold on world markets. Minpeco sent Ismael to a training program in early 1979 where he learned how to use futures contracts to reduce Minpeco's inventory risk.[94] In September 1979 Minpeco owned 3.6 million ounces of silver, so Fonseco sold short about that amount in the futures market to protect the bullion against price declines. But Ismael wanted to be a rock star rather than a stodgy bureaucrat, so when silver approached $18 in early October, he began without permission to sell more futures contracts to profit from an expected price decline. By the end of November Fonseco had sold short 15.7 million ounces of silver futures against an inventory of 3.6 million ounces of bullion, which meant that Minpeco was short the difference, or 12.1 million ounces of the white metal. Fonseco had made a bet like at the roulette wheel that would pay $12.1 million for every dollar decline in silver and would lose that amount for every dollar increase. By the time Ismael's secret speculation was discovered and offset in mid-December, silver had increased by more than $6 an ounce, producing a loss of about $80 million.[95]

Bunker had never met Ismael Fonseco but learned more about him after Minpeco sued the Hunts for manipulating prices and causing their loss. The *Wall Street Journal* reported, "Peruvian officials believe that Minpeco's need to buy [about] 10 million ounces of silver futures in late December . . . contributed to the metal's sharp rise at that time," which suggests a self-inflicted injury.[96] Bunker thought the incident showed government ineptitude, another lesson that socialism was the road to ruin, and Bunker was right—bureaucrats do not make good speculators, which is why Fonseco was fired. But the more powerful message was that Bunker had lost control of the market. Prices rose too far, too fast, in December 1979, failing to let the market breathe, and Bunker should have recognized the danger. Former Treasury secretary Henry Morgenthau, a farmer from Fishkill, New York, and a novice manipulator compared with Bunker Hunt, knew to avoid speculative excess when promoting the white metal under the Silver Purchase Act in

1934. At a news conference he had announced a thoughtful approach: "What we want is a rise in the price of silver, but we don't want a sensational price rise, because the worst thing that could happen would be to have silver go up and then have a collapse."[97]

Bunker ignored history and paid for it.

CHAPTER 19

COLLAPSE

THIEVES IN THE WEALTHY TOWNS OF WESTCHESTER COUNTY, JUST north of New York City, loosened Bunker Hunt's grip on the silver market by turning stolen sterling into bullion bars for sale on the exchanges. State troopers reported more than one hundred burglaries between November 1979 and January 1980, and silver was stolen in eighty-five cases. William Adams, a police detective in the Westchester town of North Castle, described a typical break-in: "They go into the bedroom and grab a pillowcase and then into the dining room and clean out the sideboard. They don't worry about how the pillowcase looks when they are leaving, because when they're leaving, they're running."[1] Adams added, "Flatware, consisting of knives, forks, and spoons, is the first silver item stolen." The *New York Times* quipped, "When the police saw a man running through the woods with a pillowcase over his shoulder, they knew that he wasn't on his way to the laundromat." Sometimes the thefts were inside jobs. Police in the town of Mount Kisco reported "two cases where teenagers had stolen their own family silver and tried to sell it."

The spectacular price increase had sparked the epidemic of pilfered silver. A place setting of sterling, which cost about $30 or $40 when silver was $1.29, was now worth at least $500. A Hartford, Connecticut, jeweler advertised a four-piece place setting of the Old Maryland Engraved pattern by Kirk Stieff for $637.50, making a service for twelve an attractive target worth more than $7,000.[2] One policeman said, "If the silver is stolen by 10 am it's melted down by 3 pm," but Westchester Detective Adams thought it was much quicker, having heard of a thief "running around and melting it down right in the truck."[3] Recovery is impossible after the silver becomes bullion. And by January 1980 the burglary plague had spread beyond New York suburbs. A detective in the

Houston police department, J.C. Davis, said, "The rate of metal grabs has doubled in the past six months."[4] Davis described a home burglary where "the television, the stereo, and the usual Texas gun collection were thrown into the swimming pool, but the silver and the jewelry were taken." Detectives in suburban Detroit's Oakland County complained about "advertisements by coin and metals dealers in the local papers offering to buy old gold and silver with 'no questions asked.'" Lieutenant Donald Zimmerman of Oakland's Bloomfield Township said, "Of course it's an invitation for stolen goods."

The influx of hijacked silver swamped refineries already stretched thin. The *Los Angeles Times* announced, "People Cashing In on Precious Metal Boom," and reported that the president of American Silver Recovery, Inc., a local refinery, recommended, "If you have old material (silver or gold) sell it. If it's sitting in the attic, or tucked away in a drawer, take it out and sell it."[5] Some folks went further and sold antiques that had been in their family for generations. Sebastian Musco, president of Gemini Industries, another refinery, said, "People are in a panic and the sadness of it all is they're ruining precious heirlooms. Somebody came in the other day with a sterling silver coffeepot made in the 1800s . . . and they wanted to sell it for scrap."[6] The headline "Britons Liquidate a Heritage" confirmed the mania had spread across the Atlantic.[7] U.K. bullion dealer Johnson Matthey reported, "Every item bought over the counter was immediately destroyed, including a 1748 silver salver [sterling tray] it recently took in." A manager at precious metal dealer D. Penellier & Company, located in London's Hattan Garden jewelry district, said, "It's an absolute crime," while examining a Georgian tea service he had bought for scrap.

Henry Jarecki became rich turning America's old silver coins into bullion during the 1970s but the profit incentives in January 1980 made everyone an arbitrageur. Two teenagers in Chicago, accompanied by their mother, took $200 in pre-1965 dimes and quarters inherited from their grandfather to a downtown Loop coin shop and walked away with $4,000.[8] Numismatists made money selling their coin collections for scrap, to the dismay of professional dealers. Harry Forman, a well-known Philadelphia expert, sounded as though he had lost close relatives to a pandemic when naming coins that had been scrapped, including "such one-time premium items as . . . 1931-D and S Mercury dimes, 1937-S and 1955-D Washington quarters, and 1948, 1953, and 1955 Franklin half dollars."[9] He added, "We're witnessing the great melt of the century." Joel Coen, a major New York City dealer, said, "I myself am delivering from $2 million to $4 million worth of silver coins to melters every week. And if we keep destroying all these coins, what will be left to collect in years to come?" The U.S. Treasury joined the party by scouring its vaults for hidden treasure, finding a cache of nearly one million silver dollars that had been minted between 1878 and 1893 in the now-defunct Carson City mint, and selling them at prices between $45 and $65 each.[10]

Bunker Hunt would have to buy all bullion bars, whether from newly mined silver in Mexico and Peru or from melted stocks of coin dealers and antique shops, to keep prices high. He also had to worry about increased bullion on world markets, smuggled out of India by way of Dubai, equaling about half of Mexico's annual output in early 1980.[11] Estimates of silver jewelry adorning the neck, wrists, and ankles of Indian peasants run into the billions of ounces but are immobilized by custom and law.[12] Tradition dictates that Indian women can inherit only what they are wearing so they store their wealth as gold and silver jewelry. The Indian government banned silver exports in February 1979, but the price surge since then encouraged a steady outflow of the white metal via oceangoing dhows that hid silver the size of a loaf of bread among their cargoes of cloth, rolls of carpet, and toys.[13] Ashraf Amin, one of Dubai's biggest precious metal dealers, said, "We have an open trade," which the press confirmed with the banner, "Smuggled Silver Trade Revives in Dubai."[14]

Bunker had ignored aboveground supplies until the headlines hit, wondering, "Why would anyone sell silver to get dollars? I guess they got tired of polishing it."[15] But there was at least 2.5 billion ounces of the white metal in coins, silverware, and other secondary sources in the United States, waiting silently for the right price, far more than informed experts like Henry Jarecki had estimated and enough to cover twelve years of the shortfall between world production and consumption touted by silver bulls.[16] The price was right in January 1980, and molten silver poured into bullion bars, but a shortage of refinery space prevented these secondary supplies from dominating the market and blunting the upward price pressure. A Gaithersburg, Maryland, coin dealer said, "The smelters have their hands filled. They're not buying at all right now," and the *Washington Post* confirmed, "Refiners stopped buying . . . as storerooms overflowed."[17] The refining bottleneck would eventually soften, but the Commodity Exchange could not afford to wait for supply to overwhelm demand. Silver traders had begun to melt away and Comex had to fight for its life.

✦ ✦ ✦

The daily volatility of silver prices had doubled during the last three months of 1979 compared with a year earlier, and in the first two weeks of January 1980 prices varied between a high of $43.75 an ounce and a low of $33.65, an intimidating range of 30%.[18] The increased risk had cut trading volume in half on the Commodity Exchange in early 1980, but it was not just speculators who disappeared.[19] Jewelers and precious metal dealers turned away customers to avoid the uncertainty. Eugene Berkowitz, president of Rose Industries, in the heart of Chicago's jewelry center at 29 East Madison Street, explained why he stopped buying silver from customers: "I discontinued buying this stuff . . . because of the volatile nature of the market."[20] The *Chicago Tribune* reported that John Ross, a veteran coin dealer at 12 West Madison Street, "sent speculators to the yellow pages to do their shopping," much to their displeasure.[21] Both businessmen boycotted the silver market to avoid volatility, but Comex could not afford to do that since the market *was* their business.

The Commodity Exchange Board voted on Monday evening, January 7, 1980, to impose position limits on speculators for the first time since it was established in 1933. The new rules prevented speculators from holding more than 500 futures contracts in the delivery month and limited their total net position to 2,000 contracts.[22] Comex Chairman Lowell Mintz said, "We took the action on our own initiative in order to maintain orderly markets," but everyone knew it was aimed at the Hunts, especially to prevent them from taking delivery of silver from exchange warehouses.[23] The press reported widespread "concern that a handful of large holders of silver futures, such as Hunt family interests in the United States and oil rich traders from the Middle East, might cause a squeeze on the market."[24] Bunker would have to reduce his futures position on Comex and responded to the regulations as though he were tweaking an opponent before a heavyweight championship fight: "I am more likely to take action to accept delivery on maturing silver futures contracts now that the . . . markets have set position limits."[25]

But Bunker knew when to attack and when to sidestep a jab. He lowered his profile on Comex during the week of January 14, 1980, by reducing his futures position through an EFP (exchange of futures for physicals) with industrial giant Engelhard Minerals & Chemicals, similar to the transaction with Mocatta Metals in October 1979, only bigger.[26] The agreement, initiated by Raymond Nessim, vice president of the Philipp Brothers division of Engelhard, gave the Hunts approximately 28.5 million ounces of physical silver at an average price of about $36 an ounce and gave Engelhard long positions in Comex futures contracts on the same amount of bullion. The transaction pleased both sides. Engelhard needed those futures contracts to reduce its short position, which had cost the company millions in interest on variation margin payments, and Bunker needed to reduce his futures position to avoid violating position limits. The total bill for the 28.5 million ounces was a little over $1 billion, which the Hunts agreed to pay in installments over the next few months. The largest payment of $434 million would come due on March 31, 1980, although Engelhard had the option to accelerate delivery of the bullion and receive that payment on March 3. No one suspected this was a time bomb primed to explode in Bunker's face.

Comex's new position limits produced a price decline, but the impact resembled a speed bump on the road to higher prices. On Friday, January 18, 1980, silver prices reached an all-time high of $50 an ounce during the trading day, a record that still stands, making the Hunts' 200 million ounces worth $10 billion.[27] After subtracting related borrowings of about $500 million, their silver position was worth more than the estimated value of Bunker's Libyan oil field discovery. For the country club set the $50 price meant that a sleeve of three sterling silver golf balls (a special Father's Day gift), each ball containing 1.366 troy ounces of pure silver, would cost $204.90 compared with $5.29 at the white metal's pre-1967 price of $1.29, a strong incentive to keep the ball on the fairway.[28]

History had confirmed the wisdom of Bunker's decision to buy the white metal in 1973, when prices were less than $3 an ounce, and to "double down" like a great blackjack player with the political and economic turmoil that began in 1979. Both gold and silver had jumped in value since February 1979, when the Ayatollah Khomeini had returned from exile to lead the Iranian revolution, but the more volatile silver rose about sevenfold while gold increased half as much.[29] As a result, on January 18, 1980, when gold reached its peak of $850 and silver hit $50, the price ratio of gold to silver declined to 17 to 1, close enough to the historic 16 to 1 ratio to confirm Franz Pick's bold prediction a few months earlier and to make the Hunts heroes in the century-long battle to reverse the Crime of 1873.[30] William Jennings Bryan could finally rest in peace without contemplating another presidential run.

Investors who followed Bunker's advice made a killing, but an innocent observation from precious metals analyst Bud Sward of the Shearson Loeb Rhodes brokerage firm should have worried the silver bulls. Sward claimed, "Silver isn't a poor man's metal anymore. It is really losing its appeal to any speculator who wants to trade."[31] Silver had outperformed gold, in part, because it was the metal of the people, the same reason it dominated as the medium of exchange throughout the world until the nineteenth century. Few cared that the white metal no longer served as currency as long as it remained a rock-hard asset to protect against inflation. But the Commodity Exchange needed speculators in the market to survive, which is why the exchange barred the Hunts from buying more silver after January 21, 1980.

✦ ✦ ✦

The Comex board met Monday morning, January 21 at 9 o'clock, and suspended the normal 9:40 opening of silver while considering new emergency regulations for trading the white metal.[32] The discussion lasted longer than expected and the silver opening was first delayed until 11 a.m., then to 12:30 p.m., and finally to 1:30 p.m. According to board minutes, members believed the market was "out of control" and no longer served a "legitimate economic function."[33] Board member Henry Eisenberg, representing metals dealer Brandeis, Goldschmidt & Co., said the longs "had achieved a classic corner."[34] Another member, Edward Hoffstatter of Sharps Pixley, a participant in the daily London fixing, described the price increase between January 7 and January 18 as "an indication of the congestion of the market and the fact that new longs were coming in every day."[35] He suspected these "were not new longs but just new names controlled by the same old parties." A Securities and Exchange Commission investigation later showed that at least "twenty-one Hunt family members and related entities held or traded silver."[36] At 12:30 the board voted to declare an "emergency" in silver futures and to "limit trading in Comex silver for all delivery months to liquidation only," which meant that "longs" like the Hunts could only sell (liquidate) their positions and could not buy.[37] The vote was unanimous, including two board members who had done business with the Hunts, Mocatta's Henry Jarecki and Engelhard's Raymond Nessim.[38]

During the abbreviated trading session on January 21, which started at 1:30 p.m. and ended at the normal 2:15 p.m., the spot price on Comex declined less than $3 to $44.[39] The *Wall Street Journal* commented, "It is unclear whether the Comex's controversial move will force the big speculators . . . Herbert Hunt and his brother Nelson Bunker Hunt . . . and the clients of Norton Waltuch . . . to abandon existing positions."[40] Clarity emerged the following day, Tuesday, January 22, when the Chicago Board of Trade joined Comex's attack on the alleged manipulators and imposed its own version of liquidation-only. The silver bulls had no escape from the new rules and sellers drove down the spot silver price to $34 an ounce, an unprecedented $10 decline.[41] A headline in the U.K.'s *Guardian* newspaper, "Comex Curbs Hit Bullion," memorialized the power of the larger Commodity Exchange that started it all, but the more significant drop occurred only after the

Chicago Board of Trade joined the fray, making both exchanges responsible.[42] The 30% collapse on January 21 and 22, the largest two-day price decline since the white metal began trading freely in 1967, marked the end of the long bull market and the beginning of an earthquake for the Hunts.[43]

Herbert and Bunker lost about $3 billion on Monday and Tuesday, January 21 and 22, and protested the following day in a letter to Comex president Lee Berndt. The Hunts complained that the Comex board action was a "breach of trust," liquidation-only trading was not "market neutral," and "was designed to have a downward effect" on price and to "give aid and comfort to those who were short in the market." [44] The Hunts did not mention board member Raymond Nessim by name, but as first vice-chairman of the Comex board he had set up the emergency meeting.[45] Nessim's position with the Philipp Brothers division of Engelhard Minerals & Chemicals, which was still short more than 4,000 futures contracts on January 21, the most of any Comex board member, suggested a potential conflict of interest even though it was to hedge its physical bullion.[46] Engelhard wanted lower prices to reduce crushing interest charges for margin on their short position.[47] The Hunt letter urged Comex to "reconsider" its rule and warned that failure "to rectify the Board's biased actions will inevitably result in legal and financial problems for the Board of Comex, the participants, and all concerned."[48]

Bunker went public with a reference to urban easterners taking advantage of rural westerners, saying the insiders at the exchange had been upset because "they figured that if there was any money to be made, they should make the money."[49] He complained to the press: "I bought futures under the rules that existed and suddenly the rules were changed. That doesn't seem fair." [50]

Bunker had a point. Futures trading is a contact sport like football, but America's favorite pastime establishes rules beforehand and sticks to them. Players push, grapple, and shove to win on the gridiron, risking serious injury in the process, but the home team about to kick a forty-yard field goal, for example, cannot move the goal posts forward to the thirty-yard line. Why is futures trading less evenhanded than professional football?

Henry Jarecki had worried about the fairness of changing the rules and had discussed it with his lawyer Tom Russo before the Comex board meeting. Russo made Henry smile by telling him, "Ah, but one of the rules is that futures exchanges are permitted to change the rules. Everyone knows this and must adapt."[51] The press had referred to liquidation-only as "one of the most extreme actions a futures exchange can take and is rarely invoked," but the Hunts should have paid attention to recent history.[52] In November 1979, two months before the restriction in silver, threats of a squeeze forced New York's Coffee, Sugar and Cocoa Exchange to impose liquidation-only in coffee, and Comex itself did the same in copper, although in both cases the new rules applied only to the delivery month, making them less onerous.[53] The liquidation rule inflicted a major loss on the Hunts, but the Commodity Exchange was well within its rights, so Bunker's complaint received little sympathy, except from William Proxmire, the maverick senator from Wisconsin, chairman of the Senate Banking Committee, who investigated the Hunts' charges of conflicts of interest on the Comex board: The "incredibly large short positions" give "the appearance of very substantial self-interest by the very people who were making the decisions."[54] The Hunts never sued, although Bunker accused Comex board members of positioning themselves to profit on the new rule: "I've heard at least half of them made a huge amount of money," which one eyewitness confirmed.[55] The Comex board modified the rule on Wednesday, February 13, but liquidation-only marked a turning point in the white metal that would force Bunker and Herbert to pledge their Hunt family inheritance to avoid bankruptcy.[56]

❖ ❖ ❖

The exchanges may have started the slide, but silver prices remained remarkably stable for more than a month before the next avalanche. On Monday, March 3, 1980, with the cash price of the white metal at $34.25, virtually unchanged since the liquidation orders by Comex and the CBOT crushed the market on January 22, Engelhard's Raymond Nessim notified Herbert Hunt that his company wanted to exercise its option in their EFP to deliver bullion early.[57] Herbert politely told Nessim that the Hunts' funds were fully invested until the end of the month and that it was "not convenient" for them to take delivery on March 3. Nessim just as politely insisted that the Hunts pay $1.7 million more on the mandatory delivery date, March 31, to reflect the cost of the delay, which was fair and proper since Engelhard lost interest income on the money it should have received. It was fair, but the delay by the Hunts and their willingness to accept the penalty alerted traders' antennae to a faint odor of weakness in Bunker and Herbert's finances.

The Hunts had borrowed almost a billion dollars during February and March to pay for bullion on maturing futures contracts, bringing their total silver-related loans to almost $1.5 billion.[58] But they needed more cash, in part, to help coconspirator Naji Nahas, Norton Waltuch's client, take delivery to avoid Comex position limits and to meet their own increasing margin payments.[59] On Tuesday, March 4, Barclays Bank International rejected the Hunts' request for a $100 million loan to be secured by silver bullion. Herbert and Bunker had flattered Barclays, saying their loan would be one-third of a $300 million package from top European banks, but that tactic backfired and increased Barclays' reluctance. According to an internal memorandum, Barclays refused because "the amount of silver collateral . . . was so enormous that any attempt to liquidate in the event of default would so erode the price of silver that collateral coverage could be insufficient."[60] The brothers had become too big, and Barclays' prudent concern would spread like a mudslide and smother silver prices.

The Hunts had been accused of questionable business practices in the past, including manipulating soybean prices, wiretapping an employee, and using information from their oil drilling business to front-run competitors, but they had always paid bills on time.[61] Their impeccable credit rating allowed them to borrow, without providing the usual documentation, almost $500 million from brokerage firms, including Merrill Lynch, Bache & Company, and E.F. Hutton, among the biggest companies in the securities industry.[62] All of those loans were collateralized by silver that would be dumped on the market if the Hunts defaulted—an unlikely, but catastrophic, event that would trash the price of the white metal. On Thursday, March 6, 1980, two days after Barclays' loan refusal and three days after the Hunts failed to honor Engelhard's early-delivery option, silver declined by 8.5%, the largest drop since January 22, and on Monday, March 10, after Deutsche Bank refused a similar loan request, the price fell 10.1%.[63] None of these loan rejections appeared in the press, but they displeased Bunker, and bad news seeps into the market and sinks prices like gossip destroys reputations. And more was coming.

President Jimmy Carter's March 14, 1980, announcement of a credit restraint program to control inflation seemed designed to destroy the Hunts, and silver traders panicked. Sellers drove down the spot price of the white metal by almost half over three days, from $29.30 per ounce to $17.40, anticipating that the program would reduce credit availability for speculative loans.[64] According to the *Wall Street Journal*, on Thursday, March 13, silver prices declined "following the announcement that President Carter plans to release his anti-inflation program."[65] On Friday, March 14, as details emerged before the scheduled 4:30 p.m. speech, prices dropped again.[66] And on Monday, March 17, after the market digested the facts over the weekend, prices fell by another 19%.[67] The press reported that Monday's decline surprised the professionals: "Like many in the industry, Jack Boyd, Drexel Burnham Lambert Inc.'s commodity-research chief, spent the weekend expecting futures prices to show little response to the package, as they had fallen steeply in anticipation of such measures."[68]

The absence of explicit restrictions in the president's program lulled researcher Jack Boyd into complacency, but traders with money at risk always worry and comb the press for an edge. On Monday morning, March 17, the *Wall Street Journal* delivered bad news. The *Journal* reported that a spokesman for the Federal Reserve, America's central bank, suggested that "the new measures are designed in part to insure a better distribution of credit as well as a curtailment of its growth."[69] It added that the Fed "has 'encouraged' lenders to restrain consumer lending, discourage financing of corporate takeovers . . . [and] avoid financing 'purely speculative holdings' of commodities." The antispeculation clause put silver speculators in the crosshairs, giving traders good reason to dump the white metal on Monday, March 17. The following day, the Royal Bank of Canada, Toronto Dominion Bank, and Bank of Nova Scotia each refused a $100 million borrowing request from the Hunts, suggesting that Canadian bankers would respect the Federal Reserve's caution.[70] Bunker and Herbert Hunt would be unable to borrow money needed to meet growing variation margin payments.

The Hunts were still billionaires at a time when there were fewer than a dozen in the world.[71] Bunker's racing stables, Australian farmland, and cattle ranches, and Herbert's Dallas real estate, plus their share in the family's Placid Oil Company, and their considerable silver holdings, added up. They resembled English nobility of the fourteenth century, owners of great landed estates but with little gold or silver currency, making them asset rich and cash poor. And like England's King Edward III, who needed to borrow cash from the Bardi and Peruzzi banking families of Florence to pay his Welsh archers to battle France, Bunker and Herbert needed to borrow money to make margin payments.

Jimmy Carter's credit restraint program had closed off North America's banks, forcing Bunker and Herbert to settle with their brokerage firms in silver bullion and coins. Bache & Company, which held the Hunt personal accounts, and Merrill Lynch, which held IMIC's accounts, advanced margin payments in cash as required by the exchanges and held the white metal as collateral but discounted its value 25–35% to reflect price risk.[72] When the Hunts offered their South African mining stock as collateral, Merrill discounted its value by 65%.[73] Bunker then travelled to Europe in mid-March, where his favorite institution, the Swiss Bank Corporation, did business away from the Federal Reserve's glare. The Swiss giant had already lent the Hunts $200 million, but on Thursday, March 20, the bank delivered the message that "technical problems" prevented them from advancing funds for a loan.[74] The technical problem turned out to be the Swiss Federal Banking Commission agreeing to join the Federal Reserve System in discouraging loans for speculation in gold and silver.[75]

Bunker had nowhere to turn except to his Saudi Arabian partners. On Saturday, March 22, he chartered a Lockheed Jetstar, a small four-engine business jet that seats ten, and flew with Mahmoud Fustok and Naji Nahas from Paris, where they had been staying, to the port city of Jeddah to meet with their royal backers.[76] Bunker knew this was not the time to fly commercial. When they arrived, Fustok smoothed the way with his family connections and spoke with Prince Faisal, son of Crown Prince Abdullah, suggesting that the metal's decline was temporary and favorable fundamentals would soon reassert themselves. Fustok had been encouraged by rumors that SAMA, the Saudi Arabian Monetary Agency, would diversify its reserves by buying silver.[77] Remonetizing the white metal would change everything.

Faisal spoke with his father and returned with bad news. The recent losses had convinced the royal family that silver was more complicated than Bunker had let on, especially since the futures exchanges could change the rules and the Federal Reserve could starve speculators of needed credit. Crown Prince Abdullah refused to compromise SAMA's independence by pushing for a link with the white metal. Silver had played an important role in Saudi history and that is where it would remain.

✦ ✦ ✦

Bunker returned to Paris after the failed trip to Jeddah and prepared a press release that would stun the financial world. Bache & Company had requested an immediate cash payment of $135 million for variation margin on Tuesday, March 25, 1980, and Bunker would need $434 million the following Monday, March 31, to pay Engelhard's installment on the January EFP.[78] Engelhard held 8.5 million ounces of Bunker's silver bullion as collateral, but spot silver closed at $20.20, making Engelhard's collateral worth only $172 million, less than half the Hunt obligation. Herbert Hunt told Bache that they had neither cash nor bullion to meet the margin call, and Bache responded with formal telegrams to Bunker, Herbert, Lamar, and other family members with accounts at the firm: "We are commencing efforts immediately to liquidate silver and, in our discretion, futures positions to meet this call."[79]

Everyone would get burned in a fire sale of bullion by Hunt creditors, but Bunker believed in silver more than ever. The white metal had declined by 60% from its peak value of January 18, 1980, and had become cheap relative to gold, which had dropped by less than half.[80] The price ratio of gold to silver now stood at 25 to 1, well above January's near historic 16 to 1 ratio. Bunker never wavered in his belief that eventually only five ounces of silver would be needed to buy an ounce of gold, saying, "I'll stick by my prediction of 5 to 1."[81] He was reluctant to sell anything but understood that failure to meet his financial obligations meant creditors could force him into bankruptcy proceedings, costly and embarrassing for someone worth well over a billion dollars.

In the afternoon of March 26, 1980, Bunker Hunt announced in a press release that he had agreed in principle to "join four other men with large silver holdings to market silver-backed bonds," which would be distributed "through big European banks in denominations of varying sizes."[82] The other participants in the sale were Prince Faisal of Saudi Arabia, Mahmoud Fustok, Naji Nahas, and Sheik Mohammed Al-Amoudi. The *New York Times* said the plan "comes close to remonetizing precious metals," creating securities like U.S. Treasury silver certificates, which until mid-1968 could be exchanged for bullion, except the bonds would pay interest. Andrew Racz, president of Racz International, a division of the brokerage house Philips, Appel & Walden, said, "The Hunt group would, in effect, be printing their own money," which was Bunker's intention. The Hunt announcement said that the selling group owned more than 200 million ounces of bullion, suggesting a bond sale of about $4 billion, similar in size to a U.S. Treasury issue. The offering would raise more than enough money to solve everyone's cash shortage, if it were successful.

The market responded like a guillotine, cutting the price of the white metal to $15.80 an ounce at the close on Wednesday, March 26, a drop of almost 25%.[83] The *Wall Street Journal* headline "N.B. Hunt Group Shocks Silver World with Plan for Bonds" sums up the reaction, although the *Journal* reported that prices had started to decline on Wednesday even before the Paris announcement under selling pressure from Alvin Brodsky, Bunker's favorite floor broker.[84] Traders understood the concept of silver-backed securities but Bunker's announcement seemed as desperate as trying to escape a tsunami in a rowboat. Investors knew that a $50 million sale of similar bonds had been proposed a month earlier by the Sunshine Mining Company, Bunker's former takeover target, which had engaged the investment banking firm Drexel Burnham Lambert Inc. to market the issue.[85] But Bunker had failed to identify a bank selling syndicate for his $4 billion bond issue, almost one hundred times Sunshine's size, nor did he set a timetable. He had rushed the announcement, left it incomplete, and violated the trader's cardinal rule: Sell it when you can, not when you have to. Bunker conceded as much during subsequent courtroom testimony, "It might have worked two months before . . . but [not] on a down market. . . . It was a good idea, and it's a good way to raise funds. At the wrong time you can't raise five cents with it."[86] Had the Hunts announced silver-backed bonds in a televised press conference in November 1979, right after Iranian students had taken American citizens hostage, the issue might have been oversubscribed within twenty-four hours.

Bunker added detail where it hurt. He identified bond cosponsors, Prince Faisal, Mahmoud Fustok, Naji Nahas, and Mohammed Al-Amoudi, perhaps to broaden international appeal for the proposal but also suggesting coordinated silver accumulation with the Arabs, which he had repeatedly denied. The cosponsors list elicited questions during subsequent congressional investigation into the silver debacle, forcing Bunker into evasive answers. Alabama Senator Donald Stewart asked: "Did you at any time . . . communicate either orally or through the mail with members of the Saudi Arabian royal family?" Bunker responded: "Well there are 4,000 male members of the Saudi Arabian royal family. I know a lot of Arabs and I'm not sure which ones are members of the royal family and which ones aren't."[87] Bunker's evasive quibbling impaired his country-boy image and his princely list failed to float the bond proposal, forcing him to watch his great speculation crumble the following day, March 27, 1980, forever known as Silver Thursday.

❖ ❖ ❖

Brokerage firms, led by Bache & Company and Merrill Lynch, sold the Hunts' silver positions on Thursday, March 27, to recoup

W. H. HUNT   N. B. HUNT

FIGURE 18. Herbert Hunt and Bunker Hunt promise to tell Congress the truth.

their loans to the Texas billionaires, driving down the spot price of the suddenly tarnished metal by one-third to $10.80 an ounce, eclipsing previous record declines on Comex.[88] Sales by Bache, which had the biggest exposure to the Hunts and relatively little capital, required the delicate balance of a tightrope walker. Bache had to sell Hunt silver futures to stop the hemorrhage of cash, but its selling drove down the price, increasing losses. A Securities and Exchange Commission report found that Hunt debit balances as the price of silver declined "carried the potential for losses to [the] Bache Group that were very substantial in relation to its overall financial resources."[89] The diplomatically correct report avoided the word "bankruptcy," but the SEC suspended trading in Bache stock on the New York Stock Exchange at 2:15 in the afternoon of March 27, 1980, citing "undisclosed material corporate events relating to commodities futures trading."[90] The *New York Times* headlined the spreading carnage, "Silver's Plunge Jolts Hunts' Empire and Brings Turmoil to Wall Street."[91]

Bache CEO Harry Jacobs had asked the Comex board to close the silver market to avoid the debacle and also telephoned Paul

Volcker, chairman of the Federal Reserve board, to warn him of the impending danger. Jacobs explained later that he called the six-foot-seven-inch central banker because "I thought that there was an extremely illiquid situation developing there and it was in the national interest that I call him as the senior central banker of the world."[92] Jacobs then admitted, "Secondly . . . we thought it would help put pressure on the Comex." Volcker had no direct authority over futures trading, but the formal regulatory body, the Commodity Futures Trading Commission, had shown no leadership during the entire silver episode and had deferred decision making throughout the crisis to the exchanges. Volcker knew little about futures markets and refused to push Comex to close, but Jacobs had gotten his attention. He joined the vigil on March 27 because banks had extended credit directly to the Hunt brothers and to brokerage firms like Bache, and stability of the financial system was Volcker's first order of business. He would tell the House Subcommittee on Commerce, Consumer, and Monetary Affairs, "The situation was a serious concern to financial markets. . . . When there are major brokerage houses in potential difficulty, I am concerned."[93] Volcker added a broader caution: "I don't think there is any question that an incident of this sort in what is, after all, in some sense a relatively small market—the silver market isn't the biggest market in the world—can potentially have very grave repercussions."[94]

Volcker's point that "small does not mean benign" summarizes the history of the white metal. Silver mining never contributed much to U.S. economic activity, but the white metal molded American politics since the Crime of 1873, which simply omitted coining the silver dollar, heightening the battle between the conservative rural West and the liberal urban East. FDR curried favor with the small silver bloc in the Senate during the 1930s by subsidizing the white metal, which helped Japan subjugate an economically weakened China, encouraging the Japanese march to World War II. And now Volcker worried that a small brokerage firm—Bache was the eighth largest in the country—threatened the stability of the financial system because of the Hunts' obsession with silver, continuing the "small but explosive" legacy of the white metal.

Bache waited until Friday, March 28, to sell the bulk of the Hunt futures contracts and survived by luck and prayer, trading tactics that usually spell disaster.[95] That morning bargain hunters scooped up at $12 an ounce the white metal that only two months earlier had sold for $50, allowing Bache to liquidate the Hunt silver contracts to cover the family's obligations to the firm.[96] The crisis eased, but the Hunt brothers still owed $1.7 billion to other creditors and had lost a fortune, even by Hunt standards, which they blamed on everyone but themselves.[97] In subsequent testimony before Congress Herbert cited the exchanges that "finally broke the silver market on January 21 and 22, 1980," by imposing trading for liquidation-only.[98] He failed to mention that the collapse really began in early March when the Hunt liquidity crisis rippled through the market.

Some traders made a killing during the chaotic price decline. The press reported that Armand Hammer, who ran the multinational oil and gas company Occidental Petroleum, "made $119 million on futures market silver and gold transactions . . . as prices were plunging."[99] Hammer said the company had been developing silver and gold mines in Nevada and took advantage of the price spike last January and sold silver when it was "$41 an ounce and above." He said we "closed out our silver contracts . . . in the last week or ten days," a nice example of futures markets hedging anticipated production. Henry Jarecki's head silver trader, Sal Azzara, told his boss on Friday morning, March 28, "We had a pretty good year last night."[100] Sal anticipated frenzied trading between dealers after Comex closed on Silver Thursday, so he set up a makeshift operation in Henry's Manhattan apartment at UN Plaza, which had the necessary telexes and telephones. He bought silver all night from New York brokerage firms needing to liquidate and immediately sold the bullion to European companies looking for bargains. Prices fluctuated between $8 and $12 throughout the night, and Azzara traded more than 15 million ounces, always for a profit of at least a dollar an ounce rather than the usual nickel or dime. Henry smiled because he made a lot of money and because it reminded him of arbitraging Nescafé coffee between Basel and Heidelberg.

The Hunts' downfall fit Jarecki's portrait of failure. He had warned in his March 1979 *Euromoney* article that a trader cornering the market requires an exit strategy because when he sells, "his selling, and that of those who watch his activities, rapidly causes the price to fall; the price shoots downward even more rapidly than it rose," a prophetic description of events in March 1980. Jarecki had advertised his expertise to the Hunts and in retrospect suggested: "Maybe I could have taught them how to escape if they asked. There is only one way when you've successfully undertaken a corner, and that is to transform what you own into something else. With silver, they could probably have found a sovereign oil-producing entity from which they could have bought crude oil and paid for it in silver. They could have persuaded the leaders of some such country that it would strengthen them . . . to back their money with silver. . . . The Hunts tried a variation of my idea . . . [with] silver-backed bonds. But it was all too little and too late. . . . It was done in too great a rush. . . . I could have advised them on all that, but they wouldn't have listened."[101]

◆ ◆ ◆

Bunker, Herbert, and Lamar Hunt had assets worth more than $5 billion on Friday, March 28, 1980, and owed $1.7 billion in silver-related loans and obligations, making them among the richest families in the world despite the billions they lost in silver, but they still faced the threat of bankruptcy for failure to make scheduled payments.[102] They had no cash to pay Engelhard Minerals & Chemicals the $434 million due on Monday, March 31, in connection with the January EFP that, in retrospect, was one of the worst trades in history, almost as bad as the Red Sox selling Babe Ruth to the Yankees for $100,000 cash in 1920. The Hunts, mostly Bunker and Herbert, had agreed to pay almost $700 million for silver worth about $200 million at current bullion prices.[103] Milton Rosenthal, the silver-haired chairman of Engelhard, his vice chairman, David Tendler, and his legal staff flew to the Hunt offices in Dallas on Saturday, March 29, to collect their debt, but as one Engelhard participant said, "It was pretty clear that there wasn't much free collateral around."[104] He also noted, "The Hunts weren't apologetic at all. They said those were the facts and the facts were bad. For people who had just lost $2 billion, they were as calm as any people I've ever seen." Bunker's observation during the discussions, "A billion dollars isn't what it used to be," perhaps explains their unruffled demeanor.[105]

Negotiations dragged on for three days, and in a complicated transaction the Hunts gave Engelhard a 20% interest in their Canadian oil and gas property in the Beaufort Sea, relinquished any claim to the 19 million ounces of silver in the EFP, and gave up 8.5 million ounces of bullion they had pledged as collateral.[106] The *New York Times* headline, "A Deal's a Deal, Said Engelhard," suggests a victory for the New York Stock Exchange–listed company, but Engelhard accepted a speculative package, bullion worth about $350 million and a minority stake in unproved Beaufort Sea reserves, because it had no choice.[107] Years later Engelhard wrote off the Beaufort Sea property, but at the time Rosenthal accepted it rather than declaring all-out war by putting the Hunts into bankruptcy because a default by the Hunts might have been worse.[108] Milton Rosenthal said he was confident that "we obviously could have recovered a judgment," but he worried that a lawsuit would have tied up the Hunts' assets in the courts, would have required a detailed disclosure to Engelhard stockholders, and might have created a replay of Silver Thursday that could have bankrupted some brokerage firms.[109]

Paul Volcker also worried about the financial turmoil following a bankruptcy and approved a $1.1 billion bank loan to the Hunt family's Placid Oil Company to consolidate the remaining silver-related debts of Bunker, Herbert, and Lamar, which totaled about a billion dollars after settling with Engelhard.[110] The transaction, which Volcker described as designed to "greatly strengthen the security position of the creditors," needed his approval to assure that it did not violate the prohibition against speculative bank loans in the president's credit restraint program.[111] In his testimony before Representative Benjamin Rosenthal, chairman of the House Subcommittee on Commerce, Consumer, and Monetary Affairs, Volcker admitted: "I recognize that the outcome, while plainly desirable in the interests of the creditors themselves and financial stability generally, could have as a byproduct some stabilization of the financial position of the Hunts themselves."[112] Although Volcker did not say the Hunts were "too big to fail," the thin and bespectacled Rosenthal was not pleased and pushed Volcker for details:[113]

ROSENTHAL (R): Is it a correct statement to say that the Hunts are presently negotiating a loan from a group of banks for about $1 billion?

VOLCKER (V): Yes.

R: Have you in any way indicated the Federal Reserve would be cooperative with the banks in assisting them making that loan?

V: Our principal interest in their negotiation . . . is that this credit should . . . provide the maximum assurance that it will not contribute to further speculation in the silver commodities or securities markets.

R: Are you going to make any money available to these banks?

V: No.

R: How will this affect the credit markets altogether?

V: To the extent that the position of banks and other lenders is strengthened . . . it adds stability.

R: Do you know if it is a loan to two individuals?

V: This loan . . . will not be to the Hunts or the Hunt family, it will be to the Placid Oil Company.

The distinction between the Placid Oil Company and the Hunt brothers carried dire consequences for Bunker, Herbert, and Lamar. Trusts established for the six children of Lyda Bunker Hunt jointly owned Placid Oil Company.[114] Placid was a major moneymaker, earning $153 million on revenues of $756 million in 1979 from its oil and gas businesses, including operations as producer, refiner, and pipeline owner.[115] In March 1980 the Morgan Guaranty Trust Company put the value of Bunker, Herbert, and Lamar's share of Placid at $1.9 billion.[116] But by lending money to Placid rather than to the three brothers, the banks in effect forced all the trustee owners to guarantee repayment of funds used for the benefit of the silver speculators. Bunker's oldest sister, Margaret Hunt Hill, who had a soft spot for Bunker and his lifelong battle with food, nevertheless had "never liked the way Bunker and Herbert were wheeling and dealing."[117] She forced her brothers to mortgage their property to Placid to back their obligations to the family company.

The silver crisis passed, Bache stock began trading again on Wednesday, April 2, 1980, but the list of assets pledged to Placid by Bunker, Herbert, and Lamar made headlines.[118] Under the banner "When a Billionaire's Piggy Bank Breaks," the U.K. *Guardian* gave the world a glimpse of what living like a Hunt meant.[119] The brothers pledged businesses located throughout the United States, including "Mississippi cotton plantations, . . . an old bowling alley in Dallas, . . . citrus groves in California, and car parks in Anchorage, Alaska."[120] Herbert contributed his collection of rare Roman and Greek statues, and Lamar listed personal property that might have strained his marriage, including his wife's mink coat and her diamond ring. He demonstrated fair play by pledging his Rolex watch and his Mercedes. But Bunker, of course, made the biggest splash with his list of some five hundred thoroughbred horses, including Dahlia, the filly that had won the King George VI and Queen Elizabeth Stakes at the Ascot racecourse in back-to-back years, and Trillion, which came in second at the Prix de l'Arc de Triomphe race, where he met and wooed Mahmoud Fustok and Naji Nahas.[121]

It was embarrassing but the worst was yet to come.

CHAPTER 20

THE TRIAL

REPORTERS, COMMODITIES TRADERS, AND TRIAL BUFFS PACKED THE wood-paneled courtroom in the U.S. district court on Foley Square in downtown Manhattan on Wednesday, February 24, 1988, to glimpse the Texas billionaires who had lost a legacy trading silver eight years earlier.[1] Some of the old-timers may have recalled seeing other men turn wealth into misfortune, like Jesse Livermore, who reportedly made $100 million selling short before the 1929 stock market crash only to lose it all five years later. Or Ivar Kreuger, the Swedish entrepreneur called the match king because he controlled world match production, who built an international business em-pire during the 1920s and committed suicide in 1932, when ex-posed as a fraud. But the curiosity-seekers in the federal courtroom on February 24, 1988, wanted to see the 250-pound Bunker Hunt, considered the richest person in the world a few years earlier, de-fend his reputation in a civil trial against charges by Minpeco, the Peruvian government's marketing arm, that he and his brothers, Herbert and Lamar, had manipulated the price of silver for personal gain and caused almost $150 million in damages, which could be tripled under the antitrust laws.[2] Minpeco's civil trial in federal court suspended the CFTC's Division of Enforcement proceedings against Bunker and Herbert that had begun in 1987.[3]

Federal Judge Morris Lasker, a young-looking seventy-year-old with neatly parted dark hair, sat behind the raised podium in front of the room, and six jurors plus alternates, teachers and house-wives from Manhattan and the Bronx, were boxed-off to his right. Minpeco's lawyers and two officers of the company sat facing the judge in the first pew-style bench, and behind them were lawyers for the Hunts and attorneys for Mahmoud Fustok and IMIC, also named in the complaint. But there was no sign of Bunker, Herbert, or Lamar anywhere in the courtroom, nor would there be for some time. Defense lawyers had decided to keep the brothers away to prevent plaintiff lawyers from calling them as witnesses and instead would bring them in when the defense began its case.[4] It is a common enough tactic, made possible here because the defendants lived beyond the one-hundred-mile limit to the subpoena power of the court, and defense attorneys wanted jurors to see the Hunts accompanied by a favorable narrative. Judge Lasker told the jury "there is no obligation under law for a defendant to attend the trial," but the strategy turned into a disaster.[5]

+ + +

Trials begin with opening statements by attorneys to tell the jury what they expect to prove. The plaintiff usually goes first, and Mark Cymrot, forty-one years old with a then-fashionable thick black mustache, started for Minpeco by saying the Hunts "were greedy, that they were power hungry, and that they were unscrupulous."[6] He intended to show that they "rigged the silver market [and] that they cheated, that they drove up the price of silver, and they did it intentionally."[7] He accused the Hunts of violating the Sherman Antitrust Act by conspiring with others, including Mahmoud Fustok and Naji Nahas, to manipulate prices. Judge Lasker had already explained that the Sherman Act prohibited "two or more people [from entering] . . . into an agreement . . . to fix prices" and had defined manipulation in layman's terms as "roughly speaking . . . to cause prices to rise or fall in an artificial way."[8] Cymrot told the jurors not to expect "Bunker Hunt or Herbert Hunt or Mr. Fustok or Lamar Hunt to come here and say, yes I conspired. . . . They deny it."[9] Cymrot said the evidence was "something like a jigsaw puzzle" that jurors would have to piece together but offered a compelling chart as a visual aid.[10] The panoramic picture above the windows on the wall opposite the jury showed a line tracing silver prices from 1968 through 1987. The chart stretched almost the length of the courtroom and accentuated a history of slowly rising prices, beginning at around $2 an ounce in 1968 and ending in 1987 at about $7, interrupted by a skyscraper-like spike in January 1980 to $50 an ounce.[11] The chart dominated the courtroom for the entire trial, according to one defense attorney, forcing the Hunts to disown responsibility for the abnormal jump in prices.[12]

Paul Curran, a stocky fifty-five-year-old who had served as the U.S. attorney for the Southern District of New York, opened for the Hunts by saying that Minpeco has the "burden of proving facts" and emphasized multiple layers of facts in this case.[13] He said even if Minpeco proved a conspiracy, for example, they would still have to prove that the conspiracy caused "the price of silver to go up higher than it would have gone anyway." He then explained that "the evidence as distinguished from the conjecture will show that the price rise was caused by events in the world, political and economic . . . but were at this point in history more frequent, more powerful, more compressed, than before or since. That's because silver, just like gold, is an investment commodity that people want to hold in times of turmoil."[14] Curran added that silver is "much more erratic than gold" to explain why it increased twice as much and then reminded jurors of the chaotic period eight years earlier when inflation "reached double digit levels," when "Iranian terrorists invaded the United States embassy in Teheran and seized the American hostages," and then "the Russian army invaded Afghanistan."[15]

Both Cymrot and Curran sounded persuasive and the jurors paid attention—no one dozed off just yet—but Judge Lasker had told them before the opening statements, "Whatever any of the attorneys has to say about the facts of this case does not constitute evidence. You don't start to judge the evidence until you hear the witnesses."[16] Trouble for the defense began when Cymrot, unable to call Bunker, Herbert, or Lamar to testify in person, showed the jury unflattering videotapes of the brothers.

✦ ✦ ✦

A pair of black television screens propped up in front of the jury box aired a video showing a grainy frontal image of a well-dressed Bunker Hunt seated at the head of a long mahogany table covered with file folders.[17] It looked like a casual business meeting in Bunker's dining room, with half-filled drinking glasses set in front of three or four men in shirt sleeves seated along the sides of the table, but it was a deposition, oral sworn testimony, of Bunker Hunt taken by Mark Cymrot in a conference room of a Dallas law firm. Bunker did not smile for the camera because a deposition, used to discover information from witnesses before trial, feels like a colonoscopy but worse because it is with a lawyer. The attorney pokes the witness to extract incriminating answers while the witness tries to block the lawyer from learning too much. The confrontation resembles a bare-knuckles boxing match. A court reporter sat adjacent to Bunker to record his words for subsequent transcription, lawyers sat on both sides of the table monitoring the proceedings, and a cameraman videotaped the sessions.

Cymrot began the deposition with a simple question about a well-known episode:[18]

CYMROT (C): Mr. Hunt, in March of 1980, did you issue a press release from Paris in connection with silver-backed bonds?

HUNT (H): I knew about it. . . . I don't think it's correct to say I released it.

C: (*hands Hunt a page*) Okay. Let me direct your attention to . . . a document entitled "Announcement," and at the bottom it says Mr. Nelson Bunker Hunt . . . 26–3- 1980 . . . Now is that your signature on that document?

H: (*pushes his glasses up the bridge of his nose and holds the page close to his face as though checking counterfeit currency*) I can't tell. It's pretty blurred. It's some facsimile.

C: Does it appear to be your signature?

H: I couldn't promise you it is, but it's some similarity to it.

C: (*looks surprised*) You have some doubt about whether it's your signature?

H: I've answered your question.

C: (*shrugs and moves on*) Did the press release involve a group of silver owners who owned in excess of 200 million ounces of silver at that time?

H: (*shakes his head*) I don't know.

C: (*points to a copy of the press release in front of Bunker*) Let me ask you whether that's the press release that was issued?

H: (*looks at the document and then flips it back to Cymrot*) I don't know. I don't have that . . . close a recollection of it.

Bunker's verbal sparring over a signature may be fair play at a deposition, although pointless given the press coverage accorded the original announcement, but 200 million ounces of silver would never escape the Texan's recollection. His feigned amnesia may have displeased Cymrot at the time, but it became a bonanza when shown on screen at trial. Bunker sounded evasive, uncooperative, and untrustworthy, and his body language conveyed disdain for the proceedings, convincing the jury that he was lying when he later protested innocence. In post-trial interviews members of the jury said the videotapes showed the defendants to be "less than frank in explaining their actions" and "particularly damaging was Bunker Hunt's changing his testimony about his role in the silver-backed bonds."[19]

❖ ❖ ❖

Bunker's in-person courtroom performance fared worse. Three months after the trial began Paul Curran led his client through direct testimony that allowed Bunker to tell his story. He explained his obsession with the white metal in a soft Texas drawl, saying he wanted "to invest in something I could get my hands on," and, while panning the courtroom where his brothers, Herbert and Lamar, sat among the spectators, he added, "As far as the silver market goes, it was very bullish, almost euphoric."[20] When Curran asked about the alleged conspiracy, he became indignant, "I never participated in any conspiracy with anybody at any time."[21] Bunker admitted discussing the white metal as an investment—"I talked about silver with everybody"—but insisted, "I never knew anything about Fustok's operation" and "I never knew what Nahas was doing."[22] Bunker said that he made independent trading decisions and did not conspire with anyone, including his brother Herbert. He sounded like an eagle scout until Mark Cymrot's cross-examination.

Cymrot focused on the relationship between Bunker and Herbert:[23]

C: At any time during the period 1974 through 1980, did you and Herbert Hunt agree in advance on a particular day that you would buy silver?

H: I don't recall that ever happening.

C: On occasion in the period of 1974 through 1980, when you and Herbert Hunt held the same amount of silver and the same contract . . . would you say that was a coincidence?

H: I don't recall that ever occurring but if it did occur, it would have been a coincidence.

C: (*places a fat stack of files on the table and begins showing Bunker documents with identical brotherly transactions*): Mr. Hunt, was it just a coincidence that both you and your brother in November of 1979 contracted to purchase from Swiss Bank Corporation 750,000 ounces of silver . . . as indicated in these two memos?

H: No. In this particular case, this Swiss Bank deal, as separate from the commodity exchanges, I think I did make this purchase . . . and I asked my brother if he wanted to make one. And in this case as I recall he said he did. . . .

C: (*shows him another document*) These charts indicate that both you and your brother Herbert as of January 1, 1980, held London forward contracts with prompt dates of March 11, 1980, for 600,000 ounces each. Was it a coincidence? . . .

H: I don't recall why I bought those. Someone else would have to determine whether it was a coincidence or whatnot. I just don't recall.

C: Mr. Hunt, between early May of 1979 and mid-July, 1979, both you and your brother Herbert established substantial bull spread positions on the CBOT and Comex with the long legs in February, March, and May futures contracts. Was that a coincidence?

H: No, I don't recall that. I don't know whether it was a coincidence. I wouldn't say it was.

The discussion between Mark Cymrot and Bunker Hunt of identical trades continued for about an hour, but the case was over well before that, according to Phil Geraci, a bright young lawyer on the Hunt defense team. "I thought I would throw up if I heard the word coincidence again."[24] Bunker's claim that he and Herbert had not traded together lacked credibility and undermined his denial of a conspiracy with Mahmoud Fustok, Naji Nahas, Prince Faisal, and the other participants in the silver bond announcement of March 26, 1980.

◆ ◆ ◆

After the trial members of the jury said they took only a few hours to find Bunker, Herbert, and Lamar liable for manipulation, monopolization, fraud, and conspiracy, primarily because the Hunts had been evasive and inconsistent witnesses. [25] The jurors relied on a common sense principle, "false in one, false in all," which Hunt lawyer Paul Curran had used to highlight errors in Mark Cymrot's opening statement, but the phrase came back to haunt his clients.[26] Bunker, Herbert, and Lamar had tried but failed to connect with the working-class jury by taking the subway from their hotel to the courthouse every day. No one cared. And the jury ignored when Lamar brought Willie Lanier, the former Kansas City Chief's star linebacker, to sit with him in the courtroom.[27] Jurors found it easy to convict the Hunts but fought amongst themselves for five days over the amount to award to Minpeco because witnesses had disagreed on whether the attempted manipulation raised prices.[28]

An all-star cast of economic experts offered testimony, including Harvard's Hendrik Houthakker for Minpeco and Yale's Stephen Ross, Columbia's Frank Edwards, and Stanford's Jeffrey Williams for the defendants, but their statistical models failed to connect specific Hunt purchases with price increases in silver.[29] The absence of a link should have exonerated the Hunts but political news, although considerable, also failed to fully explain prices, leaving too much to the jury's imagination.[30] According to jurors, the most persuasive connection came from plaintiff's panoramic chart above the windows picturing massive Hunt silver holdings matched in time with the price spike, linking the two like thunder and lightning during a storm.[31] Defense expert witness Jeffrey Williams said later, "As evidence becomes more complicated and a trial longer, the power of a simple memorable argument increases."[32] On Saturday, August 20, 1988, after considerable prodding by Judge Lasker and without further explanation, the jury awarded Minpeco $65.7

million in damages, tripled under the antitrust and racketeering statutes, bringing the sum to $132 million after deducting what the Peruvians had already received in other settlements.[33]

The jury got the conspiracy part right. In a civil trial the standard of proof is "preponderance of evidence," and the jurors heard too many coincidences countered by evasive Hunt testimony to reject the plaintiff's claim of collusion. But that same standard failed to demonstrate that the Hunts and their allies drove up prices. The chronology suggests that unprecedented events, the massive accumulation of bullion, and a whirlwind of provocative news swept silver prices to near mythical levels, almost like the cyclone that whipped Dorothy to the Land of Oz. But the Hunt jury had to distinguish between the defendants' accumulation and the unsettling news to measure Hunt liability, and nothing the experts offered helped. For example, plaintiffs proposed that gold prices reflected political and economic turmoil and silver increased twice as much, providing a benchmark for damage calculation.[34] But that ignores the historical evidence that the white metal is twice as volatile as the yellow in normal times.[35] The jury compromised by awarding Minpeco about one-third of its claimed damage, $65 million out of $150 million, perhaps giving each of the forces—economic, political, and conspiratorial—an equal share of the blame.[36] But Minpeco's loss was largely self-inflicted, acknowledged back then by Peruvian officials saying that their "need to buy . . . silver futures in late December . . . contributed to the metals' sharp rise at that time," which would have made the failure of Minpeco to collect even this smaller judgment an appropriate outcome.[37]

+ + +

On Wednesday, September 21, 1988, Bunker and Herbert filed for personal bankruptcy in federal court in Dallas, explaining in a formal statement released by a Hunt company executive, "Bunker and Herbert believe the jury verdict in New York is so unjust that they elected to seek Chapter 11 protection of the United States Bankruptcy Court in order to insure their ability to continue their businesses while at the same time appealing their silver case."[38] Bunker added a personal touch, "The thought of even a dime going to the government of Peru is repugnant."[39] The bankruptcy filings erected a roadblock on the path to Hunt money, temporarily suspending payment of their obligations and pushing Minpeco's claims below that of secured creditors. Minpeco would have to detour through the bankruptcy court to receive its judgment.

The white metal had already undermined the crown jewel of the Hunt fortune, forcing the Placid Oil Company into Chapter 11 in August 1986, after oil prices collapsed to under $12 a barrel and the company missed payments on the outstanding balance of the billion-dollar silver loan.[40] *Forbes* magazine still counted the Hunts among the four hundred richest Americans after Placid's bankruptcy filing but bumped them down the 1986 list, with Bunker's net worth dropping from $900 million to $400, Herbert's from $800 million to $350, and Lamar's from $500 million to $250.[41] The Hunts still made fat targets for Minpeco's claims, but, except for Lamar, who settled his smaller share of the judgment without declaring bankruptcy, the brothers made the Peruvians work for their money.[42]

Bunker's thick bankruptcy papers, filed on September 21, 1988, listed personal property worth $249 million and debts exceeding $1.2 billion, but his filing contested the biggest obligations of $600 million to the IRS and $500 million in litigation claims, including to Minpeco.[43] His uncontested debts ranged in size from $36 million owed to Manufacturers Hanover Trust Company, the New York banking giant, to 67¢ owed the tax collector in Rockdale, Texas. A former bankruptcy judge in Dallas said, "In thousands and thousands of bankruptcy schedules I've never seen anyone list a 67 cent debt to a tax collector."[44] Not to be outdone, Herbert estimated his assets at $40 million and debts of $887 million, including the $36 million owed to the New York bank, for which both he and Bunker were jointly and individually liable, and personal obligations of $27.23 owed to Dennis Brannan of Coon Rapids, Iowa, and 36¢ to Anna Belle Langley of Houston. The bankruptcy papers listed valuable personal assets, including Bunker's ancient coin collection and Herbert's museum-quality Roman and Greek bronze statues, but added distractions such as Bunker's 1979

Oldsmobile Cutlass worth $1,000 and Herbert's wardrobe valued at $3,000. The big creditors, Manufacturers Hanover Bank and Minpeco, worried that the excessive detail resembled a pickpocket's bump, a diversion to mask prebankruptcy transfers of assets by Bunker and Herbert to escape creditor claims. Hugh Ray, an attorney for the New York bank said, "We're looking at all the transfers," which presumably included Bunker's shift of capital to overseas operations in New Zealand, Libya, and Yemen and Herbert's sale of his 1973 Mercedes to pay off a $5,000 debt to his daughter, Lyda Allred Hunt.

More than a year elapsed before the Hunts and their creditors agreed on a reorganization plan under Chapter 11 to settle outstanding claims. In a crowded Dallas courtroom on Friday, December 15, 1989, federal bankruptcy Judge Harold Abramson confirmed an agreement to appoint a trustee to sell Bunker's assets, valued at about $150 million, including Australian land, the ancient coin collection, and his two-thousand-acre Circle T Texas ranch.[45] On Thursday, December 21, 1989, the judge confirmed a similar plan to sell Herbert's $125 million of assets.[46] As part of the reorganization plan the CFTC settled its judgment against Bunker and Herbert with a $10 million fine for each and a lifetime ban against trading in the American commodities markets.[47]

The bankruptcy trustees would conduct the asset sales over six years and the bulk of the proceeds, 80% of Bunker's and 70% of Herbert's, would go to the IRS to settle back taxes, with the remainder divided among the other creditors, including Minpeco, who would receive about 30¢ on the dollar.[48] The final plan made everyone unhappy, creditors because they came away with so little and the Hunts because their lives would be transformed by the Texas-size garage sale.

The liquidation of the Circle T ranch in Westlake, Texas, brought more than two thousand people to the auctioneer's stand at Bunker's favorite retreat. The crowd included art dealers, jetsetters, and bargain hunters from more than twenty-five states and seven foreign countries, with cars parked where Hunt cattle once grazed. Everything was for sale, including an oriental rug that went for

FIGURE 19. The Athenian decadrachm, Bunker's favorite.

$9,000, a Chippendale dresser that sold for $8,500, and an oak rocking chair with Bunker's name burned into the back that Dallas resident Mike McCurley grabbed for $3,500. He said, "I'm going to use this as a constant reminder that no matter how big you get, you can always fall."[49] But the most personal item sold that day was a grinning bronze bust of Bunker that Houston Hunt, Bunker's son, bought for $3,500. He explained, "We're buying back a few things that meant something to us." The press quoted an unnamed family member saying they were buying it because "we're concerned that personal items, such as the bust, might end up as objects of ridicule as a centerpiece in a tavern or restaurant."

Sotheby's auction of the family's art and antiquities collections on June 19, 1990, in New York City, attracted a more sophisticated audience. Bunker spoke philosophically about the event: "It's not a happy situation. But in life you have to do things you don't want to do. I doubt if I'll ever be in shape to collect again. If I live long enough, I may have enough money to do something, but probably not."[50] He discussed his favorite coins in the collection, mentioning the silver Athenian decadrachm, minted in the early fifth century BCE, which cost him a record $272,000 in 1974 and would fetch twice that in the auction: "You enjoy seeing these things. They're very beautiful." Herbert was equally smitten by his collection of

Byzantine coins, described by a private consultant to Sotheby's as "on a par with many museum collections." Herbert said, "I like the silver Byzantine coins. They're rarer. There're not as many of them that made it through time. They're pretty too. I just like them."

Falling in love with the white metal had cost them a fortune.

CHAPTER 21

BUFFETT'S MANIPULATION?*

ON WEDNESDAY, JANUARY 14, 1998, ALMOST TEN YEARS AFTER THE Hunt case went to trial, the *Wall Street Journal* reported that the Commodity Futures Trading Commission had "increased surveillance in the silver futures market following allegations that several market participants were manipulating prices."[1] A price increase of almost 30% during November and December 1997, bringing the white metal to an 8½-year high of almost $6 an ounce, triggered the inquiry according to the *Journal*.[2] A CFTC spokesperson said, "The Commission intensifies its surveillance efforts when unusual events or activities occur such as we've seen lately in silver markets."[3]

The CFTC had good reason to suspect foul play. Unlike 1979 and 1980, when investors took refuge in gold and silver to protect against rising inflation and political unrest, the near-30% jump in silver during the last half of 1997 came with global stability and a *decline* in gold prices of more than 13%, making manipulation the prime suspect in silver's resurgence.[4] Chase Manhattan Bank's head of commodity risk analysis, Dinsa Mehta, said, "One has to treat with suspicion an overt attempt to muscle the commodity higher."[5]

A report in the *Wall Street Journal* that "silver stockpiles at Comex Warehouses dipped to . . . the lowest level since 1985" and rumors that "a lot of that silver has left the country" sounded like the Hunts were back in business.[6] New York attorney Christopher Lovell revived names from that era by filing a lawsuit charging Phibro, the commodities trading arm of Travelers Insurance Company and originally the Philipp Brothers division of Engelhard In-

---

*Warren Buffett refused to be interviewed for this discussion. He responded to one question by e-mail through his administrative assistant, as described in an endnote below.

dustries, with moving silver from Comex warehouses to "non-reporting black hole locations" in England and elsewhere.[7] The U.K. *Guardian* spiced the international scene with the headline, "Booming Silver Market 'Rigged,'"[8] and quoted a London bullion market trader, "It seems to us someone is doing something." The *Guardian* reported that "both the Bank of England . . . and the London Bullion Market Association . . . are watching developments."[9]

The mysterious "someone" emerged from behind the curtain on Tuesday, February 3, 1998, in a press release from Warren Buffett's Berkshire Hathaway Company: "Because of recent price movements in the silver market and because Berkshire Hathaway has received inquiries about its ownership of the metal, the company is releasing certain information that it would normally have published next month in its annual report. The company owns 129,710,000 ounces of silver. Its first purchase was made on July 25, 1997, and its most recent purchase was made on January 12, 1998."[10]

Buffett, at the time a spry sixty-eight-year-old with a white-hair comb-over, the most successful American investor in the second half of the twentieth century, suggested in the press release that he had completed accumulating the white metal: "Berkshire has no present plans for purchase or sale of silver."[11] The disclaimer failed to discourage speculators, who drove up silver prices by a significant 16% in two days following the Berkshire Hathaway announcement, reaching $7.59 per ounce, the highest in almost ten years.[12] They had every reason to jump on the bandwagon. In less than six months Buffett had bought 25% of the world's annual production of the white metal, a performance worthy of Nelson Bunker Hunt.[13]

✦ ✦ ✦

Silver did not belong among Warren Buffett's investments. He had led Berkshire Hathaway for more than thirty years, priding himself on picking companies that are "understandable, possess excellent economics, and are run by outstanding people," qualities he examined as though he were considering a lifelong commitment.[14] His investments lasted longer than most modern marriages. When Robert Goizueta, the CEO of Coca Cola, Berkshire's largest holding in 1997, died in October, Buffett commented, "After his death,

FIGURE 20. Warren Buffett gives investments the taste test.

I read every one of the 100 letters and notes he had written me during the past nine years. Those messages could well serve as a guidebook for success in both business and life."[15] In discussing his acquisition of International Dairy Queen in 1997, he first gave some general information, "There are 5,792 Dairy Queen stores operating in 23 countries—all but a handful run by franchisees," and then added a personal touch, saying that he and his partner Charlie Munger, vice-chairman of Berkshire Hathaway, "bring a modicum of product expertise to this transaction. [Charlie] has been patronizing the Dairy Queens in Cass Lake and Bemidji, Minnesota, for decades and I have been a regular in Omaha. We have put our money where our mouth is."[16] But Buffett would dismiss owning assets like precious metals that "will never produce anything, but that are purchased in the buyer's hope that someone else . . . will pay more for them in the future."[17] His least favorite was gold, which he said would "remain lifeless forever."[18]

The CEO of Berkshire Hathaway gave silver a reprieve because the metal is a cross between precious and industrial, a store of wealth for millions, and productive in photography and electronics. It was also good to him early in his career, making his commitment personal as with Dairy Queen: "Thirty years ago [1967], I bought silver because I anticipated its demonetization . . . [and] ever since I have followed the metal's fundamentals but not owned it."[19] He had been watching silver longer than Bunker Hunt and made it sound like a homecoming when disclosing this "non-traditional investment" in his 1997 letter to Berkshire Hathaway shareholders: "In a way, this is a return to the past for me."

Buffett's return began on Friday, July 25, 1997, when silver was $4.33 an ounce, and he proudly reported that by the end of the year the "position produced a pre-tax gain of $97.4 million."[20] He explained his reasons for the investment, which totaled about 2% of Berkshire Hathaway's portfolio: "Charlie and I concluded that a higher price would be needed to establish equilibrium between supply and demand." Buffett liked silver because annual consumption by industry outpaced mine production, the same fundamentals attracting the Hunts to silver rather than gold, but he quickly distanced himself from the fallen billionaires: "Inflation expectations . . . play no part in our calculation of silver's value." To just about everyone else, however, the price jump in the white metal brought back memories of a squeeze and inevitable comparisons to Bunker Hunt.

The day after Berkshire Hathaway disclosed its purchases the *Washington Post* told its readers that "Buffett has amassed the biggest silver position any single individual has accumulated since the Hunt brothers were accused of trying to corner the silver market in 1980."[21] The *New York Times* drew a distinction:[22] "When the Hunts were accumulating their position, they and many investors believed that there was no way that rampant inflation could be checked. . . . Now, the opposite consensus prevails, with inflation deemed to be quiet and likely to stay that way." But the *Times* then turned Warren Buffett into a Bunker Hunt look-alike by making the technical observation that "silver has recently traded in what is called backwardation." The word "backwardation" means that silver for immediate delivery sells for a higher price than silver for delivery in the future, which is very unusual for a precious metal that incurs storage costs. The *Times* then explained that this strange phenomenon "reflects concerns about a possible squeeze on current supplies, and is an indication . . . that huge quantities of silver have been accumulated." The *Times* should have reminded readers that the CFTC had used backwardation and related concepts to charge the Hunts with manipulation.[23]

Buffett tried to soften the squeeze by saying in the original press release: "If any seller should have trouble making timely delivery, Berkshire is willing to defer delivery for a reasonable period upon payment of a modest fee."[24] Looking back he claims that Berkshire Hathaway "intentionally avoided buying an amount beyond what was easily available for delivery" but the contemporaneous backwardation in silver indicates otherwise.[25] Buffett owned a large stake in the Travelers Insurance Company and had used its commodities trading subsidiary, Phibro, to accumulate the white metal in London, draining Comex warehouses and adding to the perceived shortage.[26] The *Guardian* explained:[27] "Silver was heading for London to meet Mr. Buffett's order and once there, it disappeared behind a veil of secrecy because London publishes no figures for the bullion in its vaults." Switzerland had been the silent refuge for Hunt silver.

✦ ✦ ✦

The Berkshire Hathaway press release of February 3, 1998, ended the CFTC's investigation almost before it began, a testament to Buffett's reputation for integrity and the slippery definition of manipulation.[28] The commission's annual report never mentioned Warren Buffett by name and summarized the incident like the weather bureau on a tropical disturbance: "Silver prices rose sharply from $4 to over $7 per ounce between July 1997 and February 1998. . . . The most significant concern was the demand for silver by the holder of a sizable position in London. . . . Subsequently, prices fell and spreads loosened as the market was able to provide sufficient supplies."[29] Christopher Lovell, the New York attorney who had sued Phibro for carrying out the manipulation, joined the CFTC on the sidelines and withdrew the complaint.[30]

The subjective nature of manipulation, which requires the *intent* to distort prices, eased Buffett's treatment. Dennis A. Klejna, a lawyer who ran the CFTC's Division of Enforcement when the agency prosecuted the Hunts, said, "It is very difficult to establish manipulation under the law, because there are very legitimate reasons for people to purchase large amounts of commodity futures contracts or large amounts of physical commodities."[31] Buffett's accumulation squeezed the silver market but proving manipulation by an individual investor requires testimony by a mind reader. The jury convicted the Hunts because they conspired with other traders, a violation of the antitrust laws, while Warren Buffett's approach to investment abhors collusion. His success comes from being a contrarian, buying when everyone is selling, as explained in his 1997 letter to Berkshire Hathaway shareholders:[32] "You pay a very high price . . . for a cheery consensus . . . pessimism drives down prices to truly attractive levels." Buffett's investment in silver fits this profile.

Berkshire Hathaway never disclosed the average cost per ounce of its white metal but the pretax profit of $97.4 million reported for 1997 permits an estimate of $5.05 for 111.2 million ounces bought in 1997.[33] The remaining 18.5 million cost about $5.50.[34] Buffett had bought a bargain and paid cash, so he could have held forever, as with his Coca Cola stock.[35] But he became impatient and would scold himself: "I bought it very early and sold it very early."[36] Buffett missed the explosive advance that would soon challenge the Hunt era record of $50 an ounce.

CHAPTER 22

MESSAGE FROM OMAHA

THE NEW MILLENNIUM DULLED SILVER'S LUSTER. PRECIOUS METALS gain during economic and political chaos, but the Great Moderation that began in the mid-1980s—declining inflation, stable economic growth, and lower interest rates—made the world look as calm as a desert mirage. During the first week of September 2001 the price of the white metal averaged $4.17 an ounce, so Warren Buffet's $97.4-million paper profit of 1997 turned into a paper loss of almost $100 million, small change for Berkshire Hathaway but a disappointment to the CEO.[1]

And then came September 11.

The tragic day cost more American lives than Pearl Harbor, brought New York City to a standstill, and destroyed America's comfort zone forever. Speculators from London to Tokyo should have embraced the white metal the way Americans did when the Ayatollah Khomeini made his triumphant return to Iran. Instead they did almost nothing. Silver rose a paltry 4¢ an ounce to $4.22 in the London bullion market on September 12, about the same as a normal day's volatility, while gold increased a significant 3% to $279.50 in response to the shock.[2] By year's end neither metal deserved its reputation as a safety net. Silver closed at $4.62 an ounce on December 31, 2001, a slight increase over its pre-9/11 level, and gold settled at $279, little changed from before the terror.[3] The long slide in precious metals that began when the bubble burst in January 1980 continued to torture investors who had bought at the top. Gold had declined to less than one-third its peak and silver to under a tenth, a miserable performance over twenty years that made the precious metals market resemble West Virginia's coal country.

Warren Buffett remained undeterred. He had bought after prices had shriveled and could afford to wait for his silver seeds to flower. Buffett believed in the white metal because economic fundamentals would drive the price higher and not because silver had become a rock-hard asset after it had been demonetized. He viewed silver as an industrial commodity like copper or oil and relied on supply and demand to turn a profit. He recalled that in 1997 "silver was out of balance," with annual demand for photography, jewelry, electronics, and other uses exceeding by almost 200 million ounces mine production plus reclamation from old scrap.[4] Baby boomers melted silver cuff links and hair clips inherited from their grand-parents to close the gap. Buffett expected the annual shortfall to continue, putting upward pressure on prices, because "there are few pure silver mines—most silver is produced as a byproduct from other mining—so it's not easy to bring on added production."[5] The Berkshire Hathaway CEO also understood the power of patience, having told his stockholders when he first bought Coca Cola stock in 1988, "Our favorite holding period is forever."[6] So he waited.

By the middle of 2005 Buffett's staying power paid off. An expanding U.S. economy spurred silver prices and the *New York Times* celebrated the white metal's resurgence on Sunday, May 29, 2005, with the headline "Gold Sleeps While Silver Rocks."[7] The *Times* reported, "Silver ended last week at $7.31 an ounce, up 7.4 percent for the year," compared with gold that was "down 4.2 percent in 2005," and explained the white metal's superior performance as though it were dictated in Omaha: "Silver is more of an industrial commodity, while gold still has its monetary and safe-harbor allure. That means economic growth is good for silver." A new bull market was underway, just as Warren Buffett had predicted.

A year later, on Friday, May 5, 2006, a day before Berkshire Ha-thaway's annual meeting, silver traded at $14.15 an ounce, almost doubling over twelve months and confirming the Oracle of Oma-ha's wisdom.[8] The price advance had been slow and persistent, like a steamroller, unlike the sharp spikes of the Hunt era when prices doubled over two months (twice) only to crater when speculators ran out of cash.[9] Berkshire shareholders had much to anticipate.

+ + +

The capacity crowd at the annual meeting in the twenty-thousand-seat Quest Arena and Convention Center in downtown Omaha on Saturday morning, May 6, 2006, resembled fans gathered for a rock concert.[10] To his stockholders, Warren Buffett dwarfed Bruce Springsteen in popularity. The meeting began at 8:30 a.m. with the latest Berkshire Hathaway comedy movie, a one-hour clip featuring Buffett and his partner Charlie Munger, six years older than Warren with a similar ruddy complexion, riffing with actress Jamie Lee Curtis about their investment strategies.[11] A five-hour question-and-answer session followed the movie and both Buffett and Munger responded, although Munger often contributed his favorite line, "I have nothing further to add."[12] They answered questions on Berkshire's cash balance—"$37 billion"—and on the danger of a nuclear attack in the United States—"It will happen someday."[13] Both of those were shocking responses, but the real surprise came in the discussion of commodity bubbles. Buffett worried about speculation in copper, where prices had increased fivefold between 2001 and 2005, from 70¢ a pound to $3.50. He profiled copper's behavior as "driven by fundamentals" at the outset and then "speculation takes over." He added his favorite refrain, "What the wise man does in the beginning, fools do in the end." And then he dropped the bombshell, "We had a lot of silver at one time, but we don't have it now."

Buffett sounded apologetic: "I bought it very early and sold it very early. We made a few dollars."[14] Rumors circulated that Berkshire Hathaway had sold at $7.50 an ounce in mid-2005, soon after the *New York Times* sang silver's praises.[15] Buffett never confirmed those details, but the timing made sense. The *Times* article would have brought unhealthy follow-on speculation, making Buffett cringe, and by 2005 the excess demand by industry over mine supply, which had attracted Buffett, had declined to one-third its earlier level.[16] Berkshire Hathaway earned about $275 million on the investment of $560 million in 1997, about a 5% compound annual return over the eight years, less than they would have earned investing in U.S. Treasury bonds.[17] Charlie Munger deadpanned, "I think we've demonstrated our expertise in commodities, if you look at our activities in silver."[18] Buffett concurred: "We're not good at figuring out when a speculative game will end."

He did not realize it was about to begin.

✦ ✦ ✦

Buffett's view of silver as an industrial commodity gained credibility after the May 2006 Berkshire Hathaway annual meeting. Fabrication demand for the white metal fell by almost 100 million ounces between 2006 and 2008, a drop of 10%, primarily because digital photography thinned the need for conventional film.[19] An excess supply of the white metal drove down the price by more than 20% between Friday, May 5, 2006, and Friday, September 12, 2008.[20] Silver resembled copper, which dropped by 11% over the same time and suffered compared with gold, which increased in value by 12%.[21] The $10.87 price of the white metal on September 12, 2008, still embarrassed Buffett's sale at $7.50 but confirmed his idea that silver belonged with the base metals rather than the nobles. Then came the Great Recession.

The Chapter 11 filing of Lehman Brothers, the largest bankruptcy in American history, on Monday, September 15, 2008, turned a mild recession into the worst financial crisis since the Great Depression. The failure destroyed trust in financial assets, triggered panicked withdrawals from money market mutual funds, until then considered the equivalent of cash, and forced the U.S. Treasury to guarantee their safety. The expanded government insurance program prevented old-fashioned bank runs like those that had robbed the life savings of millions during the 1930s, but risky assets like equities remained vulnerable. Investor selling drove down U.S. stock prices by 46% in the six months after Lehman, a decline that rivaled the worst bear markets in history.[22] Shares of General Electric, a diversified multinational company founded more than one hundred years earlier by inventor Thomas Edison, fell 70%, from $26.75 on September 12, 2008, the Friday before Lehman's bankruptcy, to $7.41 on March 9, 2009, the stock market's low point.[23] A discouraged Wall Street octogenarian explained in unfashionable terms: "When they raid the brothel they take all the girls . . . even the pretty ones."[24]

The weak economy also destroyed raw material prices during those six months of economic turmoil. Crude oil dropped by more than 50% and copper lost 49%.[25] Investors turned to U.S. government bonds, where rising prices lowered yields, and bought the timeless stores of value, gold and silver, which increased in value by 20%.[26] The rise in gold surprised no one, but Buffett's industrial label for silver suggested it would decline like copper and oil. Instead, investors polished silver's twenty-first-century image to reflect its noble history.[27] Silver correlates more with gold than with copper.[28]

Aggressive government bailouts by the U.S. Treasury of General Motors, Chrysler, and insurance giant AIG, and the Federal Reserve's zero-interest rate policy, helped America weather Lehman's default, but Europe was not so lucky.[29] By the end of 2009 U.S. stock prices recovered more than three-quarters of their losses just as international lenders began to doubt the creditworthiness of Greece, Ireland, and Portugal, with Italy and Spain not far behind.[30] The European sovereign debt crisis turned the jump in gold and silver that greeted the Lehman bankruptcy into a bonanza not seen since the days of Nelson Bunker Hunt. The exploding financial chaos sparked gold prices to an all-time record $1,900 an ounce on September 5, 2011, an increase of 250% in the three years since Lehman's collapse.[31] Silver closed at $42.92 that same day, for a 400% increase, almost twice the move in gold, confirming silver's reputation for volatility.

The evidence that silver outperformed gold during the Great Recession came too late to help exonerate the Hunts, who had been blamed for manipulating that result during the last speculative boom, but it certainly taught Warren Buffett a lesson. He had been right to view silver as vulnerable to industrial forces, which is probably why it never breached the $50 record set in 1980, while gold, at $1900, more than doubled its 1980 peak. But Buffett forgot that the white metal is like a switch hitter in baseball, an industrial batter but also comfortable from the precious side of the plate. His uncharacteristic impatience cost more than he admitted. Had Buffett sold at $42.92 on September 5, 2011, well below the $48 crisis peak, he would have made $4.2 billion on his investment of $560 million.[32] His fourteen-year silver speculation would have earned a respectable 16.5% compound annual return.

◆ ◆ ◆

No one expects to sell at the top, so precious metals belong in every investor's portfolio forever, including Warren Buffett's, just like Coca Cola. His allocation of 2% to silver makes sense—not too much to cause insomnia, but enough to provide for food, clothing,

FIGURE 21. A very pretty American eagle silver dollar.

and an iPhone during the next crisis. The evidence suggests that people have learned from the three catastrophes that tested investors during the last one hundred years: the Great Depression of the 1930s; the Great Inflation of the 1970s; and the Great Recession of the new millennium. During the last two episodes investors bought gold and silver without government interference, driving up prices to dizzying heights only to watch them decline when the chaos passed. But crises will not always end in a smile, and investors understand that three tests are too few to extrapolate. In 2017, as the Great Recession faded, silver declined to about $17 an ounce, one-third its 2011 peak but three times higher than the price Buffett paid twenty years earlier. Silver has earned its reputation as a rock-hard asset in a world of fiat currency, and investors enjoy its protective shield.

The U.S. Treasury issues the American silver eagle, a dollar coin containing one troy ounce of 99.9% pure silver, sold at a friendly markup above intrinsic value since the program began in 1986.[33] The shiny white coin is as pretty as Nelson Bunker Hunt's Athenian decadrachm, with Lady Liberty etched into the front and the back engraved with an eagle and shield like the Great Seal of the United States. Between 1986 and 2007 the U.S. Mint sold an average of 7.1 million coins a year, and from 2008 through 2016 annual sales jumped fivefold to an average of 37.3 million.[34] The combined sales of silver coins by the United States, Canada, Australia, and others increased from an annual average of 30 million to 115.5 million ounces.[35] The jump in sales since 2008 suggests at least some people expect silver to make a comeback as a medium of exchange. Utah offered them hope with the Legal Tender Act of 2011 that made American silver eagles acceptable in payments at their intrinsic value within the state, but legislation elsewhere failed to pass, including Congressman Ron Paul's effort to restore both gold and silver as monetary metals.[36] Las Vegas bookmakers would place low odds on the remonetization of silver in the United States, perhaps the same line as on the richest man in the world being forced into bankruptcy, which could never happen again.

Or could it?

CHAPTER 23

THE PAST INFORMS THE FUTURE

WHEN NELSON BUNKER HUNT DIED IN OCTOBER 2014, THE *New York Times* obituary speculated that he was still a multimillionaire from trusts established by his father that had escaped the personal bankruptcy proceedings of the 1990s.[1] The *Times* was probably right about Bunker but would have been on firmer ground discussing his brother Herbert, who had returned to the ranks of billionaires in 2013 by selling oil-rich property for $1.45 billion that he had bought a few years earlier in North Dakota.[2] *Bloomberg News* reported Herbert Hunt's total net worth at $4.2 billion. The Hunts survived their infatuation with the white metal, but their name is forever linked with the silver obsession that roiled the financial system and drove prices to record levels in January 1980. Investors sought refuge in hard assets like gold and silver to protect against the economic and political turmoil back then, just like they did after the 2008 financial crisis. The Hunts preferred the white metal, like Berkshire Hathaway CEO Warren Buffett, and should have been exonerated of price manipulation charges. Their disdain for the legal proceedings and evasive courtroom behavior brought a guilty verdict, forever staining their reputations despite their enduring wealth, giving new meaning to Bunker's insight that "a billion dollars isn't what it used to be."

The white metal has lured others with its shine, making a small mining industry with a sprinkling of employees into a major force in economic and political history. Silver gained its special status as currency in the ancient world because it was valuable; it remained the key medium of exchange for centuries because it never became too valuable. Alexander Hamilton, America's first Treasury secretary, embraced silver to avoid a scarcity of circulating currency in the young

Republic, but his soft-money system, designed to promote economic growth, tarnished subsequent political careers and sprayed collateral damage beyond American borders for the next two hundred years.

U.S. Senator John Sherman, chairman of the Senate Finance Committee, used deception and misdirection to demonetize the white metal in 1873. He established gold as king of American finance, perhaps to promote his presidential aspirations, and unleashed a great deflation in the United States during the last quarter of the nineteenth century. The resulting economic turmoil fed the populist battle between the rural West and the urban East in the United States, leading to William Jennings Bryan's 1896 presidential campaign, a referendum on the gold standard. Bryan's electrifying rhetoric and "16 to 1" war cry to restore silver as a monetary standard failed to sway the voters, and the yellow metal retained its monetary crown, but pro-silver agitation persisted into the twentieth century with international repercussions.

The powerful silver bloc in the U.S. Senate, consisting of the fourteen representatives of western mining states, gave the white metal inordinate sway in the upper chamber of Congress. Key Pittman, an ambitious senator from Nevada, known as the Silver State, became the influential chairman of the Senate Foreign Relations Committee in 1933, attracting the attention of the newly elected Franklin Delano Roosevelt. FDR ensured Pittman's loyalty by supporting the Silver Purchase Act of 1934, partly reversing the Crime of 1873. The Act rehabilitated the monetary status of silver with a buying program to make the white metal 25% of America's monetary reserves. American purchases under the 1934 Act raised the metal's price, drove China off the silver standard in 1935, and tipped the balance of power in Japan away from the diplomats and towards the military. Japanese aggression had begun before the Silver Purchase Act, but the American program further weakened a China already divided by Mao Tse-tung's communist insurgents. The Sino-Japanese conflict began in 1937 and escalated globally during World War II, leading to an inflationary spiral in China that fostered the communist victory in 1949.

FDR ignored the fallout of the Silver Purchase Act on the Far East, highlighting the danger of making domestic policy without weighing the international implications, a lesson with a powerful message in the twenty-first century. Presidential tunnel vision at the dawn of the new millennium carries similar risks of international collateral damage, and as with Roosevelt's narrow-mindedness, the wreckage from "America First" policymaking may not materialize until it is too late.

The white metal continued to shape world events after Congress repealed the Silver Purchase Act in 1963. U.S. law still barred citizens from holding gold as an investment, so silver, which had been the metal of the people for centuries because it was cheaper than gold, became the refuge of choice against economic and political uncertainty, a storehouse of value in turbulent times. America's money remained linked by statute to precious metals until Congress cut the remaining connections with domestic credit in 1968. And fiat currency, paper money lacking any intrinsic value, emerged after President Nixon suspended the right of foreign central banks to convert dollars into gold on August 15, 1971.

The worldwide experiment in pure paper money that continues today almost failed at the start. The newly designed freedom from precious metals allowed America's central bank, the Federal Reserve System, to deliver easy credit in response to political pressure, spawning the Great Inflation of the 1970s. Expenditures on the Vietnam War and escalating oil prices deserve their share of the blame for the inflationary spiral, but an unchecked Federal Reserve dominates the record. The 1970s nearly destroyed the U.S. dollar and undermined America's international standing, but the chaos unleashed popular support for making price stability the primary objective of an independent central bank. During the 1980s, the Federal Reserve, under the chairmanship of Paul Volcker, tamed runaway inflation and restored monetary credibility. Since then central bank independence throughout the world has replaced gold and silver as guardian of the currency.

Will precious metals ever return to their monetary status? Not if central bankers do their job, but public support can evaporate, undermining their resolve. The U.S. Congress, for example, can abolish the Federal Reserve with a simple majority vote, suggesting that America's central bank might run a printing press when rising interest rates bring an avalanche of protest to Capitol Hill.[3] The Federal Reserve has survived the fifty-year-old trial of fiat currency, but that period is less than a heartbeat in world history. The Soviet Union's experiment with communism challenged America for world domination for the better part of the twentieth century before expiring like the worthless paper currency of the Weimer Republic. Central bankers remain on trial, and the uncertain verdict sustains the ancient role of gold and silver as storehouses of value in the new millennium.

NOTES

INTRODUCTION: OBSESSION

1. "Lamar Hunt, a Force in Football, Dies at 74," *New York Times*, December 15, 2006, p. C12.

2. The related designation "boldest futures manipulation of the twentieth century" is from Burton Malkiel, *A Random Walk Down Wall Street*, rev. ed. (New York: Norton, 2015), p. 417. The peak price was an intraday high of $50.36 for spot silver (i.e., for the January futures contract) recorded on January 18, 1980, on New York's Commodity Exchange (see *New York Times*, January 19, 1980, p. 36). An intraday high of $50.50 was recorded on the Chicago Board of Trade.

3. For Bunker's association with the John Birch Society, see Stephen Fay, *Beyond Greed* (New York: Viking Press, 1982), pp. 18–19.

4. "Bankrupt Hunt Brothers Bid Adieu to Art Collections Worth Billions," *Chicago Tribune*, May 10, 1990, p. C1.

5. "Nelson Bunker Hunt, 88, Oil Tycoon with a Texas-Size Presence, Dies," *New York Times*, October 22, 2014, p. A24.

6. "Speech Concluding the Debate on the Chicago Platform," in William Jennings Bryan, *The First Battle: A Story of the Campaign of 1896* (Chicago: W.B. Conkey Company, 1896), pp. 199–200.

7. The cash price of silver on September 12, 2008, the Friday before the investment bank Lehman Brothers announced its bankruptcy, was $10.87 per ounce. Three years later on September 12, 2011, during the height of the European sovereign debt crisis, silver was $40.26 per ounce, for an increase of 370% over the three-year period. Berkshire Hathaway closed at $103,800 on September 12, 2011, compared with a price of $68,000 on September 10, 2001, an increase of less than 100%. Note: As described in "From the Author" at the beginning of this book, cash prices after the 1930s come from the Commodity Research Bureau (CRB) database (the SI-Y series), unless noted otherwise. Berkshire Hathaway stock prices are from Yahoo! Finance.

8. I witnessed this test conducted by Donald and Angelo Palmieri of the Gem Certification & Assurance Lab (GCAL), 580 Fifth Avenue, New York City, although it was not easy for me to distinguish the colors. They also confirmed this test with a more modern X-ray fluorescence technique. For a discussion of "assaying by fire" from ancient times to the present see J.S. Forbes, *Hallmark: A History of the London Assay Office* (London: Unicorn Press, 1999), pp. 20–24. Also see http://www.sciencecompany.com/How-to-Test-Gold-Silver-and-Other-Precious-Metals.aspx.

9. See A.E. Feavearyear, *The Pound Sterling: A History of English Money* (Oxford: Clarendon Press, 1931), chap. 4; and Seymour Wyler, *The Book of Old Silver* (New York: Crown, 1937), p. 7. According to Thomas Sargent and Francois Velde, *The Big Problem of Small Change* (Princeton, N.J.: Princeton University Press, 2002), pp. 82–83, "One pound represented different amounts of gold

and silver at different times," which may be true, but both Wyler and Feavearyear confirm that Elizabeth promulgated the sterling standard of "11 ounces, 2dwt." There are 20 pennyweights (dwt) in a troy ounce so sterling meant 11.1 troy ounces, which is .925 of a troy pound (= 12 troy ounces).

10. Feavearyear, *Pound Sterling*, p. 8.

11. Daniëlle O. Kisluk-Grosheide and Jeffrey Munge, *The Wrightsman Galleries for French Decorative Arts* (New York: Metropolitan Museum of Art, 2010), p. 106.

12. William E. Brooks, "Silver," in U.S. Department of the Interior & U.S. Geological Survey. *Minerals Yearbook 2008*, vol. 1, *Metals and Minerals* (Washington, DC: Government Printing Office, 2010), p. 68.2, available at https://babel.hathitrust.org/cgi/pt?id=msu.31293031621463;view=1up;seq=902.

13. See Rhonda L. Rundle, "This War against Germs Has a Silver Lining," *Wall Street Journal*, June 6, 2006, updated 12:01 a.m. "Now, silver is showing up as a bacteria- and odor-fighting material in a range of contemporary consumer products, from sports socks to washing machines."

14. Ibid.

15. "Constantly Battling a Hidden Foe," *New York Times*, October 8, 2017, p. SP1.

16. See *World Silver Supply and Demand* at https://www.silverinstitute.org/site/supply-demand/.

17. "Teheran Students Seize U.S. Embassy and Hold Hostages," *New York Times*, November 5, 1979, p. A1.

18. The price of spot silver (i.e., for the November contract on the Commodity Exchange) closed at $16.08 on November 2, 1979 (the last trading day before the hostage taking) and reached a high of $50.36 on the Commodity Exchange on January 18, 1980 (see note 2).

19. One measure of the relative size of the gold and silver markets comes from futures markets. Data for the Commodity Exchange on December 31, 2014, show a total open interest (total number of contracts outstanding) for gold of 371,646 contracts and a total of 151,215 contracts for silver. These translate into dollar amounts as follows: Gold contracts are for 100 ounces and the cash price per ounce on December 31, 2014, was $1,184, for a total of $44 billion. Silver contracts are for 5,000 ounces at a cash price of $15.69 per ounce for a total value of $11.9 billion. These numbers are surely underestimates of the total value of gold and silver in the world, but the relative size of the two markets is confirmed by a completely different source and time period. U.S. Department of Commerce, *The Minerals Yearbook: 1932–1933 Year 1931–32* (Washington, DC: Government Printing Office, 1933), p. 12, estimates the total value (at the much lower prevailing market prices) of all gold mined since 1493 as $22.9 billion versus $14.6 billion for the total value of silver.

20. Using the same three-year time period as in the earlier note for silver, the cash price for gold on September 12, 2008 was $766 per ounce and on September 12, 2011 it was $1,814 per ounce, for an increase of 237%.

21. See Milton Friedman, *Money Mischief: Episodes in Monetary History* (New York: Harcourt Brace & Company, 1994), pp. 249–60.

22. David Ricardo, *The Principles of Political Economy and Taxation* (London: John Murray, 1817), pp. 506–7.

23. I have added silver in brackets in the quote based on a footnote in ibid., p. 503: "Whatever I say of gold coin is equally applicable to silver coin; but it is not necessary to mention both on every occasion."

24. Among the most useful of the numerous studies of this incident are: Francis A. Walker, "The Free Coinage of Silver," *Journal of Political Economy* 1, no. 2 (1893); Walter K. Nugent, *Money and American Society; 1865–1889* (New York: Free Press, 1968), esp. chap. 12–13; Friedman, *Money Mischief*, chap. 3.

25. The highest price during this twenty-five-year period was $1.29375 in 1874 and the lowest price was $.5275 in 1897. See U.S. Mint, *Annual Report of the Director of the Mint for the Fiscal Year Ended June 30, 1936* (Washington, DC: Government Printing Office, 1936), p. 88.

26. See, for example, the reference in a speech by Representative Charles H. Grosvenor of Ohio on February 3, 1896, 54th Cong., 1st sess., *Congressional Record and Appendix*, 27, pt. 7, App. p. 83.

27. I collected daily quotes published by Handy & Harman from the *Wall Street Journal* during the 1930s, and the data show a low of 24.25¢ per ounce on December 29, 1932. According to Herbert M. Bratter, *Silver Market Dictionary* (New York: Commodity Exchange, 1933), p. 99, "The New York 'official' price is determined and issued daily, usually in the late forenoon, by Handy & Harman, and is based upon the market prices prevailing that day up to the time of such determination for nearby delivery in New York of spot silver in round amounts of 50,000 ounces."

28. For a contemporary discussion, see James D. Paris, *Monetary Policies in the United States: 1932–1938* (New York: Columbia University Press, 1938), pp. 48–49.

29. Ibid., p. 42.

30. "Pittman, Silver Pact Author, Sees Export Trade Increase," *Washington Post*, December 22, 1933, p. 8

31. For a description of Chinese silver exports see "Shanghai Silver Again Moves Out," *New York Times*, September 12, 1934, p. 13 and "Lower Silver Price Seen Necessary to End Smuggling," *Wall Street Journal*, p. 1. On abandoning silver, Milton Friedman argues, "If the United States had not driven up the U.S. dollar price of silver, China would have left the silver standard later—perhaps several years later—than it actually did and under better economic and political conditions," in Friedman *Money Mischief*, pp. 177–78.

32. See John Morton Blum, *From the Morgenthau Diaries*, vol. 1, *Years of Crisis, 1928–1938* (Boston: Houghton Mifflin Company, 1959), p. 204.

CHAPTER 1: HAMILTON'S DESIGN

1. Hamilton refuted the alleged "monarchial" tendencies, according to Richard Sylla, *Alexander Hamilton* (New York: Sterling Publishing Company, 2016), p. 102.

2. Alexander Hamilton, "On the Establishment of a Mint," 1st Cong., 3d sess., January 28, 1791, *American State Papers: Finance*, 1st Cong., 3d sess., vol. 1:91–100, available at https://memory.loc.gov/cgi-bin/ampage?collId=llsp&fileName=009/llsp 009.db&recNum=3.

3. See "Establishing a mint and regulating the coins of the United States," 2d Cong., 1st sess., April 2, 1792. *Statutes at Large*, 2d Cong., 1st sess., vol. 1:246–251, available at https://memory.loc.gov/cgi-bin/ampage?collId=llsl&fileName=001 /llsl001.db&recNum=2. Section 9 of the act sets forth the precise grains of gold and silver that appear in the next sentence of the text as well as the total weight of each coin when an alloy metal (not specified) is added. The total weight of the silver dollar is specified as 416 grains, and, since there are 480 grains in a troy ounce, the silver dollar weighed 416/480 or .866 troy ounces. It contained 371.25 grains of pure (.999 fine silver) so the silver dollar was .8924 (371.25/416) pure. This was changed by the act of January 18, 1837, to .90 pure by reducing the size of the coin to 412.5 grains. Section 9 specified the ten-dollar gold eagle as containing 247.5 grains of pure gold and a total weight of 270 grains for a purity of .9166 (247.5/270) and weighing a total of .5625 troy ounces (270/480). This was later changed by a June 28, 1834 act, modified by the act of January 18, 1837, as follows: the pure gold content of the eagle was reduced to 232.2 grains with a total weight of 258, which made the eagle .9 pure gold and weighing .537 ounces (258/480). The updated details on silver appear in Dickson Leavens, *Silver Money* (Bloomington, Ind.: Principia Press, 1939), p. 20, and the updated details on gold are from H.R. Lindeman, *Money and Legal Tender in the United States* (New York: G.P. Putnam's Sons, 1879), pp. 24–27.

4. Hamilton's report of January 28, 1791, "On the Establishment of a Mint," discusses the trial of the pix [sic] in the last paragraph.

5. John Cragg, *The Mint* (London: Cambridge University Press, 1953), p. 61.

6. The quotation is from section 18 of the act of April 2, 1792, "Establishing a mint and regulating the coins of the United States."

7. Ibid., section 19.

8. See Thomas K. Delorey, "The Trial of the Pyx," at http://www.hjbltd.com /departments/articles/details.asp?inventorynumber=33&linenum=23.

9. The full quote is "To annul the use of either of the metals as money, is to abridge the quantity of circulating medium, and is liable to all the objections which arise from a comparison of the benefits of a full, with the evils of a scanty circulation." See Hamilton, "On the Establishment of a Mint," p. 93.

10. The earliest coins discovered by archeologists were made of silver and date from the middle of the Iron Age, 800–900 BCE. See Raz Kletter and Etty Brand, "A New Look at the Iron Age Silver Hoard from Eshtemoa," *Zeitschrift des Deutschen Palästina-Vereins* Bd. 114, H. 2 (1998): 139–154; and Christine M. Thompson, "Sealed Silver in Iron Age Cisjordan and the 'Invention' of Coinage," *Oxford Journal of Archaeology* 22, no. 1 (2003): 67–107. This discovery negates the story of Greek historian Herodotus, who attributed the invention of coins to King Croesus of Lydia around 600 BCE. See Peter Bernstein, *The Power of Gold: The History of an Obsession* (New York: Wiley, 2000), pp. 27–37.

11. See Arthur J. Rolnick and Warren E. Weber, "Gresham's Law or Gresham's Fallacy," *Journal of Political Economy* 94, no. 1 (1986): 17–24, for a more precise discussion.

12. Feavearyear, *Pound Sterling*, p. 155, cites Newton's report, "Gold and Silver Coin," *Cobbett's Parliamentary History* (London, T.C. Hansard, 1811), 7:525–30, showing that he did not foresee the dominance of gold: "If things be let alone till silver money be a little scarcer the gold will fall of itself."

13. Gold flakes made the *New York Times* on December 21, 2016, p. A25, with the headline "Police Identify Man They Say Took Gold Flakes from Truck." The flakes, which are shed as jewelers work with gold, are collected and stored in buckets before being shipped by armored truck to a depository. The stolen bucket weighed eighty-six pounds and was valued at $1.6 million.

14. Hamilton, "On the Establishment of a Mint," p. 94.

15. Section 9 of the act specifies the one-dollar coin as containing 371.25 grains of pure silver and the ten-dollar eagle as containing 247.5 grains of pure gold. These translate into prices as follows: An ounce contains 480 grains, so to get an ounce of pure silver you need 480/371.25 or $1.29293. The ten-dollar eagle contains 247.5 grains, so to get 480 grains of gold (an ounce) you need 480/247.5 or $19.3939.

16. The increased relative value of gold during this period arose from expanded silver production in Mexican mines that entered the United States via trade. For details see J. Laurence Laughlin, *The History of Bimetallism in the United States* (New York: D. Appleton and Company, 1897), pp. 47–48. Also see Peter Temin, "The Economic Consequences of the Bank War," *Journal of Political Economy* 76, no. 2 (1968), esp. pp. 267–70, for details on imports of silver from Mexico and exports to China.

17. Congress lowered the gold content of a dollar from 24.75 grains to 23.2 grains in 1834 and then made it 23.22 in 1837. Less gold in the dollar meant it cost more dollars to buy an ounce. Since there are 480 grains in a troy ounce, it took $20.67 (480/23.22) to buy an ounce of gold. See Leavens, *Silver Money*, p. 20.

18. Laughlin, *History of Bimetallism*, p. 61, says that there was a purposeful overvaluation of gold in 1834 to accommodate political pressure in Congress after gold was discovered in North Carolina and other southern states. Laughlin also suggests (p. 65) that Congress overvalued gold "inasmuch as the value of silver relatively [sic] to gold had been steadily falling for many years, [and Congress thought] it was quite likely to continue to fall still more in the future." The 16 to 1 ratio was designed to anticipate a further deterioration in relative market prices, which did not occur, hence the overvaluation remained and drove silver out of circulation.

19. Data on average silver prices in each year between 1833 and 1935 (based on London quotations) are in the *Annual Report of the Director of the Mint*, p. 89. Two other sources are available with similar (within a penny) numbers over that time period. Page 88 of the *Annual Report* provides estimates of the New York price from 1874 through 1935. And the NBER Macrohistory Database at http://www.nber.org/databases/macrohistory/contents/chapter04.html also records London prices like those on page 89 of the *Annual Report*. Monthly data from the Commodity Research Bureau are available from 1910 through 1946 and then are available daily beginning January 1947.

20. The annual average price of silver was $1.578 per ounce (an average of monthly data on cash silver from the Commodity Research Bureau database) in 1967, the first time the annual average exceeded $1.36 since 1859. Two spikes in daily silver prices (New York quotations) in 1919 and 1920 exceeded $1.36 (see page 88 in the *Annual Report*) but the annual averages in those years were below $1.36. Roy Jastram, *Silver: The Restless Metal* (New York: John Wiley & Sons, 1981), p. 86, reports that silver "exploded to $1.375 in November 1919." Bratter, *Silver Market Dictionary*, p. 113, writes: "The maximum price of silver recorded in New York was $1.38¼ on November 25, 1919."

21. Ronald M. James, *The Roar and the Silence: A History of Virginia City and the Comstock Lode* (Las Vegas: University of Nevada Press, 1998), esp. p. 35.

22. See the discussion and table on page 1 of the "Special Report to the Monetary Commission on the Recent and Prospective Production of Silver in the United States, Particularly from The Comstock Lode," in *Report and Accompanying Documents of the United States Monetary Commission*, organized under Joint Resolution of August 15, 1876, 2 vol., 44th Cong., 2d sess. S. Rept 703 (Washington, DC: Government Printing Office, 1877). The total production during this period for the entire United States was $100 million in silver. During 1861 the output was $2 million, all from Comstock, and in the last year output was $16 million, of which $5 million came from Comstock. I used 5/16 as my estimate for Comstock for the entire period, which is probably too low.

23. See James, *Roar and Silence*, pp. xix–xx.

24. These data on average silver prices are for the bullion market in London and come from the *Annual Report of the Director of the Mint*, p. 89.

25. The last year silver averaged less than $1.30 was in 1845, when it was $1.298.

CHAPTER 2: SOLVING THE CRIME OF 1873

1. For background see chapters 1 and 2 in *John Sherman's Recollections of Forty Years in the House, Senate, and Cabinet* (Chicago: Werner Company, Chicago, 1895), available at https://archive.org/details/johnshermansreco00sher.

2. See William Kolasky, "Senator John Sherman and the Origin of Antitrust," *Antitrust* 24, no.1 (2009): 85.

3. Ibid., for the nicknames. In *American Statesman: John Sherman* (Boston: Houghton Mifflin Company, 1906), p. 384, Theodore Burton writes about the senator's personality: "The General was fond of meeting friends and loved society. . . . The Senator . . . was much more at home in the intellectual laboratory in which his work was performed."

4. See section 14 of the Coinage Act of 1873, more formally titled, "An Act revising and amending the Laws relative to the Mints, Assay offices, and Coinage of the United States," 42d Cong., 3rd sess., February 12, 1873. *Statutes at Large*, vol. 17, chap. 131.

5. Section 15 of the Coinage Act of 1873 omits the silver dollar from the list of silver coins to be minted, and section 17 states: "That no coins, either of gold,

silver, or minor coinage, shall hereafter be issued from the mint other than those of the denominations, standards, and weights herein set forth."

6. "An Act Regulating Foreign Coins, and for Other Purposes" (February 9, 1793), *Statutes at Large*, 1:300–301.

7. This discussion relates to an earlier version of the bill, S. 859, introduced by Sherman in April 1870 and revised in December 1870, which also established gold as sole legal tender and made subsidiary silver coins legal tender only for payments up to one dollar (see sections 14, 15, and 18).

8. The *Congressional Globe*, January 9, 1871, p. 374.

9. These details are memorialized in the formal title of the legislation, "An Act revising and amending the Laws relative to the Mint, Assay Offices, and Coinage of the United States," 42d, sess. 3 (February 12, 1873).

10. See Robert R. Van Ryzin, *Crime of 1873: The Comstock Connection*, (Iola, Wisc.: Krause Publications, 2001), chap. 10.

11. Walker, "Free Coinage of Silver," p. 17n1.

12. See Paul M. O'Leary, "The Scene of the Crime of 1873 Revisited: A Note," *Journal of Political Economy* 68, no. 4 (1960): p. 390, for the reference to Weston. The quote is from *Report and Accompanying Documents of the United States Monetary Commission*, 1, p. 193.

13. Paul Barnett, "The Crime of 1873 Re-Examined," *Agricultural History* 38 (July 1964): p. 178.

14. Walker, "Free Coinage of Silver," p. 170.

15. He became chairman on March 4, 1867, when the fortieth Congress was sworn in. See Sherman, *Recollections*, p. 334. The flightless dodo became extinct during the seventeenth century.

16. Ibid., pp. 339, 420.

17. Ibid., pp. 342–43, describes this incident.

18. Ibid., p. 343.

19. See *Report of the International Conference on Weights, Measures, and Coins*, held in Paris, June 1867; and *Report of the International Monetary Conference*, held in Paris, June 1867 (London: Harrison and Sons, 1868), available at http://babel.hathitrust.org/cgi/pt?id=mdp.35112103466761;view=1up;seq=1. Propositions 5 and 6 (p. 51) discuss the advantages of gold as international money.

20. See *Report of the International Monetary Conference*. Page 52 discusses the consequence of gold discoveries: "Before the discovery of the rich mines of California, Australia, the North-west of the United States, and the American possessions of Great Britain, gold coins having a price greater than the legal rate were the first to go out of circulation, and could only be procured at a premium. After these discoveries the contrary was the case; gold having become lower than the legal rate, silver disappeared." See page 55 for the discussion of Proposition 7 (against the double standard), which was put to a vote and "adopted by a great majority."

21. *In relation to the coinage of gold and silver*, S. 217, 40th Cong., 2d sess., January 6, 1868, included the preamble: "Mr. Sherman asked, and by unanimous consent obtained, leave to bring in the following bill; which was read twice, referred to the Committee on Finance, and ordered to be printed."

22. "Opposition of Senator Morgan to the Plan of the Paris Conference for Monetary Unification," *New York Times*, June 12, 1868, p. 5.

23. S. 859 was introduced on April 28, 1870, 41st Cong., 3d sess.

24. Section 5 of the Coinage Act of 1873.

25. For example, an article in the *Chicago Tribune*, May 5, 1870, entitled "Coinage," put the demonetization of silver in the sixth paragraph.

26. Sherman, *Recollections*, p. 393.

27. See Leavens, *Silver Money*, p. 23.

28. Sherman, *Recollections*, p. 393.

29. See Henry Parker Willis, *A History of the Latin Monetary Union* (Chicago: University of Chicago Press, 1901), p. 115.

30. See Steven P. Reti, *Silver and Gold: The Political Economy of International Monetary Conferences, 1867–1892* (Westport, Conn.: Greenwood Press, 1998), pp. 53–54. The Imperial Coinage Law did not demonetize silver, but it stopped the coinage of legal tender silver and anticipated the shift to gold with the phrase: "Till the passing of a law dealing with the withdrawal of silver coins." See the discussion "Demonetization of Silver in Germany," *Report and Accompanying Documents of the United States Monetary Commission*, 1:74–78, esp. p. 75.

31. Jastram, *Silver*, p. 75.

32. Willis, *History of the Latin Monetary Union*, p. 117.

33. See Leavens, *Silver Money*, p. 33.

34. See 1) *Report and Accompanying Documents of the United States Monetary Commission*, 1, p. 98; 2) *Report from the Select Committee on Depreciation of Silver, together with the proceedings of the Committee, minutes of evidence, and appendix*, ordered by the House of Commons to be printed 5 July 1876, available at https://catalog.hathitrust.org/Record/001118659, p. iv; and 3) U.S. Department of the Treasury, *Annual Report of the Secretary of the Treasury on the State of the Finances for the Year 1889* (Washington, DC: Government Printing Office, 1889), esp. p. LXII, "Causes of the Depreciation of Silver."

35. See Laughlin, *History of Bimetallism*, p. 75, and John Walton Caughey, *The California Gold Rush* (Berkeley: University of California Press, 1948), pp. 8–10.

36. See Laughlin, *History of Bimetallism*, pp. 283, 285.

37. See *Report on Weights, Measures, and Coins*, p. 52.

38. See Feavearyear, *Pound Sterling*, pp. 211–13, for a discussion of Lord Liverpool's Coinage Act of 1816.

39. In 1894 the average quote in London was 63.5¢ per ounce. *Annual Report of the Director of the Mint*, p. 89.

40. See Laughlin, *History of Bimetallism*, chap. 15, for a full discussion of Bland-Allison.

41. Ibid., chap. 16.

42. This quote from Sherman, *Recollections*, p. 830, also appears in Leavens, *Silver Money*, p. 41.

43. See Friedman, *Money Mischief*, p. 72, for confirmation that the United States would have been on silver. Friedman also argues (p. 76) that the United States would have benefited from a more stable price level.

44. The annual rate of deflation equaled 1.5% according to Friedman, *Money Mischief*, p. 76.

45. The best interpretation is Hugh Rockoff, "The 'Wizard of Oz' as a Monetary Allegory," *Journal of Political Economy* 98, no. 4 (1990): pp. 739–60. The remainder of this paragraph uses his analogies with one exception: I interpret the cyclone as the economic and political upheaval (similar to the teacher's guide at http://www.roadmaptolastbesthope.com/files/Chapter12Lesson_LessonPlan.pdf), but he considers it the free-silver movement itself (p. 745).

46. Rockoff, "Wizard of Oz," p. 750.

47. "Denouncing the 'Goldbugs,'" *New York Times*, August 2, 1893, p. 2.

CHAPTER 3: FREE SILVER

1. "Fame Won in an Hour," *Washington Post*, March 20, 1892, p. 3.

2. Ibid.

3. Louis W. Koenig, *Bryan: A Political Biography of William Jennings Bryan* (New York: G. P. Putnam, 1971), p. 95.

4. Paxton Hibben, *The Peerless Leader: William Jennings Bryan* (New York: Farrar and Rinehart, 1929), p. 129.

5. Ibid., pp. 30–31, for this and the next quote.

6. Ibid., p. 34.

7. Ibid., p. 38.

8. Koenig, *Bryan*, p. 84.

9. See Bryan, *First Battle*, p. 39, for his debating record.

10. Hibben, *Peerless Leader*, p. 80.

11. Paolo Coletta, *William Jennings Bryan*, vol. 1, *Political Evangelist, 1860–1908* (Lincoln: University of Nebraska Press, 1964), p. 25.

12. Hibben, *Peerless Leader*, p. 124.

13. Ibid.

14. Bank suspensions in 1893 numbered 496 and the annual average for the ten years between 1883 and 1892 was 42. See U.S. Bureau of the Census, *Historical Statistics of the United States, Colonial Times to 1970*, Part 2 (Washington, DC: 1975), p. 1015 (Series X 741–55).

15. See Friedman, *Money Mischief*, p. 107, for the comparison with the 1930s. Also see Rockoff, "Wizard of Oz," p. 742.

16. Hibben, *Peerless Leader*, p. 145.

17. Coletta, *William Jennings Bryan*, p. 71.

18. Ibid., p. 150.

19. From *Annual Report of the Director of the Mint*, p. 89.

20. "Bryan's Speech for Silver Monometallism," *Chicago Tribune*, August 18, 1893, p. 4.

21. "Kansas May Be Lost," *New York Times*, July 2, 1896, p. 5.

22. This quote is from "Western Farm Mortgages," *Omaha Daily Bee*, January 20, 1890, p. 3. The newspaper article goes on to criticize the report by the New York Superintendent, defending the quality of Nebraska mortgages.

23. *New York Times*, July 18, 1896, p. 8.

24. Coletta, *William Jennings Bryan*, p. 203.

25. Ibid., p. 575.

26. Koenig, *Bryan*, p. 202.

27. This quote and the remaining ones in this paragraph are from Bryan's speech reprinted in "Boy Orator Scores a Great Hit," *Chicago Daily Tribune*, July 10, 1896, p. 11.

28. Ibid.

29. "The Noisy Georgians: They Took a Conspicuous Part Yesterday," *Atlanta Constitution*, July 10, 1896, p. 4.

30. Hibben, *Peerless Leader*, p. 161.

31. See U. S. Bureau of the Census, *Historical Statistics of the United States*, Part 1, p. 135.

32. Coletta, *William Jennings Bryan*, pp. 197–98.

33. R. Hal Williams, *Realigning America* (Lawrence: University Press of Kansas, 2010), p. 144.

34. Coletta, *William Jennings Bryan*, p. 300.

35. Williams, *Realigning America*, pp. 149–50.

36. Coletta, *William Jennings Bryan*, p. 164.

37. "Not Caught by Silver," *New York Times*, July 18, 1896, p. 8.

38. "The Battle of the Standards," *Washington Post*, August 24, 1896, p. 4.

39. "The Pivotal Point," *Washington Post*, September 13, 1896, p. 6.

40. The silver dollar contained 371.25 grains of pure silver. An ounce contains 480 grains, so the silver content of a dollar averaged (371.25/480) times 63.5, which is equal to 49¢.

41. See William L. Silber, *When Washington Shut Down Wall Street* (Princeton, N.J.: Princeton University Press, 2007), p. 151.

42. Coletta, *William Jennings Bryan*, p. 330.

43. Ibid.

44. "Bryan's Egg Illustration," *Chicago Daily Tribune*, September 24, 1896, p. 6.

45. "Eggs Thrown at Orator Bryan," *San Francisco Chronicle*, October 28, 1896, p. 3.

46. "How Bryan's 129 Cents Would Work," *Chicago Daily Tribune*, October 8, 1896, p. 6.

47. "Bismarck and Silver," *Chicago Daily Tribune*, September 30, 1896, p. 8.

48. See Friedman, *Money Mischief*, esp. pp. 119–21.

49. The Presidential Succession Act of 1947 changed the order to what it is today: vice president, Speaker of the House, president pro tempore of the Senate, and then secretary of state.

50. See Michael Kazin, *A Godly Hero: The Life of William Jennings Bryan* (New York: Alfred Knopf, 2006), pp. 285–303.

CHAPTER 4: SEEDS OF ROOSEVELT'S MANIPULATION

1. This quote and the next are from Jonathan Alter, *The Defining Moment: FDR's Hundred Days and the Triumph of Hope* (New York: Simon and Schuster, 2006), p. 41.

2. Burton Folsom Jr., *New Deal or Raw Deal: How FDR's Legacy Has Damaged America* (New York: Simon & Schuster, 2008), p. 25.

3. The biographical details in this paragraph and the next are from Betty Glad, *Key Pittman: The Tragedy of a Senate Insider* (New York: Columbia University Press, 1986), esp. pp. 4, 5, 8, 11, 14.

4. Ibid., p. 24

5. Ibid., pp. 26–27.

6. Ibid., p. 27.

7. Ibid., p. 30.

8. This quote and the next are from Fred L. Israel, *Nevada's Key Pittman* (Lincoln: University of Nebraska Press, 1963), p. 31.

9. Ibid., p. 32.

10. Glad, *Key Pittman*, p. 45.

11. Israel, *Nevada's Key Pittman*, p. 36.

12. Ibid.

13. Glad, *Key Pittman*, p. 59.

14. From July 1914 through November 1918, the wholesale price index (NBER series M04049USM052NNBR) rose from 8.7 to 19.02. The data for silver are from the Commodity Research Bureau (CRB) monthly series. Leavens, *Silver Money*, p. 137, discusses the increased demand for silver in subsidiary coins.

15. The sale price and the purchase price are for pure silver (1000 fine) and were set in Public Law 139, 65th Cong., 2d sess., April 23, 1918, chap. 63, sections 1 and 2. As S. 4292, the act was described as, "An Act to conserve the gold supply of the United States; to permit the settlement in silver of trade balances adverse to the United States; to provide silver for subsidiary coinage and for commercial use; to assist foreign governments at war with the enemies of the United States; and for the above purposes to stabilize the price and encourage the production of silver."

16. "Silver Going to India," *Wall Street Journal*, May 3, 1918, p. 9.

17. Israel, *Nevada's Key Pittman*, p. 77.

18. Leavens, *Silver Money*, p. 79, dates the drop below one dollar in May 1920 and the end of Treasury purchases in July 1923.

19. The average is based on end-of-month prices between June 1920 and July 1923, from the CRB database.

20. See "The Pittman Act Presents the Anomaly of Two Kinds of Silver," *Wall Street Journal*, June 19, 1920, p. 10; also see "Quotations in Silver Are Changed in Form," *Atlanta Constitution*, June 18, 1920, p. 11.

21. See "Would Repeal Silver Purchase Clause," *Wall Street Journal*, January 13, 1920, p. 13.

22. See "Doing Something for Silver," *New York Tribune*, June 24, 1920, p. 8.

23. "Says Pittman Act Will Stand," *Wall Street Journal*, October 5, 1921, p. 12.

24. Ibid.

25. David Lloyd George's quote was made in August 1934, after Hitler came to power (*Newsweek*, January 27, 1997, p. 86).

26. See Leavens, *Silver Money*, p. 175.

27. Ibid., p. 180. Leavens writes that prices declined by about 10% in the summer of 1926. The CRB data show a drop from 60.58¢ an ounce in September to 54.5¢ in October. The Royal Commission was published in August 1926 (Leavens, *Silver Money*, p. 175).

28. The average price of 56.23¢ is based on monthly quotes from the CRB database between October 1926 and September 1929.

CHAPTER 5: FDR PROMOTES SILVER

1. "Text of Gov. Roosevelt's Speech on Cost of Government and Pledge of Economy," *Chicago Daily Tribune*, October 20, 1932, p. 6. Also see "Roosevelt Is Opposed to Cashing Bonus Now," *Daily Boston Globe*, October 20, 1932, p. 1.

2. See Donald A. Ritchie, *Electing FDR: The New Deal Campaign of 1932* (Lawrence: University Press of Kansas, 2007), p. 141.

3. Alter, *Defining Moment*, p. 111.

4. Ibid., p. 105.

5. Ibid., p. 111.

6. Ibid., p. 105.

7. The money supply (demand deposits plus currency) measured $28.3 billion in October 1929 and $20.4 billion in June 1932, for a decline of 28% (Milton Friedman and Anna J. Schwartz, *A Monetary History of the United States, 1867–1960* (Princeton, N.J.: Princeton University Press, 1963), pp. 712–13, table A-1. The consumer price index declined by 21% (CPI for all urban consumers at http://research.stlouisfed.org/fred2), and the unemployment rate was 23.7% in June 1932 (seasonally adjusted monthly unemployment rate at http://research.stlouisfed.org/fred2).

8. "Text of Democratic Platform Submitted to Convention," *Chicago Daily Tribune*, June 30, 1932, p. 4.

9. "Governor Roosevelt's Radio Speech Interpreting Party Platform," *New York Times*, July 31, 1932, p. 2. Roosevelt began his talk by saying "I hope during this campaign to use the radio frequently to speak to you about important things that concern us all. In the olden days campaigns were conducted amid surroundings of brass bands and red lights. . . . Today common sense plays the greater part and final opinions are arrived at in the quiet of the home."

10. "Churchill Blames Money for Crisis," *New York Times*, May 9, 1932, p. 5.

11. Handy & Harman data show an all-time low of 24.25¢ per ounce on December 29, 1932.

12. Both supply and demand caused the price decline, with sales of demonetized bullion from India boosting supply and depressed economic activity cutting demand. See Senate Subcommittee of the Committee on Banking and Currency, *Purchase of Silver Produced in the United States with Silver Certificates*: Hearings on S. 3606, 72d Cong., 1st sess. May 9, 1932, esp. p. 34.

13. "Wheeler to Offer A 16–1 Silver Bill," *New York Times*, January 4, 1932, p. 2.

14. Burton K. Wheeler with Paul F. Kelley, *Yankee from the West* (Garden City, N.Y.: Doubleday & Company, 1962), p. 302.

15. "Wheeler to Offer a 16–1 Silver Bill," *New York Times*, January 4, 1932, p. 2.

16. House Committee on Foreign Affairs, "Remonetization of Silver, Part 2," May 19, 1933, p. 10 (typed).

17. "Senate Beats 16 to 1 Silver," *Chicago Tribune*, January 25, 1933, p. 1.

18. The quote is from "The President's Bank Proclamation," *New York Times*, March 6, 1933, p. 1. For details on the bank holiday, see William L. Silber, "Why Did FDR's Bank Holiday Succeed?" *Federal Reserve Bank of New York Economic Policy Review* (July 2009): pp. 19–30.

19. See Alter, *Defining Moment*, p. 269.

20. Statistical tests on silver during this period are based on daily price data I collected on silver from the *Wall Street Journal* provided by bullion dealers Handy & Harman. The President's announcement of the bank holiday was on Sunday, March 5. The price of silver on Monday, March 6 was quoted at 29.75¢ per ounce, an increase from 27.25¢ per ounce on Friday, March 4. The return (measured by log price relatives) of 8.77% is statistically significant when compared with the standard deviation of daily returns of .99% measured over the previous 90 calendar days.

21. The first four lines of T.S. Eliot's poem "The Waste Land" (1922) are: April is the cruelest month, breeding / Lilacs out of the dead land, mixing / Memory and desire, stirring / Dull roots with spring rain.

22. Wheeler with Kelley, *Yankee from the West*, pp. 302, 304.

23. Ibid., p. 304.

24. Ibid., photos 17, 18.

25. "Roosevelt Urges Speed on Farm Aid," *New York Times*, April 1, 1933, p. 3.

26. "Inflation Plan Loses 43 to 33 in Senate Test," *Chicago Daily Tribune*, April 18, 1933, p. 1.

27. See Raymond Moley, *After Seven Years* (New York: Harper & Brothers Publishers, 1939), p. 158, for the estimate of ten senators. Pittman was listed as "for the amendment" but was "paired" with another senator listed as "against" in a parliamentary move equivalent to abstaining. See "The Vote on Inflation," *New York Times*, April 18, 1933, p. 1.

28. *Encyclopedia of Oklahoma History and Culture*, s.v. "Thomas, John William Elmer" (by David D. Webb), http://www.okhistory.org/publications/enc/entry.php?entry=TH008.

29. "Seek Inflation for Farm Bill," *Wall Street Journal*, April 13, 1933, p. 12.

30. "Inflation Moves Wait," *New York Times*, April 19, 1933, p. 1.

31. "President's Action Forced by Events," *New York Times*, April 20, 1933, p. 1.

32. Moley, *After Seven Years*, p. 158.

33. "U.S. Goes Off Gold by Roosevelt Ban on Foreign Export," *Christian Science Monitor*, April 19, 1933, p. 1 continued.

34. Ibid.

35. According to "Grain Prices Soar as Dollar Drops," *New York Times*, April 20, 1933, p. 2, wheat closed up between 2–2.5¢, at 65¢ a bushel, or about 4%. According to "Buying of Cotton Heaviest in Years," *New York Times*, April 20, 1933, p. 34, cotton closed at 7.15¢ up from 6.73¢ the previous day, for a gain of about 6%.

36. The franc closed at .0438 (cents) on April 19, up from .0402 (cents) on April 18. (See "Dollar Collapses in Foreign Exchange Market—Silver Here, Up 3C., Limit for Day's Trading," *Wall Street Journal*, April 20, 1933, p. 1; and "Dollar

Drops Sharply Again," *Wall Street Journal*, April 19, p. 1.) The use of the French franc as a proxy for gold follows Paul Einzig, *The Future of Gold* (New York: Macmillan, 1935), p. 5. According to the *Manchester Guardian*, "Money and Stocks; the Paper Dollar," April 20, 1933, p. 14, "Until shortly before the United States banking stoppage, London gold prices were fixed with reference to the dollar rate, but since then the French franc has been the point of reference." *Times of India*, April 21, 1933, p. 6, "Special Service: London Market Quotations," makes the following note: "The gold price is now based on French francs rather than dollars."

37. Handy & Harman silver was quoted at 32.375¢ on April 19 compared with 28.875¢ on April 18. The 11.44% return is statistically significant compared with the daily standard deviation of returns of 1.6% over the previous 90 calendar days.

38. "Bill Is Introduced in Senate by Thomas," *Washington Post*, April 21, 1933, p. 1.

39. For a discussion of the rewriting, see Moley, *After Seven Years*, pp.159–61. Also see "President Takes Action," *New York Times*, April 20, 1933, p. 1.

40. See "Text of the Administration Measure on Inflation," *New York Times*, April 21, 1933, p. 2. This amendment was subsequently changed on April 26, 1933, to include an explicit clause authorizing the president at his discretion to mandate the unlimited coinage of silver at a fixed ratio to gold, but the price of silver did not increase on April 26, or on April 28, when the revised amendment was passed. See "Silver Plan Added to Inflation Bill," *New York Times*, April 27, 1933, p. 1. See also "Text of Thomas Amendment with Silver Provision," *Wall Street Journal*, April 29, 1933, p. 8. The price of silver declined from 36¢ to 35.5 on April 26 and the price of silver declined from 35.375 to 34.625 on April 28. The daily standard deviation of returns for silver measured 1.6% for 90 calendar days prior to April 19, 1933, so neither of those price movements is statistically significant.

41. "Robinson's Statement on Thomas Money Bill," *Washington Post*, April 21, 1933, p. 4.

42. The quote is from "Federal Reserve to Lead Credit Expansion," *Washington Post*, April 21, 1933, p. 1. The price of silver on April 20 increased to 35.5¢ from 32.375¢ on April 19. The 9.2% return is statistically significant compared with the daily standard deviation of returns of 1.6% over the 90 calendar days prior to April 19.

43. On April 20 the French franc opened at .0446 (cents), for a gain of 2% above the previous close of .0438, but it closed at .0430 (cents), for a loss of 2% (see "Foreign Monies Continue to Rise," *Wall Street Journal*, April 21, 1933, p. 1; and "Dollar Continues Exchange Decline," *New York Times*, April 21, 1933, p.3). I averaged the two numbers and report zero change for April 20. Therefore, the dollar price of gold rose over the two days by the 9% recorded on April 19. In general, silver is more volatile than gold because it is a smaller market (see *Minerals Yearbook: 1932–1933*, p. 12) so it takes less to move its price. This is consistent with the earlier discussion that after the financial crisis in 2008 silver rose by almost 400% compared with a 250% increase for gold.

44. Raymond Moley, *The First New Deal* (New York: Harcourt, Brace & World, 1966), p. 369.

CHAPTER 6: SILVER SUBSIDY

1. *Congressional Record*, 63d Cong., 2d sess., March 19, 1914, p. 5101.

2. Israel, *Nevada's Key Pittman*, p. 33.

3. Ibid., p. 88.

4. Cordell Hull, *The Memoirs of Cordell Hull* (New York: Macmillan Company, 1948), 1, p. 249.

5. Israel, *Nevada's Key Pittman*, p. 91.

6. Arthur Schlesinger Jr., *The Age of Roosevelt: The Coming of the New Deal* (Boston: Houghton Mifflin Company, 1959), p. 211.

7. Israel, *Nevada's Key Pittman*, p. 91.

8. "Silver Triumphant," *Christian Science Monitor*, July 31, 1933, p. 12

9. For more details, see "A World Conference Success," *Manchester Guardian*, July 24, 1933, p. 5; and "Text of Silver Treaty Concluded at London," *New York Times*, July 23, 1933, p. 16.

10. "Silver Triumphant," *Christian Science Monitor*, July 31, 1933, p. 12.

11. "A World Conference Success," *Manchester Guardian*, July 24, 1933, p. 5.

12. The agreement was signed on Saturday night, July 22, 1933. The Handy & Harman quote on July 22 was 35.5¢ an ounce and was 37.375 on Monday, July 24. The 5.15% return is statistically significant compared with the 2.01% daily standard deviation of returns over the previous 90 calendar days (note the increase in silver volatility during this period). Although the price increase is statistically significant, the relatively small magnitude of the increase reflects two factors: 1) Ratification by the governments involved remained uncertain; 2) The restrictions on the participating countries "represented very little self-denial," except for the United States (see Leavens, *Silver Money*, pp. 250–51).

13. Wheeler's quotes referred to the U.S. proposals at the opening of the London conference: "Wheeler Attacks Silver Plan Again," *New York Times*, June 25, 1933, p. 2

14. Ibid.

15. Israel, *Nevada's Key Pittman*, p. 93.

16. The details on Henry Morgenthau's life come primarily from Blum, *From the Morgenthau Diaries*, 1, pp. 1–27.

17. Ibid., 1, p. 12.

18. Ibid., 1, p. 15.

19. Ibid., 1, p. 20.

20. Morgenthau Diaries, vol. 00, Farm Credit Diary, April 27–November 16, 1933, p. 73, available at http://www.fdrlibrary.marist.edu/archives/collections/franklin/?p=collections/findingaid&id=535&q=&rootcontentid=188897#id188897.

21. Morgenthau Diaries, vol. 00, p. 65.

22. Ibid.

23. Ibid., p. 75.

24. Ibid. On October 29, the president said to a gathering of senior people in the administration, including Acheson, "Gentlemen . . . our buying gold is an administration policy. We are all in the same boat. If anybody does not like the boat he can get out of it" (ibid., p. 87). On November 13, FDR asked for Acheson's

resignation (ibid., p. 101). Also see "Inflationists Hail Victory as Morgenthau Replaces Woodin; Acheson Resigns," *Washington Post*, November 16, 1933, p. 1.

25. Franklin D. Roosevelt, "Fireside Chat," October 22, 1933. Online by Gerhard Peters and John T. Woolley, *The American Presidency Project*. http://www.presidency.ucsb.edu/ws/?pid=14537.

26. An excellent description of the program is in Kenneth D. Garbade, *Birth of a Market: The U.S. Treasury Securities Market from the Great War to the Great Depression* (Cambridge, Mass.: MIT Press, 2012), pp. 237–45.

27. Franklin D. Roosevelt, "Proclamation and Statement Ratifying the London Agreement on Silver," December 21, 1933. Online by Peters and Woolley, *American Presidency Project*. http://www.presidency.ucsb.edu/ws/?pid=14586.

28. The Proclamation does not mention any price but the press reported 64.5¢ and that was understood by the general public. The Proclamation implies that the Treasury purchased silver at the official price of $1.29 per ounce but only half an ounce is returned to the owner, which means each ounce brings the owner half of $1.29, which is 64.5¢. See, for example, the popular description in "How Silver Coinage Plan Will Work Under New Order," *Chicago Daily Tribune*, December 22, 1933, p. 10. The relevant text of the proclamation is: "*I, Franklin D. Roosevelt*, President of the United States of America, do proclaim and direct that each United States coinage mint shall receive for coinage into standard silver dollars any silver which such mint, subject to regulations prescribed hereunder by the Secretary of the Treasury, is satisfied has been mined, subsequent to the date of this proclamation, from natural deposits in the United States or any place subject to the jurisdiction thereof. The Director of the Mint, with the voluntary consent of the owner, shall deduct and retain of such silver so received 50 percent as seigniorage and for services performed by the Government of the United States relative to the coinage and delivery of silver dollars. The balance of such silver so received, that is, 50 percent thereof, shall be coined into standard silver dollars and the same, or an equal number of other standard silver dollars, shall be delivered to the owner or depositor of such silver. The 50 percent of such silver so deducted shall be retained as bullion by the Treasury and shall not be disposed of prior to the thirty-first day of December 1937, except for coining into United States coins." Franklin D. Roosevelt, "Proclamation 2067—Ratifying the London Agreement on Silver," December 21, 1933. Online by Peters and Woolley, *The American Presidency Project*. http://www.presidency.ucsb.edu/ws/?pid=14587.)

29. "Pittman, Silver Pact Author, Sees Export Trade Increase," *Washington Post*, December 22, 1933, p. 8.

30. "2 Silver Prices Now in Effect," *Wall Street Journal*, December 23, 1933, p. 1. The Treasury price was quoted by Handy & Harman as 64.125¢ to reflect the cost of transporting the silver to the mint.

31. The Proclamation was announced on the evening of December 21 (see "Roosevelt Order Remonetizes Silver in U.S.," *Chicago Daily Tribune*, December 22, 1933, p. 1), so the 2.865% price increase from 43 on December 21 to 44¼ on December 22 measures the price impact of the announcement. It is statistically significant compared with the 1.23% daily standard deviation of returns over the previous 90 calendar days.

32. From 1927 through the first eleven months of 1933, approximately 1,229,000 ounces were produced by Mexico, Canada, Australia, Peru, and the United States, the five principal world producers at the time. The United States accounted for about 299,000 ounces, or 24% of the total (see "2 Silver Prices Now in Effect," *Wall Street Journal*, December 23, 1933, continued on p.7).

33. "Gold Plan Aids Speculations in U.S. Silver," *Washington Post*, November 7, 1933, p. 13.

34. Ibid.

35. This quote and the next are from Morgenthau Diaries, vol. 00, p. 82.

36. This quote and the others in this paragraph are from ibid., p. 94.

37. Ibid. See the entry for November 2, 1933, which refers to the prior evening.

38. The price on October 21 was 36⅞ and the price on November 6 was 41½, which is a 12.5% increase. The daily standard deviation of returns during the 90 calendar days prior to October 21 was 1.414. There are 16 calendar days between October 21 and November 6, making the standard deviation over that time period equal to 5.66 (1.414 times the square root of 16). 12.5 divided by 5.66 gives a t-statistic of 2.21.

39. "Pittman, Silver Pact Author, Sees Export Trade Increase," *Washington Post*, December 22, 1933, p. 8.

40. This quote and the descriptions below are from "Ghost Towns to Be Revived as Government Buys Silver," *Chicago Daily Tribune*, December 23, 1933, p. 6.

41. The following description is from Israel, *Nevada's Key Pittman*, p. 95.

42. "Hint of World Gold Deal," *New York Times*, December 23, 1933, p. 1 continued.

43. Ibid.

44. Senate Committee on Foreign Relations, Commercial Relations with China, Report No. 1716, 71st Cong., 3d sess., February 17 (calendar day 20), 1931, p. 4.

45. Sir Arthur Salter, *China and Silver* (New York: Economic Forum, Inc., 1934), esp. pp. 3–6. Also see Leavens, *Silver Money*, p. 216.

CHAPTER 7: CHINA AND AMERICA COLLIDE

1. Senate Resolution 443, "Advising the President relative to our commercial relations with China, the conditions in China, and the necessity for moral, intellectual, and financial support of the National Government of China," 71st Cong., 3d sess., January 26 (calendar day February 11), 1931, p.3.

2. See Eduard Kann, *The Currencies of China: An Investigation of Silver & Gold Transactions Affecting China* (Shanghai: Kelley & Walsh, Limited, 1927), p. 234.

3. Ibid., p. 2.

4. See Leavens, *Silver Money*, pp. 86–87. Also see "An Act Regulating Foreign Coins, and for Other Purposes," February 9, 1793.

5. See Bratter, *Silver Market Dictionary*, p. 173.

6. Ibid., p. 172, defines sycee as a measure of fineness, and Kann, *Currencies of China*, chap. 3, discusses settling transactions with sycee.

7. Bratter, *Silver Market Dictionary*, p. 200. This entry refers to the "coinage law promulgated at Nanking on March 8, 1933," which is about one month earlier than the April 6, 1933, date given on page 173.

8. This paragraph is based on Franklin D. Roosevelt: "Message to Congress Recommending Legislation on the Currency System," January 15, 1934. Online by Peters and Woolley, *American Presidency Project*. http://www.presidency.ucsb.edu/ws/?pid=14868.

9. For pictures of Madonna and Bieber with gold teeth, see http://www.newnownext.com/pop-stars-summers-it-accessory-grills/08/2013/.

10. Americans were permitted to own gold as of December 31, 1974, under Presidential Executive Order 11825.

11. Roosevelt, "Message Recommending Legislation on Currency System."

12. See Garbade, *Birth of a Market*, pp. 242–43.

13. See section 43 (b) (2) of the Thomas Amendment, reprinted in Leavens, *Silver Money*, pp. 372–73.

14. "New Money Is Demanded by Senators in Gold Bill. . . . Wheeler to Insist on Silver Buying," *Washington Post*, January 25, 1934, p. 1.

15. Leavens, *Silver Money*, p. 355, table E shows total world production of 169 million ounces for 1933. The next five years averaged 240 million ounces per year. Leavens writes (p. 258): "The compulsory purchase of such a large amount of silver would have sent the price up rapidly toward the 16 to 1 ratio."

16. This quote and the next are from "Gold Bill Passed by Senate 66–23; Silver Vote Large," *New York Times*, January 28, 1934, p. 1 continued.

17. "Senate Votes Gold Bill 66 to 23, Killing Silver Rider by Slim Margin," *Hartford Courant*, January 28, 1934, p. 1.

18. "Gold Bill Passed by Senate 66–23; Silver Vote Large," *New York Times*, January 28, 1934, p. 1 continued.

19. Franklin D. Roosevelt: "Message to Congress on Silver Policy," May 22, 1934. Online by Peters and Woolley, *American Presidency Project*. http://www.presidency.ucsb.edu/ws/?pid=14882.

20. "Text of Silver Purchase Bill of 1934," *Wall Street Journal*, May 23, 1934, p. 5. Also see U.S. Department of the Treasury, *Annual Report of the Secretary of the Treasury on the State of the Finances for the Fiscal Year Ended June 30, 1935* (Washington DC: Government Printing Office, 1936), pp. 42–43. Silver certificates were first authorized and issued under the Bland-Allison Act of February 28, 1878 (see Bratter, *Silver Market Dictionary*, p. 149).

21. This quote and the previous reference to "permissive provisions" are from "President Asks Silver Base Be Ultimately 1 to 3 Gold; Wants 50% Speculation Tax," *New York Times*, May 23, 1934, p. 1 continued.

22. The price of silver was quoted at $45^{1}/_{8}$ for May 9, 1934, compared with $43\frac{3}{4}$ for May 8, 1933, by Handy & Harman. According to the *Wall Street Journal* ("Commodity Exchange, Inc.," May 9, 1934, p. 14) the price increase occurred in response to the news of "an agreement in principle looking to nationalization of existing silver stocks in the United States and inclusion of silver in the metallic reserves." That news release occurred after 2 p.m. on May 8, which is after the H&H quote for that day, so the H&H quote for May 9 reflects the impact of the news. The 3.1% price increase is significant compared with the .867% daily

standard deviation of returns over the previous 90 calendar days. There was no price impact when the bill was reported in the Senate on May 22, 1934, reflecting the report by the *Christian Science Monitor* ("U.S. Silver Plan Is Not Expected to Upset Prices," May 23, 1934, p. 2) that "Roosevelt's silver message had been so accurately forecast that its actual publication had only a slight firming effect."

23. Estimates of the ounces to be purchased under the program varied considerably. The *New York Times* ("President Asks Silver Base Be Ultimately 1 to 3 Gold; Wants 50% Speculation Tax," *New York Times*, May 23, 1934, p. 1 continued) reported a maximum of 1.7 billion ounces. Leavens, *Silver Money*, pp. 278–79, table 17, calculates the initial requirement as 1.3 billion ounces.

24. "Treasury Pushes New Silver Policy," *New York Times*, June 22, 1934, p. 31.

25. "The Treasury's Regulations for Federal Transactions in Silver," *New York Times*, June 20, 1934, p. 36.

26. See "Roosevelt Sets Sail Tonight on Vacation at Sea," *Chicago Daily Tribune*, July 1, 1934, p. 8.

27. See "Roosevelt to Retain Close Touch with Affairs," *New York Times*, June 29, 1934, p. 20.

28. The one-page memo, dated June 28, 1934, and accompanying documents are from the President's Official File (OF) 21, Box 1, Folder "Dept of Treasury, Mar-Aug 1934," Franklin D. Roosevelt Presidential Library, Hyde Park, N.Y.

29. Morgenthau Diaries, vol. 2, pt. 1, July 1–December 31, 1934, p. 3, available at http://www.fdrlibrary.marist.edu/archives/collections/franklin/?p=collections/find ingaid&id=535&q=&rootcontentid=188897#id188897.

30. "Spot Silver 48 Cents, Four-Year High," *Wall Street Journal*, August 9, 1934.

31. Morgenthau Diaries, vol. 2, pt. 1, p. 14.

32. "Pittman Sees End of Silver Question," in "Leading Countries of World Mark Time and Await Effect of U.S. Nationalizing Metal," *Christian Science Monitor*, August 10, 1934, p. 1 continued.

33. "The President's New Order Nationalizing Silver Explained," *Chicago Daily Tribune*, August 10, 1934, p. 1.

34. "Retail Sales Gain Unexpectedly in August; Outlook Brightens," *Washington Post*, September 3, 1934, p. 18.

35. See "Silverware," *Wall Street Journal*, September 19, 1934, p. 19; and "New Struggle in Silver Seen," *Wall Street Journal*, September 26, 1934, p. 9.

36. "China Pleads That U.S. Stop Buying Silver," *Christian Science Monitor*, September 29, 1934, p. 1.

37. "American Trained Monetary Expert Steadies China's Tottering Currency," *Hartford Courant*, January 13, 1935, p. D1.

38. "The Hull and Kung Notes on Silver," *New York Times*, October 15, 1934, p. 4.

39. Ming's denunciation came in June 1934 in a speech in New York, which was cited in "Denies China Plans Embargo on Silver," *New York Times*, September 30, 1934, p. 7.

40. "Shanghai Silver Again Moves Out," *Wall Street Journal*, September 12, 1934, p. 13.

41. "Silver in the Far East," *New York Times*, June 6, 1934, p. 20.

42. "The Ungrateful Chinese," *Washington Post*, September 30, 1934, p. B4.

43. Ibid.

44. "Silver Price Again Reaches New High," *Wall Street Journal*, October 13, 1934, p. 2.

45. "The Hull and Kung Notes on Silver," *New York Times*, October 15, 1934, p. 4.

46. Schlesinger, *Age of Roosevelt*, p. 191.

47. Hull, *Memoirs of Cordell Hull*, 1, pp. 207–8.

48. See Blum, *From the Morgenthau Diaries*, 1, p. 206, and Dorothy Borg, *The United States and the Far Eastern Crisis* (Cambridge, Mass.: Harvard University Press, 1964), pp. 75–82.

49. Cordell Hull to Joseph Grew, telegram, May 1, 1934, 7 p.m., in U.S. Department of State, *Foreign Relations of the United States Diplomatic Papers, 1934, The Far East* (Washington DC: Government Printing Office, 1934), 3, p. 153.

50. Cordell Hull to Edwin Cunningham, telegram, May 18, 1934, 11 a.m., in ibid., 3, p. 437.

51. This quote and the remaining in this paragraph are from "Dictated on November 27th," in Morgenthau Diaries, vol. 2, pt. 2, p.194, available at http://www.fdrlibrary.marist.edu/archives/collections/franklin/?p=collections/findingaid&id=535&q=&rootcontentid=188897#id188897.

52. "Deflation in China Gains Momentum," *New York Times*, December 9, 1934, p. N7.

53. "China Losing Her Silver," *New York Times*, December 7, 1934, p. 17.

54. "Chinese Silver Coins Imported by Chicago Firm," *Chicago Daily Tribune*, December 16, 1934, p. B8.

55. Ibid.

56. "China Is Hard Hit by Loss of Silver," *New York Times*, December 16, 1934, p. N13.

57. Morgenthau Diaries, vol. 2, pt. 2, p. 301ff.

58. Ibid., p. 303ff. The excerpts of the conversation reported below are from the full transcript of the telephone call.

CHAPTER 8: BOMBSHELL IN SHANGHAI

1. Morgenthau Diaries, vol. 2, pt. 2, p. 294ff.

2. Ibid., p. 345 and unnumbered page following p. 347.

3. This quote and the next are from Morgenthau Diaries, vol. 3, pt. 1, January 1–February 28, 1935, p. 53, available at http://www.fdrlibrary.marist.edu/archives/collections/franklin/?p=collections/findingaid&id=535&q=&rootcontentid=188897#id188897.

4. Ibid.

5. Arthur N. Young, interview by James R. Fuchs, February 21, 1974, oral history interview, Harry S. Truman Presidential Library & Museum at https://www.trumanlibrary.org/oralhist/young.htm. Young had a PhD degree in economics from Princeton University and served as an adviser to the Chinese government from 1929 until 1947.

6. See "American Trained Monetary Expert Steadies China's Tottering Currency," *Hartford Courant*, January 13, 1935, p. D1, and "Books of the Times: The Soong Dynasty," March 14, 1985.

7. This quote and the next are from Morgenthau Diaries, vol. 3, pt. 1, p. 53.

8. For Bullitt's background see: "Bullitt Confirmed as Envoy to Soviet," *New York Times*, January 12, 1934; "The Strange Case of William Bullitt," *New York Review of Books*, September 29, 1988; and Moley, *After Seven Years*, pp. 136–37.

9. FDR to William C. Bullitt, August 14, 1934, in *For the President Personal and Secret: Correspondence between Franklin D. Roosevelt and William C. Bullitt*, ed. Orville H. Bullitt (Boston: Houghton Mifflin Company, 1972), pp. 94–95.

10. FDR to William C. Bullitt, August 29, 1934, in response to Bullitt to FDR, August 5, 1934. Bullitt, *For the President Personal and Secret*, pp. 92–93, 95.

11. The telephone conversation is condensed from Morgenthau Diaries, vol. 2 pt. 2, pp. 338–43. See Bullitt, *For the President Personal and Secret*, pp. 40, 42, for the earlier interaction between Bullitt and Morgenthau.

12. Morgenthau Diaries, vol. 3, pt. 1, p. 1.

13. Ibid., p. 84.

14. This quote and the remaining in this paragraph are from *Chicago Daily Tribune*, January 2, 1935, p. 1.

15. See Tai-chun Kuo and Hsiao-ting Lin, *T.V. Soong in Modern Chinese History* (Stanford, Calif.: Hoover Institution Press, 2006), pp. 3–5.

16. This quote and the remaining in this paragraph are from the communication from Soong to Bullitt in U.S. Department of State, *Foreign Relations of the United States Diplomatic Papers, 1935, The Far East* (Washington DC: Government Printing Office, 1935), 3, pp. 532–33. "Copies were given by Mr. Bullitt to the President" appears in the footnote to the document.

17. See "Japanese Attack Towns in Chahar," *New York Times*, January 24, 1935, and "Japanese Planes Kill 44 Chinese as Chahar-Jehol Dispute Rages," *Hartford Courant*, January 26, 1935, p. 19.

18. "Japan's New Move Starts Old Alarms," *New York Times*, January 27, 1935, p. E5.

19. These quotes and those in the next two sentences are from "Japan to Offer China Union in Economic Bloc," *Chicago Daily Tribune*, January 28, 1935, p. 5.

20. "China to Melt Ornaments for Silver Stocks," *Chicago Daily Tribune*, February 15, 1935, p. 31. Leavens, *Silver Money*, p. 308, writes that the Chinese dollar was held "about 25 percent below parity with the world price of silver." The article in the *Chicago Daily Tribune* does not describe the regulations that were imposed and Leavens (p. 310) simply states "the government attempted to attract miscellaneous old silver jewelry."

21. This incident and the quotes are in Morgenthau Diaries, vol. 3, pt. 2, p. 305, available at http://www.fdrlibrary.marist.edu/archives/collections/franklin/?p=collections/findingaid&id=535&q=&rootcontentid=188897#id188897.

22. The quotes are from Arthur N. Young, *China's Nation-Building Effort, 1927–1937* (Stanford, Calif.: Hoover Institution Press, 1971), p. 227, 227n17. Young was a financial adviser to China and states that a copy of the telegram is in

his files. The substance of the telegram is confirmed in Morgenthau Diaries, vol. 3, pt. 2, p. 305.

23. Morgenthau Diaries, vol. 3, pt. 2, p. 305.

24. See U.S. Department of State, Division of Far Eastern Affairs, "China: Silver Situation, Problem and Suggested Solution," February 14, 1935, in Morgenthau Diaries, vol. 3, pt. 2, pp. 300–303. The State Department's solution was a suggestion (p. 302) "to the Chinese that they consider asking for a cooperative loan from several of the powers for assistance of China in a program of currency reform."

25. These monthly averages, which are for the first three months of 1935, come from the House Subcommittee of the Committee on Appropriations, "Treasury Department Appropriation Bill for 1938": Hearings, 75th Cong., 1st sess., p. 27. According to Leavens, *Silver Money*, pp. 278–79, table 17, silver had increased from 12% of monetary reserves to a little over 16% since mid-1934, but the required amount rose because of gold inflows to the United States.

26. The one-billion-ounce estimate is from Leavens, *Silver Money*, p. 279, and also appears contemporaneously in "Upward Revision in Statutory Price Level Viewed," *Wall Street Journal*, April 12, 1935, p. 1.

27. "Everybody's Business," *Boston Globe*, April 11, 1935, p. 23.

28. The close on April 10 was 64⅛, which is an increase of 1.77% compared with 63 on April 9 and is statistically significant given the average daily standard deviation of .56% calculated over the previous 90 calendar days.

29. "President Puts Price of Silver Up to 71 Cents," *Chicago Daily Tribune*, April 11, 1935, p. 27.

30. According to the *Wall Street Journal*, April 13, 1935, p. 8: "The 68½ cent price for silver is the highest price fixed in New York since January 9, 1926." The price increase on April 11 was 2.5% and on April 12 it was 4.1%, both of which are statistically significant given the average daily standard deviation of .56% reported above.

31. "Upward Revision in Statutory Price Level Viewed," *Wall Street Journal*, April 12, 1935, p. 1.

32. *Manchester Guardian*, April 12, 1935, p. 19.

33. "Markets of World Quickly Respond to Silver Increase," *Wall Street Journal*, April 12, 1935, p. 1.

34. "Everybody's Business: Speculation in Silver Sweeps the Market Bare and Makes Manipulation Easy," *Boston Globe*, April 24, 1935, p. 13.

35. The new subsidized price at the Treasury is 77.57¢ per ounce of 1000 fine silver and Handy & Harman adjust this to 77¢ for the industry standard 999 fine and selling fees (see "Silver: Daily Quotations by Handy & Harman," *Wall Street Journal*, April 26, 1935, p.12). The *Wall Street Journal*, April 29, 1935, p. 8, reports Handy & Harman quotes for the free market price of 77¢ on April 25 and 81¢ on April 26.

36. *New York Times*, April 25, 1935, p. 2.

37. The quote is from Morgenthau Diaries, vol. 4, pt. 3, March 1–April 22, 1935, p. 227, available at http://www.fdrlibrary.marist.edu/archives/collections /franklin/?p=collections/findingaid&id=535&q=&rootcontentid=188897#id18 8897.

38. This quote and the remaining in this paragraph are from Morgenthau Diaries, vol. 5, pt. 1, April 23–May 30, 1935, pp. 28–29, available at http://www .fdrlibrary.marist.edu/archives/collections/franklin/?p=collections/findingaid&id =535&q=&rootcontentid=188897#id188897.

39. Ibid., pp. 30–31, for this quote and the following condensed conversation.

40. "Silver Stirs World Turmoil: Mexico Closes Banks, Trading Wild in Europe," *Chicago Daily Tribune*, April 28, 1935, p. 1.

41. Allan S. Everest, *Morgenthau, The New Deal and Silver* (New York: King's Crown Press, 1950), p. 79.

42. Morgenthau Diaries, vol. 5, pt. 1, p. 38.

43. See "Silver Nations Plead with U.S. for Protection," *Christian Science Monitor*, April 27, 1935, p. 1.

44. The drop of 5.3% on April 27 is significant compared with the daily standard deviation of 1.4% over the previous 90 calendar days. This standard deviation is 2½ times larger than the .56 standard deviation of early April.

45. See Leavens, *Silver Money*, p. 284, and "Mexican Business Recovering from Monetary Changes," *Christian Science Monitor*, May 17, 1935, p. 11.

46. "Everybody's Business: Silver Market Waiting for Action by Treasury— 'Rigged' by Buying Operations," *Boston Globe*, April 29, 1935, p. 19.

47. Leavens, *Silver Money*, p. 304, reports that in 1935 smuggling estimates ranged between 112 million ounces and 172 million ounces, for an average of 142 million ounces. Smuggling occurred, according to Leavens (p. 297), because the value of silver in the yuan was fixed lower than its value in the market, and the Chinese Ministry of Finance imposed restrictions on purchases and sales of foreign exchange (p. 303) and had secured a "gentlemen's agreement" with banks to prevent exports of silver. The restrictions blunted the rise in the yuan but did not eliminate the increase. Leavens (p. 306) shows the yuan rising with the price of silver although less sharply because of controls.

48. "Japanese Rout Forces of Rebels in China," *New York Times*, May 23, 1935, p. 15; and "300 Chinese Slain Inside Great Wall," *New York Times*, May 26, 1935, p. 23.

49. This quote and the next are from "China: Japan's at It Again," *Washington Post*, May 26, 1935, p. B2.

50. "Japan Denies Plans for Invading China," *New York Times*, June 1, 1935, p. 2.

51. Ibid.

52. The telegram is dated May 31, 1935. U. S. Department of State, *United States Diplomatic Papers, 1935. Far East*, 3, p. 190.

53. Joseph Grew to Cordell Hull, telegram, June 11, 1935, ibid., 3, p. 230.

54. "Chinese Abandon Silver Standard; Note Issue Unified," *New York Times*, November 4, 1935, p. 1. There has been considerable debate among economists over the extent of the Chinese deflation and its connection to America's Silver Purchase Act. The main proponent of a close link between the American silver program and deflation in China is Milton Friedman, "FDR, Silver, and Inflation," in *Money Mischief*. This view is challenged by Loren Brandt and Thomas Sargent, "Interpreting New Evidence about China and U.S. Silver Purchases," *Journal of Monetary Economics* 23, no. 1 (1989): 31–51. Friedman's view is supported

by Richard Burdekin, *China's Monetary Challenges: Past Experiences and Future Prospects* (Cambridge, UK: Cambridge University Press, 2008), chap 5. My own judgment is that the extensive contemporary coverage, both among professional economists and journalists, confirms the Friedman view. See especially Leavens, *Silver Money*, pp. 307ff, 314.

55. The full currency reform decree appears in Young, *China's Nation-Building Effort*, pp. 484–85.

56. The discussion in this paragraph and the quote are from Morgenthau Diaries, vol. 10, September–October 31, 1935, pp. 180–81, available at http://www.fdrlibrary.marist.edu/archives/collections/franklin/?p=collections/findingaid&id=535&q=&rootcontentid=188897#id188897.

57. This quote and the next are from Morgenthau Diaries, vol. 11, November 1–November 14, 1935, pp. 50–51, available at http://www.fdrlibrary.marist.edu/archives/collections/franklin/?p=collections/findingaid&id=535&q=&rootcontentid=188897#id188897.

58. This conversation is excerpted from ibid., pp. 63–64.

59. "China's Money Plan Angers Japan," *New York Times*, November 5, 1935, p. 1.

60. Ibid.

61. This and the remaining quotes in this paragraph are from *New York Times*, November 6, 1935, p. 24.

62. "Why America Must Stand Firm in the Far East," December 27, 1934, in Joseph C. Grew, *Ten Years in Japan* (New York: Simon and Schuster, 1944), p. 148.

63. "Jap Militarists Renew Drive to Seize North China," *Chicago Daily Tribune*, November 23, 1935, p. 4.

64. "Japanese March into North China; Seize Rail Centre," *New York Times*, November 28, 1935, p. 1.

65. "Hull's Warning on China," *New York Times*, December 6, 1935, p. 16.

66. This quote and the next two are from "Japan's 'Frank Statement'," *Manchester Guardian*, December 6, 1935, p. 11.

67. "Jap Militarists Renew Drive to Seize North China, *Chicago Daily Tribune*, November 23, 1935, p. 4.

68. "New State Born in North China; Japs in Control," *Chicago Daily Tribune*, December 8, 1935, p. 5. The quote is from Barbara Tuchman, *Stilwell and the American Experience in China, 1911–45* (New York: Grove Press, 1970), p. 151.

69. "North China Plans Its Own Currency," *New York Times*, December 17, 1935, p. 18.

70. "China: Warned and Bombed," *Washington Post*, December 22, 1935, p. B2. Also see "Tojo and 6 Others Hanged by Allies as War Criminals," *New York Times*, December 23, 1948, p. 1.

71. See Borg, *United States and the Far Eastern Crisis*, p. 299.

72. George B. Roberts, "The Silver Purchase Program and Its Consequences," *Proceedings of the Academy of Political Science* 17, no. 1 (1936): p. 23.

73. For the initial favorable impact, see Leavens, *Silver Money*, p. 323, who writes, "Contrary to the misgivings of many, the new currency system was emi-

nently successful . . . during 1936 and 1937." The inflation under wartime pressure is discussed in Everest, *Morgenthau, New Deal and Silver*, p. 123, who writes, "Kung . . . took the easy way out and printed paper. Circulating currency rose from a billion and a half dollars in 1937 to a trillion in 1946; prices followed a similar trend until V-J day they stood at 2,500 times the prewar level." Also see Friedman, *Money Mischief*, p. 179: "The issue of notes multiplied 300-fold from 1937 to 1945, or an average of 100 percent a year. . . . Prices rose even faster . . . or an average of 150 percent a year." Friedman (p.181) acknowledges that "war . . . would have led to inflation. . . . However, in the absence of the silver purchase program, the Nationalists would probably have had an extra year or two during which inflation would have been low. . . . The existence of the silver standard would have been a check on inflation."

74. Morgenthau Diaries, vol. 13, December 1–December 12, 1935, p. 90, available at http://www.fdrlibrary.marist.edu/archives/collections/franklin/?p=collections /findingaid&id=535&q=&rootcontentid=188897#id188897.

75. Ibid., p. 89. Morgenthau writes that "silver can only be gotten into Japan by smuggling it out of China and somebody is making the difference between 40¢, approximately what you can buy silver for in China, and 65¢, the world price."

76. This quote and the remaining in this paragraph are from ibid.

77. All of the quotes in this paragraph are from ibid., p. 90.

78. Handy & Harman's free market price varied between 65.75¢ and 65.375¢ during the four-month period.

79. *Wall Street Journal*, December 10, 1935, p. 1.

80. "New York Mystified," *Manchester Guardian*, December 11, 1935, p. 14.

81. Ibid.

82. This and the following quotes are from Morgenthau Diaries, vol. 13, p. 218.

CHAPTER 9: SILVER LINING

1. The information in this paragraph is based on "Moving of Silver to Vault Is Begun," *New York Times*, July 6, 1938, p. 5; and on "Huge Silver Vault Gets First Deposit," *New York Times*, July 7, 1938, p. 21.

2. The 45,000-ton estimate comes from the approximately 1.3 billion ounces purchased under the Silver Purchase Act (see Leavens, *Silver Money*, p. 273, table 15), when converted from troy ounces into avoirdupois ounces by multiplying the troy ounce total by a factor of 1.1. The 70,000 tons mentioned in the July 7, 1938, *New York Times* article refers to the total capacity of the West Point depository at that time. See "U.S. to Send Silver Here," *New York Times*, May 9, 1938, p. 29.

3. Roberts, "Silver Purchase Program and Its Consequences," p. 22.

4. Ibid., p. 23.

5. "Treasury Department Appropriation Bill for 1938," p. 34.

6. The silver dollar coin contains 371.25 grains of silver according to the Mint Act of April 2, 1792. Since there are 480 grains in a troy ounce, the silver dollar contains 371.25/480 = .7734375 ounces of pure (999 fine) silver. The $1.29 price of an ounce is 1/.7734 = 1.292929.

7. The formal order forcing Americans to divest their gold holdings was issued on April 5, 1933, "Executive Order 6102—Requiring Gold Coin, Gold Bullion and Gold Certificates to Be Delivered to the Government," April 5, 1933. Online by Peters and Woolley, *American Presidency Project*.

8. "Silver's Subsidy," *Washington Post*, December 28, 1937, p. 7

9. See Richard Burdekin and Marc Weidenmier, "The development of 'nontraditional' open market operations: Lessons from FDR's silver purchase program," in *The Origins and Development of Financial Markets and Institutions from the Seventeenth Century to the Present*, ed. Jeremy Attack and Larry Neal, pp. 319–44 (Cambridge, UK: Cambridge University Press, 2009).

10. The data in this sentence and the next are from Y.S. Leong, *Silver: An Analysis of Factors Affecting Price* (Washington, DC: Brookings Institution, 1933), p. 97.

11. Franklin D. Roosevelt, "Annual Budget Message," January 5, 1942. Online by Peters and Woolley, *American Presidency Project*. http://www.presidency.ucsb.edu/ws/?pid=16231.

12. See Franklin D. Roosevelt, "Executive Order 9024 Establishing the War Production Board," January 16, 1942, Online by Peters and Woolley, *American Presidency Project*.

13. The U.S. Department of the Treasury, *Annual Report of the Secretary of the Treasury, for the Fiscal Year Ended June 30, 1941* (Washington, DC: Government Printing Office, 1942), p. 254, reports that the West Point depository contained 1,542,694,885 ounces of silver bullion.

14. Roosevelt, "Executive Order 9024," *American Presidency Project*.

15. "Wartime Curb on Newspaper Size Predicted," *Chicago Daily Tribune*, January 28, 1942, p. 25.

16. "WPB Plans to Build Stockpile of Cloth," *New York Times*, January 29, 1942, p. 29.

17. "Brass Discontinued for Shoe Eyelets," *Washington Post*, January 28, 1942, p. 22.

18. "WPB Halts Output of Metal Zippers," *New York Times*, March 31, 1942, p. 33.

19. Ibid.

20. The steel penny was launched in February 1943, and distribution was ended in the last week of December 1943. See U.S. Department of the Treasury, *Annual Report of the Secretary of the Treasury, for the Fiscal Year Ended June 30, 1943* (Washington, DC: Government Printing Office, 1944), p. 263.

21. "Steel Pennies Move into Use Quickly; Complaints Grow," *Chicago Daily Tribune*, September 5, 1943, p. 4.

22. "Minting of Steel Pennies to End This Year: New Coin to Be of Salvaged Cartridge Shells," *New York Times*, October 23, 1943, p. 15; and "End of a Bad Penny," *New York Times*, December 28, 1943, p. 16.

23. For a description of free silver and the 1.3-billion-ounce estimate see *Annual Report of the Secretary of the Treasury for 1943*, p. 364.

24. Morgenthau Diaries, vol. 512, April 1–2, 1942, p. 86, available at http://www.fdrlibrary.marist.edu/archives/collections/franklin/?p=collections/findingaid&id=535&q=&rootcontentid=188897#id188897.

25. This quote and the next are from "Using Silver for War," *Washington Post*, March 30, 1942, p. 11.

26. "Morgenthau Advocates Wiping Out Silver Laws," *New York Times*, February 4, 1943, p. 10.

27. "Treasury Weighs Use for Its Silver: Seeks Way under Law to Meet WPB's Desire to 'Lend' It for Industrial Use," *New York Times*, March 31, 1942, p. 33.

28. Edward Foley to Henry Morgenthau, memorandum, March 30, 1942, Morgenthau Diaries, vol. 514, pt. 1, April 7–9, 1942, pp. 76–79, and Henry Morgenthau to Francis Biddle, April 1, 1942, Morgenthau Diaries, vol. 512, p. 86, available at http://www.fdrlibrary.marist.edu/archives/collections/franklin/?p=collections/finding aid&id=535&q=&rootcontentid=188897#id188897.

29. Biddle's letter is in Morgenthau Diaries, vol. 514, pt. 1 pp. 81–86; and the public announcement is in "40,000 Tons of Silver 'Loaned' for Busbars," *New York Times*, April 8, 1942, p. 8 (the dateline on the story is April 7).

30. "40,000 Tons of Silver 'Loaned' for Busbars," *New York Times*, April 8, 1942, p. 8.

31. For the start of the program, see U.S. Department of the Treasury, *Annual Report of the Secretary of the Treasury, for the Fiscal Year Ended June 30, 1942* (Washington, DC: Government Printing Office, 1943), pp. 45, 184.

32. Morgenthau Diaries, vol. 564, August 29–31, 1942, pp. 15–17, available at http://www.fdrlibrary.marist.edu/archives/collections/franklin/?p=collections/find ingaid&id=535&q=&rootcontentid=188897#id188897. Clear photocopies of these pages were provided by Kendra Lightner, Archives Technician, FDR Presidential Library and Museum.

33. Six thousand tons translates into 175 million troy ounces as follows: 2,000 avoirdupois pounds times 6,000 tons equals 12 million avoirdupois pounds times 16 avoirdupois ounces equals 192 million avoirdupois ounces, which must be divided by 1.097 to take account of the extra weight in a troy ounce, which produces 175,022,789 troy ounces.

34. Leslie R. Groves, *Now It Can Be Told: The Story of the Manhattan Project* (New York: Harper & Row Publishers, 1962), pp.107–8.

35. According to Stimson, Morgenthau was not happy about being kept in the dark, angry that he was not "fit to be trusted with the secret." See Robert S. Norris, *Racing for the Bomb* (South Royalton, Vt.: Steerforth Press, 2002), pp. 203 and 337–38.

36. See Cameron Reed, "From Treasury Vault to the Manhattan Project, *American Scientist* 99, no. 1 (January 2011): p. 44.

37. Ibid.

38. Norris, *Racing for the Bomb*, p. 203.

39. Reed, "From Treasury Vault," p. 44.

40. Ibid., p. 45.

41. This quote and the next are from Elting E. Morison, *Turmoil and Tradition: A Study of the Life and Times of Henry L. Stimson* (Boston: Houghton Mifflin Company, 2003), p. 621.

42. Groves, *Now It Can Be Told*, p. 109.

43. Ibid.

CHAPTER 10: COSTLY VICTORY

1. For a concise biographical sketch of McCarran see http://www.onlinene
vada.org/articles/patrick-anthony-mccarran.

2. See Michael J. Ybarra, *Washington Gone Crazy: Senator Pat McCarran and the Great American Communist Hunt* (Hanover, N.H.: Steerforth Press, 2004), p. 29.

3. Jerome E. Edwards, *Pat McCarran: Political Boss of Nevada* (Reno: University of Nevada Press, 1982), p. 45.

4. See ibid., p. 147, for McCarran and McCarthy, and ibid., p. 132 for McCarran and Franco.

5. For biographical information, see Erwin L. Levine, *Theodore Francis Green: The Washington Years* (Providence, R.I.: Brown University Press, 1971) and "Theodore Francis Green of Rhode Island," at http://knoxfocus.com/2013/08 /theodore-francis-green-of-rhode-island/.

6. See Senate Subcommittee of the Committee on Banking and Currency, "To Authorize the Use for War Purposes of Silver Held or Owned By the United States": Hearings on S. 2768, 77th Cong., 2d sess., October 14, 1942, p. 26.

7. "Subcommittee Backs Bill for Silver Sale," *New York Times*, October 15, 1942, p. 9.

8. See Senate Subcommittee of the Committee on Banking and Currency, "To Authorize Use for War Purposes," p. 6.

9. The McCarran quote is in "Subcommittee Backs Bill for Silver Sale," *New York Times*, October 15, 1942, p. 9.

10. The restriction on Treasury sales is in section 4 of the Silver Purchase Act, which contains an exception if the value of silver stocks in the Treasury exceeds 25% of the total value of gold and silver. This exception was not operative.

11. Morgenthau Diaries, vol. 578, October 10–15, 1942, pp. 24–25, available at http://www.fdrlibrary.marist.edu/archives/collections/franklin/?p=collections/find ingaid&id=535&q=&rootcontentid=188897#id188897.

12. "McCarran Halts Senate on Silver," *New York Times*, December 9, 1942, p. 47.

13. "McCarran Succeeds in Killing Silver Bill," *New York Times*, December 12, 1942, p. 8.

14. "Silver for War Work," *New York Times*, November 23, 1942, p. 22.

15. See "Senate Vote Silver Bill for Its Use in Industry," *New York Times*, June 19, 1943; and "Bill to Release U.S. Silver Goes to White House," *Christian Science Monitor*, July 6, 1943, p. 14.

16. "Bill to Sell Federal Silver Gets Approval," *Christian Science Monitor*, May 12, 1943, p. 18.

17. The balance at West Point is reported at 235 million ounces on June 30, 1945, U.S. Department of the Treasury, *Annual Report of the Secretary of the Treasury, for the Fiscal Year Ended June 30, 1945* (Washington, DC: Government Printing Office, 1946), p. 230, and at 172 million ounces on June 30, 1946, U.S. Department of the Treasury, *Annual Report of the Secretary of the Treasury, for the Fiscal Year Ended June 30, 1946* (Washington, DC: Government Printing Office, 1947), p. 216.

18. See Charles Merrill and Helena Meyer, "Gold and Silver," in U.S. Bureau of Mines, *Minerals Yearbook 1946* (Washington, DC: Government Printing Office, 1948), p. 561 for domestic production, and p. 577 for industrial consumption, available at http://digital.library.wisc.edu/1711.dl/EcoNatRes.MinYB1946. Also see Everest, *Morgenthau, New Deal and Silver*, pp. 164–66.

19. The amount of free silver in the Treasury's General Fund was valued on a cost basis as $324 million on June 30, 1945, and at $102 million on June 30, 1946. See the table entitled "Condition of the Treasury Exclusive of Public Debt Liabilities" in the *Annual Report of the Secretary of the Treasury for 1945* (p. 612) and *1946* (p. 430).

20. "Acute Shortage Threatens Many Silver Producers," *Hartford Courant*, April 20, 1946, p. 14.

21. "Senate Delays on Silver Cuts Supply of Film," *Wall Street Journal*, June 17, 1946, p. 4.

22. "Acute Shortage Threatens Many Silver Producers," *Hartford Courant*, April 20, 1946, p. 14.

23. "West's Silver Bloc Seeking 19 Cent Boost: Remonetization Expected in Two Years," *Chicago Daily Tribune*, April 26, 1946, p. 31.

24. "Senators for Silver Sales at 90 cents; McCarran Sees Re-monetization," *New York Times*, April 26, 1946, p. 1.

25. "Congress Sets Price of Silver at 90.5 cents; Agreement Frees Postal and Treasury Pay," *New York Times*, July 20, 1946, p. 26.

26. "House, Senate Accept 90.5 Cent silver Price," *Christian Science Monitor*, July 20, 1946, p. 15. For a reprint of the bill see the *Annual Report of the Secretary of the Treasury for 1946*, p. 325.

27. "Both Houses Pass Silver Legislation: Koppleman Hails Reduction from $1.29 for Treasury Metal," *Hartford Courant*, July 20, 1946, p. 2.

28. There was, of course, a tiny spread between the Treasury's buying price (bid), which was 90.41¢, and its selling price (offer), which was 90.91¢, to cover expenses and perhaps make a little profit. See Handy & Harman, *Annual Review of the Silver Market, 31st, 1946* (New York: Pandick Press, 1947), p. 7.

CHAPTER 11: JFK'S DOUBLE CROSS

1. LBJ wrote of the Warren Commission investigation: "Russia was not immune. Neither was Cuba. Neither was the State of Texas. Neither was the new President of the United States." See Robert Caro, *The Passage of Power* (New York: Random House, 2012), p. 440.

2. *Report of the President's Commission on the Assassination of President Kennedy* (Washington, DC: Government Printing Office, 1964), pp. 367–69. Henceforth, this will be referred to as the "Warren Commission Report."

3. No reference appears to silver or silver bloc senators in the "Warren Commission Report."

4. The letter, along with Kennedy's reply, is reprinted (pp. 1102–4) in J. P. Ryan and Katheen M. McBreen, "Silver," in U.S. Bureau of Mines, *Minerals Yearbook 1961*, vol. 1, *Metals and Minerals (except fuels)* (Washington, DC: Government

Printing Office, 1962), available at http://digital.library.wisc.edu/1711.dl/EcoNat Res.MinYB1961v1.

5. The data are from Handy & Harman, *The Silver Market in 1963, 48th Annual Review* (New York: 1964), pp. 20–21.

6. "Hi-Yo, Silver," *New York Times*, November 30, 1961, p. 36.

7. The quote from the CRB (Commodity Research Bureau) database for November 28, 1961, is 91.375¢ and for November 29 it is $1.00¾. The price was unchanged at 91⅜ for the entire year until then because of pegging by the U.S. Treasury's purchases and sales at that price. A spot check comparison of CRB records with daily price quotations for silver during this period from Handy & Harman confirms the reliability of the quotations.

8. "Mining Men Cheer Kennedy Order on Silver," *Los Angeles Times*, November 29, 1961, p. C9.

9. "U.S. Silver Decision Reverberates," *Christian Science Monitor*, November 30, 1961, p. 20.

10. The quotes are from Kennedy's letter, reprinted in Ryan and McBreen, "Silver," *Minerals Yearbook 1961*, pp. 1102–4, available at http://digital.library .wisc.edu/1711.dl/EcoNatRes.MinYB1961v1.

11. Mel Carnahan had served as the Democratic governor of Missouri and was elected posthumously as U.S. senator in 2000 after being killed in a plane crash three weeks before the election.

12. For the biographical details in this paragraph see "C. Douglas Dillon Dies at 93; Was in Kennedy Cabinet," *New York Times*, January 12, 2003.

13. See the entry for Douglas Dillon at http://www.anb.org/articles/07/07-00 862.html.

14. William L. Silber, *Volcker: The Triumph of Persistence* (New York: Bloomsbury, 2012), p. 28.

15. Paul Volcker and Toyoo Gyohten, *Changing Fortunes* (New York: Times Books, 1992), p. 22.

16. "Mint Director Loses Authority to Supervise Silver Policies," *New York Times*, October 27, 1961, p. 19.

17. Silber, *Volcker*, pp. 27–28.

18. "Mint Chief Confirmed," *New York Times*, September 24, 1961, p. 80.

19. "Silver Backer to Head Mint—Minus Powers," *Los Angeles Times*, October 29, 1961, p. D1.

20. Dillon's quote is from "Woman Sworn in as Mint Director," *New York Times*, October 31, 1961, p. 16.

21. See Kennedy letter in Ryan and McBreen, "Silver," *Minerals Yearbook 1961*, pp. 1102–4, available at http://digital.library.wisc.edu/1711.dl/EcoNatRes .MinYB1961v1.

22. "Excerpts from President Kennedy's Economic Report to the Congress," *New York Times*, January 23, 1962, p. 16.

23. For the end-of-year number for 1961 see Board of Governors of the Federal Reserve System, *Banking and Monetary Statistics: 1941–1970* (Washington, DC: Government Printing Office, 1976), p. 620, available at https://fraser .stlouisfed.org/scribd/?title_id=41&filepath=/docs/publications/bms/1941-1970 /BMS41-70_complete.pdf. The volume of silver certificates on June 30, 1934, was

$401 million. See Board of Governors of the Federal Reserve System. *Banking and Monetary Statistics: 1914–1941* (Washington, DC: Government Printing Office, 1943), p. 409, available at https://fraser.stlouisfed.org/docs/publications/bms/1914 -1941/BMS14–41_complete.pdf.

24. See Dillon's letter to Kennedy in Ryan and McBreen, "Silver," *Minerals Yearbook 1961*, pp. 1102–4, for the statement "nearly 1.7 billion ounces." The precise number of ounces backing the $2.12 billion of silver certificates outstanding on December 31, 1961, is .7734 (the fraction of an ounce of silver in a silver dollar) times 2.12, which is 1.62396 billion ounces. Recall that a silver certificate could be exchanged for a silver dollar (not an ounce of silver). According to the Board of Governors of the Federal Reserve System, *Banking and Monetary Statistics: 1941– 1970* (p. 620), Federal Reserve notes outstanding on December 31, 1961, totaled $28.7 billion, or more than ten times the volume of silver certificates.

25. The Federal Reserve Act of December 23, 1914, section 16, entitled "Note Issues," permits the issuance by the Federal Reserve Banks for circulation "notes of the denominations of $5, $10, $20, $50, and $100, as may be required." The omission of one-dollar denomination notes was explicit but not commented on in the legislation. Perhaps it had something to do with the silver bloc in the Senate promoting the circulation of silver dollars and one-dollar silver certificates.

26. See U.S. Department of the Treasury, *Annual Report of the Secretary of the Treasury, for the Fiscal Year Ended June 30, 1962* (Washington, DC: Government Printing Office, 1963), p. 177.

27. See Bratter, *Silver Market Dictionary*, for the definition of subsidiary coin. Subsidiary coins had limited legal tender status from the act of June 9, 1879, which specified that such coins must be accepted in payments up to ten dollars but not necessarily above that amount. Title III of the Thomas Amendment of May 12, 1933, specified that "All coins and currencies of the United States . . . should be legal tender for all debts public and private," but that may or may not have applied to subsidiary coin. According to a 1960 memorandum prepared by the U.S. Treasury, "the legal tender quality of subsidiary silver has never been ruled upon by the courts." See "Coins and Currency of the United States," reprinted in Senate Committee on Banking and Currency, *Federal Reserve Direct Purchases—Old Series Currency Adjustment Act*: Hearings on S. 3702 and S. 3714, 86th Cong., 2d sess., June 24, 1960, pp. 21–40, esp. p. 28. The ambiguity was resolved by Public Law 89–81 of July 23, 1965, section 102: "All coins and currencies of the United States (including Federal Reserve notes and circulating notes of Federal Reserve banks and national banking associations) regardless of when coined or issued shall be regarded as legal tender for all debts, public and private, public charges, taxes, duties and dues."

28. The news story "U.S. Moves to End Backing of Silver," *New York Times*, February 22, 1962, p. 33, dates the introduction of the bill as February 20, but the bill itself, S. 2885, "A Bill to Repeal Certain Legislation Relating to the Purchase of Silver and for Other Purposes," carries the date February 22, 1962.

29. This quote and the next are from "U.S. Moves to End Backing of Silver," *New York Times*, February 22, 1962, p. 33.

30. Bible's remarks and the other comments are in Senate Subcommittee on Minerals, Materials, and Fuels of the Committee on Interior and Insular Affairs,

"Gold and Silver Production Incentives": Hearings on S.J. Res. 44, 87th Cong., 2d sess., March 15 and June 8, 1962, pp. 6–7.

31. Ibid.

32. "Administration Bid to Repeal Silver Acts Appears Doomed, at Least for This Year," *Wall Street Journal*, March 15, 1962, p. 5.

33. This quote and the next are from "Critical Coin Shortage Hits Christmas Buying," *Boston Globe*, December 11, 1962, p. 17.

34. "Mint Employees Work Weekends to Ease Yule Coin Shortage," *Wall Street Journal*, November 27, 1962, p. 8.

35. "Critical Coin Shortage Hits Christmas Buying," *Boston Globe*, December 11, 1962, p. 17.

36. "Coin Shortage Held Likely by Treasury Boss," *Los Angeles Times*, January 31, 1963, p. B7.

37. Ibid.

38. "Dillon Backs Change in U.S. Silver System," *Chicago Tribune*, March 12, 1963, p. 5

39. "This quote and the next are from "Coins Remain Scarce in Many U.S. Cities; Treasury Seeks Funds to Build New Mint," *Wall Street Journal*, March 26, 1963, p. 32.

40. The data are from Handy & Harman, *The Silver Market in 1963, 48th Annual Review* (New York, 1964), pp. 20–21.

41. "Silver Act Repeal Plan Wins House Approval," *New York Times*, April 11, 1963, p. 61.

42. "Campaign to Get Congress to Sever Silver's Link to Paper Currency Is Opened by Dillon," *Wall Street Journal*, January 31, 1963, p. 6.

43. "Bill to Cut Silver's Paper-Currency Link Is Passed in House," *Wall Street Journal*, April 11, 1963, p. 20.

44. Senate Committee on Banking and Currency, "Repeal of Silver Purchase Acts": Hearing, 88th Cong., 1st sess., April 29, 1963, p. 4.

45. This quote and the next are from ibid., pp. 4–5.

46. In 1961 Idaho produced 17 million ounces, while Arizona, the next biggest, produced 5 million ounces. A similar relationship held for the previous five years. See Ryan and McBreen, "Silver," *Minerals Yearbook 1961*, p. 1108, available at http://digital.library.wisc.edu/1711.dl/EcoNatRes.MinYB1961v1.

47. Senate Committee on Banking and Currency, "Repeal of Silver Purchase Acts," p. 81.

48. This quote and the others in this paragraph are from ibid., pp. 72–74.

49. This quote and the next are in ibid., p. 81.

50. These quotes and the next are from Dillon's testimony reprinted in U.S. Department of the Treasury, *Annual Report of the Secretary of the Treasury, for the Fiscal Year Ended June 30, 1963* (Washington, DC: Government Printing Office, 1963), pp. 400, 404.

51. Ibid., p. 405, for a reprint of Public Law 88–36.

52. The vote was 68–10 as reported in "Senate Votes End to Silver Backing," May 24, 1963, *New York Times*, p. 1. Support by Dodd, Pell, Pastore, and Keating appears in Senate Committee on Banking and Currency, "Repeal of Silver Purchase Acts," p. 8.

53. "Cutting the Silver Chord," *Washington Post*, May 26, 1963, p. E6.

54. "Silver Is Traded on Open Market: Hectic Trading as Brokers Enter the 'Silver Ring' for the First Time in 29 Years," *New York Times*, June 13, 1963, p. 59.

55. "Silver Hits Price Treasury Quotes for Its Holdings," *Wall Street Journal*, September 10, 1963, p. 32.

56. See "Silver Is Bought from U.S. Stocks," *New York Times*, September 13, 1963, p. 19; and "Cashing Bills to Get Silver Now Feasible," *Chicago Tribune*, September 15, 1963, p. D3

57. See "Delivery of Silver Bullion in Exchange for Silver Certificates," in *Federal Register* (July 24, 1963), vol. 28, no. 143, reprinted in Handy & Harman, *Silver Market in 1963*, pp. 27–28.

58. Detailed data on Treasury silver appears in U.S. Department of Treasury, *Treasury Staff Study of Silver and Coinage* (Washington, DC, 1965), table 5 (p.16). The Treasury owned 1,584 million troy ounces at the end of 1963.

59. "Senate Drops Dollar's Silver," *Newsday*, May 24, 1963, p. 2.

60. Ibid.

61. The quotes in this paragraph are from the "Warren Commission Report," pp. 40–41.

62. Ibid., p. 296.

63. See chapter 2, last paragraph.

CHAPTER 12: LBJ NAILS THE COFFIN SHUT

1. Caro, *Passage of Power*, p. 356.

2. Ibid., picture following p. 426.

3. Ibid., p. 429.

4. Ibid., p. 430.

5. See *Annual Report of the Secretary of the Treasury for 1963*, p. 400.

6. "Long Lines Form to Buy Silver Dollars at Treasury," *New York Times*, March 24, 1964, p. 10.

7. "Dillon Asks New Silver Dollars as Trading in Old Ones Goes On," *Washington Post*, March 24, 1964, p. A1.

8. This quote and the remaining in this paragraph are from "Mansfield Fights to Keep Cartwheels Rolling," *Boston Globe*, March 22, 1964, p. 33.

9. "State Residents Flip Over New JFK Halves," *Hartford Courant*, March 26, 1964, p. 10A.

10. "Kennedy Half Dollar Due Today with Limit of 40 to Customer," *Washington Post*, March 24, 1964, p. A3.

11. "Bank Workers Profit on Kennedy Halves," *Washington Post*, June 26, 1964, p. A1.

12. "Fruit of the Mints," *New York Times*, November 29, 1964, p. X34.

13. "Problem of Sinking Silver Supply Draws Multitude of Plans," *Chicago Tribune*, October 27, 1964, p. C5.

14. The Coinage Act of 1853 made the silver content of a dollar's worth of subsidiary coin equal to 345.6 grains, or .72 (345.6/480) per troy ounce. Section 15 of The Coinage Act of 1873 slightly increased the silver content to 347.229

grains or to .72339+ per troy ounce. Therefore, after 1873, subsidiary coins bought a troy ounce of silver at 1/.72339 = $1.3824. See Laughlin, *History of Bimetallism*, p. 82, for a discussion of the 1853 Act and Laughlin (p. 305) for section 15 of the 1873 Act. The slight change occurred because in the 1853 Act the total size of the half-dollar was defined as 192 grains while in the 1873 Act it was defined as 12½ grams, which is 192.905 grains (each gram contains 15.4234 grains). Since each coin contained 90% silver, the silver in each half-dollar after 1873 was 173.6145 grains or 347.229 for two half-dollars.

15. "Coin Business Is High Finance," *Hartford Courant*, November 15, 1964, p. 10C3.

16. Each of these nickels contained 56% copper, 9% manganese, and 35% silver. The silver content of each coin weighed .05626 ounces, which is worth 7.274¢ at silver's price of $1.293. See http://silvercoinmeltvalues.net/jefferson-nickels-1942 -1945/.

17. For this quote and the remaining discussion in this paragraph see "Grocery Chains Plan to Issue Own 'Money' to Meet Coin Needs," *Wall Street Journal*, June 8, 1964, p. 1.

18. Ibid.

19. "Wooden Nickel Test Foiled by Treasury," *Hartford Courant*, June 1, 1964, p. 12A.

20. Ibid.

21. "Paper Scrip Plan Ruled Illegal in Treasury Advisory Opinion," *New York Times*, June 13, 1964, p. 27.

22. "Johnson OK's Around-Clock Work at Mints," *Chicago Tribune*, May 4, 1964, p. E6.

23. Ibid.

24. "Silver Dollar Legislation Signed," *Washington Post*, August 4, 1964, p. A13.

25. "News of Coins: President Gets the Bill to Freeze 1964 Date," *New York Times*, September 6, 1964, p. X24.

26. See U.S. Department of the Treasury, *Treasury Staff Study*, p. 16, table 5.

27. Ibid., p. 7, table 1.

28. "Treasury Delays Minting of Silver Dollars; Will Seek to Cut All Coins' Silver Content," *Wall Street Journal*, December 28, 1964, p. 9.

29. For the volume of silver certificates in 1964 see Board of Governors of the Federal Reserve System, *Banking and Monetary Statistics: 1941–1970*, p. 620, available at https://fraser.stlouisfed.org/scribd/?title_id=41&filepath=/docs/publi cations/bms/1941-1970/BMS41-70_complete.pdf. See U.S. Department of the Treasury, *Treasury Staff Study*, p. 16, table 5, for the required silver bullion to back those certificates. Recall that each certificate was entitled to the amount of bullion in a silver dollar, which was .77344 ounces. The $1.232 billion certificates outstanding times .77344 equals 952 million ounces.

30. Ibid., p. 16, table 5, col. 2.

31. Ibid., p. 7, table 1. Also see the discussion on the influence of price on consumption on pp. 30–32.

32. "It's Silver Time in the Rockies as Mines Come Alive," *New York Times*, December 10, 1964, p. 75.

33. Ibid.

34. Ibid.

35. Ibid.

36. See U.S. Department of the Treasury, *Treasury Staff Study*, p. 28.

37. See *Washington Post*, January 1, 1965, p. C5, for the headline and for the remaining quotes in this paragraph.

38. The quotes in this paragraph and the discussion in the next appear in "Text of President Johnson's Message to Congress on Changing the Nation's Coinage," *New York Times*, June 4, 1965, p. 18.

39. "U.S. Won't Mint Cartwheels," *Boston Globe*, May 25, 1965, p. 28.

40. "Text of President Johnson's Message to Congress on Changing the Nation's Coinage," *New York Times*, June 4, 1965, p. 18.

41. The source of Fowler's nickname had been obscured by history until I spoke with Roy Smith, his son-in-law and my colleague here at the Stern School of Business, who explained the origin. Also see "Perfect Fit: The Appointment of Fowler," *Washington Post*, March 22, 1965, p. A18.

42. House Committee on Banking and Currency, *Coinage Act of 1965*: Hearings on H.R. 8746, 89th Cong., 1st sess., June 4, 7, 8, 1965, p. 19.

43. "Reaction to President's Coin Proposal Is Mixed," *New York Times*, June 4, 1965, p. 18.

44. This quote and the next are from House Committee on Banking and Currency, *Coinage Act of 1965*, pp. 17–19.

45. Ibid., p. 22.

46. Wright Patman, interview (1) by Joe B. Frantz, August 11, 1972, oral history transcript, LBJ Presidential Library, available at http://transition.lbjlibrary.org/files/original/49e8dd04e2a6a1db3aaa8ef58993cbdc.pdf.

47. The following interchange is from House Committee on Banking and Currency, *Coinage Act of 1965*, pp. 20–21.

48. See chapter 11, note 27.

49. Public Law 89–3, March 3, 1965, *An Act to Eliminate the Requirement that Federal Reserve Banks Maintain Certain Reserves in Gold Certificates against Deposit Liabilities*.

50. The following quotes are from the Senate Committee on Banking and Currency, "Gold Reserve Requirements": Hearings on S. 797, S. 743, S. 814, 89th Cong., 1st sess., February 2, 3, 4, 9, 10, 1965, pp. 142–44.

51. Congress would sever the last link between precious metals and domestic money creation in the United States in 1968. On March 18, 1968, President Johnson signed PL 90–269 eliminating the requirement that each Federal Reserve Bank maintain reserves in gold certificates of not less than 25% of its Federal Reserve notes (currency) in actual circulation. See "President Wins Battle to Remove Gold Cover," at https://library.cqpress.com/cqalmanac/document.php?id=cqal68-1283478.

52. This quote and the remaining two in this paragraph are from Robert Barro, "United States Inflation and the Choice of Monetary Standard," in *Inflation: Causes and Effects*, ed. Robert E. Hall, 104 (Chicago: University of Chicago Press, 1982).

53. "Mr. Fowler's Unwieldy Legacy," *Wall Street Journal*, April 1, 1965, p. 12.

CHAPTER 13: PSYCHIATRIST'S MELTDOWN

1. Eugene Lichtenstein, "Our Silver Dolors," *Fortune*, March 1965, p. 126ff.

2. Ibid., p. 128.

3. "U.S. Won't Mint Cartwheels," *Boston Globe*, May 25, 1965, p. 28.

4. The details of Henry Jarecki's life are based on an autobiographical manuscript referred to as Jarecki Manuscript, as well as on interviews with him.

5. Ibid., chap. 1, p. 5.

6. Ibid., chap. 1, p. 15.

7. Ibid., chap. 2, p. 22.

8. Ibid., chap. 3, pp. 7, 30–31.

9. Ibid., chap. 4, pp. 7–9

10. Ibid., chap. 3, pp. 34–36.

11. Quote is from an interview with Jarecki and the subsequent story is in Jarecki Manuscript, chap. 5, p. 6.

12. Jarecki Manuscript, chap. 4, p. 14.

13. Ibid., chap. 3, p. 7.

14. Ibid., chap. 4, p. 14.

15. Russell Barnhart, *Beating the Wheel* (New York: Kensington Publishing Company, 1992), p. 93.

16. "Treasury Halts Silver Dollar Run, Offers Bullion for Paper Money," *Washington Post*, May 26, 1964, p. A1.

17. Interview with Jarecki and in Henry Jarecki, *An Alchemist's Road: My Transition from Medicine to Business* (privately printed, October 1989), p. 1.

18. Ibid.

19. "Treasury Acts to Guard Silver," *New York Times*, May 19, 1967, p. F55.

20. Handy & Harman, *The Silver Market in 1967, 52nd Annual Review* (New York, 1968), p. 7.

21. Ibid.

22. According to the *New York Times*, "Silver Futures All Set Records," May 19, 1967, p. F61. The news on Thursday, May 18 came out after the close of trading, although "there was a riptide of enthusiasm for silver futures" even before the announcement. The $1.49 price quotation is for the close of business on Friday, May 19, for the spot May contract on Comex (see *Wall Street Journal*, May 22, 1967, p. 4, "Silver Price Spiral Is Seen Affecting Gold as Crises, New U.S. Rules Shake Markets"). The previous peak price for silver comes from the U.S. Department of the Treasury, *Annual Report of the Secretary of the Treasury, for the Fiscal Year Ended June 30, 1920* (Washington, DC: Government Printing Office, 1921), p. 595.

23. The CRB database shows July silver futures rising the daily permissible limit of 5¢ on Thursday, May 18, Friday, May 19, Monday, May 22, and Tuesday, May 23. It closed at $1.544 on Wednesday, May 24, up 2¢ on the day, which means that was the first unconstrained response in futures contracts to the May 18 announcement.

24. Jarecki, *Alchemist's Road*, p. 1.

25. See http://sabr.org/research/mlbs-annual-salary-leaders-1874-2012 and https://sportslistoftheday.com/2011/12/05/major-league-baseballs-average-salaries-1964-2010/.

26. Jarecki suggests that delivery cost is about four cents an ounce in Jarecki Manuscript, chap. 6, p. 6, but writes in the *Alchemist's Road*, p. 1, that silver must be above $1.35 an ounce compared with $1.29 to cover costs, suggesting a six-cent delivery cost. But he adds in "nuisance" in the latter estimate so that slightly less than five cents was probably the best estimate.

27. There were $547 million silver certificates outstanding in May 1967, according to the Board of Governors of the Federal Reserve System, *Banking and Monetary Statistics: 1941–1970*, p. 621.

28. See *New York Times*, August 3, 1967, p. 48.

29. This story is from Jarecki, *Alchemist's Road*, p. 3.

30. *Washington Post and Times Herald*, July 7, 1967, p. F7.

31. This quote and the next are from Jarecki, *Alchemist's Road*, p. 5.

32. Public Law 90–29, 90th Cong., "An act to authorize adjustments in the amount of silver certificates outstanding and for other purposes," in U.S. Department of the Treasury, *Annual Report of the Secretary of the Treasury, for the Fiscal Year Ended June 30, 1967* (Washington, DC: Government Printing Office, 1968), p. 400. Also see Handy & Harman, *The Silver Market in 1967, 52nd Annual Review* (New York, 1968), p. 6.

33. "Treasury Halting Sales of Its Silver at $1.29 An Ounce," *New York Times*, July 15, 1967, p. 32.

34. Ibid.

35. The closing price of the spot contract (July) on Comex, Monday, July 17, 1967, was $1.795 compared with the closing price of $1.6985 on Friday, July 14, 1967, for a 5.7% increase.

36. "Silver Certificates and Certain Nickels Draw Premiums as Dealers Seek Easy Gain," *Wall Street Journal*, August 14, 1967, p.18.

37. Jarecki, *Alchemist's Road*, p. 6.

38. "Treasury to Restrict Silver Sales to Grades Needing More Refining," *Wall Street Journal*, October 13, 1967, p. 19.

39. "Prices of Silver in Sharp Advance," *New York Times*, October 14, 1967, p. 30.

40. Franz Pick, *Silver: How and Where to Buy and Hold It*, rev. and enl. 3d ed. (New York: Pick Publishing Corporation, [1974]), p. 39.

41. Ibid., p. 41.

42. The conversation is from Jarecki, *Alchemist's Road*, pp. 9–10.

43. The data are from the spot silver series of the CRB database.

44. This quote and the remaining in this paragraph are from "Silver Now at Bryan's 16 to 1 Ratio," *New York Times*, December 25, 1967, p. 42. The $2.10 spot price was reached on December 12 and remained there through the end of the year.

45. This quote and the next two are from "Price Rise Beginning to Worry Experts," *Washington Post and Times Herald*, December 24, 1967, p. B1.

46. *Economic Report of the President*, transmitted to the Congress, February 1968, together with the *Annual Report of the Council of Economic Advisers* (Washington, DC: Government Printing Office, 1968), p. 96.

47. "Commodities: Speculators Continue to Trade Precious Metals," *New York Times*, November 28, 1967, p. 75.

48. Handy & Harman, *Silver Market in 1967*, p. 22.

49. Ibid., p. 24.

50. "British Devalue Pound," *Boston Globe*, November 19, 1967, p. 1

51. "How Sound Is Your Dollar?" *Chicago Tribune*, October 30, 1967, p. 16.

52. See "Gold Pool Dropped to End Speculation: Two Prices Adopted by 7 Nations," *Washington Post*, May 18, 1968, p. A1; and "The Gold Rush Threatens the Entire System," *New York Times*, March 17, 1968, p. E3.

53. These are the spot gold and silver prices from the CRB database.

54. This incident and the quotes are from Jarecki, *Alchemist's Road*, p. 15.

CHAPTER 14: BATTLE LINES

1. This paragraph and the next are based on "Two Men Are Seized, Charged with Illegal Melting of Coins," *Wall Street Journal*, December 5, 1968, p. 29; and "State Man Seized in Coin Melting," *Hartford Courant*, December 5, 1968, p. 12.

2. "Two Men Are Seized, Charged with Illegal Melting of Coins," *Wall Street Journal*, December 5, 1968, p. 29.

3. Recall that the silver content of subsidiary coins is worth $1.38¼. The premium at $2.00 per ounce is 44.7%.

4. This quote and the next are from "Opening Statement of the Secretary before the Meeting of the Joint Coinage Committee," May 12, 1969, reprinted in U.S. Department of the Treasury, *Annual Report of the Secretary of the Treasury on the State of the Finances, for the Fiscal Year Ended June 30, 1969* (Washington, DC: Government Printing Office, 1970), p. 379.

5. Ibid., p. 375, for this quote and the next.

6. See the Board of Governors of the Federal Reserve System, *Banking and Monetary Statistics: 1941–1970*, p. 621.

7. There were $547 million silver certificates outstanding in May 1967, backed by .77 ounces of silver for a total of 421 ounces. There were $2.68 billion in subsidiary coin outstanding in December 1965, containing .72 ounces of silver for a total of 1.929 billion ounces, which is more than 4.5 times bigger than 421 million ounces.

8. Jarecki, *Alchemist's Road*, p. 22.

9. "Speculators and Melters Rush for Silver Coins," *Christian Science Monitor*, May 15, 1969, p. 17.

10. This quote and the next are from Jarecki, *Alchemist's Road*, p. 18.

11. The book was published in 1971 by J.B. Lippincott, New York.

12. Interview with Henry Jarecki.

13. The 1684 date is in "Along Wall Street: London's 'Four Just Men,'" *Wall Street Journal*, June 13, 1937, p. 47. The 1720 date is in "Notes on 'Precious Heritage: three hundred years of Mocatta & Goldsmid,'" available at http://www.barrow-lousada.org/PDFdocs/PreciousHeritage.pdf.

14. "U.S. Silver Plan: Leading London Bullion Firm Believes Purchase Program May Not Be Completed," *Wall Street Journal*, January 21, 1937, p. 4.

15. "London Gold Market Reopened for First Day's Trading Since '39," *New York Times*, March 23, 1954, p. 35.

16. "Broker Forecasts a Silver Shortage," *New York Times*, January 3, 1961, p. 41.

17. Jarecki, *Alchemist's Road*, p. 23.

18. "Suzy Says: London Doings," *Chicago Tribune*, May 6, 1969, p. B1.

CHAPTER 15: NELSON BUNKER HUNT

1. *Wall Street Journal*, April 25, 1966, p. 12. The headline reads "Big Oil Discovery Well." I have transposed the words Well and Discovery to make it read properly.

2. "Dallas Was Trying to Polish Image Tarnished by Rightists," *Washington Post and Times Herald*, September 28, 1964, p. A18.

3. "The Biggest Pipeline," *Daily Telegraph*, December 14, 1964, p. 15.

4. For Margaret's quote see Margaret Hunt Hill, *H.L. and Lyda* (Little Rock, Ark.: August House Publishers, 1994), p. 251; and for Getty's observation see Jerome Tuccille, *Kingdom: The Story of the Hunt Family of Texas* (Ottawa, Ill.: Jameson Books, 1984), p. 268.

5. Tuccille, *Kingdom*, p. 227.

6. The $6 to $8 billion estimate is in Bryan Burrough, *The Big Rich: The Rise and Fall of the Greatest Texas Oil Fortunes* (New York: Penguin Press, 2009), p. 296. Fifteen years later, in 1982, the first year *Forbes* published its list of wealthiest Americans, there were only 13 billionaires in the world. See http://www.forbes.com/sites/seankilachand/2012/09/20/the-forbes-400-hall-of-fame-36-members-of-our-debut-issue-still-in-ranks/.

7. The quote is from Bunker Hunt's testimony in Congress in 1980 and appears in House Subcommittee of the Committee on Government Operations, "Silver Prices and the Adequacy of Federal Actions in the Marketplace, 1979–80": Hearings, 96th Cong., 2d sess., March 31; April 14, 15, 29, 30; May 2, 22, 1980, p. 313.

8. "Suzy Says: London Doings," *Chicago Tribune*, May 6, 1969, p. B1.

9. This quote and the remaining in this paragraph are from "Decies Sold to Texan for 110,000 Guineas," *The Times*, December 5, 1969, p. 15.

10. Hill, *H.L. and Lyda*, p. 50.

11. Burrough, *Big Rich*, p. 119, for these details.

12. Hill, *H.L. and Lyda*, p. 243.

13. Harry Hurt III, *Texas Rich: The Hunt Dynasty from the Early Oil Days through the Silver Crash*, (New York: W.W. Norton & Company, 1981), p. 106.

14. Tuccille, *Kingdom*, p. 227.

15. Hurt, *Texas Rich*, p. 106.

16. Burrough, *Big Rich*, p. 157.

17. Tuccille, *Kingdom*, p. 228.

18. Hill, *H.L. and Lyda*, p. 15.

19. Ibid., p. 253.

20. Ibid., p. 229.

21. Fay, *Beyond Greed*, p. 14.

22. Hill, *H.L. and Lyda*, p. 239.

23. Hurt, *Texas Rich*, p. 370.

24. Tuccille, *Kingdom*, p. 312.

25. Hurt, *Texas Rich*, p. 371.

26. The 1957 date is given in "Britain Protests Libya's Seizure of Oil Operations," *Wall Street Journal*, December 9, 1971, p. 4.

27. Tuccille, *Kingdom*, pp. 227–28.

28. Burrough, *Big Rich*, p. 296.

29. Hurt, *Texas Rich*, p. 21.

30. Burrough, *Big Rich*, pp. 62–65, 124–25, 274–75.

31. Hill, *H.L. and Lyda*, p. 264.

32. Hurt, *Texas Rich*, p. 379.

33. "U.S., British Rights Threatened by Coup," *Chicago Tribune*, September 2, 1969, p. 4.

34. "Libya Rocks Mideast," *Christian Science Monitor*, September 3, 1969, p. 1.

35. "New Libyan Regime Charts Radical Course Except for Oil," *Boston Globe*, December 28, 1969, p. 25.

36. "Libya Seizes BP Plants Worth 60 Million Pounds," *Guardian*, December 8, 1971, p. 1.

37. "Libya Denies Threat of More Takeovers," *Guardian*, December 10, 1971, p. 4.

38. "Libya Summons Oil Men," *New York Times*, June 10, 1972, p. 40.

39. "Libyan Bid Eyed by U.S. Oilmen," *Washington Post*, November 6, 1972, p. A20.

40. Ibid.

41. "Libyan Chief, Citing U.S. Aid to Israel, Seizes Oil Concern," *New York Times*, June 12, 1973, p. 1.

42. "U.S. Oil Firm Nationalized by Qaddafi," *Washington Post and Times Herald*, June 12, 1973, p. A1.

43. This and the following quotes are from "Libya Seizes Hunt's Stake in Sarir Oil Field; Nigeria Negotiates 35% Holding in Shell BP," *Wall Street Journal*, June 12, 1973, p. 17.

44. Burrough, *Big Rich*, p. 352.

45. "Consumer Prices up .7% for June; Food Again Leads," *New York Times*, July 23, 1973, p. 57.

46. *Economic Report of the President*, Transmitted to the Congress, February 1974, together with the *Annual Report of the Council of Economic Advisers* (Washington, DC: Government Printing Office, 1974), p. 21.

47. "Controls a Way of Life," *New York Times*, July 15, 1973, p. 136.

48. Hurt, *Texas Rich*, p. 325.

49. According to the CRB database, the cash price of silver was $2.47 on June 24, 1968, the date silver certificate redemption ended, and sold for $1.80 on December 31, 1969. The low price for silver was $1.288 on November 3, 1971.

50. The quote is from Handy & Harman, *The Silver Market, 1970* (New York: Handy & Harman, 1971), p. 2.

51. The January 1970 date for Bunker Hunt's first investment in silver is from page 1 of "Silver Chronology," a document submitted in connection with the lawsuit *Minpeco S.A. v. ContiCommodity Services*, September 3, 1987.

52. Hurt, *Texas Rich*, p. 317.

53. "N.B. Hunt Purchases Mississippi Project," *Los Angeles Times*, August 20, 1972, p. J8.

54. "U.S. Investors Scurry for Land in Australia's Big Northern Territory," *Wall Street Journal*, February 9, 1970, p. 1.

55. "When It Is Far Cheaper to Buy than Breed," *Observer*, February 20, 1972, p. 18.

56. "Yanks' New Owners Got Deal They Couldn't Refuse," *New York Times*, January 11, 1973, p. 45.

57. "Dahlia, American-Owned Filly, Captures Richest English Race," *New York Times*, July 29, 1973, p. S1.

58. Handy & Harman, *The Silver Market in 1968, 53rd Annual Review* (New York, 1969), p. 8.

59. J.R. Welch, "Silver," in U.S. Bureau of Mines, *Minerals Yearbook 1973*, vol. 1, *Metals and Minerals (except fuels)* (Washington, DC: Government Printing Office, 1975), 1, p. 1123, available at http://digital.library.wisc.edu/1711.dl/EcoNat Res.MinYB1973v1.

60. For an analysis of the dominance of the New York Stock Exchange, see Kenneth D. Garbade and William L. Silber, "Dominant and Satellite Markets: A Study of Dually-Traded Securities," *Review of Economics and Statistics* 61, no. 3 (1979): pp. 455–60.

61. Handy & Harman, *The Silver Market in 1972, 57th Annual Review* (New York, 1973), p. 8.

62. See Handy & Harman, *The Silver Market in 1974, 59th Annual Review* (New York, 1975), p. 5. *The 1973 Annual Review* (p. 5) states: "the Handy & Harman price, which is issued at noon each business day, reflects the level of prices on Comex at that time."

63. For a discussion of price discovery, see Kenneth D. Garbade and William L. Silber, "Price Movements and Price Discovery in Cash and Futures Markets," *Review of Economics and Statistics* 65, no. 2 (1983), pp. 289–97.

64. The *New York Times* (March 10, 1974, p. 157, "The World of Gold") writes, "Dr. Jarecki . . . heads the nation's largest gold bullion and coin trading house." Mocatta became a major Kodak supplier according to Jarecki Manuscript, chap. 9, p. 8.

65. Michael MacCambridge, *Lamar Hunt: A Life in Sports* (Kansas City, Mo.: Andrews McMeel Publishing, 2012), p. 82.

66. Ibid., p. 91.

67. Ibid., pp. 99–100.

68. Burrough, *Big Rich*, p. 302.

69. This quote and the next are from Roy Rowan, "Talkfest with the Hunts," *Fortune*, August 11, 1980, p. 164.

70. Jerome F. Smith, *Silver Profits in the Seventies* (West Vancouver, BC: ERC Publishing Company, 1972).

71. Ibid., p. 5.

72. Ibid., p. 18.

73. Ibid., p. 24. The 40% silver half-dollar was discontinued by Public Law 91–607 signed by President Nixon on December 31, 1970. See Handy & Harman, *The Silver Market in 1970, 55th Annual Review* (New York, 1971), pp. 8–9.

74. Smith, *Silver Profits*, pp. 26, 44.

75. Ibid., p. 43, invokes the 16 to 1 ratio and applies it to gold at $70 for an implied silver price of $4.38. I take the same 16 to 1 and apply it to data for September 28, 1973, the last trading day of the third quarter and right before the Hunts began to buy in bulk. The $100 price for gold is the afternoon fixing from the London bullion market for September 28, 1973. I used the London bullion market $2.70 quote for silver on the same date.

76. Tuccille, *Kingdom*, pp. 312–13.

77. This quote and the next are in Smith, *Silver Profits*, p. 48.

78. Ibid., p. 47, for this quote and the remaining in this paragraph.

CHAPTER 16: HEAVYWEIGHT FIGHT

1. The record of Hunt transactions reported here is based on congressional testimony by Charles Mattey, a vice president at Bache & Company and president of the Commodity Exchange, in Senate Committee on Agriculture and Forestry, *Commodity Futures Trading Commission Act*: Hearings on S. 2485, S. 2578, S. 2837, H.R. 13113, 93d Cong., 2d sess., pt. 2, May 16, 17, 20, 1974, pp. 475–76, 481(which reproduces an article from the financial weekly, *Barron's*, dated February 11, 1974). The record is confirmed in testimony by William Bledsoe, a former Hunt employee, in House Committee on Government Operations, "Silver Prices and the Adequacy of Federal Actions." The industrial use of silver in France is in Handy & Harman, *Silver Market in 1972*, p. 20.

2. The CRB database is the source for the December Comex futures contract. The profit was calculated as follows: The average daily closing price of the December contract during November 1973 was $2.865. The closing price on December 3 was $3.04, for a difference of 17.5¢ per ounce. Multiplying 17.5¢ by 20 million ounces produces $3.5 million.

3. Bache took delivery of 1,071 contracts on the first delivery day of December, according to Ron Scherer in "Who's Trying to Corner the Market in Silver?" *Christian Science Monitor*, December 12, 1973, p. 10. According to Securities and Exchange Commission, *The Silver Crisis of 1980: A Report of the Staff of the U.S. Securities and Exchange Commission* (Washington, DC: 1982), pp. 50–51, Bache took delivery of five million ounces for the Hunts in December 1973. Part of the discrepancy may be due to the incorrect use of 5,000 ounces per contract assumed by the SEC staff study, which did not go into effect until September 1974. In December 1973 the contract size was still 10,000 ounces, so the contemporary report of 1,071 contracts by Ron Scherer makes it at least 10 million ounces. In addition, the SEC mentions other brokerage houses—Reynolds Securities—that did business for the Hunts, so part of the 20 million ounces may have been delivered there.

4. This quote and the remainder in this paragraph are from "Who's Trying to Corner the Market in Silver?" *Christian Science Monitor*, December 12, 1973, p. 10.

5. This quote and the remainder in this paragraph are from Richard A. Donnelly, "Commodities Corner," *Barron's*, February 11, 1974, reprinted in Senate

Committee on Agriculture and Forestry, *Commodity Futures Trading Commission Act*, pp. 480–81.

6. Note 2 above gives $2.865 as the average price of those November purchases, so with cash silver selling at $5.37 (CRB database), the per ounce profit is $2.505 times 20 million ounces, which equals $50,100,000.

7. The $6.70 price is for cash silver from the CRB database.

8. The total of 50 million ounces during the 1973–1974 period was confirmed in testimony by William Bledsoe, in House Committee on Government Operations, "Silver Prices and the Adequacy of Federal Actions," p. 558.

9. Donnelly, "Commodities Corner," p. 481.

10. The quote is from "Precious Metals Post Price Gains: Silver and Platinum Futures Follow Activity in Gold," *New York Times*, February 9, 1974, p. 41. Gold prices for December 3, 1973, and February 26, 1974, are from the cash gold price in the CRB database.

11. This quote and remaining in this paragraph are from *The Congressional Record—House*, February 28, 1974, p. 4803.

12. Senate Committee on Agriculture and Forestry, *The Commodity Futures Trading Commission Act of 1974*: Hearing, November 15, 1974, p. 122.

13. "Who's Trying to Corner the Market in Silver?" *Christian Science Monitor*, December 12, 1973, p. 10.

14. See Testimony by Henry Jarecki in House Committee on Agriculture, *Commodity Futures Trading Commission Act of 1974*, Hearings on H.R. 11955, 93d Cong., 2d sess., pt. 2, January 23, 24, 29, 30, 31, 1974, p. 190.

15. For details on marketmaker behavior, see William L. Silber, "Marketmaker Behavior in an Auction Market: An Analysis of Scalpers in Futures Markets," originally published in *Journal of Finance* 39, no. 4 (Sept 1984): pp. 937–53, and reprinted in *Futures Markets*, ed. A.G. Maliaris (Edward Elgar Publishing Co., 1997).

16. This quote and the remaining story in this paragraph are based on Jarecki Manuscript, chap. 8, pp. 9–10, supplemented by Jarecki interviews.

17. Jarecki Manuscript, chap. 9, p. 14.

18. The five-million-ounce short position is from Jarecki Manuscript, chap. 8, pp. 24–25. Jarecki recalls that he had a multimillion-dollar loss, which I estimate as follows: The price of silver on February 26, 1974, was $6.70 and Jarecki (chap. 8, p. 24) writes that he was short at an average price of $2.00 an ounce, which means a loss of $4.70 per ounce. Multiplying $4.70 by 5,000,000 equals $23,500,000.

19. Jarecki Manuscript, chap. 8, p. 25.

20. Ibid.

21. Ibid., chap. 8, p. 26.

22. This discussion and the remaining in this paragraph are from ibid., chap. 9, pp. 5–6.

23. Hurt, *Texas Rich*, p. 325.

24. *Economic Report of the President*, Transmitted to the Congress, February 1975, together with the *Annual Report of the Council of Economic Advisers* (Washington, DC: Government Printing Office, 1975), p. 304.

25. Ibid., p.128.

26. The discussion in this paragraph is based on Bledsoe testimony in House Committee on Government Operations, "Silver Prices and the Adequacy of Federal Actions," p. 560; and the discussion in Hurt, *Texas Rich*, p. 324.

27. The quote is from http://www.au.af.mil/au/awc/awcgate/navy/log_quotes _navsup.pdf.

28. Jarecki Manuscript, chap. 14, pp. 1–4.

CHAPTER 17: SAUDI CONNECTION

1. For biographical details see "Ibn Saud, Arabian Ruler, 73, Dies; Won Desert Kingdom with Sword," *New York Times*, November 10, 1953, p. 1; "Ibn Saud, Ally in War, Dies; Ruler Built Modern Arabia," *Washington Post*, November 10, 1953, p. 14; and "The Saga of Ibn Saud," *Boston Globe*, November 15, 1953, p. C7.

2. According to Arthur N. Young, "Saudi Arabian Currency and Finance," *Middle East Journal* 7, no. 3 (1953): p. 365, there were 270 million silver riyals outstanding in 1952, each containing .34375 troy ounces of silver, giving a total of 92.8 million troy ounces of pure silver. The population of Saudi Arabia in 1950 was 3.8 million (see http://www.bluemarblecitizen.com/world-population/Saudi-Arabia), which comes to 24.4 troy ounces per capita, or 2 troy pounds per person.

3. Young, "Saudi Arabian Currency," p. 369.

4. See Arthur N. Young, "Saudi Arabian Currency and Finance: Part II," *Middle East Journal* 7, no. 4 (1953): pp. 539–56.

5. Ibid., p. 539.

6. See Bledsoe testimony in House Committee on Government Operations, "Silver Prices and the Adequacy of Federal Actions," p. 558, for the Iran trip and the plan for the trip to Saudi Arabia.

7. "Faisal, Rich and Powerful, Led Saudis into 20th Century and to Arab Forefront," *New York Times*, March 26, 1975, p. 10.

8. See "King Faisal Slain by Nephew," *Los Angeles Times*, March 25, 1975, p. 1; and "Hint Revenge Motive in King's Death," *Chicago Tribune*, March 26, 1975, p. 15.

9. Harold Drake, "Silver," in U.S. Bureau of Mines. *Minerals Yearbook 1977*, vol. 1, *Metals and Minerals* (Washington, DC: Government Printing Office, 1980) 1, p. 829 (table 1), available at https://catalog.hathitrust.org/Record/003909435.

10. "Hunts Making Offer for Sunshine Mining," *New York Times*, March 22, 1977, p. 64. The Hunts bid $15.75 per share for up to 2 million shares. There were 5.8 million shares outstanding.

11. Patrick Ryan, "Silver," in U.S. Bureau of Mines, *Minerals Yearbook 1965*, vol. 1, *Metals and Minerals* (except fuels) (Washington, DC: Government Printing Office, 1966) 1, p. 831, available at https://catalog.hathitrust.org/Record/00 3909435.

12. For discussion of the fire see "Steel Union Aide Assails Company in Idaho Mine Fire," *New York Times*, May 16, 1972, p. 8; and for the strike and aftermath see Drake, "Silver," *Minerals Yearbook 1977*, p. 830, available at https:// catalog.hathitrust.org/Record/003909435.

13. "Sunshine Mining: Why Hunts Want It," *New York Times*, June 24, 1977, p. 76.

14. The CBOT introduced silver trading on November 3, 1969, according to Handy & Harman, *The Silver Market in 1969, 54th Annual Review* (New York, 1970), p. 11.

15. See William Silber, "Innovation, Competition and New Contract Design in Futures Markets," *Journal of Futures Markets* (Summer 1981), for a discussion of first-mover advantages in futures markets, including silver.

16. This paragraph is based on information in "Commodity Agency Accuses 7 Hunt Heirs of Violations in Soybean-Futures Trades," *Wall Street Journal*, April 29, 1977, p. 36.

17. Fay, *Beyond Greed*, p. 75.

18. "Commodity Agency Accuses 7 Hunt Heirs of Violations in Soybean-Futures Trades," *Wall Street Journal*, April 29, 1977, p. 36.

19. See "Court Frees Hunts to Act on May Soybean Deliver," *New York Times*, May 13, 1977, p. 84; and "U.S. Wins Suit against Hunts as Court Backs Curb on Futures Holdings," *New York Times*, June 8, 1977, p. 85. Also see Jerry W. Markham, *Law Enforcement and the History of Financial Market Manipulation* (Armonk, N.Y.: M.E. Sharpe, 2014), pp. 174–75.

20. See Markham, *Law Enforcement*, pp. 175–77, for a discussion of the conflict between the CFTC and the CBOT over regulatory issues in connection with the March 1979 wheat emergency.

21. Fay, *Beyond Greed*, pp. 73–74.

22. See "Silver Futures Follow Soybean Lead," *New York Times*, August 21, 1976, for Bunker Hunt's desire to move silver to the CBOT warehouses to avoid the Comex-approved Iron Mountain Depository owned by Mocatta Metals.

23. The CBOT contract was always for 5,000 ounces. Comex reduced the size of its contract from 10,000 ounces to 5,000 on September 27, 1974.

24. Deposition of William Herbert Hunt, Minpeco S.A., et al., Plaintiff, against Nelson Bunker Hunt, et al., Defendants, October 29, 1986, p. 143.

25. Cash silver in the CRB database was $6.125 on October 26, 1978, the first time it broke through the six-dollar level since May 14, 1974, when it was $6.06.

26. Cash silver traded at $3.85 on January 20, 1976. Cash gold was $130.40 on February 2, 1976, and reached $225 on October 10, 1978.

27. "Alleged Easy Winner in l'Arc de Triomphe," *Los Angeles Times*, October 2, 1978, p. D10.

28. This discussion is based on Fay, *Beyond Greed*, pp. 81–84, 94–100; and the testimony by Norton Waltuch in Senate Subcommittee on Agricultural Research and General Legislation, "Price Volatility in the Silver Futures Market," Hearing, 96th Cong., 2d sess., pt. 2, June 26, 1980.

CHAPTER 18: SILVER SOARS

1. The 6.2% return of silver on February 5 is statistically significant given the 1.3% standard deviation of daily returns over the previous 90 calendar days. As always, I used cash silver prices from the CRB database to run the significance test.

2. "Gold Prices at Record in Near-Panic Buying," *New York Times*, February 6, 1979, p. D12.

3. "Khomeini Arrives in Teheran; Urges Ouster of Foreigners; Millions Rally to Greet Him," *New York Times*, February 1, 1979, p. A1.

4. "A Prophet Returns to His Own Land—With Honor," *New York Times*, February 4, 1979, p. E1.

5. Jarecki Manuscript, chap. 8, pp. 15–16.

6. Ibid.

7. Henry Jarecki, "A Squeeze in Silver: How Likely?" *Commodities Magazine*, March 1979, pp. 56–58.

8. Henry Jarecki, "Silver Threads Among the Gold," *Euromoney*, March 1979. This quote is on page 149.

9. Ibid., p. 139.

10. Ibid., p. 149.

11. Ibid., p. 142.

12. Ibid.

13. Ibid.

14. This quote and the next are from Jarecki Manuscript, chap. 9, pp. 11–12.

15. Herbert Hunt's letter and related material is from the 1988 trial *Minpeco S.A. v. Nelson Bunker Hunt, et al.* The correspondence from plaintiff attorney Mark Cymrot to Judge Lasker, dated April 15, 1988, includes a copy of the letter from Herbert Hunt to Scott Dial.

16. The Hunt use of straddles for the first time is referenced on page 2 of Mark Cymrot's letter to Judge Lasker and in CFTC Docket No. 85–12, Complaint and Notice of Hearing. In the Matter of Nelson Bunker Hunt, et. al., pp. 17–18. The Hunts claim they began using straddles because of tax advantages. See Jeffrey Williams, *Manipulation on Trial: Economic Analysis and the Hunt Silver Case* (Cambridge, UK: Cambridge University Press, 1995), p. 30.

17. "Hunt International, Sunshine Mining Co. Settle Their Disputes," *Wall Street Journal*, June 8, 1979, p. 24.

18. CFTC Docket No. 85–12, p. 15.

19. Harry Hurt III, "Silverfinger," *Playboy*, September 1980, pp. 230–31.

20. Deposition of William Herbert Hunt, Minpeco S.A., et al., Plaintiff, against Nelson Bunker Hunt, et al., Defendants, October 29, 1986, p. 231.

21. Ibid., p. 304.

22. See Silber, *Volcker*, p. 143.

23. The first quote is in "Gas Crunch Will Hit Entire Nation: Carter," *Chicago Tribune*, May 6, 1979, p. 1. The second quote is in "From the Gas Lines; Anger and Frustration," *Boston Globe*, June 17, 1979, p. 25.

24. "Silver Prices Set Highs for Third Day in Row; Gold Increases Slightly," *Wall Street Journal*, July 12, 1979, p. 30.

25. See Silber, *Volcker*, pp. 143–44.

26. See "Gold, Silver Prices' Unfathomable Surge Stirring Rumors of 'Big Money' Invasion," *Wall Street Journal*, September 6, 1979, p. 30.

27. Ibid.

28. Ibid.

29. "Silver, Gold Futures Soar in Buying by Speculators," *Los Angeles Times*, September 6, 1979, p. E15.

30. "Gold Price Falls in London, Posts Rise in New York," *Wall Street Journal*, September 14, 1979, p. 12.

31. I became a member of Comex in 1984, where I traded gold and silver options, and I recently spoke to a trader who was present in the silver ring during 1979 and 1980. He prefers to remain anonymous but was generous in providing many of the details described below.

32. The conversation is from Senate Subcommittee on Agricultural Research, and General Legislation, "Price Volatility in the Silver Futures Market," pp. 28–29.

33. CFTC Docket No. 85–12, p. 5.

34. The conversation is from Senate Subcommittee on Agricultural Research, and General Legislation, "Price Volatility in the Silver Futures Market," pp. 45–46.

35. CFTC Docket No. 85–12, p. 15.

36. "Gold Mart a 'Nightmare' as Price Jumps $22," *Chicago Tribune*, September 19, 1979, p. C1.

37. Ibid.

38. "Frenzied Trading Sends Gold Price to Record High," *Washington Post*, September 19, 1979, p. A1.

39. Ibid. The gold price is from the CRB cash gold price series.

40. Ibid.

41. The daily standard deviation of returns for gold was 1.5% during the previous 90 calendar days.

42. The silver price is from the CRB cash silver price series.

43. The greater normal volatility of silver compared with gold is confirmed by the daily standard deviation of returns of the two metals between 1987–2014, a period when neither metal was controlled by government policy or alleged manipulation. The daily standard deviation of the London PM gold fixing was 1.1% compared with 1.96% for silver during that period, suggesting that silver is normally about twice as volatile as gold. One explanation for this, discussed in the introductory chapter, is that silver is a much smaller market so that exogenous shifts in demand or supply have a bigger price impact. One measure of the relative size of the gold and silver markets comes from futures markets. Data for the Commodity Exchange on December 31, 2014, show a total open interest (total number of contracts outstanding) for gold of 371,646 contracts and a total of 151,215 contracts for silver. These translate into dollar amounts as follows: Gold contracts are for 100 ounces and the price per ounce on December 31, 2014, was $1,199, for a total of $44.5 billion. Silver contracts are for 5,000 ounces at a closing price of $16.25 per ounce, for a total value of $12.3 billion. The quote in the sentence is from "Frenzied Trading Sends Gold Price to Record High," *Washington Post*, September 19, 1979, p. A1.

44. "Silver Surge Roils Market, So Exchanges Sharply Increase Margin Requirements," *Wall Street Journal*, September 19, 1979, p. 38.

45. For these details see SEC, *Silver Crisis of 1980*, p. 58n37.

46. See Fay, *Beyond Greed*, p. 127.

47. Ibid.

48. "Talkfest with the Hunts," *Fortune*, August 1980, p. 166.

49. Ibid., p.167.

50. In the Jarecki Manuscript (chap. 9, p. 16) Henry writes "Mocatta owned about 40 million ounces of silver," so the numbers in the text should be doubled. The reason for using 20 million ounces is that the Jarecki Manuscript (chap. 9, p. 21) also claims "the EFP deal caused our position to go almost to zero." As described later in the text, the EFP involved 23 million ounces of silver.

51. For a detailed discussion of how hedging properly with futures contracts accounts for interest on variation margin payments see Stephen Figlewski, Yoram Landskroner, and William Silber, "Tailing the Hedge: Why and How," *Journal of Futures Markets* (April 1991).

52. "Talkfest with the Hunts," *Fortune*, August 1980, p. 167.

53. See Silber, *Volcker*, p. 167. The 9% jump on October 1 is significant given the 3.5% standard deviation of daily returns during the previous 90 calendar days.

54. "Talkfest with the Hunts," *Fortune*, August 1980, p. 167.

55. Ibid.

56. Ibid.

57. Also see the discussion in Williams, *Manipulation on Trial*, p. 38n22, for the role of silver coins as bank reserves.

58. "Talkfest with the Hunts," *Fortune*, August 1980, p. 167.

59. Interview with Tom Russo, February 15, 2017.

60. Williams, *Manipulation on Trial*, p. 33, table 2.2, shows as of August 31, 1979, that the Hunts and IMIC were long 36,815 contracts and short 13,254, for a net long position of 23,561 contracts. Williams (p. 31) also notes that they *bought* approximately 500 contracts a day between "late" July 1979 through early September. Also see SEC, *Silver Crisis of 1980*, pp. 27–28.

61. At the October 29, 1979, Comex board meeting Jarecki said there was no evidence of a "squeeze or a manipulation" with respect to December silver. See Senate Subcommittee on Agricultural Research, and General Legislation, "Price Volatility in the Silver Futures Market," p. 484.

62. This quote and the next are from "Talkfest with the Hunts," *Fortune*, August 1980, p. 167.

63. Members of the Comex board are listed in Senate Committee on Banking, Housing, and Urban Affairs, "Information Related to Futures Contracts in Financial Instruments," Hearing, 96th Cong., 2d sess., pt. 1, July 1980, pp. 9–10.

64. The cash price of silver was $8.94 on August 1, 1979, and $18.00 on October 1, 1979.

65. Senate Subcommittee on Agricultural Research, and General Legislation, "Price Volatility in the Silver Futures Market," p. 31.

66. Fay, *Beyond Greed*, p. 138.

67. Ibid.

68. CFTC Docket No. 85–12, p. 26.

69. The quotes in this paragraph are all from "Commodities: Squeezing the Market in Silver," *New York Times*, October 29, 1979, p. D2.

70. See Burrows, CFTC Report, mimeo., undated, Chapter 1, p. 4.

71. Cash gold averaged $227 and silver averaged $6.25 in January 1979, for a ratio of 36.3 to 1. In October 1979, gold averaged $392.70, and silver averaged

$16.73, for a ratio of 23.4 to 1. The increase in silver was 167% compared with an increase of 73% for gold.

72. See Fay, *Beyond Greed*, p. 135.

73. See N.H. Gale and Z.A. Stos-Gale, "Ancient Egyptian Silver," *Journal of Egyptian Archaeology* 67, no. 1 (1981): p. 103, for evidence that silver was worth more than gold. Also see Arthur R. Burns, *Money and Monetary Policy in Early Times* (New York: Alfred A. Knopf, 1927), p. 186. In Genesis the Bible lists silver before gold in stories of the Patriarchs, and a proximity study of gold and silver in Genesis, conducted at my request by Bernard Septimus, Jacob E. Safra Professor of Jewish History and Sephardic Civilization at Harvard, confirms that relationship (he cautions, however, that there are reasons other than relative value for word ordering in the Bible). Silver's medicinal use was well known even back then, according to Rhonda L. Rundle, "This War against Germs Has a Silver Lining," *Wall Street Journal*, June 6, 2006. She writes: "Since ancient times, people have known of the germ-fighting qualities of silver. Dead bodies were wrapped in silver cloth to ward off bad odors. Milk stored in silver vessels didn't spoil as quickly." For a technical discussion, see A. Lansdown, "Silver in Health Care: Antimicrobial Effects and Safety in Use," in *Biofunctional Textiles and the Skin*, ed. U.-C. Hipler and P. Eisner (Basel; New York: Karger, 2006).

74. Phillip McBride Johnson, *Commodities Regulation* (Boston: Little Brown and Company, 1982), 2, p. 233

75. See Williams, *Manipulation on Trial*, p. 5.

76. There were many lawsuits and legal proceedings concerning the allegations of manipulation of silver prices during this period, but there were two that dominate the record. The first is the CFTC Division of Enforcement hearings that began in 1987 before an administrative law judge following the 1985 charges in CFTC Docket No. 85–12. The second was a civil trial that began in 1988 in the U.S. District Court, Southern District of New York, Minpeco S.A., et al., Plaintiff, against Nelson Bunker Hunt, et al., Defendants. Neither of these cases were criminal prosecutions, which are normally undertaken by the Department of Justice (see Johnson, *Commodities Regulation*, 1, p. 183). The discussion in the text reflects both of these cases.

77. These charges are detailed in CFTC Docket No. 85–12, esp. para. 36, 49, 51, and table 3. In 1978 the four countries mentioned in the text produced 162 million ounces of silver according to Handy & Harman, *The Silver Market in 1978* (New York, 1979), p. 21. Total noncommunist world production was 265 million ounces.

78. See CFTC, *Report of the Commodity Futures Trading Commission on Recent Developments in the Silver Futures Markets*," [prepared for] Senate Committee on Agriculture, Nutrition, and Forestry (Washington, DC: Government Printing Office, 1980), p. 68.

79. Williams, *Manipulation on Trial*, pp. 6–7, provides an excellent discussion of the alternative definitions of manipulation and suggests the "pump and dump" analogy. Also see Albert S. Kyle and S. Viswanathan, "Price Manipulation in Financial Markets: How to Define Price Manipulation," *American Economic Review* 98, no. 2 (2008).

80. "Rush of Silver-Delivery Offers Spurs Fall in Prices as Speculator Showdown Mounts," *Wall Street Journal*, November 30, 1979, p. 38.

81. "The Lone Ranger: Hunt Rides Silver Out of the Market," *Wall Street Journal*, February 29, 1980, p. 12.

82. The quote is from "Commodities: Squeezing the Silver Market," *New York Times*, October 29, 1979.

83. Average daily trading volume on Comex in silver during October 1979 was 8,339 contracts compared with a daily average of 19,026 contracts from January 1, 1979 through September 30 (based on the CRB database).

84. This quote and the next are from Deposition of Lamar Hunt, Minpeco S.A., et al., Plaintiff, against Nelson Bunker Hunt, et al., Defendants, October 21, 1986, 1, pp. 51–52.

85. According to SEC, *Silver Crisis of 1980*, pp. 31–32, Lamar Hunt held approximately 8.1 million ounces of silver in January 1980, compared with 195 million ounces for Bunker and Herbert Hunt (including IMIC). The Kansas City Chiefs went 7–9 in 1979.

86. The cash price of silver was $1.81 on January 12, 1970, a day after the Super Bowl. On October 31, 1979, it was $16.40, or 9 times higher.

87. *Wall Street Journal*, December 4, 1979, p. 3.

88. *New York Times*, December 27, 1979, p. D11.

89. "Gold and Silver at Peaks; Dollar Ends Year Mixed," *New York Times*, January 1, 1980. The CRB database records a cash price of $23.65 for December 21 and gives a price of $28.00 for December 31, 1979, unchanged from the previous day. The spot Comex contract (for January 1980, delivery) closed at $34.45 on December 31, up $5.10 from the previous close. I used the Comex close because it seems that the Handy & Harman cash price (reported in the CRB data) was not updated or that the Comex price moved after Handy & Harman posted its 12 noon quote. The $34.45 close is confirmed in CFTC Docket No. 85–12, p. 29.

90. Williams, *Manipulation on Trial*, pp. 114–15, shows the connection between the Soviet invasion of Afghanistan and silver during the last week of 1979.

91. The first quote is from "Price of Gold Tops $500 for First Time," *New York Times*, December 27, 1979, p. D11; the second quote is from "Gold's Price Edges Up to $517.80 an Ounce for Another Record," *Wall Street Journal*, December 31, 1979, p. 5.

92. The average price of $8 reflects the following calculation: The Hunts bought approximately 500 contracts a day through IMIC over a two-month period, between "late" July 1979 through early September, according to Williams, *Manipulation on Trial*, p. 31. Therefore, they accumulated 20,000 contracts representing 100 million ounces at an average price during that period of about $10. They already owned about 100 million ounces from their earlier purchases in 1973 through 1977 (see SEC, *Silver Crisis of 1980*, p. 32). The average price back then was about $5. The average cost, therefore, was about $7.50, which I rounded up to $8.00 to reflect slippage. My estimate of the size and profitability of the Hunt position is supported in Hurt, *Texas Rich*, p. 419.

93. Fay, *Beyond Greed*, p. 135.

94. This discussion is based on *Minpeco S.A., plaintiff v. ContiCommodity Services, et.al.* Civil no. 81–7619 (M.E.L.) Fourth Amended Complaint, p.93ff; and Fay, *Beyond Greed*, pp. 147–50.

95. These numbers are from Williams, *Manipulation on Trial*, p. 43n27.

96. "Peru Sustained Loss of About $80 Million because of Speculation in Silver Futures," *Wall Street Journal*, February 15, 1980, p. 30.

97. "Treasury Pushes New Silver Policy," *New York Times*, June 22, 1934, p. 31

CHAPTER 19: COLLAPSE

1. The quotes and information in this paragraph are from "Silver Thefts: A High Yield," *New York Times*, February 24, 1980, p. WC1.

2. "As Silver Market Reaches Record Highs, So Does Price of Flatware," *Hartford Courant*, January 19, 1980, p. 14.

3. "Silver Thefts: A High Yield," *New York Times*, February 24, 1980, p. WC1.

4. This quote and the remaining in this paragraph are from "Gold and Silver Prices Cause Rash of Thefts throughout the Country," *New York Times*, February 1, 1980, p. A1.

5. "People Cashing in on Precious Metal Boom," *Los Angeles Times*, February 6, 1980, p. C1.

6. Ibid.

7. The headline "Britons Liquidate a Heritage" and the remaining quotes in this paragraph are from the *New York Times*, January 23, 1980, p. D1.

8. "Metal Fever Hits—'Mom's Teeth' Sold," *Chicago Tribune*, January 20, 1980, p. 3.

9. This and the remaining quotes in this paragraph are from "Too Many Coins into the Melting Pot," *New York Times*, January 20, 1980, p. D41.

10. "Declining Dollar? Not 90%-Silver Ones Involved in U.S. Sale," *Wall Street Journal*, February 8, 1980, p. 4.

11. Handy & Harman, *The Silver Market, 1980, 65th Annual Review* (New York, 1981) gives the estimated export from India as 25.7 million ounces in 1980 (p. 18). Mexico's production was 51.5 million ounces (p. 25).

12. See Allen Boraiko, "Silver: A Mineral of Excellent Nature," *National Geographic*, September 1981; an estimate of 3.4 billion ounces in India is found in W.J. Streeter, *The Silver Mania* (Dordrecht, Neth.: D. Reidel Publishing Company, 1984), p. 109.

13. "Smuggled Silver Trade Revives in Dubai," *Times of India*, March 3, 1980, p. 8.

14. Ibid.

15. "The Lone Ranger: Hunt Rides Silver Out of the Market," *Wall Street Journal*, February 29, 1980, p. 12.

16. See U.S. Bureau of Mines, *The Price Responsiveness of Secondary Silver* (Washington, DC, 1982), pp. 7, 117. In "Silver Threads," *Euromoney*, p. 136, Henry Jarecki had reported an estimated total world supply of 600 to 800 million ounces, but his calculation is less reliable than the detailed study released in March 1982.

17. The first quote is from "Scrap Silver Market Saturated," *Washington Post*, January 19, 1980, p. C7; and the second quote is from "Canadian Silver Sellers' Checks Bounce as Refiners Stop Buying," *Washington Post*, January 21, 1979, p. D13.

18. The daily standard deviation of returns between October 1 and December 31 was 1.3% in 1978 and 3.2% in 1979. The first ten trading days in January 1980 began on January 2 and ended on January 15. The cash price of $33.65 was on January 9, 1980, and the cash price of $43.75 was on January 15, 1980.

19. Daily trading volume during the first ten trading days of 1980 was 8,882 contracts compared with 17,197 contracts for the first ten trading days of 1979. Although the dollar volume of trading was higher in 1980 because the price of silver was more than double, the Commodity Exchange and brokers earn commissions per contract, so the decline hurt their business.

20. "Metal Fever Hits—'Mom's Teeth' Sold," *Chicago Tribune*, January 20, 1980, p. 3.

21. Ibid.

22. For further details see CFTC, *Report of the Commodity Futures Trading Commission on Recent Developments in the Silver Futures Markets*, at the request of Committee on Agriculture, Nutrition, and Forestry, 96th Cong., 2d sess. (Washington, DC: Government Printing Office, 1980), pp. 73–74.

23. "Limits on Silver Futures Touches Off Price Drop," *New York Times*, January 9, 1980, p. D1.

24. "Position Limits Adopted in Comex Silver Futures," *New York Times*, January 8, 1980, p. D1.

25. "Limits on Silver Futures Touches Off Price Drop," *New York Times*, January 9, 1980, p. D1.

26. Details of the EFP with Engelhard come from SEC, *Silver Crisis of 1980*, pp. 36–37.

27. The intraday high in spot silver on Comex was reported as $50.36 and the intraday high on the Chicago Board of Trade was $50.50 (see *New York Times*, January 19, 1980, p. 36).

28. There are no sterling silver golf balls (perhaps a patent pending now?), but if there were they would weigh the regulation 1.62 ounces (avoirdupois), which is 1.47675 troy ounces. Sterling is 92.5% pure so each ball would contain 1.366 troy ounces of pure silver. Three balls contain 4.098 troy ounces, which is worth $5.29 at $1.29 per ounce and $204.90 at $50 an ounce.

29. On February 1, 1979, the closing price of spot gold was $229.60 and silver was $6.66. Using the peak closing prices on January 18, 1980, in the next note gives an increase in silver of 7.6 times and an increase in gold of 3.7 times.

30. Here are two precise calculations. The closing price on Comex of spot gold was $822 and the closing price of silver was $46.80, for a ratio of 17.56 to 1. The high for spot gold on Comex was $850 and dividing that by the high of $50.36 for silver gives a price ratio of 16.88 to 1.

31. "Comex, in Bid to Cool Silver Market, Bans Traders from Taking New Positions," *Wall Street Journal*, January 22, 1980, p. 39.

32. This discussion is based on an untitled and undated 112-page report that appears to be a CFTC document summarizing the Comex meeting and follow-up discussions. It cites transcript testimony dated 1984, so it was prepared after that date, and is partially redacted. This pdf file was provided to me by Henry Jarecki and my page citations are based on the pdf. It is referenced below as CFTC-Jarecki Pdf.

33. CFTC-Jarecki Pdf, p. 3.

34. Ibid.

35. Ibid., p. 4.

36. SEC, *Silver Crisis of 1980*, p. 31.

37. CFTC-Jarecki Pdf, p. 2.

38. CFTC-Jarecki Pdf, p. 3, reports the vote was ten in favor, none opposed, and five abstentions.

39. The price decline was $2.80 for the January Comex contract (see *Washington Post*, January 22, 1980, p. D15), for a log return of –6.2%. The daily standard deviation of returns during the previous 90 calendar days was 5%, so the decline on January 21 is not statistically significant.

40. "Comex, in Bid to Cool Silver Market, Bans Traders from Taking on New Positions," *Wall Street Journal*, January 22, 1980, p. 39

41. "Chicago Board Limits Futures Trading," *New York Times*, January 23, 1980, p. D12. The spot price is for the January contract on Comex (see *Washington Post*, January 23, 1980, p. B10) and the log return of –25.8% is statistically significant given the daily standard deviation of returns of 5% during the previous 90 calendar days.

42. "Comex Curb Hits Bullion," *Guardian*, January 23, 1980, p. 15.

43. The two-day log return from $46.8 to $34 of –32% is significant given the daily standard deviation of returns of 5% over the 90 calendar days ending with January 18, 1980.

44. These excerpts are from Herbert Hunt's letter in CFTC-Jarecki Pdf, pp. 12–13.

45. Williams, *Manipulation on Trial*, p. 44.

46. CFTC-Jarecki Pdf, p. 4, shows Engelhard short 4,918 contracts on January 21, 1980.

47. See "A Study of the Silver Market," in "Report to the Congress in Response to Section 21 of the *Commodity Exchange Act*, Public Law No. 96–276," 96th Cong., 2d sess., section 7, pt. 2, June 1, 1980. *Statutes at Large*, 94, p. 133 (542).

48. See CFTC-Jarecki Pdf, pp. 12–13.

49. "Country-Boy Hunt King of Silver Hill," *Chicago Tribune*, March 2, 1980, p. N1.

50. "The Lone Ranger: Hunt Rides Silver Out of the Market," *Wall Street Journal*, February 29, 1980, p. 12.

51. Interview with Tom Russo, February 15, 2017.

52. "Copper Futures Curbed to Prevent a Squeeze," *New York Times*, November 16, 1979, p. D1.

53. "Coffee Futures Curbed to Prevent a Squeeze," *New York Times*, November 22, 1979, p. D8.

54. "Self Interest Charged in Comex Silver Rulings," *Chicago Tribune*, May 31, 1980, p. A6

55. The quote is from "Talkfest with the Hunts," *Fortune*, August 11, 1980, p. 168. The eyewitness prefers to remain anonymous but confirms that a number of board members sold thousands of gold spreads, which collapsed in value in sympathy with silver after the January 21 announcement.

56. The liquidation rule was actually terminated and replaced by a less oner-ous restriction on new positions. See CFTC, *Report on Recent Developments in the Silver Futures Markets,* p. 80.

57. The information in this paragraph is from the SEC, *Silver Crisis of 1980,* pp. 36–38.

58. Ibid., pp. 34, 38. The Hunts borrowed $896 million between January 17, 1980, and March 27, 1980.

59. See CFTC Docket No. 85–12, pp. 33–38.

60. SEC, *Silver Crisis of 1980,* p. 39.

61. The soybean manipulation is discussed above. The wiretapping incident is discussed in Hurt, *Texas Rich,* chap. 12. See Bledsoe testimony in House Com-mittee on Government Operations, "Silver Prices and the Adequacy of Federal Actions," pp. 561–62, for allegations that the Hunts exploited supposedly con-fidential information received from their Penrod Drilling Company to buy drill-ing rights from under their competitor's noses.

62. See SEC, *Silver Crisis of 1980,* p. 35, for the loans outstanding to Merrill Lynch, Bache, and E.F. Hutton. See p. 136 for the absence of documentation at Merrill Lynch.

63. The price of the spot silver contract (for March delivery) on March 5 was $36.05 and on March 6 it was $33.10, for a log return of −8.54%. The spot price on March 7 was $32.90 and on March 10 it was $29.75, for a log return of −10.06% (these spot prices were taken from the CRB database for March 1980 futures). The standard deviation of returns over the previous 90 days is 6.98% so neither of these is significant, but they are both responses to nonpublic informa-tion and are similar to a price run-up before a merger is announced. The cumula-tive log return from March 5 through March 17 (see the continuing discussion in the text) of −72.84% is significant.

64. All prices in this paragraph refer to the spot contract on Comex as re-ported in the CRB database.

65. "Precious Metals Prices Plunge as Carter Sets Anti-Inflation Speech," *Wall Street Journal,* March 14, 1980, p. 38. The price of spot silver declined from $29.30 on March 12 to $25.50 on March 13, for a log return of −13.9%.

66. The details of Carter's program appeared in Friday morning's newspapers, such as "Carter to Unveil Anti-Inflation Plan," *Chicago Tribune,* March 14, 1980, p. 3, and "Anti-Inflation Plan to Be Unveiled Today, with Credit Curbs Expected," *Wall Street Journal,* March 14, 1980, p. 3. The spot price declined from $25.50 on March 13 to $21.00 on March 14, for a log return of −19.4%.

67. The spot price declined to $17.40 on March 17, for a log return of −18.8%.

68. "Prices Suffer Broad, Steep Decline Triggered by Early Drop in Europe," *Wall Street Journal,* March 18, 1980, p. 36.

69. This quote and the next are from "Reserve Board, in New Attack on In-flation, Is Stressing Restraint on Debt Rather Than Higher Interest Rates," *Wall Street Journal,* March 17, 1980, p. 2.

70. SEC, *Silver Crisis of 1980,* p. 39.

71. In 1982, the first year *Forbes* published its list of wealthiest Americans, there were only 13 billionaires in the world. See http://www.forbes.com/sites/sean

kilachand/2012/09/20/the-forbes-400-hall-of-fame-36-members-of-our-debut
-issue-still-in-ranks/.

72. Williams, *Manipulation on Trial*, p. 47.

73. SEC, *Silver Crisis of 1980*, p. 156.

74. Ibid., p. 153.

75. Fay, *Beyond Greed*, p. 200.

76. Ibid., pp. 201–10.

77. Ibid., p. 98.

78. SEC, *Silver Crisis of 1980*, p. 83n72.

79. Ibid.

80. The spot price of gold on March 25, 1980, was $496.50. The peak on January 18, 1980, was $850, or a decline of 42%. The price ratio of gold to silver was $496.50/20.20 = 24.6.

81. See "Talkfest with the Hunts," *Fortune*, August 11, 1980, p. 168.

82. This quote and the rest in this paragraph are from "Hunt Group Sets Silver-Backed Bonds," *New York Times*, March 27, 1980, p. 81.

83. The log return of 15.80/20.20 is –24.6%.

84. "N.B. Hunt Group Shocks Silver World with Plan for Bonds," *Wall Street Journal*, March 27, 1980, p. 12.

85. "Sunshine Planning Sale of Silver-Backed Notes," *New York Times*, February 5, 1980, p. D1.

86. Deposition of Nelson Bunker Hunt, Minpeco S.A., et al., Plaintiff, against Nelson Bunker Hunt, et al., Defendants, April 10, 1986, pp. 90–92.

87. See "Senate Subcommittee on Agricultural Research, and General Legislation, "Price Volatility in the Silver Futures Market," p. 215.

88. The spot price of $10.80 on March 27 is for the April Comex contract (See *New York Times*, March 28, 1980, p. D8). When the March contract stopped trading on the 26th, it closed at $15.80.

89. SEC, *Silver Crisis of 1980*, p. 87.

90. "Silver's Plunge Jolts Hunts' Empire and Brings Turmoil to Wall Street," *New York Times*, March 28, 1980, A1.

91. Ibid.

92. This quote and the next are from SEC, *Silver Crisis of 1980*, p. 92.

93. House Committee on Government Operations, "Silver Prices and the Adequacy of Federal Actions," p. 218.

94. Ibid., p. 223.

95. CFTC, *Report on Recent Developments in the Silver Futures Markets*, p. 86.

96. The Comex April futures contract opened at $12 on March 28, traded as high as $13 and as low as $10.90, and closed at $12 (see *Washington Post*, March 29, 1980, p. D12).

97. The Hunt debts are summarized in the Federal Reserve's "Interim Report on Financial Aspects of the Silver Market Situation in Early 1980," published in House Committee on Government Operations, "Silver Prices and the Adequacy of Federal Actions," p. 244.

98. House Committee on Government Operations, "Silver Prices and the Adequacy of Federal Actions," p. 282.

99. This quote and the next two are from "Markets Rebound; Silver Lining for Occidental," *Boston Globe*, March 29, 1980, p. 14.

100. This quote and the story are from Jarecki Manuscript, chap. 9, p. 37.

101. Ibid.,, chap. 9, pp. 39–40.

102. The $5 billion calculation comes from the net worth pledged as collateral for the loan to the family's Placid Oil Company. See SEC, *Silver Crisis of 1980*, pp. 24–25. The SEC report suggests that the collateral was really worth much less than $5 billion, but it also ignores other assets that were not pledged, so $5 billion seems like a fair estimate.

103. The original EFP called for 28.5 million ounces but only 19 million remained outstanding. The price agreed to in January was about $36 an ounce for a total payment of $684 million. At the closing price of $12 an ounce on March 28 the bullion was worth $228 million.

104. This quote and the next are from Peter Bernstein, "Engelhard's Not So Sterling Deal with the Hunts," *Fortune*, May 19, 1980, p. 86.

105. Ibid.

106. Ibid., p. 84.

107. "A Deal's a Deal, Said Engelhard," *New York Times*, April 6, 1980, p. F1.

108. The write-off of the Beaufort Sea property was disclosed to me in an interview on November 22, 2016, with Hal Beretz, president of the Philipp Brothers division of Engelhard at the time of the Hunt transaction.

109. Bernstein, "Engelhard's Not So Sterling Deal," p. 86.

110. See SEC, *Silver Crisis of 1980*, pp. 42–43, for details of the loan to Placid. Also see the Federal Reserve's "Interim Report on Financial Aspects of the Silver Market Situation in Early 1980," published in House Committee on Government Operations, "Silver Prices and the Adequacy of Federal Actions," pp. 250–57.

111. House Committee on Government Operations, "Silver Prices and the Adequacy of Federal Actions," p. 209.

112. Ibid.

113. Ibid., pp. 218–19, for the interchange below.

114. According to the SEC, *Silver Crisis of 1980*, p. 26, there are six trusts that own Placid. Testimony by William Bledsoe, a former Hunt employee in House Committee on Government Operations, "Silver Prices and the Adequacy of Federal Actions," p. 554, says there were only five trusts.

115. SEC, *Silver Crisis of 1980*, p. 26.

116. Ibid., p. 31.

117. The quote is from Hurt, *Texas Rich*, p. 415.

118. See SEC Release No. 16715, April 1, 1980.

119. "When a Billionaire's Piggy Bank Breaks," *Guardian*, May 28, 1980, p. 4.

120. Ibid.

121. "Hunt Mortgages 500 Thoroughbreds," *Washington Post*, May 25, 1980, p. F12. For discussion of Dahlia's second victory see "Dahlia Wins $194,976 in Ascot Race," *New York Times*, July 28, 1974, p. 181.

CHAPTER 20: THE TRIAL

1. "Trial of Hunt Brothers in Silver Case Begins," *New York Times*, February 25, 1988, p. D2.

2. Plaintiff's attorney Mark Cymrot uses $150 million in his opening statement (see Transcript, *Minpeco S.A., Plaintiff v. Nelson Bunker Hunt, et. al., Defendants*, February 24, 1988, p. 418). But immediately before the case went to trial, Judge Morris Lasker reduced Minpeco's claim from $252 million to $75 million, which could then be subject to treble damages. See "Hunts Hail Silver Ruling," *New York Times*, January 7, 1988, p. D14.

3. See Williams, *Manipulation on Trial*, p. 3. Note that Lamar Hunt was not charged by the CFTC, although he was named in the Minpeco lawsuit.

4. Ibid., pp. 194–95.

5. Transcript, *Minpeco S.A., Plaintiff v. Nelson Bunker Hunt, et. al., Defendants*, February 24, 1988, p. 403.

6. Ibid., p. 417.

7. Ibid., p. 418.

8. Ibid., pp. 410–11.

9. Ibid., p. 481.

10. Ibid., p. 482

11. Ibid., p. 425.

12. From an interview on January 14, 2015, with Phil Geraci, a lawyer with Kay, Scholer, the New York law firm representing the Hunts at the trial.

13. This quote and the next are from transcript, *Minpeco S.A., Plaintiff v. Nelson Bunker Hunt, et al., Defendants*, February 24, 1988, p. 518.

14. Ibid., p. 521.

15. Ibid., pp. 522–23, 527.

16. Ibid., p. 414.

17. The description of the layout in court is from "Hunts Still Fighting Losses from Silver Crisis," *Washington Post*, March 20, 1988, p. H1. The description and detail of what is on the videotape comes from copies of tapes that I received from an anonymous source.

18. This dialogue comes from a transcription of Bunker Hunt's deposition, dated April 10, 1986, 1, pp. 8–11, and a videotape of that deposition.

19. Williams, *Manipulation on Trial*, pp. 194–95.

20. "Nelson Hunt Denies Trying to Corner the Silver Market," *Wall Street Journal*, June 1, 1988, p. 43.

21. "Nelson Hunt Denies Plotting to Manipulate Silver Market," *Los Angeles Times*, June 2, 1988, p. E12.

22. "Hunt Says He Was Just 'Bullish' on Silver," *Los Angeles Times*, June 3, 1988, p. D14.

23. The remaining discussion between Cymrot and Bunker Hunt are excerpts from Mark Cymrot, "Cross-Examination in International Arbitration," *Dispute Resolution Journal* 62, no.1 (2007). A detailed description of the interchange came from an interview with Hunt Lawyer Phil Geraci, January 14, 2015.

24. From an interview with Hunt lawyer Phil Geraci, January 14, 2015.

25. See Williams, *Manipulation on Trial*, p. 194.

26. Transcript, *Minpeco S.A., Plaintiff v. Nelson Bunker Hunt, et. al., Defendants*, February 24, 1988, p. 509.

27. From an interview with Hunt lawyer, Phil Geraci, January 14, 2015.

28. For an excellent summary of the disputed evidence see chapter 4, "Testing for the Cause of the Price Rise in Silver," Williams, *Manipulation on Trial*.

29. Ibid., pp. 104–9.

30. Ibid., p. 114.

31. The visual image was important because the statistical evidence showing the impact of Hunt holdings and silver price levels had serious statistical problems. See Williams, *Manipulation on Trial*, pp. 109–10 for a discussion.

32. Ibid., p. 195.

33. Ibid., p. 190, and see "Hunts Are Ruled Part of Scheme to Control Silver," *New York Times*, August 21, 1988, p. 1.

34. See Williams, *Manipulation on Trial*, pp. 115–18, 124, for a discussion of plaintiff's attempt to identify gold with political events. Also see ibid., pp. 92–96, for a related discussion of the gold-silver price ratio.

35. I calculated the standard deviation of returns on gold and silver from January 1981 through July 2017 with London bullion market data. Using daily returns, the standard deviation of silver is 2.45% versus 1.1% for gold. To avoid temporary volatility of daily returns I used month-end values over that same period, producing a monthly standard deviation of returns for silver of 8.34% versus 4.76% for gold.

36. Williams, *Manipulation on Trial*, p. 194, describes the jury's award as "a compromise," although different from what is suggested here.

37. The quote, cited at the end of chapter 18, is from "Peru Sustained Loss of about $80 Million because of Speculation in Silver Futures," *Wall Street Journal*, February 15, 1980, p. 30.

38. "2 Hunts File for Personal Bankruptcy," *New York Times*, September 22, 1988, p. D1.

39. Ibid.

40. "3 Hunt Brothers Put Oil Concern into Bankruptcy," *New York Times*, August 30, 1986, p. 1. Crude oil was $11.57 in July 1986, according to the West Texas Intermediate Crude Oil series in https://fred.stlouisfed.org/series/OILPRICE and https://fred.stlouisfed.org/series/MCOILWTICO.

41. "It Takes $180 Million to Make *Forbes* List of Richest in the U.S.," *Wall Street Journal*, October 14, 1986, p. 8.

42. "Lamar Hunt Pays $17 million in Damages to Peru's Minpeco," *Washington Post*, October 21, 1988, p. F2.

43. "Hunt Brothers' Debts Dwarf Their Texas-Sized Fortunes," *Chicago Tribune*, November 27, 1988, p. G12B.

44. This quote and the remaining in this paragraph are from "Hunts, Proving No Detail Too Small, List 67 Cent Debt in Bankruptcy Filing," *Wall Street Journal*, November 23, 1988, p. B5.

45. "Hunts' Assets Will Pay Creditors, Court Rules," *New York Times*, December 17, 1989, p. 36.

46. "William Hunt's Bankruptcy Plan Cleared," *New York Times*, December 22, 1989, p. D6.

47. "2 Hunts Fined and Banned from Trades," *New York Times*, December 21, 1989.

48. "Hunts' Assets Will Pay Creditors, Court Rules," *New York Times*, December 17, 1989, p. 36.

49. This quote and the remaining in this paragraph are from "Hunt's Treasure: Oil Baron's Belongings Go on the Block," *Chicago Tribune*, July 29, 1990, p. C6C.

50. This quote and the remaining in this paragraph are from "Bankrupt Hunt Brothers Bid Adieu to Art Collections Worth Millions," *Chicago Tribune*, May 10, 1990, p. C1.

CHAPTER 21: BUFFETT'S MANIPULATION?

1. "CFTC Boosts Surveillance of Silver-Futures Market," *Wall Street Journal*, January 14, 1998, p. C1.

2. The cash price of silver in the CRB database closed at $5.93 on December 31, 1997. It traded above $6 an ounce from December 18 through December 30.

3. "CFTC Boosts Surveillance of Silver-Futures Market," *Wall Street Journal*, January 14, 1998, p. C1.

4. The cash price of gold was $333.70 on June 30, 1997 and $288.8 on December 31, 1997, for a decline of 13.5%. Silver was $4.63 on June 30 and $5.93 on December 31, for an increase of 28%. All data are from the CRB cash price series for gold and silver.

5. "Silver Futures Rally as Analysts Say Market Is Refocused on Fundamentals," *Wall Street Journal*, January 7, 1998, p. C15.

6. "Gold Rises from 12½ Year Lows as Silver Surges," *Wall Street Journal*, December 11, 1997, p. C17.

7. "Phibro and Others Sued Over Silver Prices," *Wall Street Journal*, January 29, 1998, p. C18.

8. "Booming Silver Market 'Rigged,'" *The Guardian*, January 13, 1998, p. 18.

9. Ibid.

10. Berkshire Hathaway press release, dated February 3, 1998.

11. Ibid.

12. The daily standard deviation of returns in the 90 calendar days before February 3, 1998, is 1.9%. The two-day standard deviation is 2.698%. The 10.7% return on February 4 and the 4% return on February 5 are each significant and so is the combined two-day return.

13. Henry E. Hilliard, "Silver," in Bureau of Mines, *Minerals Yearbook 1998*, vol. 1, *Metals and Minerals* (Washington, DC: Government Printing Office, 2000), 1, p. 69, available at https://catalog.hathitrust.org/Record/003909435. Global mine production in 1998 was reported at 16,400 metric tons. There are 32,150.7 troy ounces in a metric ton, translating into 527 million troy ounces. Berkshire bought 129.7 million troy ounces, which is 24.61% of the total.

14. This quote and the remaining in this paragraph are from the Berkshire Hathaway 1997 Chairman's Letter available at http://www.berkshirehathaway.com/1997ar/1997.html.

15. Ibid.

16. Ibid.

17. Warren Buffett, "Why Stocks Beat Gold and Bonds," *Fortune*, February 27, 2012.

18. Ibid.

19. See Berkshire Hathaway 1997 Chairman's Letter for this quote and the remaining in this paragraph.

20. Ibid., for this quote and the remaining in this paragraph.

21. "Buffett Discloses Big Silver Purchases," *Washington Post*, February 4, 1998, p. C13.

22. The remaining quotes in this paragraph are from "Buffett's Company Is Amassing Silver, Pushing Up Prices," *New York Times*, February 4, 1998, p. A1.

23. See CFTC Docket No. 85–12, p. 7, for a discussion of the "manipulative period" of the Hunt accumulation and the impact on "distorted price relationships." This section of the CFTC complaint is based on the expert report of Professor Albert Kyle, "Report on the Behavior of Silver Prices and Economic Evidence of Manipulative Activities," February 19, 1987. Kyle argues (DX2220–7ff) that during the period of the Hunt manipulation, September 1979 through March 1980, Comex silver spreads failed to reflect full cost of carry, which is a less stringent indication of distortion than backwardation. Also see Kyle and Viswanathan, "Price Manipulation in Financial Markets," p. 276.

24. Berkshire Hathaway press release, dated February 3, 1998.

25. Buffett's quote is from an e-mail exchange I had through his executive assistant, Joanne Manhart, June 21, 2017.

26. The Phibro connection appears in "Buffett Silver Gambit Stirs Silver Again," *Wall Street Journal*, February 5, 1998, p. C1.

27. "The $10 Billion Man, on a Silver Buying Spree, Keeps Horde in Secretive London Market," *Guardian*, February 5, 1998, p. 3.

28. The CFTC investigation "fell silent," according to "In This Corner, a Silver Bull. In That Corner, India," *Wall Street Journal*, February 18, 1998, p. A23. A search of the 1998 annual report of the CFTC shows no mention of Warren Buffett and the only place silver appears is in the section entitled "Division of Economic Analysis," which is summarized in the text. On August 14, 2017, I submitted a written request to the CFTC under the Freedom of Information Act (FOIA) for "all communications" between the CFTC and Buffett or Berkshire Hathaway during that period. On November 22, 2017, I received the following response: "Our search of the CFTC's records did not identify any record that would respond to your request."

29. CFTC, *1998 Annual Report* (Washington, DC: Government Printing Office, [1999]), pp. 58–59.

30. "In This Corner, a Silver Bull. In That Corner, India," *Wall Street Journal*, February 18, 1998, p. A23.

31. "Buffett's Purchases Push Silver Past $7 an Ounce," *New York Times*, February 5, 1998, p. D1.

32. Berkshire Hathaway 1997 Chairman's Letter.

33. The calculation is as follows: The Berkshire Hathaway 1997 Chairman's Letter reports that they bought 111.2 million ounces by the end of 1997 and earned a mark-to-market profit of $97.4 million in 1997. The closing cash price

on December 31, 1997, was $5.93 per ounce. The $97.4 million profit on 111.2 million ounces works out to a per ounce profit of $0.876. Subtracting $0.876 from $5.93 equals $5.054.

34. On January 12, 1998, the date of Buffett's last purchase, cash silver closed at $5.49 an ounce, but it is unlikely that he bought the entire 18.5 million then. The average price during the first 12 calendar days of 1998 was $5.8457, so the $5.50 cost is probably an underestimate.

35. Joanne Manhart's e-mail (see earlier note) says, "It was all paid for in cash." According to the *Berkshire Hathaway 2016 Annual Report* (p. 19) the company owned 400 million shares of Coke, Buffett's third largest stock investment. His 1997 letter quoted above implies that he bought Coca Cola nine years earlier, or in 1989.

36. From Whitney Tilson's "2006 Berkshire Hathaway meeting notes," May 6, 2006, at http://www.designs.valueinvestorinsight.com/bonus/bonuscontent/docs/Tilson_2006_BRK_Meeting_Notes.pdf.

CHAPTER 22: MESSAGE FROM OMAHA

1. The paper loss on silver, calculated just for the 111.2 million ounces held on December 31, 1997, is estimated as follows: The average cost of $5.05 per ounce minus the average cash price of $4.17 in the first week of September gives a loss of 88¢ per ounce, producing a mark-to-market loss of $97.85 million on 111.2 million ounces.

2. The daily standard deviation of returns on silver during the previous 90 calendar days was .82% and for gold it was .69%. The four-cent increase in silver was an insignificant increase of .96%, while gold's 2.98% jump was clearly significant. I use the London bullion market prices because the New York markets were disrupted by the attack. The gold price reported here is the morning fixing from September 12 versus the morning fixing for September 11, which is comparable to the timing of the silver fix. The London afternoon fixing on September 11 occurred after the attacks and jumped to $287, which represents an almost 6% increase. The afternoon fix on September 12 was $279, in line with the morning fix on September 12. There are allegations that the London fixing has been subject to manipulation by the fixing members. See Andrew Caminschi, "Too Precious to Fix: The London Precious Metals Fixings and Their Interactions with Spot and Futures Markets," (PhD diss., University of Western Australia, 2016).

3. These are from the respective cash series in the CRB database.

4. The data on silver are from CPM Group, *The CPM Silver Yearbook 2016* (New York, 2016), pp. 6–7. The quote is from Tilson, "2006 Berkshire Hathaway meeting notes."

5. The quote is from Tilson, "2006 Berkshire Hathaway meeting notes."

6. Berkshire Hathaway 1988 Chairman's Letter.

7. This and the remaining quotes in this paragraph are from "Gold Sleeps While Silver Rocks," *New York Times*, May 29, 2005, p. B8.

8. According to the CRB database the high in cash silver was $14.15, and it closed at $13.97.

9. The cash price of silver on October 1, 1979, was $18.00 compared with $8.94 on August 1, 1979. The cash price on January 2, 1980, was $37.75 compared with $16.32 on November 1, 1979.

10. No recordings or videotapes were permitted at Berkshire Hathaway annual meetings at that time, but a number of attendees took notes and published them. This discussion of the 2006 annual meeting is based on the following sources, with specific quotes noted separately. 1) Jason Zweig, "Buffett: Real Estate Slowdown Ahead," May 8, 2006, CNN Money, available at http://money.cnn.com/2006/05/05/news/newsmakers/buffett_050606/index.htm?section=money_latest; 2) J.V. Bruni & Co., "The 2006 Berkshire Hathaway Annual Meeting: Top 20 Questions," available at http://www.jvbruni.com/Berkshire2006annualmeeting.pdf; 3) Whitney Tilson, "2006 Berkshire Hathaway meeting notes," May 6, 2006, at http://www.designs.valueinvestorinsight.com/bonus/bonuscontent/docs/Tilson_2006_BRK_Meeting_Notes.pdf; 4) "Notes from Berkshire Hathaway Annual Meeting," available at https://www.gurufocus.com/news/1569.

11. See "Notes from Berkshire Hathaway Annual Meeting."

12. See Zweig, "Buffett."

13. This quote and the remaining in this paragraph are from Tilson, "2006 Berkshire Hathaway meeting notes."

14. Ibid.

15. See Adam Doolittle, "Analyzing Warren Buffett's Investment in Silver," available at http://www.silvermonthly.com/analyzing-warren-buffetts-investment-in-silver/.

16. See CPM Group, *CPM Silver Yearbook 2016*, pp. 6–7, showing the excess of fabrication demand over mine plus secondary supply equal to 67 million ounces in 2005 compared with an excess of 175 million ounces in 1997.

17. The 111.2 million ounces purchased in "mid-1997" cost $5.05 per ounce or a total of $561 million. Selling those 111.2 ounces in "mid-2005" at $7.50 per ounce produced $834 million. The annual compound growth over 8 years is 5.08%. Ten-year Treasury bonds yielded an average of 6.075% during the last 6 months of 1997 (see *Economic Report of the President*, Transmitted to the Congress February 1998, together with the *Annual Report of the Council of Economic Advisers* (Washington, DC: Government Printing Office, 1998), p. 367.

18. This quote and the next are from Tilson, "2006 Berkshire Hathaway meeting notes,"

19. See CPM Group, *CPM Silver Yearbook 2016*, pp. 6–7, showing the excess of fabrication demand over mine plus secondary supply equal to 67 million ounces in 2005 compared with an excess supply of 67.5 million ounces in 2008.

20. Cash silver in the CRB database closed at $13.97 on May 5, 2006, versus $10.87 on September 12, 2008.

21. In the CRB database cash gold was $682.57 on May 5, 2006, versus $766.19 on September 12, 2008. Copper was $3.597 per pound on May 5, 2006 and $3.209 on September 12, 2008.

22. The start date I used is September 12, 2008, the Friday before the Lehman bankruptcy and the end date is March 9, 2009, the low for the S&P500. The S&P index was 1251.7 on September 12, 2008, and was 676.5 on March 9, 2009, for a drop of 45.9%.

23. The price data for GE are from Yahoo! Finance.

24. Anonymous, of course.

25. The cash price of West Texas Intermediate crude oil was $101.18 on September 12, 2008, and $47.07 on March 9, 2009. The cash copper price was $3.209 on September 12, 2008, and $1.6295 on March 9, 2009. All data are from the CRB cash series.

26. Cash gold was $766.19 on September 12, 2008, and $922.78 on March 9, 2009, an increase of 20%. Cash silver was $10.87 on September 12, 2008, and $13.01 on March 9, 2009, an increase of 19.69%.

27. The precious metals proved their safe haven status during the week of Lehman's bankruptcy, when three-quarters of the increase occurred. Silver closed at $12.61 on Friday, September 19, 2008, an increase of 16% over the previous Friday, and gold closed at $873.44, an increase of 14%. Both of those returns are statistically significant using the standard deviation of returns calculated over the previous 90 calendar days ending September 12, 2008. Gold had a daily standard deviation of returns equal to 1.52%, and silver had a daily standard deviation of returns equal to 2.68%.

28. The correlation coefficient between daily returns on silver and gold is .71 compared with .136 between silver and copper, using daily data from the London Bullion Market Association between January 1987 and December 2014.

29. See Alan Blinder, *After the Music Stopped* (New York: Penguin Press, 2013), for a nice discussion of the government rescue programs.

30. On December 31, 2009, the S&P500 closed at 1115.10. The drop from 1251.7 on the Friday before the Lehman bankruptcy was now 10.9% compared with the low of 46% on March 9, 2009. For a nice discussion of the European debt crisis see Philip R. Lane, "The European Sovereign Debt Crisis," *Journal of Economic Perspectives* 26, no. 3 (2012): pp. 49–68.

31. See the cash price series of the CRB database for gold and for silver in the next sentence.

32. The peak in silver was $48.42 on April 28, 2011. The $4.2 billion profit is calculated as follows: The profit per ounce was $42.92 less $5.05 equals $37.87, multiplied by 111.2 million ounces, equals $4,203,570,000.

33. The production of the coins was authorized by Public Law 99–61 of July 9, 1985, available at https://www.gpo.gov/fdsys/pkg/STATUTE-99/pdf/STATUTE-99 -Pg113.pdf.

34. The coin production data from 1986 through 2015 are available at http://silvereagleguide.com/mintages/. The 2016 number comes from "American Eagle silver bullion coins struck at three facilities in FY 2016" at http://www .coinworld.com/news/precious-metals/2017/02/silver-eagle-production-spread -between-three-mints.all.html#.

35. See CPM Group, *CPM Silver Yearbook 2016*, pp. 6–7.

36. "Utah Law Makes Coins Worth Their Weight in Gold (or Silver)," *New York Times*, May 30, 2011, p. A1. Also see the draft of the legislation at https:// le.utah.gov/~2011/bills/hbillint/hb0317s01.htm#. Ron Paul introduced H.R. 4248 in 2009, a bill "To repeal the legal tender laws, to prohibit taxation on certain coins and bullion, and to repeal superfluous sections related to coinage." See https://www.ronpaul.com/2009-12-10/break-the-monopoly-ron-paul-introduces -hr-4248-the-free-competition-in-currency-act.

CHAPTER 23: THE PAST INFORMS THE FUTURE

1. See "Nelson Bunker Hunt, Texas Tycoon, Dies at 88," *New York Times*, October 22, 2014, p. A24: "Like his siblings, Bunker still had millions in trusts set up by his father, and *Forbes* reported in 2001 that, while he had long ago dropped off the list of the richest Americans, he had recently bought eighty racehorses for $2.5 million, and that a filly called Hattiesburg, which he picked up for $20,000, had won $357,000."

2. "Hunt Becomes Billionaire on Bakken Oil after Bankruptcy," March 28, 2013, Bloomberg News at https://www.bloomberg.com/news/articles/2013-03-28/hunt-becomes-billionaire-on-bakken-oil-after-bankruptcy.

3. For additional detail see Paul Wachtel, "Central Bank Independence: More Myth than Reality" (paper, Colloquium on Money, Debt and Sovereignty, University de Picardie Jules Verne, Amiens, France, December 11–12, 2017).

SELECTED BIBLIOGRAPHY

BOOKS, ARTICLES, AND REPORTS

Alter, Jonathan. 2006. *The Defining Moment: FDR's Hundred Days and the Triumph of Hope*. New York: Simon and Schuster.

The American Presidency Project. Various dates. Available at http://www.presidency.ucsb.edu.

Atlanta Constitution. Various dates.

Barnhart, Russell. 1992. *Beating the Wheel*. New York: Kensington Publishing Company.

Barro, Robert J. 1982. "United States Inflation and the Choice of Monetary Standard," in *Inflation: Causes and Effects*, edited by Robert E. Hall. Chicago: University of Chicago Press.

Berkshire Hathaway Annual Report. Various dates.

Berkshire Hathaway 1997 Chairman's Letter, available at http://www.berkshirehathaway.com/1997ar/1997.html.

Bernstein, Peter L. 1980. "Engelhard's Not So Sterling Deal with the Hunts," *Fortune*, May.

———. 2000. *The Power of Gold: The History of an Obsession*. New York: Wiley.

Blinder, Alan. 2013. *After the Music Stopped*. New York: Penguin Press.

Blum, John Morton. 1959. *From the Morgenthau Diaries*, vol. 1, *Years of Crisis, 1928–1938*. Boston: Houghton Mifflin Company.

Board of Governors of the Federal Reserve System. 1943. *Banking and Monetary Statistics: 1914–1941*. Washington, DC.

———. 1976. *Banking and Monetary Statistics: 1941–1970*. Washington, DC.

Boraiko, Allen. 1981. "Silver: A Mineral of Excellent Nature," *National Geographic*. September.

Bordo, Michael D. and Athanasios Orphanides, eds. 2013. *The Great Inflation: The Rebirth of Modern Central Banking*. Chicago: University of Chicago Press.

Borg, Dorothy. 1964. *The United States and the Far Eastern Crisis*. Cambridge, Mass.: Harvard University Press.

Boston Globe. Various dates.

Brandt, Loren and Thomas Sargent. 1989. "Interpreting New Evidence about China and U.S. Silver Purchases," *Journal of Monetary Economics* 23.

Bratter, Herbert M. 1933. *Silver Market Dictionary*. New York: Commodity Exchange.

Bryan, William J. 1896. *The First Battle: A Story of the Campaign of 1896*. Chicago: W.B. Conkey Company.

Buffett, Warren. 2012. "Why Stocks Beat Gold and Bonds," *Fortune*, February.

Bullitt, Orville H. 1972. ed. *For the President Personal and Secret: Correspondence between Franklin D. Roosevelt and William C. Bullitt*. Boston: Houghton Mifflin Company.

Burrough, Bryan. 2009. *The Big Rich: The Rise and Fall of the Greatest Texas Oil Fortunes*. New York: Penguin Press.

Burdekin, Richard. 2008. *China's Monetary Challenges: Past Experiences and Future Prospects*. Cambridge, UK: Cambridge University Press.

Burdekin, Richard and Marc Weidenmier. 2009. "The Development of 'Nontraditional' Open Market Operations: Lessons from FDR's Silver Purchase Program." In *The Origins and Development of Financial Markets and Institutions from the Seventeenth Century to the Present*, edited by Jeremy Attack and Larry Neal. Cambridge, UK: Cambridge University Press.

Burns, Arthur R. 1927. *Money and Monetary Policy in Early Times*. New York: Alfred A. Knopf.

Burton, Theodore. 1906. *American Statesman: John Sherman*. Boston: Houghton Mifflin Company.

Caminschi, Andrew. 2016. "Too Precious to Fix: The London Precious Metals Fixings and their interactions with spot and futures markets." PhD diss., University of Western Australia.

Caro, Robert. 2012. *The Passage of Power*. New York: Random House.

Caughey, John Walton. 1948. *The California Gold Rush*. Berkeley: University of California Press.

CFTC-Jarecki PDF. Undated. mimeo.

Chicago Daily Tribune. Various dates.

Christian Science Monitor. Various dates.

Coletta, Paolo. 1964. *William Jennings Bryan,* vol. 1, *Political Evangelist, 1860–1908*. Lincoln: University of Nebraska Press.

Commodity Futures Trading Commission. Various years. *Annual Report*. Washington, DC.

CPM Group. 2008, 2016. *The CPM Silver Yearbook*, New York.

Cragg, John. 1953. *The Mint*. London: Cambridge University Press.

Cymrot, Mark. 2007. "Cross-Examination in International Arbitration," *Dispute Resolution Journal* 62, no.1.

Daily Telegraph. Various dates.

Detre, Thomas P. and Henry G. Jarecki. 1971. *Modern Psychiatric Treatment*. New York: J. B. Lippincott.

Doolittle, Adam. Undated. "Analyzing Warren Buffett's Investment in Silver," available at http://www.silvermonthly.com/analyzing-warren-buffetts-investment-in-silver.

Economic Report of the President, transmitted to the Congress, together with the *Annual Report of the Council of Economic Advisers*. Various dates. Washington, DC: Government Printing Office.

Edwards, Jerome E. 1982. *Pat McCarran: Political Boss of Nevada*. Reno: University of Nevada Press.

Einzig, Paul. 1935. *The Future of Gold*. New York: Macmillan Company.

Everest, Allan S. 1950. *Morgenthau, the New Deal and Silver*. New York: Columbia University Press.

Fay, Stephen. 1982. *Beyond Greed*. New York: Viking Press.

Feavearyear, A.E. 1934. *The Pound Sterling: A History of English Money*. Oxford, UK: The Clarendon Press.

Figlewski, Stephen, Yoram Landskroner, and William Silber. 1991. "Tailing the Hedge: Why and How," *Journal of Futures Markets*, April.

Folsom, Burton, Jr. 2008. *New Deal or Raw Deal: How FDR's Legacy Has Damaged America*. New York: Simon and Schuster.

Forbes. Various dates.

Forbes, J. S. 1999. *Hallmark: A History of the London Assay Office*. London: Unicorn Press.

Fortune. Various dates.

Friedman, Milton. 1994. *Money Mischief: Episodes in Monetary History*. New York: Harcourt Brace & Company.

Friedman, Milton and Anna J. Schwartz. 1963. *A Monetary History of the United States*. Princeton, N.J.: Princeton University Press.

Gale, N.H. and Z.A. Stos-Gale. 1981. "Ancient Egyptian Silver," *Journal of Egyptian Archaeology* 67.

Garbade, Kenneth D. and William L. Silber. 1979. "Dominant and Satellite Markets: A Study of Dually-Traded Securities," *Review of Economics and Statistics* 61, no. 3.

———. 1983. "Price Movements and Price Discovery in Cash and Futures Markets," *Review of Economics and Statistics* 65, no. 2.

Garbade, Kenneth D. 2012. *Birth of a Market: The U.S. Treasury Securities Market from the Great War to the Great Depression*. Cambridge, Mass.: MIT Press.

Glad, Betty. 1986. *Key Pittman: The Tragedy of a Senate Insider*. New York: Columbia University Press.

Grew, Joseph C. 1944. *Ten Years in Japan*. New York: Simon and Schuster.

Groves, Leslie R. 1962. *Now It Can Be Told: The Story of the Manhattan Project*. New York: Harper & Row Publishers.

The Guardian. Various dates.

Handy & Harman. Various years. *The Silver Market, Annual Review*.

Hartford Courant. Various dates.

Hibben, Paxton. 1929. *The Peerless Leader: William Jennings Bryan*. New York: Farrar and Rinehart.

Hull, Cordell. 1948. *The Memoirs of Cordell Hull*. New York: Macmillan Company.

Hunt Hill, Margaret. 1994. *H.L. and Lyda*. Little Rock, Ark.: August House Publishers.

Hurt, Harry, III. 1980. "Silverfinger," *Playboy*, September.

———. 1981. *Texas Rich: The Hunt Dynasty from the Early Oil Days through the Silver Crash*. New York, London: W.W. Norton & Company.

Israel, Fred L. 1963. *Nevada's Key Pittman*. Lincoln: University of Nebraska Press.

J.V. Bruni & Co. 2006. "The 2006 Berkshire Hathaway Annual Meeting: Top 20 Questions," available at http://www.jvbruni.com/Berkshire2006annualmeeting.pdf.

James, Ronald M. 1998. *The Roar and the Silence: A History of Virginia City and the Comstock Lode*. Las Vegas: University of Nevada Press.

Jarecki, Henry. 1979. "Silver Threads among the Gold," *Euromoney*, March.

———. 1979. "A Squeeze in Silver: How Likely?" *Commodities*, March.

———. 1989. *An Alchemist's Road: My Transition from Medicine to Business*. Privately printed.

Jarecki, Henry. Undated. Manuscript.

Jastram, Roy. 1981. *Silver: The Restless Metal*. New York: John Wiley & Sons.

Johnson, Phillip McBride. 1982. *Commodities Regulation*. Boston: Little Brown and Company.

Kann, Eduard. 1927. *The Currencies of China: An Investigation of Silver & Gold Transactions Affecting China*. Shanghai: Kelley & Walsh, Limited.

Kazin, Michael. 2006. *A Godly Hero: The Life of William Jennings Bryan*. New York: Alfred Knopf.

Kisluk-Grosheide, Daniëlle O. and Jeffrey Munge. 2010. *The Wrightsman Galleries for French Decorative Arts*. New York: Metropolitan Museum of Art.

Kletter, Raz and Etty Brand. 1998. "A New Look at the Iron Age Silver Hoard from Eshtemoa," *Zeitschrift des Deutschen Palästina-Vereins* Bd. 114, H. 2.

Koenig, Louis W. 1971. *Bryan: A Political Biography of William Jennings Bryan*. New York: G.P. Putnam.

Kolasky, William. 2009. "Senator John Sherman and the Origin of Antitrust," *Antitrust* 24, no. 1.

Kuo, Tai-chun and Hsiao-ting Lin. 2006. *T.V. Soong in Modern Chinese History*. Stanford, Calif.: Hoover Institution Press.

Kyle, Albert S. and S. Viswanathan. 2008. "Price Manipulation in Financial Markets: How to Define Price Manipulation," *American Economic Review* 98, no. 2.

Lane, Philip R. 2012. "The European Sovereign Debt Crisis," *Journal of Economic Perspectives* 26, no. 3.

Lansdown, A. 2006. "Silver in Health Care: Antimicrobial Effects and Safety in Use." In *Biofunctional Textiles and the Skin*, edited by U.-C. Hipler and P. Eisner. Basel: Karger.

Laughlin, J. Laurence. 1897. *The History of Bimetallism in the United States*. New York: D. Appleton and Company.

Leavens, Dickson. 1939. *Silver Money*. Bloomington, Ind.: Principia Press.

Leong, Yau Sing. 1933. *Silver: An Analysis of Factors Affecting Price*. Washington, DC: Brookings Institution.

Levine, Erwin L. 1971. *Theodore Francis Green: The Washington Years*. Providence, R.I.: Brown University Press.

Lichtenstein, Eugene. 1965. "Our Silver Dolors," *Fortune*, March.

Lindeman, H.R. 1879. *Money and Legal Tender in the United States*. New York: G.P. Putnam's Sons.

Los Angeles Times. Various dates.

MacCambridge, Michael. 2012. *Lamar Hunt: A Life in Sports*. Kansas City, Mo.: Andrews McMeel Publishing.

Malkiel, Burton. 2015. Revised and Updated. *A Random Walk Down Wall Street*. New York: Norton.

Manchester Guardian. Various dates.

Markham, Jerry W. 2014. *Law Enforcement and the History of Financial Market Manipulation*. Armonk, N.Y.: M.E. Sharpe.

Moley, Raymond. 1939. *After Seven Years*. New York: Harper & Brothers Publishers.

———. 1966. *The First New Deal*. New York: Harcourt, Brace & World.

Morgenthau, Henry, Jr. *Morgenthau Diaries*. Various dates.

Morison, Elting E. 2003. *Turmoil and Tradition: A Study of the Life and Times of Henry L. Stimson*. Boston: Houghton Mifflin Company.

Newsday. Various dates.

Newsweek. Various dates.

New York Times. Various dates.

Norris, Robert S. 2002. *Racing for the Bomb*. South Royalton, Vt.: Steerforth Press.

Nugent, Walter K. 1968. *Money and American Society; 1865–1889*. New York: Free Press.

O'Leary, Paul M. 1960. "The Scene of the Crime of 1873 Revisited: A Note," *Journal of Political Economy* 68, no. 4.

Paris, James D. 1938. *Monetary Policies in the United States: 1932–1938*. New York: Columbia University Press.

Pick, Franz. Undated. *Silver: How and Where to Buy and Hold It*. Rev. and enlarged 3rd ed. New York: Pick Publishing Corporation.

Reed, Cameron. 2011. "From Treasury Vault to the Manhattan Project, *American Scientist* 99, no. 1.

Report from the Select Committee on Depreciation of Silver, together with the proceedings of the Committee, minutes of evidence, and appendix, ordered by the House of Commons to be printed 5 July 1876. Available at https://catalog.hathitrust.org/Record/001118659.

Report of the International Conference on Weights, Measures, and Coins, Paris, June 1867, London: Harrison and Sons, available at http://babel.hathitrust.org/cgi/pt?id=mdp.35112103466761;view=1up;seq=1.

Reti, Steven P. 1998. *Silver and Gold: The Political Economy of International Monetary Conferences, 1867–1892*. Westport, Conn.: Greenwood Press.

Ricardo, David. 1817. *On the Principles of Political Economy and Taxation*. London: John Murray.

Ritchie, Donald A. 2007. *Electing FDR: The New Deal Campaign of 1932*. Lawrence: University Press of Kansas.

Roberts, George B. 1936. "The Silver Purchase Program and Its Consequences," *Proceedings of the Academy of Political Science* 17, no. 1.

Rockoff, Hugh. 1990. "The 'Wizard of Oz' as a Monetary Allegory," *Journal of Political Economy* 98, no. 4.

Rolnick, Arthur J. and Warren E. Weber. 1986. "Gresham's Law or Gresham's Fallacy," *Journal of Political Economy* 94, no. 1.

Rowan, Roy. 1980. "Talkfest with the Hunts," *Fortune*, August.

Ryan, J. P. and Katheen M. McBreen. 1962. "Silver." In Bureau of Mines, *Minerals Yearbook, Metals and Minerals (except fuels) 1961*, vol. 1. Washington, DC: Government Printing Office.

Salter, Sir Arthur. 1934. *China and Silver*. New York: Economic Forum, Inc.

Sargent, Thomas and Francois Velde. 2002. *The Big Problem of Small Change*. Princeton, N.J.: Princeton University Press.

Schlesinger, Arthur M., Jr. 1959. *The Age of Roosevelt: The Coming of the New Deal*. Boston: Houghton Mifflin Company.

Securities and Exchange Commission. 1982. *The Silver Crisis of 1980: A Report of the Staff of the U.S. Securities and Exchange Commission*. Washington, DC.

Sherman, John. 1895. *Recollections of Forty Years in the House, Senate, and Cabinet*. Chicago: Werner Company.

Silber, William L. 1981. "Innovation, Competition, and New Contract Design in Futures Markets," *Journal of Futures Markets*, Summer.

———. 1984. "Marketmaker Behavior in an Auction Market: An Analysis of Scalpers in Futures Markets," *Journal of Finance* 39, no. 4.

———. 2007. *When Washington Shut Down Wall Street*. Princeton, N.J.: Princeton University Press.

———. 2009. "Why Did FDR's Bank Holiday Succeed?" *Federal Reserve Bank of New York Economic Policy Review*. July.

———. 2012. *Volcker: The Triumph of Persistence*. New York: Bloomsbury.

Smith, Jerome F. 1972. *Silver Profits in the Seventies*. West Vancouver, BC: ERC Publishing Company.

Streeter, W.J. 1984. *The Silver Mania*. Dordrecht, Neth.: D. Reidel Publishing Company.

Sylla, Richard. 2016. *Alexander Hamilton*. New York: Sterling Publishing Company.

Temin, Peter. 1968. "The Economic Consequences of the Bank War," *Journal of Political Economy* 76, no. 2.

Thompson, Christine M. 2003. "Sealed Silver in Iron Age Cisjordan and the 'Invention' of Coinage," *Oxford Journal of Archaeology* 22, no. 1.

Tilson, Whitney. 2006. "Berkshire Hathaway Meeting Notes," available at http://www.designs.valueinvestorinsight.com/bonus/bonuscontent/docs/Tilson_2006_BRK_Meeting_Notes.pdf.

Times of India. Various dates.

Tuccille, Jerome. 1984. *Kingdom: The Story of the Hunt Family of Texas*. Ottawa, Il.: Jameson Books.

Tuchman, Barbara. 1970, 1985. *Stilwell and the American Experience in China, 1911–45*. New York: Grove Press.

U.S. Bureau of the Census. 1975. *Historical Statistics of the United States, Colonial Times to 1970*. Washington, DC.

U.S. Bureau of Mines. Various dates. *The Minerals Yearbook*. Washington, DC: Government Printing Office.

———. 1982. *The Price Responsiveness of Secondary Silver*. Washington, DC: Government Printing Office.

U.S. Department of Commerce. 1933. *The Minerals Yearbook: 1932–1933 Year 1931–32*. Washington, DC: Government Printing Office.

U.S. Department of the Interior & U.S. Geological Survey. Various dates. *Minerals Yearbook*. Washington, DC: Government Printing Office.

U.S. Department of State. 1934 & 1935. *Foreign Relations of the United States Diplomatic Papers*, vol. 3, *The Far East* available at http://digicoll.library.wisc.edu/cgi-bin/FRUS/FRUS-idx?type=browse&scope=FRUS.FRUS1.

U.S. Department of the Treasury. Various dates. *The Annual Report of the Secretary of the Treasury*. Washington, DC: Government Printing Office.

———. 1965. *Treasury Staff Study of Silver and Coinage*. Washington, DC: Government Printing Office.

U.S. Mint. 1936. *The Annual Report of the Director of the Mint.* Washington, DC: Government Printing Office.

Van Ryzin, Robert R. 2001. *Crime of 1873: The Comstock Connection.* Iola, Wisc.: Krause Publications.

Volcker, Paul and Toyoo Gyohten. 1992. *Changing Fortunes.* New York: Times Books.

Wachtel, Paul. 2017. "Central Bank Independence: More Myth than Reality," a paper presented at the Colloquium on Money, Debt and Sovereignty, University de Picardie Jules Verne, Amiens, France, December 11–12.

Walker, Francis A. 1893. "The Free Coinage of Silver," *Journal of Political Economy* 1, no. 22.

Wall Street Journal. Various dates.

Washington Post. Various dates.

Wheeler, Burton K. with Paul F. Kelley. 1962. *Yankee from the West.* Garden City, N.Y.: Doubleday & Company.

Williams, Jeffrey C. 1995. *Manipulation on Trial: Economic Analysis and the Hunt Silver Case.* Cambridge, UK: Cambridge University Press.

Williams, R. Hal. 2010. *Realigning America.* Lawrence: University Press of Kansas.

Willis, Henry Parker. 1901. *A History of the Latin Monetary Union.* Chicago: University of Chicago Press.

Wyler, Seymour. 1937. *The Book of Old Silver.* New York: Crown.

Ybarra, Michael J. 2004. *Washington Gone Crazy: Senator Pat McCarran and the Great American Communist Hunt.* Hanover, N.H.: Steerforth Press.

Young, Arthur N. 1953. "Saudi Arabian Currency and Finance," *Middle East Journal* 7, no. 3.

———. 1953. "Saudi Arabian Currency and Finance: Part II," *Middle East Journal* 7, no. 4.

———. 1971. *China's Nation-Building Effort, 1927–1937.* Stanford, Calif.: Hoover Institution Press.

Zweig, Jason. 2006. "Buffett: Real Estate Slowdown Ahead," May 8, available at http://money.cnn.com/2006/05/05/news/newsmakers/buffett_050606/index.htm?section=money_latest.

CONGRESSIONAL HEARINGS AND REPORTS

An Act Regulating Foreign Coins, and for Other Purposes, 2d Cong., 2d sess., February 9, 1793. *Statutes at Large of USA,* vol. 1, chap. 5.

An Act revising and amending the Laws relative to the Mints, Assay offices, and Coinage of the United States (The Coinage Act of 1873), 42d Cong., 3d sess., February 12, 1873. *Statutes at Large,* vol. 17, chap. 131.

Commodity Futures Trading Commission. 1980. *Report of the Commodity Futures Trading Commission on Recent Developments in the Silver Futures Markets,* [prepared for] Senate Committee on Agriculture, Nutrition, and Forestry. Washington, DC: Government Printing Office.

Congressional Record. Various dates.

"Establishing a Mint and Regulating the Coins of the United States," 2d Cong., 1st sess., April 2, 1792. *Statutes at Large*, vol. 1, chap. 14, 15, 16

Hamilton, Alexander. "On the Establishment of a Mint." 1st Cong., 3d sess. January 28, 1791. *American State Papers, Finance*, vol. 1, item 24.

"Report and Accompanying Documents of the United States Monetary Commission," organized under Joint Resolution of August 15, 1876, 2 vol., 44th Cong., 2d sess. S. Rept 703 Washington, DC: Government Printing Office, 1877.

"Report of the President's Commission on the Assassination of President Kennedy," September 24, 1964. Washington, DC: Government Printing Office, 1964.

"Report to the Congress in Response to Section 21 of the *Commodity Exchange Act*, Public Law No. 96–276," 96th Cong., 2d sess., sect. 7, pt. 2: "A Study of the Silver Market." June 1, 1980. *Statutes at Large*, vol. 94 (542).

U.S. Congress. House Committee on Banking and Currency. *Coinage Act of 1965*: Hearings on H.R. 8746, 89th Cong., 1st sess., June 4, 7, 8, 1965.

———. House Subcommittee of the Committee on Appropriations. "Treasury Department Appropriation Bill for 1938": Hearings, 75th Cong., 1st sess.

———. House Subcommittee of the Committee on Government Operations. "Silver Prices and the Adequacy of Federal Actions in the Marketplace, 1979–80": Hearings, 96th Cong., 2d sess., March 31; April 14, 15, 29, 30; May 2, 22, 1980.

———. House [Subcommittee of the] Committee on Government Operations. "Silver Prices and the Adequacy of Federal Actions in the Marketplace, 1979–80," Seventeenth Report, . . . together with Separate and Dissenting Views," December 11, 1981.

———. House Subcommittee on Conservation, Credit, and Rural Development of the Committee on Agriculture. "Joint Agency Reports on Silver Markets": Hearing, 97th Cong., 1st sess., October 1, 1981.

———. Senate Committee on Agriculture and Forestry. *Commodity Futures Trading Commission Act*: Hearings on S. 2485, S. 2578, S. 2837, H.R. 13113, 93d Cong., 2d sess., pt. 2, May 16, 17, and 20, 1974.

———. Senate Committee on Banking and Currency. "Federal Reserve Direct Purchases—*Old Series Currency Adjustment Act*: Hearings, 86th Cong., 2d sess., June 24, 1960.

———. Senate Committee on Banking and Currency. "Gold Reserve Requirements": Hearings on S. 797, S. 743, S. 814, 89th Cong., 1st sess., February 2, 3, 4, 9, 10, 1965.

———. Senate Committee on Banking and Currency, "Repeal of Silver Purchase Acts": Hearing, 88th Cong., 1st sess., April 29, 1963.

———. Senate Committee on Banking, Housing, and Urban Affairs. "Information Related to Futures Contracts in Financial Instruments": Hearing, 96th Cong., 2d sess., pt. 1, July 1980.

———. Senate Committee on Foreign Relations. "Commercial Relations with China." Report No. 1716, 71st Cong., 3d sess., February 17 (calendar day 20), 1931.

———. Senate Subcommittee of the Committee on Banking and Currency. "Purchase of Silver Produced in the United States with Silver Certificates": Hearings on S. 3606, 72d Cong., 1st sess., May 9, 1932.

———. Senate Subcommittee of the Committee on Banking and Currency. "To Authorize the Use for War Purposes of Silver Held or Owned by the United States": Hearing on S. 2768, 77th Cong., 2d sess., October 14, 1942.

———. Senate Subcommittee on Agricultural Research and General Legislation. "Price Volatility in the Silver Futures Market": Hearings, 96th Cong., 2d sess., pt. 1–2, May 1–2 and June 26, 1980.

———. Senate Subcommittee on Minerals, Materials, and Fuels of the Committee on Interior and Insular Affairs. "Gold and Silver Production Incentives": Hearings on S.J. Res. 44, 87th Cong., 2d sess., March 15 and June 8, 1962.

TRIAL DOCUMENTS

Burrows, James. CFTC Report. mimeo.

CFTC Docket No. 85–12, Complaint and Notice of Hearing, In the Matter of Nelson Bunker Hunt, et. al.

Deposition of Lamar Hunt, Minpeco S.A., et al., Plaintiff, against Nelson Bunker Hunt, et al., Defendants, October 21, 1986, vol. 1.

Deposition of Nelson Bunker Hunt, Minpeco S.A., et al., Plaintiff, against Nelson Bunker Hunt, et al., Defendants, April 10, 1986.

Deposition of William Herbert Hunt, Minpeco S.A., et al., Plaintiff, against Nelson Bunker Hunt, et al., Defendants, October 29, 1986.

Kyle, Albert S. "Report on the Behavior of Silver Prices and Economic Evidence," February 19, 1987, mimeo.

Minpeco S.A. plaintiff v. ContiCommodity Services, et al. Civil no. 81–7619 (M.E.L.) Fourth Amended Complaint.

Trial Transcripts, *Minpeco S.A. Plaintiff v. Nelson Bunker Hunt, et al., Defendants.* Various dates.

Videotape Depositions. Various dates.

ABOUT THE AUTHOR

WILLIAM L. SILBER IS THE MARCUS NADLER PROFESSOR OF Economics and Finance at the Stern School of Business, New York University. He received NYU's Distinguished Teaching Medal in 1999 and was voted Professor of the Year by Stern MBA students in 1990, 1997, and 2018. He received his PhD in economics from Princeton University and has written about monetary economics and financial history, including seven books, most recently, *Volcker: The Triumph of Persistence*, which chronicles the career of former Federal Reserve Chairman Paul Volcker. The Volcker biography won the China Business News Financial Book of the Year in 2013, was a finalist in the Goldman Sachs / Financial Times Business Book of the Year in 2012, and was named "One of the Best Business Books of 2012" by Bloomberg Businessweek. His first book, *Money*, coauthored with Lawrence Ritter, made a serious topic fun to read.

ILLUSTRATION CREDITS

FIGURE 1. National Photo Company Collection, Prints & Photographs Division, Library of Congress, LC-DIG-npcc-24200

FIGURE 2. Everett Historical / Shutterstock.com

FIGURE 3. Brady-Handy Collection, Prints & Photographs Division, Library of Congress, LC-DIG-cwpbh-04797

FIGURE 4. Prints & Photographs Division, Library of Congress, LC-USZ62-22703

FIGURE 5. Prints & Photographs Division, Library of Congress, LC-USZ62-86702

FIGURE 6. Bettmann / Contributor / Getty Images

FIGURE 7. nsf / Alamy Stock Photo

FIGURE 8. Bettmann / Contributor / Getty Images

FIGURE 9. National Numismatic Collection, National Museum of American History

FIGURE 10. Sueddeutsche Zeitung Photo / Alamy Stock Photo

FIGURE 11. National Numismatic Collection, National Museum of American History

FIGURE 12. (*top*) Photograph by Dimitri Karetnikov; (*bottom*) United States Mint

FIGURE 13. John Marmaras Photography

FIGURE 14. AP Photo/Charles Wenzelberg

FIGURE 15. Central Press / Stringer / Hulton Archive / Getty Images

FIGURE 16. doomu / Shutterstock.com

FIGURE 17. Bettmann / Contributor / Getty Images

FIGURE 18. Bettmann / Contributor / Getty Images

FIGURE 19. Classical Numismatic Group, Inc. www.cngcoins.com

FIGURE 20. Bloomberg / Contributor / Getty Images

FIGURE 21. United States Mint

Index

Page numbers in **boldface** refer to illustrations

Abdullah bin Abdul-Aziz, 181, 186, 214
Abramson, Harold, 233
Acheson, Dean, 55, 57, 267n24
Adams, Alva, 63
Adams, Bud, 161
Adams, Edward R., 123
Adams, Eva, 107–8, 110, 114
Adams, William, 202
Advicorp PLC, 189
Affara, Mohammed, 186
Afghanistan, Russian invasion of, 199,
    302n90
Agricultural Adjustment Act, 49; Thomas
    Amendment to, 50, 51, 61, 67, 266n40,
    283n27
Al-Amoudi, Mohammad Aboud, 186,
    215, 216
Allison, William, 24
Allott, Gordon, 117
Alter, Jonathan, 262n1
Amau Doctrine, 67
Amelkin, Sol, 138
American Bimetallic League, 26, 30, 118
American Silver Recovery, Inc., 203
American Smelting and Refining Company,
    43, 116, 136
Amin, Haji Ashraf, 204
anti-communism, 153–54, 157, 176
anti-Semitism, 132, 133, 154
Apuzzo, Patricia, xiii
Ariyoshi, Akira, 76–77
Arnold-Hamilton, Carol, xiv
Astaire, Fred, 67
Australia: Hunt's farmland in, 151, 158,
    213, 233; silver production in, 21,
    23–24, 53, 248, 269n32
Azzara, Sal, 219

Bache & Company, 158, 165–66, 194,
    211, 213, 214, 216–19, 223, 294n3
backwardation, 239–40
Bailey, Benton, 125
Bankers Trust Company, 140
bank holidays, 48–49, 80–81, 265n20

Bank of New York, 10, 32
Barclays Bank International, 211
Barnett, Paul, 259n13
Barnhart, Russell, 288n15
Barro, Robert, 129, 287n52
Baruch, Bernard M., 75
Baum, L. Frank. See *Wonderful Wizard
    of Oz, The*
Beatles, the, 120
Belgium, 23
Beretz, Hal, 308n108
Berkowitz, Eugene, 205
Berkshire Hathaway Company, 4, 237,
    239–45, 253n7
Berndt, Lee, 209
Bernstein, Peter L., 256n10, 308n104
Bethlehem Steel Company, 40
Bible, Alan, 107, 110, 114
biblical references, xi, 27–28, 187, 301n73
Biddle, Francis, 95
Bieber, Justin, 61, 270n9
bimetallism, xvii, 12–15, 22, 30, 33, 63
Bismarck, Otto von, 20, 23, 24, 36
Blake, Geoffrey, xiii
Bland, Richard, 24
Bland-Allison Act, 24–25
Bledsoe, William, 294n1
Blinder, Alan, 315n29
Blum, John Morton, 255n32, 267n16
Boleyn, Anne, 5
Boraiko, Allen, 303n12
Bordo, Michael D., and Athanasios Or-
    phanides, 317
Borg, Dorothy, 272n48
Boyd, Jack, 212
Brandeis, Goldschmidt & Co., 208
Brandt, Loren, 275n54
Brannan, Dennis, 232
Bratter, Herbert M., 255n27, 258n20
Brennan, Pat, 149
Brimmer, Andrew, 194
Brodsky, Alvin, 158, 165–67, 171, 215
Brooks, William F., 254n12
Broun, Heywood, 45

Bruns, Franklyn R., 120
Bryan, Silas and Mariah Elizabeth, 27–29
Bryan, William Jennings, ii, 3–4, 8, 16, 26, 27–37, **28**, **37**;40, 47, 50, 80, 99, 105–6, 137, 207, 250; biographical sketch of, xvii; "Cross of Gold" speech by, xvii, 3, 33, 62, 143; on silver pricing, 30–31, 34–36, 49, 102, 145, 163; in *The Wonderful Wizard of Oz*, xvii
Buffet, Warren, iii, 4, 236n, **238**; biographical sketch of, xx; silver investments by, xx, 3, 237–47, 249
Bullitt, Orville H., 273n9
Bullitt, William C., 72–73, 75–76, 77, 85
Burdekin, Richard, 276n54
Burns, Arthur R., 192–93
Burr, Aaron, 14–15
Burrough, Bryan, 291
Burrows, James, 300n70
Burton, Theodore, 258n3

California Gold Rush, 21, 23–24
Caminschi, Andrew, 313n2
Canada, 36, 168, 176, 196, 213, 248, 269n32
Cárdenas, Lázaro, 80
Carnahan, Mel, 282n11
Caro, Robert, 281n1
Carroll, John, 110
Carter, Jimmy, 12, 186–87, 212, 213
Carusi, Ugo, 57
Castro, Fidel, 2
Caughey, John Walton, 260n35
Chiang Kai-shek, xviii, 8, 65, 71, 76–77, 87
Chicago Board of Trade (CBOT), 177, 179–80, 191–92, 194–95, 208–9
Chico, Luis, 169, 170–71
China, xviii, 3, 4, 8–9, 42, 44, 58–59, 60–62, 65–89, 162, 218, 255n31; currency system in, 60–61, 87, 275n47, 276n73; Silver Purchase Act and, 77, 82, 89, 250, 275n54. *See also* silver smuggling: in China and Japan; Sino-Japanese War
China Development Finance Company, 75
Church, Frank, 106, 117
Churchill, Winston, 46–47, 97, 154
Civil Rights Act, 119, 124
Clark, Worth, 101
Clayton Brokerage, 185
Coen, Joel, 147–48, 204

Coinage Act of 1873 ("Crime of 1873"), xvii, 4, 16, 17–26, 33, 80, 142, 170, 207, 218, 250, 258nn4–5, 285n14; Adams on, 63; McCarran on, 102; Robertson on, 112; Warner on, 118; Wheeler on, 53
Coinage Acts: of 1792, 4, 10, 12, 13, 18, 31, 256n3, 257n15; of 1834 and 1837, 256n3; of 1853, 285n14; of 1965, 126–29
coin collecting, 111, 120–22, **122**, 124, 148, 203–4, 205; Hunt brothers' coin collections, 232–35, **234**, 247
coins. *See* silver: currency uses of; silver dollars; subsidiary coins
coin shortages, 41, 110–11, 113, 122–26, 131
Coletta, Paolo, 261n11
Colorado Mining Association, 58
Comex (New York Commodity Exchange), xiv, xv, xix, 64, 115–16, 137, 140, 158, 159–60, 163–64, 170–71, 178–80, 191–92, 205; barring of Hunts from, 207–10; Nelson Bunker Hunt's visit to, 171; new regulations by, 194–95, 205–6, 208–10; Silver Thursday and, 217–18; Special Silver Committee of, 194–95; Waltuch's presence at, 187–88
Commodities Future Trading Commission (CFTC), 178–79, 189, 191, 192, 194–96, 218, 233, 240; founding of, 167; in 1990s, 236, 240–41
Commodity Exchange Act, 196
Commodity Futures Trading Act, 168
Comstock Lode, 15–16, 24, 258n22
ContiCommodity Investor Services, 187–88, 194
Coolidge, Calvin, 39
copper, 93–96, 100, 210, 244, 245–246
cornering: defined, 165; Jarecki's advice on, 184–86, 220
Couzins, Bart, 191, 193
Cox, James, 39
Cragg, John, 256n5
Crime of 1873. *See* Coinage Act of 1873
Croesus, 256n10
Crowl, William, 148
Cummings, Homer, 55, 57
Curran, Paul, 226, 228, 230
Curtis, Jamie Lee, 244
Cymrot, Mark, 225–30

Daley, Richard, 104
Darrow, Clarence, 36

Darwin, Charles, 36
Davis, J.C., 203
Defense Plant Corporation, 96
Delorey, Thomas K., 256n8
Denmark, 23
Despres, Leon, 45–46
Detre, Thomas P., 148
Dial, Scott, 185–86
Dillon, Douglas, 105–9, 111, 115, 117, 120, 127, 131
Dillon Read & Company, 106
Ditchik, Seth, xiv
Dodd, Thomas, 115
Doihara, Kenji, 86
Dominick, Peter, 117, 128, 129, 144
Donnelly, Richard A., 294n5
Doolittle, Adam, 314n15
Dougherty, Peter, xiv
D. Penellier & Company, 203
Drake, Harold, 296n9
Drexel Burnham Lambert Inc., 216
Dubai, 204
DuPont, 180

Eastman Kodak Company, 5–6, 105, 160, 164, 168–69, 170, 178, 180, 293n64
Eccles, Marriner, 45
Edison, Thomas A., 245
Edward III, 213
Edwards, Frank, 230
Edwards, Jerome E., 280n3
E.F. Hutton, 194, 211
EFP transactions, 193, 206
Egypt, ancient, 5, 196
Einzig, Paul, 266n36
Eisenberg, Henry, 208
Eisenhower, Dwight D., 106
Eliasoph, Gene, 145
Eliot, T.S., 49, 265n21
Elizabeth I, 5, 13, 254n9
Elizabeth II, 159
Engelhard Minerals & Chemicals Corporation, 116–17, 125, 146, 194, 206, 209, 210–12, 214, 220–21, 236–37
Estes, Alicia, xiv
Ethiopia, 87
Everest, Allan S., 275n41, 277n73

Faisal bin Abdul-Aziz, 176
Faisal bin Abdullah, 186, 214, 215, 216, 230
Faisal bin Musaid, 176

Farm Credit Association (FCA), 55
Fay, Stephen, 253n3
Feavearyear, A.E., 253n9
Federal Coin & Currency, Inc., 138, 147
Federal Resources Company, 125
Federal Reserve Act, 114
Federal Reserve Bank, 107, 117, 136
Federal Reserve System, xix, 32, 45, 51, 91, 117–18, 129, 144, 157, 251–52; currency notes issued by, 109–11, 114–15, 283n25; antispeculation guidance by, 212–14
fiat currency. See paper currency
Figlewski, Stephen, 300n51
Financial Crisis of 2008, 4, 6, 245–46, 249
Foley, Edward, 95
Folsom, Burton, Jr., 262n2
Fonseco, Ismael, 199–200
Forbes, J.S., 253n8
Ford, Gerald, 172
Forman, Harry, 203–4
Fowler, Henry ("Joe"), 127–29, 147, 287n41
France, 5, 19, 20, 24, 36; French franc, 21–22, 23, 51, 265n36, 266n43
Franco, Francisco, 99
Friedman, Milton, 46, 260n43, 264n7; on China crisis, 255n31, 275n54, 277n73
Funck, N.R., 69–70
Fustok, Mahmoud, 181–82, 188–89, 214, 215, 216; Hunts trial and, 223, 224–25, 228, 230

Gale, N.H., and Z.A. Stos-Gale, 301n73
Garbade, Kenneth D., xiv, 268n26, 293n60
Garner, John Nance, 74
Gem Certification & Assurance Lab, xiii, 253n8
Gemini Industries, 203
George III, 10
George V, 44
Geraci, Phil, xiii, 229, 309n12
Germany, 24, 36, 41, 44, 133, 252; Imperial Coinage Law in, 23, 260n30
Getty, J. Paul, 150
Gibson, Paul, 139
Glad, Betty, 263n3
Glass, Carter, 32
Goizueta, Robert, 237–38
gold: Buffet on, xx, 238; currency uses of, 12–15, 18, 21, 23–24, 31; discoveries

gold (*continued*)
in 1850s of, 21, 23–24, 259n20; flakes of, 13, 257n13; Hamilton on, 12; Hunt and, 163; investment in, xx, 6, 107, 144, 163, 167, 171, 172, 180, 190, 243, 245–46; Jennings's opposition to, 33; Roosa on, 107; Roosevelt and, 55–57, 61, 144, 267n24
"gold fixing," 148–49
gold mining, 23–24, 219
Gold Reserve Act, 61–62
Goldschmidt, Walter, 194
Goldsmith Brothers Smelting and Refining Company, 68
gold standard, xvii, xviii, 4, 7, 21, 23–24, 30, 35–36, 46, 87, 106, 129, 250; Roosevelt's suspension of, 50–51, 55, 105; "sound currency" euphemism for, 46, 48
Goldwater, Barry, 32
Goodnight, Emily, xiii
Gorham Manufacturing Company, 65
Grant, Ulysses S., 17, 26
Great Britain, 10–12, 19, 23, 36, 42–43, 64–65, 87; gold sovereign in, 133; Libyan oil operations and, 155–57; London forward market in, 141–42, 229; pound sterling in, 5, 13, 35, 83, 144, 253n9; silver scrapping in, 203; silver storage in, 240
Great Crash of 1929, 44, 224
Great Depression, xviii, 3; 8, 30, 33, 37, 46, 48–49, 52, 66, 91, 247
Great Inflation, xix, 120, 129, 157, 167, 172, 181, 186–87, 226, 239, 247, 251
Great Moderation, 242
Great Recession, 245–47
Great War. *See* World War I
Great Western United, 177, 179
Greece, 4, 246
Green, Theodore, 99–101
Greenspan, Alan, 172
Gresham, Thomas (and Gresham's law), 13, 14, 21, 25, 127
Grew, Joseph C., 85, 276n62
Grosvenor, Charles H., 255n26
Groves, Leslie R., 98
Gut, Rainer, 190
Gyohten, Toyoo, 282n15

Hambros, Jocelyn, 148, 170
Hamilton, Alexander, ii, 7, 10–15, **11**, **14**, 18, 22, 25, 30, 63, 249–50; biographical

sketch of, xvii; silver price set by, ii, xvii, xix, 13, 15, 72, 102, 116, 143, 172
Hammer, Armand, 219
Handy & Harman, xv, 43, 56, 65, 78, 144, 158, 160, 164, 255n27, 266n37
Hanna, Mark, 34
Hardy, Robert, 105
Hayes, Rutherford B., 17
Henry VIII, 5
Herodotus, 256n10
Hertesbergh, Giles de, 11
Hibben, Paxton, 27
Hilliard, Henry E., 311n13
Hirota, Koki, 76, 85–86
Hitler, Adolf, 47
Hoffstatter, Edward, 208
Holland, 23
Hoover, Herbert, 45
Houthakker, Hendrik, 230
Hughes, Sarah, 119
Hull, Cordell, 52, 65, 67, 72, 77, 82, 86
Hunt, Caroline, 151, 154
Hunt, Douglas, 178
Hunt, Elizabeth, 178
Hunt, Ellen, 178
Hunt, Hassie, 152–53
Hunt, Herbert, xx, 1–3, 152–55, **153**, 161–63, 165, 185–86, 191–93, 210–11, 214, **217**, 219, 229; post-trial life of, 232–35, 249. *See also* Hunt brothers
Hunt, H.L., 2, 150, 151–55, 172, 199, 249
Hunt, Houston, 178, 234
Hunt, Lamar, xx, 1–3, 152, **153**, 154, 161, 197, **198**, 222–23; post-trial life of, 232; silver investments of, 214, 220, 224–25, 230, 302n85
Hunt, Lamar, Jr., 1
Hunt, Lyda Allred, 233
Hunt, Lyda Bunker, 151–52, 155
Hunt, Mary, 178
Hunt, Nelson Bunker, xiii, **xiii**, 2, 9, 150–51, **153**, **159**, **217**, 248; background of, 151–55; biographical sketch of, xix–xx; death of, xiii, 249; horse ownership of, 151, 158–59, 181–82, 223, 316n1; Iran and, 176, 183; Kennedy opposition by, 117–18, 150; oil business of, xx, 2, 150, 152, 156–57, 158, 159, 161, 174, 176, 195, 207; post-trial life of, 231–34, 249, 316n1; Saudi connections of, 176, 180–82, 186–87, 193, 216;

silver-backed bonds scheme of, 215, 220, 227–28; silver investments of, xx, 1–3, 151, 157–68, 174, 178–79, 181, 189, 196, 200–201, 204, 206–7, 209, 211, 214–15, 228–29, 237, 239. *See also* Hunt brothers

Hunt, Sharron, 1

Hunt brothers: bankruptcy filings of, 231–33; House Subcommittee investigation of, 216, **217**, 218, 219; Jarecki and, 149, 169–70, 179–80, 174, 179, 185–86, 190–94, 208, 220; oil and gas businesses of, 154–55, 161, 211, 221, 222, 249; silver investments of, xix, xx, 1–3, 4, 5, 7, 161, 164, 165–68, 171–72, 177, 179, 185–86, 190–91, 195–97, 199, 206–9, 213–20, 236, 239, 246, 302n85; soybean market and, 177–78, 195, 211; trial of, xiii, 3, 186, 216, 224–31, 241, 301n76, 309n2; unapologetic attitude of, 3, 219, 220–21, 225, 231–32

Hunt Hill, Margaret, 3, 150, 151, 154, 222–23, 291n4

Hurt, Harry, III, 154, 291n13

Ibn Saud, Abdul-Aziz, 175–76, 181

Idris of Libya, 2, 154

illegal coin and silver melting, 146–47, 202

India, xviii, 3, 42–43, 44, 88, 162, 204

International Metals Investment Company (IMIC), 186, 193, 213, 224

International Silver Company, 65, 105

Iran, 6, 176, 183, 187, 190; hostage crisis in, 199, 216, 226

Ireland, 4, 246

Israel, Fred L., 263n8, 269n95

Italy, 4, 23, 246

Jacobs, Harry, 217–18

James, Ronald M., 258n21

Japan, xviii, 44, 67–68, 72, 73–78, 84–85, 87, 88, 101, 277n75; military aggression by, 3, 8–9, 73, 75–76, 81–82, 85–87, 89, 218, 250. *See also* Sino-Japanese War

Jarecki, Gloria, 134, 137–38, 140, 145

Jarecki, Henry, xiii, **143**; background of, 132–35; biographical sketch of, xix; Hunt brothers and, 149, 169–70, 179–80, 174, 179, 185–86, 190–94, 208, 220; paranoia and, 173–74; silver arbitraging by, 131–32, 135–42, 145, 147–49,

162–64, 168–71, 179–80, 183, 190–92, 203, 204, 210, 219–20, 295n18; "Silver Threads among the Gold" article by, 184–86, 220

Jarecki, Max, 132, 134, 148

Jarecki, Richard, 131, 132, 135–36

J. Aron & Company, 194

Jastram, Roy, 258n20

Jay, John, 10

Jefferson, Thomas, 14

Jewel Tea Company currency, 123

John Birch Society, xix, 2, 104, 117–18, 150

Johnson, Lyndon Baines, 32, 104, 119; biographical sketch of, xix; gold politics of, 129, 287n51; silver politics of, 120, 124–30, 136, 139, 159, 162; on Warren Commission, 281n1

Johnson, Nelson, 82, 87

Johnson, Phillip McBride, 301n74

Johnson, Sam, 128

Johnson Matthey, 203

Jones, James K., 34

Jones, John P., 20

Kann, Eduard, 269n2, 268n6

Kaufman, Henry, 190

Kawashima, Yoshiyuki, 85–86

Kazin, Michael, 262n50

Keating, Kenneth, 115

Kelley, Paul F., 264n14

Kennedy, David, 147

Kennedy, Jacqueline, 119

Kennedy, John Fitzgerald: assassination of, xviii–xix, 104, 117–19, 150; biographical sketch of, xviii–xix; Kennedy half-dollar, 121, **122**, 126; silver politics of, 103, 104–10, 114–20, 137

Kennedy, Joseph P., Sr., 106

Key, Francis Scott, 114

Keynes, John Maynard, 35

Khalid Ibn Abdul-Aziz, 176

Khomeini, Ruhollah, 183, 187, 207, 242

Kisluck-Grosheide, Daniëlle, and Jeffrey Munge, 254n11

Klejna, Dennis A., 240–41

Kletter, Raz, and Etty Brand, 256n10

Klondike Gold Rush, 39, 139

Koenig, Louis W., 261n3

Kohnstamm, Louis, 32

Kolasky, William, 258n2

Kopplemann, Herman, 103
Kreiling, Randy, 172
Kreuger, Ivar, 224
Kung, H.H., 65, 67, 71, 77, 82–84, 277n73
Kunstmann, Arthur, 132
Kunstmann, Gerda, 132
Kuo, Tai-chun, and Hsiao-ting Lin, 273n15
Kuwait, 195
Kyle, Albert S., 312n23

La Follette, Robert, 48
Landskroner, Yoram, 300n51
Lane, Francis K., 38
Lane, Philip R., 315n30
Langley, Anna Belle, 232
Lanier, Willie, 230
Lansdown, Alan B.G., 301n73
Lasker, Morris, 224–25, 230
Laughlin, J. Laurence, 30, 257nn16 and 18
Leavens, Dickson, 263nn18 and 27,
    267n12, 270n15; on China crisis,
    273n20, 275n47, 276n73
Legal Tender Act, 248
Lehman Brothers, iii, 245–46
Leith-Ross, Frederick, 83, 84
Lenin, Vladimir, 99, 183
Leong, Yau Sing, 278n10
Lester, Richard A., 66
Levine, Erwin L., 280n5
Libyan oil fields, xx, 2, 150, 154, 155–57,
    161, 195, 207
Lichtenstein, Eugene, 288n1
Lightner, Kendra, 279n32
Li Ming, 66, 271n39
Lincoln, Abraham, 17, 29
Lindeman, H.R., 256n3
Lindley, Ernest K., 95
Lippmann, Walter, 50
Livermore, Jesse, 224
Lloyd George, David, 44
Lombardi, Vince, 1
London Bullion Market Association, xv,
    237
López, Roberto, 80–81
Louis XIV, 5
Lovell, Christopher, 236–37, 240
Lowe, John, 110

MacCambridge, Michael, 293n65
Madonna, 61, 270n9
Madison, James, 10

Malkiel, Burton, 253n2
Malthus, Thomas, 33
Manhart, Joanne, 236n, 312n25, 313n35
Manhattan Project, 97–98, 100
manipulation, definitions of, 196, 225,
    240–41, 301n79
Mansfield, Mike, 112, 121, 124
Manufacturers Hanover Trust Company,
    232–33
Mao Tse-tung, xviii, 8, 85, 87, 250
Markham, Jerry W., 297nn19–20
Marshall, John C., 97
Marx, Groucho, 79
Mattey, Charles, 294n1
Mays, Willie, 137
McCarran, Pat, 99, 100–102, 105, 107–8
McCarthy, Joseph, 99
McCurley, Mike, 234
McDonald, Jesse, 58
McFadden, L.T., 43
McKinley, William, 8, 17, 27, 33–34, 102,
    107, 146
Mehta, Dinsa, 236
Merrill, Charles, and Helena Meyer, 281n18
Merrill Lynch & Company, 158, 194, 211,
    213, 216–17
Mexico, 36, 80–81, 88, 90, 168–70, 176,
    196, 204, 257n16, 269n32
Minpeco S.A., 200, 224–26, 230–33
Mint Act, 126, 277n6
Mintz, Lowell, 205
Mirror Manufacturers Association, 102
Mobruk, Ezzeldin, 155–56
Mocatta, Moses, 148
Mocatta & Goldsmid, 141–42, 145,
    148–49, 195
Mocatta Metals Corporation, xiii, xix,
    149, 160, 168–70, 179–80, 184–85,
    190–94, 206, 293n64, 300n50. See also
    Jarecki, Henry
Moley, Raymond, 51, 66, 265n27
Morashti, Omer, xiv
Morgan, Edwin, 21
Morgenthau, Elinor, 81
Morgenthau, Henry, Jr., 8–9, 53, 54, 62–
    65, 90–91, 97, 171, 200–201; biographi-
    cal sketch of, xviii; China silver crisis and,
    67–75, 78, 277n75; Manhattan Project
    and, 96–97, 279n35; Roosevelt and, 53–
    55, 57, 64, 67–68; World War II and,
    95–97, 100

Morison, Elting E., 279n41
Munger, Charlie, 238–39, 244
Murdock, Abe, 101
Murphy's Law, 13
Musco, Sebastian, 203
Mussalem, Ali bin, 186

Nahas, Naji, 181–82, 188–89, 211, 214, 215, 216, 223; Hunts trial and, 225, 228, 230
Napoleon III, 20
Nelson, Donald, 95–96
Nessim, Raymond, 206, 208–9, 210–11
Nevada (as Silver State), xvii, 15, 39–40, 43, 58, 90, 93, 99, 107–8, 114, 124, 219, 250
Nevada Hills Extension Mining Company, 40
New England Manufacturing Jewelers and Silversmiths Association, 100, 167
Newton, Isaac, 13, 257n12
New York Gold Refining Company, xiii
Niagara Hudson Power Company, 100
Nixon, Richard M., 7, 104, 147, 157, 251, 293n73
Norris, Richard, 121
Norris, Robert S., 279n35
Nugent, Walter K., 255n24

Occidental Petroleum, 219
O'Leary, Arthur, 146–47
O'Leary, Paul M., 259n12
Oliphant, Herman, 55, 83
Oppenheimer, Bob, xiv
Oswald, Lee Harvey, xviii–xix, 104, 118

Pacific State Telephone Company, 40
Pahlavi, Mohammad Reza, 176, 183
Palmieri, Don and Angelo, xiii, 253n8
Panic of 1893, 30, 33
paper currency, 7, 35, 46, 92, 109, 113, 114–15, 123, 187, 251–52; in Asia and the Middle East, 60, 82–83, 87, 175; Hunt's contempt for, 157, 171, 181
paranoia and success, 173
Paris, James D., 255n28
Paris Monetary Conference, 20–21, 24
Pastore, John, 115
Patman, Wright, 111, 127–29
Patton, George, 172
Paul, Ron, 248, 315n36

Pell, Claiborne, 115
Penrod Drilling Company, 306n61
Peru, 168, 170, 176, 196, 200, 204, 269n32
Peters, Gerhard, and John T. Woolley, 268n25
Phibro, 236–37, 240
Pick, Franz, 127, 141, 195–96, 207
Pierce, Franklin, 45
Pittman, Key: background of, 39–44; biographical sketch of, xvii–xviii; China and, 58, 60, 61, 65, 74–75; death of, 99; India and, 3; Morgenthau and, xviii; photographs of, iii, 42, 74; Roosevelt and, xviii, 8, 38, 41, 49, 51, 52, 57, 250; silver politics of, 52–53, 56, 62, 63, 65, 67, 80, 89, 90, 108, 172; wild side of, 52–53, 151
Pittman, Mimosa, 39–40, 41
Pittman Act, xviii, 43–44, 137, 263n15
Placid Oil Company, 2, 155, 161, 213, 221–23, 232
Platt, Edward, 43
Platt, Robert, xiv
Portugal, 19, 246
private currency, 123, 215
Progressive Ring Company, 100
Proxmire, William, 210

Qaddafi, Muammar, xx, 2, 155–57, 159, 161

Racz, Andrew, 215
Ray, Hugh, 233
Ray, Ruth, 155
Reagan, Ronald, 32
Reconstruction Finance Company, 55–56, 101
Redlich, Fritz, 135
Reed, Cameron, 279n36
Reti, Steven P., 260n30
Revere, Paul, xiii, xix, 107
Reynolds Securities, 294n3
Ricardo, David, 7
Ritchie, Donald A., 264n2
Robert, Albert, xiii
Roberts, George B., 87, 90–91
Robertson, A. Willis, 112, 118
Robinson, Joseph, 49, 51
Robinson, Nathaniel, 146–47
Rockefeller, Laurence, 106

Rockefeller, Nelson, 2, 106
Rockoff, Hugh, 261n45
Rogers, James H., 67
Rogers, Will, 48
Rolnick, Arthur J., and Warren E. Weber, 257n11
Rosenthal, Benjamin, 221–22
Rosenthal, Milton, 220–21
Roosa, Robert, 107
Roosevelt, Franklin D., 3, 37, 44, 52, **54**, **74**, 104, 157; Asia and, 72, 73–74, 75, 77; biographical sketch of, xviii; early career of, 38–39, 45, 54; gold politics of, 55–57, 61, 267n24; silver politics of, xviii, 8–9, 45–51, 55, 57–58, 61–64, 68, 71, 78–79, 84, 87–89, 103, 116, 141, 172, 218, 250–51; World War II and, 93–94, 154
Roosevelt, James and Sara, 38
Roosevelt, Theodore, 17, 38
Ross, John, 205
Ross, Stephen, 230
Rowan, Roy, 293n69
Ruby, Jack, 104
Ruggles, Samuel, 21
Rundle, Rhonda L., 254n13, 301n73
Russia, 23–24, 199, 302n90
Russo, Tom, 192, 210
Ruth, Babe, 220
Rutledge, David, 197
Ryan, J.P., and Kathleen M. McBreen, 281n4
Ryan, Patrick, 296n11

Salter, Arthur, 59, 269n45
Sargent, Thomas, 253n9, 275n54
Saudi Arabia, 4, 175–76, 180–82, 190, 296n2
Saudi Arabian Monetary Agency, 175–76, 214
Schacht, Hjalmer, 53
Schlesinger, Arthur, Jr., 267n6
Schwab, Charles M., 40
Schwartz, Anna J., 264n7
Scopes, John Thomas, 36
Scopes Trial, 36–37
Scrugham, James, 101
September 11 attacks, 242, 313n2
Septimus, Bernard, xiv, 301n73
Shane, Nat, 138
Sherer, Ron, 294n3

Sherman, Charles and Mary, 17
Sherman, John, 16, 17–26, **18**, 112, 118, 250, 258n3; biographical sketch of, xvii
Sherman, William Tecumseh, 17
Sherman Antitrust Act, xvii, 17, 225
Sherman Silver Purchase Act, 24–25
Shoemaker, Willie, 181
Silber, Lillian, xiv
silver, **173**;: in antiquity, 3, 12, 31, 196, 234–35, 249, 256n10, 301n73; appeal of, 4–5, 31, 196; currency uses of, xix, 3–5, 7–8, 10, 12–14, 16, 18–19, 21, 24–25, 31–34, 41, 46, 108, 109, 120–28, 147, 207, 247–48, 249–50; in golf balls, 207, 304n28; industrial uses of, 5–6, 56, 65, 68, 95–98, 101–2, 105, 108, 117, 125–26, 144, 162, 180, 239, 243–45; medicinal uses of, 196, 301n73; nationalization of, xviii, 62, 64–66, 116, 141; "secondary," 91; theft and burglary of, 202–3; wartime uses of, 95–98, 100–101
Silver Act (1946), 102–3, 109
Silver Agreement (Proclamation and Statement Ratifying the London Agreement on Silver), 52–53, 56–58, 61, 63, 74, 78, 89, 103, 268n28
"silver bloc" senators, xvii–xviii, 8–9, 49, 62, 66–67, 71, 74, 78–79, 89, 91, 93, 99–101, 218, 250; after World War II, 103, 106–12, 115, 117, 127
silver certificates, 91–93, **92**, 109–10, **113**, 115–17, 125, 128, 144, 157, 215, 270n20; Jarecki and, 131, 135, 137–42, 147–48
silver dollars, 7, 10, 24, 32, 34, 43, 61, 91–92, **122**, 204, 247, **247**, 262n40, 277n6; Coinage Act of 1873 and, 4, 16, 19, 22, 112, 218, 258n5; in 1960s, 120–22, 124, 126, 131, 135
silver futures trading, xiv, 64, 115–16, 137, 141, 167–69, 209–10, 219, 254n19; Comex and, 160, 163–64, 165–66; Fonseco and, 200; Jarecki and, 184–85, 191–92
"silverites" vs. "goldbugs," 25, 43, 51. See also "silver bloc" senators
Silvermann, Susan, 138, 147–48
silver mining, 15–16, 31, 39, 93, 102, 125, 176–77, 218, 243, 249, 257n16
silver prices (cash prices): charts of, ii–iii, 225–26, 230; during 1800s, 7–8, 15, 16,

22, 23, 24–25, 30, 47, 258n25; during
1910s, 41–43, 258n20; during 1930s,
47, 51, 53, 56–57, 61, 63–65, 68, 78,
81, 88, 90–92, 266n40, 270n22; during
1940s, 100–103; during the 1960s, 105,
112, 116–17, 121–22, 124, 131, 135–37,
139, 142–44, 258n20; during 1970s, 1,
2, 6, 157–58, 165–67, 170–72, 180–81,
183, 185, 186–87, 190–94, 199–200,
202, 226–27, 243, 254n18; during
1980s, 3, 205, 206–7, 208–9, 212, 215,
217, 219, 225; during 1990s, 236, 237,
239, 240; during twenty-first century, 6,
242–43, 245, 246–47, 253n7, 315n27.
See also under Bryan, William Jennings;
Hamilton, Alexander
Silver Purchase Act (1934), xviii, 8, 62–64,
67–68, 73, 77–79, 90–91, 93, 100, 108,
280n10; impact on China of, 77, 82, 89,
250, 275n54; repeal of, xix, 108–17, 251
silver ring (on Comex), xiv, 158, 170, 188,
194, 299n31
silversmithing, xiii, 4, 5, 101–2, 107
silver smuggling: in China and Japan, xviii,
8, 68, 73, 76, 81–82, 87–88, 275n47,
277n75; in India and Dubai, 204
silver speculators, xix, 6; in 1930s, 63–64,
66, 78–80; after World War II, 124–25,
127, 136–37, 141, 144, 158, 162–64,
195, 212–13
silver standard, xviii, 8, 14, 23, 25, 42, 44,
61, 80, 87, 255n31
Silver Thursday, 216–17, 219, 221
Silver Users Association, 102
silverware, jewelry, and housewares, 65,
100, 102, 105, 184, 202–4, 243
Sinclair, James, 183, 197
Sino-Japanese War, xviii, 9, 87, 250
"16 to 1" gold to silver price ratio, 14–15,
30–31, 196, 207, 215, 257n18, 270n15,
294n75; Bryan and, 36–37, 47–48, 143,
145, 163, 250; Wheeler and, 48–49, 52,
58, 62
Smith, Al, 45
Smith, Elizabeth R., 109
Smith, Jerome F., 162–64
Smith, Keith, 141–42, 145, 147–48
Smith, Roy, 287n41
Somers, Andrew, 48
Soong, T.V., 71, 74–76
soybeans, 167, 177–78, 195

Spain, 19, 246
Springsteen, Bruce, 244
squeezing. See cornering
Stahl, Charles, 166
Stalin, Joseph, 99, 154
Steen, Charles, 105–6
Steinbrenner, George, 158
Stephenson, Edward, 181
sterling standard, 5, 11, 146–47
Stern, Jean, 158
Stern, Siegfried, 69–70
Stevenson, Adlai, 117
Stewart, Donald, 188–89, 216
St. Germain, Fernand, 167–68
Stieff, Kirk, 202
Stimson, Henry, 96–98, 279n35
straddles, 184–85, 186, 298n16
Strauss, Simon, 116
Streeter, W.J., 303n12
Streussel (chauffeur), 132
subsidiary coins, 109, 129, 263nn14–15,
283n27
Sunshine Mining Company, 105, 176–77,
178–79, 186, 216
Sun Yat-sen, 68, 71
Super Bowl trophies, 1, 5, 161, 197
Sward, Bud, 207
Sweden, 23
Swiss Bank Corporation, 213, 229
Switzerland, 23, 133; Hunt bank deposits
in, 163–64, 172–73, 195, 240
Sylla, Richard, xiv, 255n1
Sze, Alfred Sao-ke, 71–72, 77, 83–84

Taft, William Howard, 96
Tea Party, 2, 7
Temin, Peter, 257n16
Tendler, David, 220
Terminal Trading Company, 138, 142
Thoesen, M.E., 34
Thomas, Elmer, 50–51, 58
Thomas, John, 101
Thompson, Christine M., 256n10
3M Company, 168, 170, 180
Thurber, William, 102
Tiffany & Company, 1, 161
Tilson, Whitney, 314n10
Tonopah Extension Mining Company, 40, 52
Trial of the Pyx, 10–12
Trump, Donald, 251
Tuccille, Jerome, 291n4

Tuchman, Barbara, 276n68
Tuchman, Bruce, xiv
Turner, R.H., 102
Twain, Mark, 16
Tye, Frania, 155

U.S. Assay Commission, 12
U.S. Government, financiers' mistrust of,
    6–7, 163; Hunt family, xx, 2, 4, 157,
    159, 163, 173, 200
U.S. Metals Refining Company, 97
U.S. Secret Service, 146

Van Ryzin, Robert R., 259n10
Velde, François, 253n9
vending machines, 39, 94–95, 108, 111
Vietnam War, 120, 143, 251
Viner, Jacob, 69
Viswanathan, S., 312n23
Volcker, Paul, 107, 217–18, 221–22, 251

Wachtel, Paul, xiv, 316n3
Wadsworth, A.W., 111
Walker, Francis A., 19–20, 255n24
Wall Street Crash. See Great Crash of 1929
Waltuch, Norton, 187–89, 194, 195, 208
Warburg, James, 52–53
Warner, A.J., 26, 118
War Production Board (WPB), 93–96,
    100, 101
Warren Commission, xix, 104, 118, 281n3;
    LBJ on, 281n1

Washington, George, 10, 152
Weidenmier, Marc, 278n9
Weisman, John, 140
Welch, J.R., 293n59
Weston, George M., 19–20
West Point Depository, 90, 92–93, 96–98,
    100, 101, 102, 140
Wheeler, Burton, 47–50, 52, 58, 62, 91
White, Compton, 112–13
Williams, Jeffrey, xiii, 230, 298n16
Williams, John Henry, 68–69
Williams, R. Hal, 262n33
Williams, Roger, 99
Willis, Henry Parker, 260n29
Wilson, Joseph, 39
Wilson, Woodrow, 36, 38–41, 54
Wonderful Wizard of Oz, The (Baum), xvii,
    4, 25–26, 231, 261n45
Woody Herman and His Orchestra, 151
World Monetary and Economic Confer-
    ence, 52–53
World War I, 3, 35, 38, 41–43; debts from,
    51
World War II, 9, 47, 49, 87, 93–101
Wyler, Seymour, 253n9

Ybarra, Michael J., 280n2
Young, Arthur N., 175–76, 272n5,
    273n22, 296n2

Zimmerman, Donald, 203
Zweig, Jason, 314n10